Complete
Taste of Life

Complete Taste of Life

BETTER LIVING THROUGH BETTER EATING

Low fat ◆ low cholesterol ◆ no added sugar or salt ◆ high fiber

JULIE STAFFORD

Charles E. Tuttle Company, Inc.
Boston • Rutland, Vermont • Tokyo

First published in 1993 by RD Press
a registered business name of
Reader's Digest (Australia) Pty Limited
26–32 Waterloo Street, Surry Hills, NSW 2010

Produced by Viking O'Neil
56 Claremont Street, South Yarra, Victoria 3141, Australia
A Division of Penguin Books Australia Ltd

First published in the United States in 1993 by
Charles E. Tuttle Company, Inc. of Rutland, Vermont & Tokyo, Japan,
with editorial offices at 77 Central Street, Boston, Massachusetts 02109.

ISBN 0-8048-1843-6
Library of Congress Catalog Card Number 92-62594

Text designed by Meredith Parslow
Cover designed by Cathy Larsen
Illustrations by Lorraine Ellis
Typeset in Perpetua by Midland Typesetters, Victoria, Australia
PRINTED IN HONG KONG

CONTENTS

INTRODUCTION

I changed my family's eating habits some ten years ago, after my husband, Bruce, was diagnosed as having cancer. We opted for a diet that was low in fat and cholesterol, high in nutrients and natural fibre and contained no added refined sugar and salt. We substituted vegetables, pasta, brown rice, wholegrains, cereals, fruit and fish for the roast dinners, deep-fried foods, rich casseroles, eggs and bacon, cheeses and salami, cream-covered desserts and cakes we had grown up with.

The new diet gave Bruce's body a chance to heal after the effects of chemotherapy and radiation, but it had other benefits, too: I was able to lose weight and maintain my new weight easily, and we both experienced an increase in energy and reduced cholesterol levels, which remain in the 'very acceptable' range.

We had two children to raise, and I was determined to give them the healthiest possible start in life. Why knowingly wait until you reach thirty or forty years of age to change poor eating habits and try to heal a body that has endured years of food abuse?

Once upon a time eating healthy foods was considered trendy. Today, eating healthily is essential for anyone who is seriously interested in avoiding the degenerative diseases of our Western world, such as heart disease, which are now widely recognised as being caused in part or whole by our excessive, unhealthy diets.

Why a low-fat, low-cholesterol, low-salt, sugar-free diet?

Heart disease is the leading cause of deaths in the Western world. Medical studies show that there are three major factors associated with it.

1 High blood cholesterol.
2 High blood pressure (hypertension). If blood pressure is above 160/95, compared with under 140/90, the risk of having a heart attack is doubled, and is five times greater for a stroke.
3 Smoking. Smokers compared with non-smokers are twice as likely to have a heart attack. Men under the age of 45 who are heavy smokers (more than twenty-five a day) are fifteen times more likely than non-smokers to have a heart attack.

Other factors that increase the risk of heart disease are stress, obesity, lack of exercise and diseases such as diabetes.

World heart foundations believe that, with diet modifications, many of the deaths from heart disease are preventable. Diets that are rich in non-essential saturated fat (from a high consumption of meats, dairy foods and cooking fats), high in dietary cholesterol, refined sugar and salt, and low in fibre need to change.

The second leading cause of deaths is cancer. Cancer of the colon, breast and prostate, as well as other forms of cancer, have been directly linked to diet and lifestyle, too. Other diet-related degenerative diseases include adult-onset diabetes, diverticular disease, gallstones, kidney disease, gout, arthritis, arteriosclerosis, blood disorders, constipation, obesity and auto-immune diseases.

One of the biggest problems with our diet is the amount of saturated fat and excess kilojoules we consume, especially in the form of processed foods. In Third World countries, where very little, if any, saturated fat is consumed and kilojoule intake is more controlled, there is little or no evidence of degenerative diseases and obesity. We store the excess kilojoules as fat, which is not only bad for our hearts but bad for our image. It has been said that, at any given time, at least one in four people is on a diet trying to lose this fat. Unfortunately, statistics show that for every hundred people who lose this fat, ninety-five will regain it within two years. To avoid degenerative diseases, to control and maintain our ideal weight, and to have the energy we require to live a fulfilling life, we need to follow a lifetime plan for healthy eating.

The recipes included in this book have been designed to help you do just that. They are low in saturated fat and cholesterol, have no added refined sugar or salt, and are high in both soluble and insoluble fibre. They encourage you to use natural foods, especially foods in season, and to enhance the flavour of foods with natural ingredients such as fresh herbs and spices rather than salt or sugar. The dishes are prepared and cooked in a way that maintains their maximum level of nutrition.

For years we have been changing the natural structure, appearance and flavour of foods in an attempt to win the taste buds of the consumer. All too often we forget that food is, first, for survival, and the quality of our survival is determined by the quality of the food we eat. When developing recipes, I take into account more than just the 'taste test', although the result will surprise many people who thought that healthy food could not possibly taste good and be good for you.

Our ability to taste food in its natural state is often diminished by the addition of so many other ingredients that are high in fat, salt, sugar or artificial chemical components. But it does not take long to eliminate the need for these flavours in your food. Many people who follow for just a short time a low-fat, low-sugar, low-salt diet, without chemicals and preservatives, are pleasantly surprised at the 'new' taste sensation of healthy food. There is no doubt about it, healthy food can taste great!

We now recognise more than ever that it is important that all the family members are conscious of the foods they eat. Health problems associated with poor dietary habits do not start at the age of forty: they begin at childhood, when our eating habits and patterns are formed. If we grow up eating all the wrong types of foods, we place ourselves at a high risk of developing diet-related diseases. If, on the other hand, we eat a balanced, nutritious diet most of the time, we are at least living in a way that will prevent the onset of many common diseases. Whether you use these recipes all of the time or only some of the time you will be contributing to your wellbeing.

Choosing Low-cholesterol Foods

Excess cholesterol and saturated fat in the diet can be brought about by too often choosing foods from animal sources, and by frying foods in butter and solid fats. Choose from the following food groups to create a balanced daily menu and protect against heart disease and other diet-related diseases.

FOOD GROUP	SPECIAL NOTES
Dairy Foods Choose from: ■ skim milk or reduced-fat soymilk ■ low-fat evaporated milk ■ non-fat or low-fat yoghurt ■ low-fat cottage cheese ■ low-fat ricotta cheese (use moderately) ■ low-fat grating cheese (use moderately) ■ ice cream (home-made ice creams using low-fat evaporated milk) ■ geska herb cheese or grated parmesan cheese (use moderately)	Full-cream milk and its products (cheeses, butter, yoghurt, cream cheese, etc.) are high in both fat and cholesterol. Keep these to a minimum and substitute the non-fat or low-fat alternatives listed opposite. There is still the same amount of protein and calcium in the skim-milk dairy products as there is in their full-cream counterparts.
Meat All meat should be lean. Meat includes: ■ beef (rump steak, fillet, topside, oyster blade and gravy beef) ■ pork ■ veal ■ lamb ■ rabbit ■ venison	Red meat is a good source of protein, iron, minerals and vitamins, but only small quantities should be eaten per day, and all visible fat should be removed before cooking the meat. Avoid organ and gland meats. They are very high in fat and cholesterol. Cook meat by grilling (fat should drip away from the meat), or roasting (in an oven bag), or cook in a casserole with added vegetables. Add meat to soups, but remove fat from top of soup before eating. Marinate meat for barbecuing. Rabbit and venison are particularly healthy meats because their fat is higher in polyunsaturated fats than that of domesticated animals. One serve is 125 g/¼lb. Do not eat more than one serve per day.

FOOD GROUP	SPECIAL NOTES
Fish and Seafood This group includes: ■ all fresh fish ■ oysters ■ scallops ■ mussels ■ water-packed canned tuna ■ water-packed sardines	You should aim to eat about 125 g / ¼ lb of fish if it is your major source of protein for the day. Prawns, lobster, crayfish, crab, sardines in oil and calamari are high in fat and cholesterol and should be limited to special occasions.
Poultry Choose between: ■ chicken ■ turkey	Duck and goose have a much higher fat and cholesterol level than chicken and turkey, so should be avoided or their consumption limited. All skin and fat should be removed from chicken and turkey before cooking. Chicken and turkey can be microwaved, baked, roasted in oven bags, cooked in a casserole with vegetables, marinated for the barbecue or steamed. A serve should be about 125 g / ¼ lb. Do not eat more than one serve per day.
Eggs Egg whites only	To limit your cholesterol intake egg yolks should be kept to a minimum. If your blood cholesterol level is low and you are not overweight, an occasional egg yolk in a balanced diet should not cause too many health problems. Two egg whites can be successfully substituted for 1 whole egg in most cakes, biscuits and pastries. **Note** 1 whole egg contains more than twice the recommended daily cholesterol intake.
Nuts and Seeds Choose from the following: ■ sunflower seeds ■ pumpkin seeds ■ sesame seeds ■ pine nuts ■ almonds ■ pecan nuts ■ walnuts ■ hazelnuts	Nuts and seeds have a high fat content so use them sparingly in recipes rather than eating them in handfuls! Most of the nuts and seeds listed contain polyunsaturated fat. Avoid any roasted nuts (they have added fat), macadamias, cashews and coconuts. These are all high in saturated fats. **Note** Use almonds, pecan nuts, walnuts and hazelnuts sparingly.

FOOD GROUP	SPECIAL NOTES
Fats and Oils Use the following sparingly: ■ safflower oil ■ sunflower oil ■ grapeseed oil ■ light olive oil	The oils listed opposite are polyunsaturated (with the exception of olive oil, which is mono-unsaturated), and therefore are considered more favourable than saturated fats and oils (for example, butter, ghee, copha, cooking margarine – usually a combination of butter and margarine – and coconut oil). **Note** Cold-pressed grapeseed oil is used as an ingredient in cakes, muffins and pastries. Only use as directed in recipes. 　Light olive oil is occasionally used in some vegetable and meat recipes to enhance the flavour. Only use the amount specified in the recipes.
Beans and Pulses Among this group are: ■ navy beans ■ kidney beans ■ lima beans ■ brown or green lentils ■ split peas ■ garbanzo beans (chick peas)	These are a good source of protein without lots of fat and cholesterol. They also contain good amounts of soluble fibre. Beans and lentils can be substituted for a meat dish in a daily menu plan.
Grains These include: ■ wholegrain breads and rolls ■ brown rice ■ rolled oats ■ oat bran ■ rice bran ■ wholewheat / semolina / soy pasta ■ wheat bran ■ wholemeal flour ■ rye flour ■ buckwheat flour ■ millet ■ tapioca and sago	Breads, cakes, biscuits, desserts, pastries and breakfast cereals can be made at home using these ingredients. They are good sources of fibre, vitamins and minerals, without any saturated fat or cholesterol. They provide good sources of energy.

FOOD GROUP	SPECIAL NOTES
Fruit and Vegetables Because the composition of our body is approximately 70 per cent water, it stands to reason that a great deal of the food we eat should be high in water content. Fresh fruit and vegetables are the foods with the highest water content and they contain minimal fat and no cholesterol. They contain most of our nutritional requirements in the form of vitamins, minerals, amino acids, enzymes, proteins, complex carbohydrates and fats that the body requires to maintain health and survive. If we eat fresh fruit and vegetables regularly, the processes of digestion, assimilation, and elimination of wastes will almost be guaranteed to occur on a regular basis. Fruit and vegetables should become the basis of our energy supply. They are not a burden to the body because little energy is required to utilise their goodness in the body and to expel the wastes. Research has shown that the oldest people in the world, who are relatively disease free, have followed diets based mainly on fruit and vegetables.	Fruit and vegetables are best eaten raw. If cooking, lightly steam to maximise the nutritional value and fibre content. Limit avocados because they are high in fat. It is best to eat avocado on a meat-free day, using it as the fat source for that day. Limit olives because they are high in fat and salt. Use them sparingly over a pizza or in a casserole for added flavour. Canned fruits and vegetables are suitable if they are packaged in natural juices. For vegetables canned in water and salt, simply drain and place under cold running water for a few moments to get rid of excess salt.

Conversions

In each of the recipes in this book the ingredients are given in metric and imperial measurements, while a third set of measures gives volume quantities for readers in the United States (for example, 65 ml/2 fl oz/¼ cup lemon juice). Please note that because the American tablespoon is smaller than the metric tablespoon the conversion is given as follows: 1 tablespoon/ 1 tablespoon plus 1 teaspoon. Small inconsistencies sometimes occur because conversions have been adjusted slightly to give convenient working measurements. It is important to follow only one style of measurement – never mix them.

Oven Temperatures

	°C	°F
Low or cool	95	200
Very slow	120	250
Slow or warm	150	300
Moderate	180	350
Hot	200	400
Very hot	230	450

Glossary for American Cooks

Although some of the language and spellings in this book may be unfamiliar to the American home cook, most of the information is straightforward and easy to decipher. But to help you get the most from the recipes, we have assembled a glossary of ingredients and terms.

agar powder: natural gelling agent made from seaweed; substitute gelatin
bean shoots: bean sprouts
beetroot: beets
bicarbonate of soda: baking soda
blade steak: chuck
brown onion: common yellow onion
burghul: bulghur
butternut pumpkin: butternut squash
calcium ascorbate: vitamin C powder
capsicum, red and green: bell pepper
champignons: mushrooms
chilli: jalapeno or other hot chilli pepper
cold-pressed oil: the least processed oil available, regardless of type of oil; look for terms "expeller pressed" and "unrefined"
cornflour: cornstarch
flaked almonds: slivered almonds
gemfish: substitute whiting (also called silver hake) or similar saltwater fish
geska herb cheese: substitute Parmesan
golden syrup: a type of cane syrup
grapeseed oil: substitute safflower, sunflower or canola oil
grating cheese: hard, aged cheese suitable for grating such as Parmesan
gravy beef: rump or round
horseradish paste: substitute horseradish sauce, to taste
Jonathon apples: available mostly in the Midwest; substitute McIntosh apples
ice blocks: ice cubes
instant lasagne: requires no pre-cooking; substitute cooked lasagne noodles
king prawns: substitute jumbo shrimp
lamb steaks: boned lamb, cut into steaks
mignonette lettuce leaves: baby lettuce leaves, such as Bibb
minced beef, lamb, pork: ground beef (hamburger), lamb, pork
odourless onions: sweet onions such as Vidalia, Walla-Walla and Maui
Packham pears: substitute Bartlett pears
papaw: papaya
pappadams: puffed lentil wafers
peppermint essence: peppermint extract

pickling onions: pearl onions
plain flour: bleached all-purpose flour
Pontiac potatoes: use any firm white- or red-skinned potato
prawns: medium and large shrimps
pulses: legumes (beans, lentils)
pumpkin: substitute American pumpkin, squash or unsweetened pumpkin purée for blue Max, golden nugget, Queensland blue, sweet or Windsor black pumpkins
pumpkin kernels: pumpkin seeds
red globe onions: Bermuda or red onions
Robinson potatoes: use any firm white- or red-skinned potato
seafood marinara mixture: mixture of shrimp, scallops and other seafood
shrimps: tiny shrimp
silver beet leaves: substitute spinach
soyaroni: pasta made from soyflour
sultanas: golden raisins
swedes: substitute rutabaga
sweet chillies: sweet peppers such as anaheim
tamari: aged soy sauce traditionally made with no added wheat
Thai spice: piquant seasoning available in Asian markets
topside steak: top round
trevally fillets (fish): substitute sole
vanilla essence: vanilla extract
unbleached white plain flour: bleached all-purpose flour
wholemeal: whole wheat (breadcrumbs, flour, spaghetti)

Cooking and Baking Terms

cook under a grill: broil
kilojoules: calories
mince: chop very fine; grind
muffin tray: muffin pan
paper patty cups: paper baking cups; paper cupcake liners
pipped: pitted
slice tin: rectangular baking pan; substitute a 9- by 13-inch baking pan

SOUPS

A vision that so easily comes to mind from my childhood is the big old wooden stove in our farmhouse kitchen. The aromas that emanated from it would fill the house, and the aroma that lingered the most was of the herbs, vegetables and meats simmering in the big old soup pot. Never have I captured that wonderful aroma when opening a can of soup, and I am ever grateful that Mum shared with me the secrets of many a good soup.

There are really only 'secrets', not rules, to soup making: certain herbs complement certain ingredients; certain cuts of meat and bones create a well-balanced, delicious stock; certain vegetables work well together. However, these secrets vary according to the soup maker, as they are based on individual taste.

Serve chilled and light soups as a prelude to a main course and heartier, chunkier soups as a meal in themselves.

Vegetable Stock

xxxxxxxxxxxxxxxxxxxxxxxxxxxxxxxxxxxxxxxxxxxxxxxxxxxxxxxxxxxxxxxxxxxxxxxxxxxxxxxxxxxxx

potatoes
carrots
onions
celery head
celery leaves
spinach
swede
turnip
parsnip
tomatoes
½ lemon (optional)
black pepper (optional)
65 ml/2 fl oz/¼ cup dry sherry
   (optional)
65 ml/2 fl oz/¼ cup unsweetened
   orange juice (optional)
65 ml/2 fl oz/¼ cup salt-free tomato
   juice or 75 g/2½ oz/¼ cup salt-free
   tomato paste

All or any of these vegetables in a combination would be suitable to make a vegetable stock. Chop the vegetables, place them in a large saucepan, cover them with water and add any optional extras. Bring to the boil and simmer for 20 minutes. Cover and leave to stand. When cold, strain. Purée the vegetable pulp in a food processor or blender and set aside (the pulp can be used to thicken soups). The strained stock can be used as required as a base for soup. (See right colour plate between pages 56 and 57.)

Chicken Stock

xxxxxxxxxxxxxxxxxxxxxxxxxxxxxxxxxxxxxxxxxxxxxxxxxxxxxxxxxxxxxxxxxxxxxxxxxxxxxxxxxxxxx

MAKES 2 LITRES/3½ PINTS/
8 CUPS

1 × 1.5 kg/3½ lb chicken or chicken
   carcass (all skin and fat removed)
1 stick celery, roughly chopped
1 carrot, roughly chopped
1 onion, roughly chopped
a little freshly chopped parsley
6 black peppercorns
2 litres/3½ pints/8 cups water

Place the chicken in a large saucepan with the celery, carrot, onion, parsley, peppercorns and water. Simmer for 2 hours. Strain off the stock, discarding the bones, meat and vegetables. Cool and refrigerate. Discard any congealed fat before using.

   This stock can be frozen and used as desired. For small amounts, pour stock into ice-cube trays and freeze. Remove cubes from trays and store in a plastic bag in the freezer. Add to soups, casseroles and gravies for extra flavour.

Chinese Chicken Stock

xxxxxxxxxxxxxxxxxxxxxxxxxxxxxxxxxxxxxxxxxxxxxxxxxxxxxxxxxxxxxxxxxxxxxxxxxxxxxxxxxxxxx

MAKES 2 LITRES/3½ PINTS/
8 CUPS

1 kg/2¼ lb chicken meat or chicken
   pieces (all skin and fat removed)
2 litres/3½ pints/8 cups water
4-cm/1½" piece fresh ginger, sliced
4 black peppercorns
1 onion, sliced
3 sprigs parsley

Place all the ingredients in a large saucepan, bring to the boil and simmer for 1½ hours. Allow to cool and remove any scum. Strain the liquid and use as required or remove the chicken and any bones, purée the remaining ingredients and liquid, and use as required. You can also chop the chicken meat and add it to the strained liquid or the liquid to be puréed.

   Chinese Chicken Stock is an excellent stock to use in the preparation of Minestrone (see page 25). (See right colour plate between pages 56 and 57.)

Lamb Shank Stock

MAKES 3 LITRES/5 PINTS/
12 CUPS

6 lamb shanks
3 litres/5 pints/12 cups water
1 onion, chopped
3 sticks celery with leaves, roughly
  chopped
½ lemon
sprigs of parsley
6 peppercorns (optional)

Place all the ingredients in a large saucepan and bring to the boil. Turn down and simmer for 3 hours.

Strain, cool and refrigerate. Discard any congealed fat before using.

Use as required in soups and to add flavour to casseroles.

Beef Stock

MAKES 2 LITRES/3½ PINTS/
8 CUPS

2 kg/4½ lb beef bones
1 onion, chopped
2 bay leaves
2 sticks celery with leaves, chopped
1 carrot, chopped
6 black peppercorns (optional)
2 litres/3½ pints/8 cups water

Remove all visible fat from the beef bones. Place all the ingredients in a large saucepan and bring to the boil. Turn down and simmer for at least 3 hours. Strain, cool and refrigerate. Discard any congealed fat before using.

Use as required in soups and to add flavour to casseroles.

Fish Stock

MAKES 2 LITRES/3½ PINTS/
8 CUPS

1 kg/2¼ lb fish heads or bones
1.5 litres/2½ pints/6¼ cups water
500 ml/16 fl oz/2 cups unsweetened
  apple juice or dry white wine
2 large white onions or leeks (thoroughly
  washed), chopped
2 carrots, chopped
large handful finely chopped fresh parsley
3 bay leaves
sprig of thyme or marjoram
½ lemon

Place all the ingredients in a large saucepan and bring to the boil. Turn down and simmer for 30 minutes. Strain, and then pour the strained liquid through a piece of fine cheesecloth.

Use as required to add flavour to fish-based soups or casseroles.

Chicken Vegetable Soup

xxxxxxxxxxxxxxxxxxxxxxxxxxxxxxxxxxxxxxxxxxxxxxxxxxxxxxxxxxxxxxxxxxxxxxxxxxxxxxxx

SERVES 4–6

1 onion, chopped
1 teaspoon crushed garlic
500 ml/16 fl oz/2 cups Chicken Stock
  (see p. 14)
500 g/1 lb 2 oz carrots
500 g/1 lb 2 oz zucchini
500 g/1 lb 2 oz celery
500 g/1 lb 2 oz leeks, thoroughly
  washed
200 g/7 oz parsnips
200 g/7 oz swedes
200 g/7 oz turnips
2 chicken drumsticks (all skin and fat
  removed)
500 ml/16 fl oz/2 cups salt-free tomato
  juice
1 teaspoon dried basil
1 teaspoon dried oregano
black pepper to taste

Cook the onion and garlic in a large saucepan with a little Chicken Stock, until the onion softens.

Chop all the remaining vegetables finely, and add to the saucepan with the remaining Chicken Stock and all the other ingredients. Cook until the vegetables are soft and the chicken is tender – about 30–40 minutes. Cool and refrigerate. Discard congealed fat.

Remove the chicken from the bones, discard the bones and return the meat to the soup. (See colour plate opposite.)

Vegetable and Barley Soup

xxxxxxxxxxxxxxxxxxxxxxxxxxxxxxxxxxxxxxxxxxxxxxxxxxxxxxxxxxxxxxxxxxxxxxxxxxxxxxxx

SERVES 4–6

185 g/6 oz/1 cup barley
1.5 litres/2½ pints/6 cups water
185 g/6 oz/2 cups chopped carrot
90 g/3 oz/1 cup chopped onion
2 cloves garlic, crushed
40 g/1½ oz/½ cup grated swede
185 g/6 oz/2 cups grated parsnip
90 g/3 oz/1 cup green beans, roughly
  chopped
425 g/15 oz canned whole tomatoes in
  natural juice, salt-free
2 tablespoons/2 tablespoons plus
  2 teaspoons salt-free tomato paste
2 tablespoons/2 tablespoons plus
  2 teaspoons wine vinegar or dry
  sherry
½ teaspoon dried marjoram

In a large saucepan, cook the barley in the water until soft but not mushy. Drain the barley and reserve the liquid. In a food processor or blender blend half the barley with a little of the liquid until smooth. Return this to the remaining liquid in the saucepan. Add the carrot, onion, garlic, swede, parsnip and bean pieces. Cook until the vegetables are tender. Add the tomatoes, tomato paste, vinegar and marjoram. Add additional water if necessary and simmer for a further 40 minutes.

Chicken Vegetable Soup (opposite page);
Artichoke and Leek Pizza Slice (page 172).

Sweet-potato Curry and Mint Soup (opposite page); Broccoli and Cauliflower Muffins (page 219).

Sweet-potato Curry and Mint Soup

SERVES 4–6

1 onion, chopped
500 g / 1 lb 2 oz sweet potato, peeled
* and chopped*
2 teaspoons curry powder
1 litre / 1¾ pints / 4 cups Vegetable
* Stock or Chicken Stock (see p. 14)*
2 teaspoons finely chopped fresh mint

Combine all the ingredients except the mint and simmer until the sweet potato is tender. Purée in a food processor or blender and stir through the mint. (See colour plate opposite.)

Variation
■ Cook 90 g / 3 oz / ½ cup of brown or red lentils and add to the soup before puréeing.

Potato Curry Soup

SERVES 4–6

2 onions, finely chopped
2 leeks, thoroughly washed and chopped
65 ml / 2 fl oz / ¼ cup unsweetened
* orange juice*
6 large potatoes, peeled and cubed
1.5 litres / 2½ pints / 6 cups Chicken
* Stock (see p. 14) or Lamb Shank*
* Stock (see p. 15)*
1 teaspoon curry powder (more if desired)
½ teaspoon ground ginger
1 bay leaf
small handful freshly chopped parsley

Cook the onion and leek in the orange juice over a gentle heat until soft and transparent. Add the potato and cook for 3 minutes, gently tossing it through the onion and leek.

Add the stock, curry powder, ginger and bay leaf. Cover, and simmer for 30 minutes or until the potato is soft. Stir through the parsley before serving. (See right colour plate between pages 24 and 25.)

Curried Vegetable Soup

SERVES 6–8

750 ml / 1⅓ pints / 3 cups Beef Stock
* (see p. 15)*
small piece fresh ginger, crushed
1 teaspoon curry powder
200 g / 7 oz leeks, thoroughly washed and
* roughly chopped*
125 g / ¼ lb parsnips, chopped
225 g / ½ lb pumpkin, peeled and
* chopped*
1 zucchini, cut into rounds
425 g / 15 oz canned whole tomatoes in
* natural juice, salt-free*
250 ml / 8 fl oz / 1 cup water

Combine all the ingredients in a large saucepan and simmer for 3 hours. Stir occasionally so that the vegetables do not stick to the bottom of the saucepan.

Chicken Broth

MAKES 1 LITRE/1¾ PINTS/
4 CUPS

3 kg/6½ lb chicken meat and bones or
carcasses (all skin and fat removed)
2 cloves garlic, chopped
2 teaspoons chopped fresh ginger
6 black peppercorns
1 large carrot, chopped
1 small parsnip, chopped
2 sticks celery, chopped
1 litre/1¾ pints/4 cups water
finely chopped spring onion or *finely
chopped fresh parsley (optional)*
finely grated lemon rind (optional)

Place all the ingredients in a large saucepan and bring to the boil. Simmer for at least 1 hour. Strain, cool and refrigerate. Discard congealed fat before using.

For added flavour, add finely chopped spring onion and finely grated lemon rind.

The broth can also be used as a chicken stock to enhance the flavour or be the base of other soups.

Vegetable Broth

MAKES 3 LITRES/5 PINTS/
12 CUPS

4 litres/7 pints/16 cups water
*½ bunch celery (the half with green
leaves)*
2 large brown onions
2 large carrots, chopped
large handful fresh parsley, chopped
*1 tablespoon/1 tablespoon plus
1 teaspoon pink peppercorns*

Combine the water and celery in a saucepan. Top and tail the onions and wash the skins. Cut the onions in half, leaving the skins on, and add to the saucepan with the remaining ingredients. Bring to the boil. Turn down and simmer for 2½–3 hours. Strain, cool and refrigerate.

This is a very clear liquid full of goodness and flavour, which is excellent served as a clear broth with finely chopped fresh herbs; or grate some vegetables, add to the broth and bring to the boil so the vegetables are just cooked.

The broth can also be used as a vegetable stock to enhance the flavour or be the base of other soups.

Asparagus and Spinach Broth

SERVES 2

*500 ml/16 fl oz/2 cups Vegetable
Broth (see this page)*
100 g/3½ oz fresh asparagus spears
½ small onion, finely chopped
*100 g/3½ oz fresh spinach, torn into
small pieces*
black pepper to taste

Prepare the Vegetable Broth according to the recipe. Add the asparagus and onion and simmer until they are tender. Add the spinach and cook until it has just changed to a bright green colour. Season with black pepper.

Broccoli and Cauliflower Broth

SERVES 4

1 litre/1¾ pints/4 cups Vegetable Broth (see p. 18)
2 cloves garlic, crushed
200 g/7 oz finely sliced broccoli
200 g/7 oz finely sliced cauliflower
a little freshly chopped marjoram for garnishing
a little freshly chopped thyme for garnishing

Prepare the Vegetable Broth according to the recipe and bring it to a gentle simmer. Add the garlic, broccoli and cauliflower. Cover and cook until the vegetables are just tender.

Serve garnished with the freshly chopped herbs.

Asparagus Soup

SERVES 4 – 6

750 ml/1⅓ pints/3 cups Chicken Stock (see p. 14)
3 sticks celery with leaves, roughly chopped
500 g/1 lb 2 oz potatoes, peeled and chopped
400 g/14 oz cooked asparagus
125 ml/4 fl oz/½ cup asparagus cooking liquid
1 tablespoon/1 tablespoon plus 1 teaspoon lemon juice
extra cooked asparagus for garnishing

Combine all the ingredients and cook for 1 hour. Purée and serve. Garnish with the extra cooked asparagus or purée a small amount of extra cooked asparagus, add a little to each bowl prior to serving and lightly stir through.

Avocado Soup

SERVES 3

1 avocado
200 g/7 oz celery
310 g/10½ oz carrots
squeeze of lemon juice
black pepper to taste
handful of finely chopped fresh chives for garnishing (optional)

This is a raw chilled soup. Purée the avocado flesh and juice the celery and carrots in a food processor or blender. Add the juice to the avocado and continue to purée for a thick, creamy, smooth-textured soup. Season with lemon juice and black pepper. Garnish with chopped chives and serve chilled.

You can extend this soup by thinning it with Vegetable Broth (see page 18).

Cream of Carrot Soup

xxxxxxxxxxxxxxxxxxxxxxxxxxxxxxxxxxxxxxxxxxxxxxxxxxxxxxxxxxxxxxxxxxxxxxxxxxxxxxxxxxxxxx

SERVES 6–8

750 ml/1⅓ pints/3 cups Chicken
   Stock *(see p. 14)*
250 ml/8 fl oz/1 cup unsweetened
   orange juice
1 leek, thoroughly washed and chopped
1 kg/2¼ lb baby carrots, chopped
1 teaspoon freshly chopped thyme or
   ¼ teaspoon dried thyme
1 teaspoon non-fat or low-fat yoghurt
a little finely chopped fresh parsley
black pepper to taste

Combine all the ingredients in a large saucepan. Cook over a gentle heat until the carrot is quite tender. Remove from heat and purée. Return to a clean saucepan and reheat, without boiling.

Serve in individual soup bowls with the yoghurt, a sprinkling of parsley and black pepper to taste.

Carrot and Herb Soup

xxxxxxxxxxxxxxxxxxxxxxxxxxxxxxxxxxxxxxxxxxxxxxxxxxxxxxxxxxxxxxxxxxxxxxxxxxxxxxxxxxxxxx

SERVES 2

500 ml/16 fl oz/2 cups carrot juice,
   chilled
large handful finely chopped mixed fresh
   herbs (e.g. parsley, chives, thyme,
   oregano, marjoram, basil)
1 stick celery, finely sliced

This is a raw chilled soup. Combine all the ingredients and serve.

Carrot, Leek and Zucchini Soup

xxxxxxxxxxxxxxxxxxxxxxxxxxxxxxxxxxxxxxxxxxxxxxxxxxxxxxxxxxxxxxxxxxxxxxxxxxxxxxxxxxxxxx

SERVES 6

1 litre/1¾ pints/4 cups Chicken Stock
   (see p. 14)
250 ml/8 fl oz/1 cup water
2 leeks, thoroughly washed
3 carrots
3 zucchini
black pepper to taste
2 tablespoons/2 tablespoons plus 2
   teaspoons freshly chopped parsley

In a large saucepan, bring the stock and water slowly to the boil and then simmer. Remove the outer skin and roots from the leeks, and cut into 2.5-cm/1″ lengths. Cut the carrots and zucchini into 2.5-cm/1″ chunks. Add the leek, carrot, zucchini and black pepper to the simmering stock.

Cook slowly for 1 hour. Do not boil again. Add parsley just prior to serving.

Carrot and Lemon Soup

SERVES 2

500 ml/16 fl oz/2 cups carrot juice, chilled

2 tablespoons/2 tablespoons plus 2 teaspoons lemon juice

finely grated rind of 1 lemon (more if desired)

1 tablespoon/1 tablespoon plus 1 teaspoon finely chopped fresh thyme or marjoram for garnishing

This is a raw chilled soup. Combine all the ingredients except the chopped thyme and pour into serving bowls. Add the thyme and stir into the soup to make a circular pattern.

Carrot, Tomato and Basil Soup

SERVES 4

500 ml/16 fl oz/2 cups carrot juice, chilled

500 ml/16 fl oz/2 cups salt-free tomato juice, chilled

lots of black pepper

large handful finely chopped fresh basil

a little celery powder (optional)

This is a raw chilled soup. Combine all the ingredients except the celery powder, mix well and serve. If the tomato juice is too acidic, you could add a little celery powder.

Carrot and Turnip Soup with Coriander

SERVES 4–6

225 g/½ lb baby carrots, sliced

225 g/½ lb turnips, sliced

1 litre/1¾ pints/4 cups Chicken Stock (see p. 14)

black pepper to taste

2 tablespoons/2 tablespoons plus 2 teaspoons non-fat or low-fat yoghurt

2 teaspoons ground coriander

1 teaspoon ground cummin

1 tablespoon/1 tablespoon plus 1 teaspoon finely chopped fresh coriander

In a large saucepan, cook the carrot and turnip in 65 ml/2 fl oz/¼ cup of the Chicken Stock for approximately 6 minutes, stirring now and then. Heat the remaining stock and add it to the vegetables. Bring to the boil, add black pepper and simmer, covered, for 30 minutes. Purée and return to a clean saucepan. Reheat and add the yoghurt and more black pepper if necessary. Add the spices and the coriander, mix well, and stand for 5 minutes before serving.

Carrot and Walnut Soup

SERVES 4

60 g/2 oz/¼ cup walnuts
500 ml/16 fl oz/2 cups carrot juice,
    chilled
500 ml/16 fl oz/2 cups Vegetable
    Broth (*see p. 18*)
a little ground nutmeg for garnishing

This is a raw chilled soup. Ensure the walnuts are fresh or they will give a bitter taste.

Place the walnuts in a food processor and process until powdery. Add the carrot juice, then the Vegetable Broth. Serve in individual bowls and garnish with the nutmeg.

Creamy Cauliflower Soup

SERVES 4–6

2 cloves garlic, crushed
1 small leek (*thoroughly washed*) or
    onion, chopped
1 teaspoon light olive oil (*optional but
    creates an excellent flavour; substitute
    1 tablespoon/1 tablespoon plus
    1 teaspoon water if desired*)
400 g/14 oz cauliflower, chopped
200 g/7 oz potatoes, peeled and chopped
1 litre/1¾ pints/4 cups Vegetable
    Broth *or* Chicken Broth (*see p. 18*)
250 ml/8 fl oz/1 cup low-fat evaporated
    skim milk
chopped chives or parsley or thyme for
    garnishing

Sauté the garlic and leek in the oil over a very gentle heat until the leek is soft. Add all the remaining ingredients and simmer until the vegetables are soft. Purée in a food processor or blender. Add the milk, return to the heat but do not boil.

Garnish with the chopped chives.

Cream of Cauliflower and Parsnip Soup

SERVES 6–8

185 g/6 oz leeks, thoroughly washed and
    finely sliced
65 ml/2 fl oz/¼ cup water
200 g/7 oz/1¼ cups grated parsnip
400 g/14 oz chopped cauliflower
½ teaspoon ground nutmeg
black pepper to taste
2 litres/3½ pints/8 cups Lamb Shank
    Stock (*see p. 15*)

In a large saucepan, cook the leek in the water until soft. Add all the other ingredients and simmer for 1½ hours. Remove from the heat and purée. Return to a clean saucepan, reheat and serve.

Celery Soup

SERVES 4

1 litre/1¾ pints/4 cups Vegetable
    Stock *or* Chicken Stock *(see p. 14)*
150 g/5 oz chopped leek
500 g/1 lb 2 oz celery
2 potatoes, peeled and chopped
small piece fresh ginger, finely chopped
1 tablespoon/1 tablespoon plus
    1 teaspoon lemon juice
finely grated rind of 1 lemon
250 ml/8 fl oz/1 cup water
3 sticks extra celery, finely sliced

Combine all the ingredients, except the extra celery, in a large saucepan. Simmer for 1½ hours. Purée in a food processor or blender. Return the soup to a clean saucepan. Add the extra celery and stir through. Reheat and serve. (See right colour plate between pages 24 and 25.)

Gazpacho

SERVES 4–6

1 kg/2¼ lb ripe tomatoes
200 g/7 oz carrots
150 g/5 oz cucumber
2 large cloves garlic, crushed
2 tablespoons/2 tablespoons plus 2
    teaspoons finely chopped mixed fresh
    herbs (e.g. basil, oregano, thyme)
lots of black pepper

This is a raw chilled soup. Juice the tomatoes, carrots and cucumber. Add the remaining ingredients and stir through. Chill and stir occasionally to develop the flavours. (See colour plate opposite page 25.)

Hearty Lamb Shank Vegetable Soup

SERVES 4–6

1 onion, chopped
1 teaspoon crushed garlic
500 ml/16 fl oz/2 cups water
500 g/1 lb 2 oz carrots
500 g/1 lb 2 oz zucchini
500 g/1 lb 2 oz celery
500 g/1 lb 2 oz washed leeks
200 g/7 oz parsnips
200 g/7 oz swedes
200 g/7 oz turnips
2 lamb shanks
500 ml/16 fl oz/2 cups salt-free tomato
    juice
1 teaspoon dried mixed herbs
black pepper to taste
40 g/1½ oz/½ cup cooked kidney beans
    or peas

In a large saucepan cook the onion and garlic in a little of the water until the onion is soft. Chop all the remaining vegetables finely and add to the saucepan along with the lamb shanks, tomato juice, herbs, seasoning and the rest of the water. Cook for 1–1½ hours or until the vegetables are soft and the lamb is tender. Cool and refrigerate. Discard any congealed fat.

Remove all the meat from the lamb shanks, return it to the soup and discard the bones. Finally, add the kidney beans, reheat and serve. (See right colour plate between pages 24 and 25.)

Summer Cucumber Yoghurt Soup

SERVES 6

2 large cucumbers
500 ml/16 fl oz/2 cups non-fat or
    low-fat yoghurt
125 ml/4 fl oz/½ cup skim milk
2 tablespoons/2 tablespoons plus 2
    teaspoons finely chopped chives or
    spring onion
2 teaspoons finely chopped fresh dill
1 Jonathan apple, finely sliced for
    garnishing

Peel and halve the cucumbers. Remove the seeds and grate the flesh. Combine the remaining ingredients and mix well with the grated cucumber. Chill for several hours so that the flavour can develop. Garnish with the apple slices. (See colour plate opposite.)

Fish Soup

SERVES 6–8

2 small leeks, thoroughly washed and
    green leaves removed or 2 medium-
    sized onions, finely sliced
2–3 cloves garlic, crushed
125 ml/4 fl oz/½ cup unsweetened
    orange juice
500 g/1 lb 2 oz ripe tomatoes, skinned,
    seeded and chopped
2 tablespoons/2 tablespoons plus 2
    teaspoons salt-free tomato paste
black pepper to taste
2 litres/3½ pints/8 cups Fish Stock
    (see p. 15)
1 tablespoon/1 tablespoon plus 1
    teaspoon chopped basil
1 small carrot, cut into julienne strips
40 g/1½ oz/½ cup extra thoroughly
    washed and finely sliced leek
40 g/1½ oz/½ cup finely sliced celery
30 g/1 oz/⅓ cup finely sliced fennel
    (optional)
1 kg/2¼ lb white fish fillets, cut into
    small strips
8 scallops, washed
handful of finely chopped fresh parsley
    for garnishing

Place the leek, garlic and orange juice in a large saucepan and cook over a gentle heat for 5–10 minutes or until all the juice is absorbed. Add the tomato and tomato paste. Season with black pepper. Cook for a further 5 minutes. Add the Fish Stock, basil, carrot, leek, celery and fennel. Bring to the boil and simmer for 10 minutes with the lid on. Add the fish and simmer for a further 5 minutes with the lid on. Add the scallops and simmer for 4 minutes.

Serve immediately in a large soup tureen, garnish with the chopped parsley, and serve with hot crispy wholemeal bread. (See left colour plate overleaf.)

Summer Cucumber Yoghurt Soup
(opposite page).

Fish Soup (page 24).

Potato Curry Soup (page 17); Celery Soup (page 23); Hearty Lamb Shank Vegetable Soup (page 23).

Quick-as-a-wink Pumpkin Soup and Minestrone (opposite page); Gazpacho (page 23).

Minestrone

✕✕✕

SERVES 4–6

2 cloves garlic, crushed

1 large onion, chopped

2.25 litres/4 pints/9 cups Vegetable
   Stock or Chicken Stock or Chinese
   Chicken Stock (see p. 14)

2 large carrots, chopped

3 sticks celery with leaves, chopped

1 large potato, chopped

3 small zucchini, chopped

10 green beans, chopped

850 g/2 lb sliced mushrooms

850 g/2 lb canned whole tomatoes in
   natural juice, salt-free

black pepper to taste

185 g/6 oz/1 cup haricot beans, cooked

30 g/1 oz/2 tablespoons plus 2
   teaspoons brown rice or 60 g/2 oz
   wholemeal macaroni, cooked

1 teaspoon dried marjoram

Cook the onion and garlic for 6 minutes in 125 ml/4 fl oz/
½ cup of the stock in a large saucepan. Add the remaining
stock, fresh vegetables and tomatoes. Season with black
pepper. Bring to the boil, turn down and simmer for 1 hour,
stirring occasionally.

Purée 500 ml/16 fl oz/2 cups of the soup in a food processor or blender and return this to the saucepan. Add the
haricot beans, rice and marjoram and heat through for a
further 5 minutes. (See colour plate opposite.)

Quick-as-a-wink Pumpkin Soup

✕✕✕

SERVES 6–8

1 onion, chopped

1 teaspoon finely chopped fresh ginger

1 clove garlic, crushed (optional)

2 tablespoons/2 tablespoons plus
   2 teaspoons water

850 g/2 lb pumpkin, peeled and finely
   chopped

1 litre/1¾ pints/4 cups Chicken Stock
   (see p. 14) or 500 ml/16 fl oz/
   2 cups unsweetened orange juice and
   500 ml/16 fl oz/2 cups water

60 g/2 oz/3 tablespoons plus 3
   teaspoons salt-free tomato paste

½ teaspoon ground cummin (optional)

sprigs of parsley for garnishing

In a large saucepan cook the onion, ginger and garlic in the
water for 3 minutes or until transparent. To get the best
flavour from onion without cooking in oil, always place the
lid on the saucepan while the onion is cooking. Add all the
other ingredients. Cook for 15–20 minutes or until the
pumpkin is tender. Purée in a food processor or blender. Serve
with a thin slice of orange, and garnish with parsley. (See
colour plate opposite.)

Green Soup

*any combination of the following: lettuce,
 spinach, a little cabbage, parsley,
 kale, wild carrot tops, radish tops,
 cress, wheat grass, alfalfa sprouts,
 comfrey, cucumber, celery and
 especially celery leaves*
chopped red and green capsicum
finely sliced celery
finely sliced cucumber
finely chopped fresh chives
lemon juice or *black pepper to taste*

This is a raw chilled soup. The benefits of green vegetable juices are thought to be many: they supply chlorophyll and many vitamins and minerals, trace elements, enzymes and other components of nature's 'natural medicines'.

Place your selection of green vegetables in a juicer and juice. Place the juice in a bowl and add some red and green capsicum, celery, cucumber, and fresh chives. Season with lemon juice. Chill well before serving.

Mushroom Soup with Chervil

SERVES 3 – 4

225 g / ½ lb mushrooms
*1 litre / 1¾ pints / 4 cups Chicken Stock
 (see p. 14)*
250 ml / 8 fl oz / 1 cup skim milk
juice of ½ lemon
black pepper to taste
handful of freshly chopped chervil

Wipe mushrooms clean with a damp cloth. Do not peel. Chop them, stalks and all. Heat the stock and add almost all the chopped mushroom (the reserved mushroom will be used as a garnish). Simmer for 15 minutes and cool slightly. Purée in a food processor or blender, add the milk and stir until smooth. Add the lemon juice and black pepper. Pour into a clean saucepan and reheat, adding the chopped chervil a few moments before serving. Garnish with the reserved mushroom pieces.

Potato Soup

SERVES 6

*1.5 litres / 2½ pints / 6 cups Vegetable
 Broth (see p.18)*
2 onions, chopped
2 cloves garlic, crushed
1 teaspoon ground cummin
½ teaspoon ground ginger
¼ teaspoon turmeric
¼ teaspoon ground nutmeg
¼ teaspoon dry mustard
1 kg / 2¼ lb potatoes, peeled and chopped
200 g / 7 oz chopped celery

Prepare the Vegetable Broth according to the recipe. In a separate saucepan, cook the onion and garlic in a little broth until soft, then add the spices and cook for a few minutes. Add the remaining ingredients and simmer until the potato is soft.

Purée the soup, return to the saucepan to reheat, and serve.

Potato and Dill Soup

SERVES 4

750 ml/1⅓ pints/3 cups Vegetable
    Stock (see p. 14)
½ teaspoon dried dill
¼ teaspoon black pepper
1 onion, chopped
2 sticks celery, chopped
3 large potatoes, peeled and chopped
500 ml/16 fl oz/2 cups skim milk
finely chopped fresh dill or sprig of dill
    for garnishing

In a large saucepan, bring the stock to the boil and add the dill, pepper, onion, celery and potato. Turn the heat down and simmer for 20 minutes or until the vegetables are tender. Purée. Add the milk and reheat, but do not boil. Garnish lightly with the dill.

Peppery Pumpkin Bean Soup

SERVES 4–6

1 large onion, chopped
1 teaspoon crushed garlic
1 tablespoon/1 tablespoon plus 1
    teaspoon Vecon (natural vegetable
    stock available at health-food stores)
1.25 litres/2¼ pints/5 cups water
750 g/1½ lb pumpkin, peeled and
    chopped
¼ teaspoon black pepper
750 g/1½ lb canned mixed cooked beans
handful of finely chopped fresh chives or
    a little finely chopped fresh thyme

In a large saucepan cook the onion and garlic with the Vecon and 125 ml/4 fl oz/½ cup of the water until the onion has softened. Add the remaining water, pumpkin and pepper. Cook until the pumpkin is soft and then purée the contents of the saucepan. Return to the pan.

Rinse the beans under running water to wash off excess salt and sugar. Add the beans and the fresh herbs to the soup. Heat through and serve.

Pumpkin and Coriander Soup

SERVES 4

1 litre/1¾ pints/4 cups Vegetable
    Broth (see p.18) or water
2 onions, chopped
1 tablespoon/1 tablespoon plus 1
    teaspoon finely chopped fresh ginger
1 teaspoon turmeric
2 teaspoons ground coriander
500 g/1 lb 2 oz pumpkin, peeled and
    chopped

Prepare the Vegetable Broth according to the recipe.

Place the onion and ginger in a saucepan. Cover and cook on a gentle heat until the onion is soft and almost transparent (if the onion and ginger are sticking the cooking temperature is too high – adding just a little water will ease the foodstuffs off the bottom of the saucepan).

Add the spices and cook for a further minute. Add the pumpkin and broth and cook until the pumpkin is tender.

Purée the soup, return to the saucepan to reheat, and serve.

Corn Chowder

xxxxxxxxxxxxxxxxxxxxxxxxxxxxxxxxxxxxxxxxxxxxxxxxxxxxxxxxxxxxxxxxxxxxxxxxxxxxxx

SERVES 6

Chicken Stock

1 × 1 kg/2¼ lb chicken (all skin and fat removed)
2 corn cobs, husks removed
1 onion, chopped
1 carrot, chopped
2 sprigs parsley
small piece fresh ginger
water

Soup

1 teaspoon finely chopped fresh ginger
1 onion, chopped
2 teaspoons toasted sesame seeds
2 tablespoons/2 tablespoons plus 2 teaspoons dry sherry (optional)
40 g/1½ oz/¼ cup cornflour
65 ml/2 fl oz/¼ cup water
2 egg whites
2 tablespoons/2 tablespoons plus 2 teaspoons extra water
6 spring onions, finely chopped

You will use approximately 225 g/½ lb/1 cup of shredded chicken meat for this soup. The remaining chicken can be stored for other meals. A large chicken ensures a tasty chicken stock, but you can substitute chicken carcasses or chicken breasts.

Place the Chicken Stock ingredients in a large saucepan and cover with water. Bring to the boil, turn down and simmer for 1½ hours. Remove the chicken and cover immediately with cold water. This will keep the chicken meat very moist. Remove from the water when completely cold, and refrigerate.

Shred 225 g/½ lb/1 cup of chicken and set aside. Strain the stock and discard the ingredients except the corn. Reserve 1.5 litres/2½ pints/6 cups of stock. Use a sharp knife to cut through the corn kernels in the centre from top to bottom. Use the back edge of the knife to press the corn flesh out without pulling away the skin of the kernel. Set aside.

Place the chopped ginger, onion and sesame seeds in a large non-stick saucepan and cook gently over dry heat for approximately 2–3 minutes or until the onion begins to soften. If the onion begins to stick, add a little stock and turn down the heat. Add the chicken stock, shredded chicken, corn and sherry and bring to the boil. Mix the cornflour with the water to make a paste. Stir through the soup until it thickens and then turn down the heat. Beat the egg whites lightly with 2 tablespoons/2 tablespoons plus 2 teaspoons of water. Add this to the soup, stirring continuously. Remove from the heat, add the spring onion and serve.

Chick Pea Soup

xxxxxxxxxxxxxxxxxxxxxxxxxxxxxxxxxxxxxxxxxxxxxxxxxxxxxxxxxxxxxxxxxxxxxxxxxxxxxx

SERVES 6

185 g/6 oz/1 cup chick peas
225 g/½ lb chicken meat (all skin and fat removed)
2 onions, chopped
1 leek, washed and sliced
2 bay leaves
¼ teaspoon dried thyme
¼ teaspoon dried marjoram
2 litres/3½ pints/8 cups Chicken Stock (see p. 14) or water
2 sticks celery with leaves, chopped
2 large cabbage leaves, finely chopped
150 g/5 oz/1 cup broken wholemeal spaghetti pieces

Wash the chick peas thoroughly and then put into a saucepan with the water. Bring to the boil and boil for 2 minutes. Remove from the heat and cover. Leave for 1 hour.

Drain the chick peas. Add the chicken meat, onion, leek, bay leaves, thyme, marjoram and Chicken Stock. Cover and simmer for 1½ hours. Add the celery and cabbage, cover, and simmer for about 30 minutes. Remove the chicken meat, cut up very finely, and return to the saucepan. Add the broken spaghetti pieces and cook for 15–20 minutes or until tender.

Serve with hot crusty wholemeal bread.

Winter Bean and Lentil Brew

SERVES 6–8

400 g/14 oz/2 cups mixed pulses (e.g.
   red kidney beans, baby lima beans,
   lentils, chick peas, split peas)
1 large leek, thoroughly washed and
   chopped
2 cloves garlic, crushed
125 ml/4 fl oz/½ cup unsweetened
   orange juice
90 g/3 oz/1 cup peeled, seeded and
   freshly chopped tomato
2 litres/3½ pints/8 cups stock of your
   choice
1½ sticks celery with leaves, chopped
40 g/1½ oz/½ cup grated parsnip
40 g/1½ oz/½ cup grated carrot
large handful finely chopped fresh parsley
½ teaspoon dried basil
½ teaspoon dried oregano
1 teaspoon dried rosemary
black pepper to taste (optional)

Rinse the pulses and soak them overnight or cover them with boiling water, place the lid on the saucepan and leave for 2 hours. Drain. Cook the leek and garlic in the orange juice over a gentle heat until soft and transparent. Add the tomato and cook for 3–4 minutes. Add all the remaining ingredients and simmer with the lid on for 2 hours or until the pulses are soft. Stir occasionally, so that the brew does not stick to the bottom of the saucepan.

Quick-and-easy Tomato Soup

SERVES 4

1 onion, chopped
½ teaspoon dried oregano
½ teaspoon dried basil
2 sticks celery with leaves, chopped
a little water
850 g/2 lb canned whole tomatoes in
   natural juice, salt-free
2 tablespoons/2 tablespoons plus 2
   teaspoons salt-free tomato paste

Cook the onion, herbs and celery in a little water for approximately 3 minutes until soft. Purée the tomatoes and tomato paste in a food processor or blender until smooth. Add to the onion and cook gently for 10–15 minutes. Purée again and serve immediately.

Variations
- Add 90 g/3 oz/1 cup of grated raw carrot before serving.
- Add 90 g/3 oz/1 cup of finely sliced celery before serving.
- Add 90 g/3 oz/1 cup of finely chopped mixed red and green capsicum before serving.
- Add a handful of finely chopped fresh chives.
- Add 2 teaspoons of fresh ginger juice when cooking the onion.
- Serve chilled tomato soup with non-fat or low-fat yoghurt and a sprinkle of the fresh herbs of your choice.

Delicious Summer Soup

xxxxxxxxxxxxxxxxxxxxxxxxxxxxxxxxxxxxxxxxxxxxxxxxxxxxxxxxxxxxxxxxxxxxxxxxx

SERVES 4

500 g/1 lb 2 oz ripe tomatoes, skinned,
*   seeded and chopped*
1 cucumber, peeled and chopped
1 clove garlic, crushed
200 ml/7 fl oz/¾ cup dry sherry
*   (optional)*
black pepper to taste
75 ml/3 fl oz/⅓ cup non-fat or low-fat
*   yoghurt or handful of finely chopped*
*   fresh parsley*
slices of cucumber or finely chopped
*   shallot for garnishing*

Blend the tomato, cucumber, garlic, sherry and black pepper in a food processor until very smooth. Chill for several hours. Before serving, stir in either the yoghurt or the parsley.

Serve garnished with the cucumber or the chopped shallot.

Melon Soup

xxxxxxxxxxxxxxxxxxxxxxxxxxxxxxxxxxxxxxxxxxxxxxxxxxxxxxxxxxxxxxxxxxxxxxxxx

SERVES 2

200 g/7 oz peeled and seeded cantaloup
200 g/7 oz peeled and seeded honeydew
*   melon*
4-cm/1½" piece fresh ginger
a little freshly chopped mint

This is a raw chilled soup. Juice the melons and ginger. Stir the mint through the juice. Serve well chilled.

Watermelon and Chive Soup

xxxxxxxxxxxxxxxxxxxxxxxxxxxxxxxxxxxxxxxxxxxxxxxxxxxxxxxxxxxxxxxxxxxxxxxxx

SERVES 2–4

1 litre/1¾ pints/4 cups watermelon
*   juice, chilled*
2 tablespoons/2 tablespoons plus 2
*   teaspoons finely chopped fresh chives*

This is a raw chilled soup. To obtain watermelon juice for this recipe, it is best to push the watermelon flesh through a fine sieve, to obtain a clear liquid. (Using a food processor will make the juice pale and frothy.)

Combine the juice with the chives and serve.

Variation

■ Place a small piece of fresh ginger in a garlic press and add the ginger juice to the above mixture. The quantity will be determined by the flavour you desire.

HORS-D'OEUVRES, DIPS, PÂTÉS & TERRINES

Hors-d'oeuvres are small parcels or portions of food originally devised to stimulate the appetite for the main meal to follow. This is still the custom but today, with changing food trends towards lighter, healthier meals, these dips and dishes are often complemented with breads and salads to make a meal on their own.

Fish Pâté

xxxxxxxxxxxxxxxxxxxxxxxxxxxxxxxxxxxxxxxxxxxxxxxxxxxxxxxxxx

SERVES 4–6

small can crab meat
200 g/7 oz canned red salmon
125 g/¼ lb canned sardines
3 tablespoons/3 tablespoons plus 3
    teaspoons Soymilk Mayonnaise
    (see p. 139)
2 teaspoons gelatine
2 tablespoons/2 tablespoons plus 2
    teaspoons boiling water
1 tablespoon/1 tablespoon plus 1
    teaspoon lemon juice
lots of black pepper
finely chopped fresh chives for garnishing

Drain the cans of fish well, and combine in a food processor or blender with the Soymilk Mayonnaise. Process until smooth.

Dissolve the gelatine in the boiling water and add, with the lemon juice, slowly to the fish mixture while the food processor is operating.

Spoon the mixture into a mould and refrigerate overnight.

To serve, unmould and press the chopped chives over the top. This pâté is excellent with crudités or wholemeal toast fingers. (See colour plate opposite.)

Vegetable Crudités

xxxxxxxxxxxxxxxxxxxxxxxxxxxxxxxxxxxxxxxxxxxxxxxxxxxxxxxxxx

red, yellow and green capsicum, cut into
    strips
carrot, cut into sticks
zucchini, cut into sticks
cucumber, cut into sticks
celery, cut into sticks
fennel, sliced into thin strips
large tomatoes, quartered or whole
    cherry tomatoes
green beans, blanched
asparagus spears, blanched
broccoli, cut into florets and blanched
cauliflower, cut into florets and blanched
whole spring onions
whole radishes

Crudités are pieces of raw or lightly cooked, chilled vegetables. Have a crudité container in your refrigerator filled with any one of the ingredient groups here for snacks during the day. (See colour plate opposite.)

Pita Crisps

xxxxxxxxxxxxxxxxxxxxxxxxxxxxxxxxxxxxxxxxxxxxxxxxxxxxxxxxxx

SERVES 2–4

2 small wholemeal pita breads
1 teaspoon onion powder or garlic
    powder
2 tablespoons/2 tablespoons plus 2
    teaspoons grated parmesan cheese

Preheat the oven to 200°C/400°F.

Split the pita pocket circles in half and cut each round into four pieces. Sprinkle with the onion powder and parmesan cheese. Place on a non-stick baking sheet or a baking tray and cook until browned. Cool and store in an airtight container. Use the pita crisps for a tasty, crunchy snack with your favourite dip. (See colour plate opposite.)

Variation
- Before baking, spread a thin layer of salt-free tomato paste on the pita breads and sprinkle with sesame seeds.

*Fish Pâté with fresh vegetables and Vegetable Crudités, served with Pita Crisps
(opposite page).*

*Triangle Puffs, Stuffed Mushrooms and Marinated Fruit Kebabs (opposite page);
Poppyseed Log (page 35).*

Triangle Puffs

MAKES 16

8 sheets wholemeal filo pastry
2 teaspoons fresh ginger juice (press
  ginger through a garlic crusher)
1–2 cloves garlic, crushed
125 ml/4 fl oz/½ cup non-fat or
  low-fat yoghurt
90 g/3 oz/1 cup carrot, grated
2 potatoes, peeled, grated and drained
30 g/1 oz/¼ cup green beans, finely
  chopped, or peas
30 g/1 oz/¼ cup finely chopped
  capsicum
½ onion, chopped
125 ml/4 fl oz/½ cup Curry Sauce (see
  Curried Scallop and Potato Pie, p. 75)

Preheat the oven to 200°C/400°F.

Place one sheet of pastry on top of another. Using a sharp knife or scissors, cut the pastry lengthwise into four equal strips. This will give you 16 pieces.

Combine the ginger juice, garlic and yoghurt and mix well. Add all the remaining ingredients and mix well.

To make the triangles, place a rectangle of two sheets of filo on a bench. Fold one corner over to form the first triangle. Place a spoonful of filling inside this triangle.

Turn the corner of the filo, folding the filling over on itself to form the triangle. Continue to fold in triangles to the end of the filo. The filling will now be completely concealed. Place on a lightly greased non-stick baking tray. Repeat with the remaining mixture and filo. Bake for 15 minutes. Turn over and cook for a further 15 minutes. (See colour plate opposite.)

Stuffed Mushrooms

SERVES 9

36 mushrooms
225 g/½ lb/1 cup mashed potato
handful finely chopped fresh herbs (e.g.
  oregano, chives, parsley)
30 g/1 oz/¼ cup finely chopped spring
  onion
30 g/1 oz/¼ cup finely grated low-fat
  grating cheese
60 g/2 oz/1 cup fresh wholemeal
  breadcrumbs

Preheat the oven to 230°C/450°F.

Wash the mushrooms thoroughly and remove the stems. Combine the potato, herbs, spring onion and cheese and mix well. Spoon the mixture onto the mushrooms and sprinkle the breadcrumbs over the top. Bake for 5 to 8 minutes, or place under a hot grill to brown the top. (See colour plate opposite.)

Marinated Fruit Kebabs

any combination of the following fruits,
  cut into kebab pieces: cantaloup,
  pineapple, apple, orange, honeydew
  melon, green grapes, pear, peach,
  nectarine, watermelon, strawberries,
  purple grapes, kiwi fruit
vinaigrette of your choice
lettuce leaves or grapefruit or melon for
  serving

This is a refreshing way to start a main meal on a hot summer's day. Use 10-cm/4″ long kebab sticks. Thread on bite-sized pieces of fruit using two to four variations on each stick. Put the kebabs in a shallow dish and pour the vinaigrette over the top. Leave to marinate in the refrigerator until you are ready to serve. Serve two or three on a bed of lettuce leaves or halve the grapefruit or melon and stick the kebabs into each half. (See colour plate opposite.)

Asparagus Roll-ups

MAKES 10

1 bunch asparagus
squeeze of lemon juice
10 slices wholemeal bread, crusts removed
125 g / ¼ lb / ½ cup low-fat cottage
  cheese
handful of finely chopped fresh tarragon
  (optional)

Lightly steam the asparagus, drain, and squeeze lemon juice over the top. Purée in a food processor or blender, cool and chill.

Using a wooden rolling pin, roll out the bread slices until they are very thin. Refrigerate for at least 30 minutes. Push the cottage cheese through a fine sieve. Spread the bread slices with the cottage cheese, then with the asparagus, and sprinkle the tarragon over the top. Roll up and secure with a small toothpick. Repeat to make 10 roll-ups.

Refrigerate for at least 1 hour and remove toothpicks before serving.

Carrot Wheels

MAKES 24

6 slices wholemeal bread, crusts removed
125 ml / 4 fl oz / ½ cup tomato relish
150 g / 5 oz / 1½ cups finely grated carrot

Using a rolling pin, roll out the bread slices until they are very thin. Lightly spread each piece of bread with tomato relish. Top with grated carrot. Roll up very tightly, wrap securely in foil, and refrigerate overnight.

Unwrap carefully and, using a very sharp knife or an electric knife, cut each roll into four wheels. Place on a serving platter and serve.

Curried Eggs

MAKES 12

6 hard-boiled eggs, shelled
225 g / ½ lb / 1 cup cold mashed potato
½ teaspoon turmeric
1 teaspoon curry powder
90 g / 3 oz / 1 cup peas, cooked, puréed
  and chilled

Using a sharp knife, carefully cut the eggs in half and remove the egg yolk. Place the egg whites on a serving platter. Combine the potato, turmeric and curry powder, and mix well. Spoon some of the mixture into the egg whites so that half the cavity is filled. Spoon the puréed pea mixture into the remaining space. Using the top end of a spoon, swirl the two mixtures together. Chill before serving.

Stuffed Dried Fruits

large stoned dates
whole dried figs
whole dried peaches
whole dried nectarines
low-fat cottage cheese
low-fat ricotta cheese
a little vanilla essence (optional)

Cut a small pocket in the dried fruit. Mix equal quantities of the cheeses until creamy and smooth. Fill the fruits with the cheese. The blandness of the cheese complements the flavour of the fruit but you can add a little vanilla essence for extra flavour.

Variation

- Nutmeg, cayenne pepper, finely chopped fresh chives or glacé ginger can be used instead of the vanilla essence.

Spicy Nuts and Crunch

SERVES 6

1 tablespoon/1 tablespoon plus 1
  teaspoon light olive oil
2 cloves garlic, crushed
1 teaspoon turmeric
1 teaspoon ground cummin
1 teaspoon curry powder
1 teaspoon ground coriander
150 g/5 oz/1 cup raisins
350 g/¾ lb/2 cups raw cashews
185 g/6 oz/1 cup dry roasted chick peas
90 g/3 oz/½ cup pumpkin kernels
60 g/2 oz/⅓ cup sunflower seeds

Put the oil, garlic and spices in a shallow saucepan. Heat and add the raisins, cashews, chick peas, pumpkin kernels and sunflower seeds. Toss until all the ingredients are well coated.

This mixture can be eaten hot or cold and is delicious with drinks. Remember that cashews are high in saturated fats, though, and should be eaten sparingly.

Variation
- Peanuts or a mixture of your favourite nuts can be used instead of raw cashews.

Poppyseed Log

SERVES 6–8

225 g/½ lb/1 cup low-fat cottage cheese
1 tablespoon/1 tablespoon plus 1
  teaspoon finely chopped fresh sage
2 tablespoons/2 tablespoons plus 2
  teaspoons finely chopped fresh chives
1 tablespoon/1 tablespoon plus 1
  teaspoon finely chopped fresh parsley
60 g/2 oz/¼ cup poppyseeds

Press the cottage cheese through a fine sieve, add the herbs and form into a log shape. Tear off a sheet of foil, and place the poppyseeds on it. Roll the log backwards and forwards through the poppyseeds to coat it thoroughly. Refrigerate the log, wrapped in foil, for at least 2 hours.

Serve with celery sticks, carrot slices and bunches of green and purple grapes. (See colour plate opposite page 33.)

Tomato Sorbet

SERVES 6–8

500 g/1 lb 2 oz/2 cups fresh tomato
  purée (made from skinned and seeded
  tomatoes)
250 ml/8 fl oz/1 cup unsweetened
  orange juice or grapefruit juice
250 ml/8 fl oz/1 cup Chicken Stock
  (see p. 14)
a few drops Tabasco
1 tablespoon/1 tablespoon plus 1
  teaspoon dry sherry
1 teaspoon finely grated orange rind
1 teaspoon finely grated ginger
1 egg white
6 small oranges for serving
sliced cucumber for garnishing

Purée all the ingredients except the egg white, oranges and cucumber in a food processor or blender until well combined. Pour the purée into a metal freezer tray. Freeze until mushy, stirring occasionally with a fork. Transfer to a bowl. Beat the egg white until stiff and fold into the tomato mixture. Return immediately to the freezer tray and freeze until firm.

Cut a top off each orange and remove flesh. Chill orange cups in freezer until required. Scoop out spoonfuls of tomato sorbet and fill the oranges, garnish with the cucumber, and serve. (See left colour plate between pages 120 and 121.)

Broad Bean Pâté

SERVES 6

1 kg/2¼ lb broad beans, shelled
½ lemon
125 g/¼ lb/¼ cup low-fat cottage
  cheese
2 tablespoons/2 tablespoons plus 2
  teaspoons chopped parsley
juice of 1 lemon
finely grated lemon rind
black pepper to taste

In a saucepan, cover the beans with water, add the lemon half, and cook until the beans are soft. Drain well and purée to a paste in a food processor or blender. Beat through the cheese, parsley, lemon juice and rind, and pepper. Press into a pâté dish and refrigerate until firm.

Serve chilled with fresh wholemeal bread slices or wholemeal toast fingers, or with celery sticks.

Tomato Moulds

SERVES 4

1 tablespoon/1 tablespoon plus 1
  teaspoon gelatine
300 ml/10 fl oz/1¼ cups salt-free
  tomato juice
300 ml/10 fl oz/1¼ cups vegetable juice
225 g/½ lb/1 cup low-fat cottage cheese
175 ml/6 fl oz/⅔ cup non-fat or
  low-fat yoghurt
2 tablespoons/2 tablespoons plus 2
  teaspoons lemon juice
lettuce leaves for serving
sprigs of watercress and tomato slices for
  garnishing

Dissolve the gelatine in 2 tablespoons/2 tablespoons plus 2 teaspoons of the tomato juice. Mix the remaining tomato juice and the vegetable juice with the cottage cheese and yoghurt in a food processor or blender. Stir in the lemon juice and add the gelatine mixture. Pour through a strainer into moulds. Chill in the refrigerator until set.

To serve, turn onto a bed of lettuce leaves and garnish with the watercress and tomato slices. A herb-flavoured sauce makes a good accompaniment to Tomato Moulds.

Carrot Terrine

SERVES 10–12

500 g/1 lb 2 oz carrots, chopped
225 g/½ lb potatoes, peeled and chopped
1 large onion, finely chopped
2 bay leaves
125 ml/4 fl oz/½ cup salt-free tomato
  juice
65 ml/2 fl oz/¼ cup Vegetable Stock
  or Chicken Stock (see p. 14)
60 g/2 oz/½ cup wholemeal plain flour
½ teaspoon dried sage
2 teaspoons dried basil
1 teaspoon dried oregano
4 egg whites

Preheat the oven to 200°C/400°F.

Simmer the carrot, potato, onion, bay leaves, tomato juice and stock in a covered saucepan for 20 minutes or until the vegetables are soft. Remove the bay leaves and purée the contents of the saucepan. Add the flour and herbs and then mix well.

Beat the egg whites until light and fluffy. Fold through the mixture. Pour into a lightly greased glass terrine dish (approximately 20 cm × 10 cm/8″ × 4″). Cover with foil. Bake for 40–60 minutes. The terrine is cooked when a knife inserted into the centre comes out clean. Rest for 5–10 minutes before serving. It is best eaten cold so refrigerate after the terrine is cooled.

Serve in wholegrain rolls or in salt-free, oil-free rye crispbread, or with salad or crudités.

Salmon and Ricotta Terrine

SERVES 5

a little finely chopped red capsicum
a little finely chopped celery
finely chopped fresh herbs (optional)
½ teaspoon agar powder
125 ml/4 fl oz/½ cup unsweetened
    apple juice

Terrine
425 g/15 oz canned red salmon
225 g/½ lb/1 cup low-fat ricotta cheese
1 teaspoon wholegrain mustard
1 teaspoon hot English mustard
1 tablespoon/1 tablespoon plus 1
    teaspoon salt-free tomato paste
1 tablespoon/1 tablespoon plus 1
    teaspoon gelatine
1 tablespoon/1 tablespoon plus 1
    teaspoon boiling water
2 tablespoons/2 tablespoons plus 2
    teaspoons lemon juice
2 tablespoons/2 tablespoons plus 2
    teaspoons finely chopped red capsicum
2 tablespoons/2 tablespoons plus 2
    teaspoons finely chopped celery
black pepper to taste

Lightly grease the inside of a 20 cm × 10 cm/8″ × 4″ terrine dish. Place the chopped vegetables and fresh herbs on the base of the dish (which will appear on the top when the terrine is removed from the dish).

Dissolve the agar powder in the apple juice over heat and pour this over the vegetables. Refrigerate until just set.

To make the Terrine, blend the salmon, ricotta, mustards and tomato paste in a food processor until smooth.

Dissolve the gelatine in the boiling water and add the lemon juice. Add this to the salmon and cheese mixture. Fold in the vegetables and add the black pepper. Spoon into the prepared terrine dish and refrigerate to set.

To unmould the terrine, sit the dish for 5–10 seconds in a sink of hot water that comes up to the top edge of the dish. Turn the dish upside-down on a platter, shake out the terrine and cut into slices to serve.

Sorrel Trout Terrine

SERVES 4 – 8

20 large sorrel or spinach leaves,
    blanched for 20 seconds and drained
500 g/1 lb 2 oz trout flesh, cooked and
    mashed or 425 g/15 oz canned
    salmon
60 g/2 oz/1 cup fresh wholemeal
    breadcrumbs
2 egg whites
2 Granny Smith apples, peeled, cored
    and grated
1 tablespoon/1 tablespoon plus 1
    teaspoon lemon juice
2 tablespoons/2 tablespoons plus 2
    teaspoons green peppercorns
65 ml/2 fl oz/¼ cup non-fat or low-fat
    yoghurt
wholemeal French loaf for serving

Preheat the oven to 160°C/325°F.

Place a single layer of sorrel leaves slightly overlapping in the base of a terrine dish (approximately 20 cm × 10 cm/8″ × 4″). Combine the remaining ingredients and place half the mixture over the sorrel leaves, pressing down firmly. Arrange another layer of sorrel leaves on top of the fish mixture. Repeat with another layer of fish and sorrel leaves. Cover with foil and place in a baking dish containing 2 cm/¾″ of warm water. Bake in the lower half of the oven for 40 minutes. Allow to cool and refrigerate overnight.

Remove the terrine from the dish. Cut into slices and arrange on a serving platter with the sliced French loaf. This dish is ideal for a luncheon for four, accompanied by salads.

Avocado and Tahini Dip

SERVES 8

2 avocados
125 ml/4 fl oz/½ cup lemon juice
200 ml/7 fl oz/¾ cup firm, non-oily
    tahini
2 cloves garlic, finely chopped
500 ml/16 fl oz/2 cups non-fat or
    low-fat yoghurt
2 spring onions, finely chopped
lots of black pepper
cayenne pepper to taste

Mash the avocados with the lemon juice. Add the tahini, and mix well. Add all the remaining ingredients. Cover and chill well.

Avocado and Vegetable Dip

SERVES 8

2 avocados
65 ml/2 fl oz/¼ cup lemon juice
1 large clove garlic, finely chopped
½ teaspoon ground coriander
4 drops Tabasco
2 tablespoons/2 tablespoons plus 2
    teaspoons finely chopped fresh parsley
2 tablespoons/2 tablespoons plus 2
    teaspoons finely chopped red and
    green capsicum
2 tablespoons/2 tablespoons plus 2
    teaspoons peeled, seeded and chopped
    cucumber
2 tablespoons/2 tablespoons plus 2
    teaspoons finely chopped carrot
2 tablespoons/2 tablespoons plus 2
    teaspoons chopped spring onion
lots of black pepper

Mash the avocados with the lemon juice, and fold through all the remaining ingredients. Cover and chill well.

Minted Sambal Dip

MAKES 250 ML/8 FL OZ/1 CUP

4 spring onions, finely chopped
250 ml/8 fl oz/1 cup non-fat or low-fat
    yoghurt
1 teaspoon finely grated fresh ginger
1 tablespoon/1 tablespoon plus 1
    teaspoon curry powder
large handful freshly chopped mint
1 clove garlic, crushed

Combine all the ingredients. Cover and chill well. The flavour will improve as the dip stands.

Cucumber Yoghurt Dip

MAKES 350 ML/12 FL OZ/1½ CUPS

½ large cucumber
250 ml/8 fl oz/1 cup low-fat yoghurt
2 teaspoons dried dill
1 clove garlic, crushed

Peel and remove the seeds from the cucumber. Grate it and then combine all the ingredients and mix well.

Indian Curry Dip

MAKES 250 ML/8 FL OZ/1 CUP

250 ml/8 fl oz/1 cup low-fat yoghurt
1 teaspoon curry powder
1 teaspoon ground cummin

Add a little of the yoghurt to the spices and blend well. Add the remaining yoghurt and mix through. Cover and chill.

Homous Dip

SERVES 8

310 g/10½ oz/1½ cups raw chick peas
¼ teaspoon ground cummin
¼ teaspoon ground coriander
¼ teaspoon ground ginger
¼ teaspoon dry mustard
¼ teaspoon turmeric
¼ teaspoon paprika
125 ml/4 fl oz/½ cup unsweetened
   orange juice
65 ml/2 fl oz/¼ cup firm, non-oily
   tahini
4 drops Tabasco
2 tablespoons/2 tablespoons plus 2
   teaspoons cider vinegar
3 cloves garlic, crushed
3 spring onions, finely chopped
1–2 teaspoons tamari

Soak the chick peas overnight. Cook for 1½–2 hours or until very tender. Mash the cooked chick peas and add all the remaining ingredients.

Carrot Dip

SERVES 4–6

1 bunch baby carrots
equal parts lemon juice or unsweetened
   orange juice diluted with water
extra squeeze of lemon juice
½–1 teaspoon ground nutmeg
225 g/½ lb/1 cup low-fat cottage cheese

Clean and chop the carrots. Cover the carrot with equal parts of water and lemon juice and simmer gently until the carrot is tender. Purée with the extra lemon juice, nutmeg and cottage cheese. Spoon into a bowl. Refrigerate until well chilled. Serve with vegetable sticks or salt-free wholewheat crackers.

Salmon Dip

SERVES 4 – 6

425 g/15 oz canned red salmon, drained
225 g/½ lb/1 cup low-fat cottage cheese
3 tablespoons/3 tablespoons plus 3
    teaspoons salt-free tomato paste
1 tablespoon/1 tablespoon plus 1
    teaspoon lemon juice
black pepper to taste
3 shallots, finely chopped

Blend all the ingredients except the chopped shallot in a food processor or blender. Stir through the shallot, cover, and chill well before serving with a platter of vegetables.

Salmon Mousse

SERVES 8

425 g/15 oz canned red salmon, drained
65 ml/2 fl oz/¼ cup cider vinegar
65 ml/2 fl oz/¼ cup lemon juice
1 tablespoon gelatine
65 ml/2 fl oz/¼ cup boiling water
250 ml/8 fl oz/1 cup low-fat yoghurt
1 tablespoon/1 tablespoon plus 1
    teaspoon Dijon mustard
30 g/1 oz/¼ cup finely chopped celery
30 g/1 oz/¼ cup finely chopped green
    capsicum
1 tablespoon/1 tablespoon plus 1
    teaspoon finely grated horseradish

Purée the salmon, vinegar and lemon juice in a food processor or blender. Dissolve the gelatine in the boiling water. Add the yoghurt and mustard to the salmon mixture, and then purée. Add the gelatine and mix well. Fold through the remaining ingredients and pour into a glass mould. Refrigerate until quite firm. Serve with salad. (See colour plate opposite.)

Tomato Mousse

SERVES 4 – 6

boiling water
1 kg/2¼ lb ripe tomatoes
125 ml/4 fl oz/½ cup extra boiling
    water
2 tablespoons/2 tablespoons plus 2
    teaspoons gelatine
2 tablespoons/2 tablespoons plus 2
    teaspoons salt-free tomato paste
250 ml/8 fl oz/1 cup low-fat yoghurt
2 tablespoons/2 tablespoons plus 2
    teaspoons finely chopped red capsicum
2 tablespoons/2 tablespoons plus 2
    teaspoons finely grated cucumber
2 tablespoons/2 tablespoons plus 2
    teaspoons finely chopped mixed fresh
    herbs (e.g. parsley, basil, oregano)

Pour boiling water over the tomatoes and leave to stand until the skins begin to break, approximately 3–5 minutes. Drain the tomatoes, and peel. Cut in half and scoop out as many seeds as possible. Pour 125 ml/4 fl oz/½ cup of boiling water over the gelatine and stir to dissolve. Leave to cool slightly.

Place the tomatoes and tomato paste in a food processor or blender and purée until smooth. Add the gelatine and then the yoghurt. Fold through the red capsicum, grated cucumber and herbs. Beat the egg white until stiff. Fold through the mixture until just combined. Pour into individual moulds and refrigerate until quite firm. (See colour plate opposite.)

*Tomato Mousse and Salmon Mousse
(opposite page).*

Mushroom Pie (page 45).

Mushroom and Tomato Roll (page 46); fruit platter; Tomato Spicer (page 254).

Curried Vegetables and Yoghurt Dip
(page 53).

VEGETARIAN DISHES

A vegetarian diet is becoming more popular today. Some people are looking for what they see to be healthier alternatives to meat dishes, while others choose a vegetarian diet for ecological reasons.

Whatever the reason for following a vegetarian diet, it is important to balance a vegetarian meal carefully so that it provides essential nutrients.

Meals can be all vegetable or combined with legumes, beans and grains. They can be served with extra legumes, beans and cooked grains, brown rice, pasta and bread.

Keep whole eggs to a minimum, because they are high in cholesterol and fat, and use low-fat cheese in these dishes.

Vegetarian meals offer high complex carbohydrates without the fat. They are an excellent choice for weight watchers, because they tend to be very filling, yet low in kilojoules (calories).

Cabbage Chop Suey

SERVES 6–8

1 teaspoon finely chopped fresh ginger
1 clove garlic, crushed
*2 tablespoons/2 tablespoons plus 2
    teaspoons low-salt soy sauce*
*1 tablespoon/1 tablespoon plus 1
    teaspoon salt-free tomato paste*
*2 tablespoons/2 tablespoons plus 2
    teaspoons dry sherry or Chinese wine*
*350 ml/12 fl oz/1½ cups Vegetable
    Stock (see p. 14)*
125 g/¼ lb mushrooms, chopped
125 g/¼ lb beans, chopped
4 sticks celery, diagonally sliced
2 onions, cut into thin wedges
500 g/1 lb 2 oz Chinese cabbage
1 large carrot, chopped
1 small red capsicum, chopped
1 small green capsicum, chopped
*1 tablespoon/1 tablespoon plus 1
    teaspoon cornflour*
200 g/7 oz fresh bean shoots
*225 g/½ lb lightly steamed chicken meat,
    cut into bite-sized pieces (optional)*
*225 g/½ lb cooked prawns, shelled and
    deveined (optional)*
*60 g/2 oz/½ cup dark-brown roasted
    almonds (optional)*

Place the ginger, garlic, soy sauce, tomato paste, sherry, 125 ml/4 fl oz/½ cup of the Vegetable Stock and mushroom in a cold wok. Slowly bring to the boil and simmer, covered, for 1 minute.

Remove the lid and add the beans, celery and onion. Toss to combine all the ingredients. Cook, covered, for 2 minutes.

Shred the cabbage. Remove the lid and add the carrot, capsicum and cabbage. Toss to combine all the ingredients. You will need to do this at least twice as the cabbage softens. Cook, covered, for 3 minutes.

Remove the lid and add the remaining stock combined with the cornflour. Stir through until the sauce boils and begins to thicken. Add the bean shoots and one of the optional extras if desired. Toss the ingredients to combine and cook for a further 2–3 minutes. Serve immediately.

Note
If including the almonds, remember that roasted nuts are high in saturated fats and should be eaten sparingly.

Carrot and Broccoli Quiche

SERVES 6

Base
*185 g/6 oz/3 cups fresh wholemeal
    breadcrumbs*
*2 tablespoons/2 tablespoons plus 2
    teaspoons salt-free tomato paste*

Filling
200 g/7 oz broccoli florets
200 g/7 oz carrots, cut into chunks
*250 ml/8 fl oz/1 cup low-fat evaporated
    skim milk*
*200 g/7 oz/⅔ cup low-fat cottage
    cheese*
4 egg whites
*60 g/2 oz/1 cup mixed fresh herbs (e.g.
    chives, parsley, basil), finely chopped*

Preheat the oven to 180°C/350°F.

To make the Base, combine the breadcrumbs and tomato paste in a food processor or blender until the mixture just begins to stick together. Press into a lightly greased quiche dish, ensuring the sides are even and come up to the top of the dish. Firm the base and edges, otherwise the quiche will be crumbly. Bake for 10 minutes. Set aside to cool.

To make the Filling, steam the broccoli florets and carrot chunks until just tender. Drain well. Place the milk, cheese, egg whites and herbs in a food processor or blender. Blend until well mixed and the cheese is smooth. Place the vegetables across the cooked base and pour the cheese mixture over the top.

Bake until the centre is firm (approximately 30–40 minutes).

Carrot Mousse with White Parsley Sauce

SERVES 4

500 g/1 lb 2 oz carrots (preferably baby carrots)
2 teaspoons fresh ginger juice (press ginger through a garlic crusher)
30 g/1 oz/¼ cup wholemeal plain flour
250 ml/8 fl oz/1 cup low-fat evaporated milk
¼ teaspoon ground nutmeg
4 egg whites

White Parsley Sauce
350 ml/12 fl oz/1½ cups skim milk
2 tablespoons/2 tablespoons plus 2 teaspoons cornflour
2 tablespoons/2 tablespoons plus 2 teaspoons finely chopped fresh parsley
black pepper to taste

Preheat oven to 180°C/350°F.

Cook the carrots until just tender. Blend the carrot and ginger in a food processor or blender until smooth. Place the flour in a small saucepan and cook on low heat for a few seconds. Pour in the milk and stir briskly until thick. Add the nutmeg, and pour the mixture over the carrot in the food processor and blend until all the ingredients are combined. Add the egg whites and blend for 15 seconds. Pour into lightly greased individual moulds. Cover with foil. Place in a baking dish containing water and bake for 40 minutes. Remove from the oven and let stand for 5 minutes before turning out.

To make the White Parsley Sauce, combine a little of the milk with the cornflour and make a paste. Heat the remaining milk until boiling. Stir in the cornflour. Cook until the sauce thickens, and then add the parsley.

Serve the mousses with the White Parsley Sauce, perhaps accompanied by broccoli and cherry tomatoes.

Carrot Strudels with Lemon Sauce

SERVES 2

200 g/7 oz/2¼ cups grated carrot
90 g/3 oz/1 cup grated pumpkin
1 teaspoon finely chopped fresh ginger
2 tablespoons/2 tablespoons plus 2 teaspoons freshly chopped chives
310 g/10½ oz/1 cup cooked brown lentils
4 sheets filo pastry
1 egg white
2 tablespoons/2 tablespoons plus 2 teaspoons cold water

Lemon Sauce
30 g/1 oz/¼ cup cornflour
250 ml/8 fl oz/1 cup unsweetened orange juice
500 ml/16 fl oz/2 cups Vegetable Stock (see p. 14)
1 tablespoon/1 tablespoon plus 1 teaspoon lemon juice
1 tablespoon/1 tablespoon plus 1 teaspoon apple juice concentrate

Preheat the oven to 180°C/350°F.

Combine the carrot, pumpkin, ginger, chives and lentils and mix well. Cut the filo sheets in half. Mix the egg white and water together. Brush most of this mixture over the top of the pastry, especially around the edges.

Place equal amounts of filling in the centre of each pastry. Roll up securely, using more egg white and water. Pinch the ends together to make a bonbon shape. Brush more egg white and water over the top of the strudels.

Bake on a non-stick baking tray for 25–30 minutes.

To make the Lemon Sauce, mix the cornflour with a little of the orange juice to make a paste. Add the paste to the remaining ingredients in a saucepan. Stir well over heat until the sauce boils and thickens. Cook for 2 minutes. This sauce can also be used over chicken, fish or steamed vegetables.

Carrot Strudel

xxxxxxxxxxxxxxxxxxxxxxxxxxxxxxxxxxxxxxxxxxxxxxxxxxxxxxxxxxxxxxxxxxxxx

SERVES 8

*1 tablespoon/1 tablespoon plus 1
    teaspoon light olive oil*
1 egg white
8 sheets wholemeal filo pastry
125 ml/4 fl oz/½ cup water
575 g/1¼ lb carrots, grated
400 g/14 oz pumpkin, grated
2 teaspoons finely chopped fresh ginger
2 teaspoons dried dill
*2 tablespoons/2 tablespoons plus 2
    teaspoons lemon juice*
225 g/½ lb/1 cup low-fat cottage cheese

Preheat the oven to 200°C/400°F.

Combine the oil, egg white and water and lightly wipe between the filo sheets. Do not saturate. Combine the remaining ingredients, and mix well. Leave to stand in a colander for 30 minutes. Squeeze out excess moisture before wrapping in the filo. Wipe all edges well so filling does not escape in the cooking process.

Place the parcel carefully on a baking tray lined with baking paper. Cook for 30 minutes. Turn the heat down to 160°C/325°F and cook for a further 20 minutes. Remove from the oven to a cooling tray.

Cauliflower Cheese Bake

xxxxxxxxxxxxxxxxxxxxxxxxxxxxxxxxxxxxxxxxxxxxxxxxxxxxxxxxxxxxxxxxxxxxx

SERVES 4

310 g/10½ oz carrots, cut into rounds
500 g/1 lb 2 oz cauliflower florets
500 ml/16 fl oz/2 cups soymilk
2 bay leaves
black pepper to taste
*2 tablespoons/2 tablespoons plus 2
    teaspoons finely chopped fresh parsley*
30 g/1 oz/¼ cup cornflour
*100 g/3½ oz/1 cup low-fat grating
    cheese, finely grated*

Preheat the oven to 200°C/400°F.

Steam the carrot and cauliflower until just tender. Combine the remaining ingredients, except the cornflour and cheese, in a small saucepan. Mix the cornflour with a small amount of water to make a paste. Bring the soymilk and herbs to just below boiling. Stir through the cornflour briskly to make a thick sauce. Remove the bay leaves.

Place the carrots on the base of a shallow casserole dish. Top with the cauliflower and pour the white sauce over the top. Sprinkle with the cheese. Bake for 10–15 minutes or until the top is browned.

Mushroom Quiche

xxxxxxxxxxxxxxxxxxxxxxxxxxxxxxxxxxxxxxxxxxxxxxxxxxxxxxxxxxxxxxxxxxxxx

SERVES 6

Base
*185 g/6 oz/3 cups fresh wholemeal
    breadcrumbs*
*2 tablespoons/2 tablespoons plus 2
    teaspoons salt-free tomato paste*

Filling
20 mushrooms
*250 ml/8 fl oz/1 cup low-fat evaporated
    skim milk*
225 g/½ lb/1 cup low-fat cottage cheese
4 egg whites
lots of black pepper
90 g/3 oz/1 cup chopped spring onion

Preheat the oven to 180°C/350°F.

Combine the breadcrumbs and tomato paste in a food processor or blender until the mixture just begins to stick together. Press into a lightly greased quiche dish.

Cook for 10 minutes. Remove from oven and cool.

Steam the mushrooms until soft. Drain, and add the juice to the milk. Combine the milk, cottage cheese and egg whites in a food processor or blender and blend until smooth. Add the black pepper and fold in the spring onion.

Pour the mixture across the cooked base and place the mushrooms, tops up, evenly in the mixture.

Bake until the centre is firm, approximately 30–40 minutes.

Mushroom Pie

SERVES 6–8

Base

125 g / ¼ lb / 2 cups fresh wholemeal
　breadcrumbs
40 g / 1½ oz / ½ cup finely chopped
　shallot
1 egg white
1 tablespoon / 1 tablespoon plus 1
　teaspoon toasted sesame seeds

Filling

3 zucchini, grated
2 tomatoes, sliced
1 teaspoon dried basil
1 teaspoon dried oregano
200 g / 7 oz mushrooms, finely sliced
4 egg whites
125 ml / 4 fl oz / ½ cup low-fat
　evaporated skim milk
60 g / 2 oz / 1 cup fresh parsley, finely
　chopped
65 ml / 2 fl oz / ¼ cup non-fat or low-fat
　yoghurt
30 g / 1 oz / ¼ cup grated low-fat grating
　cheese
60 g / 2 oz / 1 cup fresh wholemeal
　breadcrumbs

Preheat the oven to 180°C/350°F. To make the Base, blend the Base ingredients in a food processor or blender until the breadcrumbs begin to stick together. Do not overblend. Lightly grease a fluted-edged pie dish and press the breadcrumbs firmly over the base and sides. Cook for 15 minutes.

Turn up the oven to 200°C/400°F.

To make the Filling, spread the zucchini over the base. Top with tomato slices, basil and oregano. Add the mushroom. Beat the egg whites and milk, add the parsley and pour over the mushroom. Spoon the yoghurt in a circle over the mushroom. Sprinkle the cheese over the yoghurt, and the breadcrumbs over the top. Cook for 40–50 minutes. (See left colour plate between pages 40 and 41.)

Mushroom and Potato Pie

SERVES 4–6

1 kg / 2¼ lb potatoes, peeled and cubed
a little skim milk (if necessary)
4 sticks celery, finely chopped
1 onion, finely chopped
2 cloves garlic, crushed
2 tablespoons / 2 tablespoons plus 2
　teaspoons water (if necessary)
1 carrot, grated
400 g / 14 oz mushrooms, finely sliced
2 tablespoons / 2 tablespoons plus 2
　teaspoons cornflour
250 ml / 8 fl oz / 1 cup skim milk
2 tablespoons / 2 tablespoons plus 2
　teaspoons finely chopped fresh parsley
1 teaspoon dried thyme
2 teaspoons lemon juice
pinch of cayenne pepper

Preheat the oven to 190°C/375°F.

Cook the potato in boiling water until tender. Drain and mash until smooth. Add a little skim milk if necessary.

Place the celery, onion and garlic in a saucepan and cook until soft and transparent. If necessary, add 2 tablespoons / 2 tablespoons plus 2 teaspoons of water to avoid sticking at the base of the saucepan. Add the carrot and mushroom and cook for a further 10 minutes.

Blend the cornflour and milk and stir into the mushroom. Add the parsley, thyme, lemon juice and cayenne pepper. Simmer for 5 minutes. Pour the mixture into a lightly greased ovenproof dish. Spoon the mashed potatoes over the top, and spread evenly. Cook for 20 minutes or until the potato begins to brown.

Mushroom and Tomato Rolls

SERVES 4

310 g/10½ oz mushrooms
125 ml/4 fl oz/½ cup water
4 cooked tomatoes and juice
2 tablespoons/2 tablespoons plus 2
    teaspoons freshly chopped parsley
2 tablespoons/2 tablespoons plus 2
    teaspoons freshly chopped chives
pinch of ground nutmeg (optional)
2 tablespoons/2 tablespoons plus 2
    teaspoons cornflour
65 ml/2 fl oz/¼ cup extra water
4 wholemeal bread rolls

Cook the mushrooms in the water over a gentle heat for 10 minutes. Add the tomatoes and juice, parsley and chives. Cook for a further 5 minutes. Add the nutmeg. Mix the cornflour and the extra water, and stir through the mushrooms until thick.

Remove the tops from the rolls and hollow out the centre of each. Place the rolls under the grill until well browned on the top and bottom. Place each roll on individual serving plates and spoon the mushroom and tomato mixture into each roll. Serve. (See right colour plate between pages 40 and 41.)

Potato Stew

SERVES 8–10

1 kg/2¼ lb potatoes
1 sweet potato
1 parsnip
2 carrots
1 zucchini
2 onions, quartered
1 tablespoon/1 tablespoon plus 1
    teaspoon Vecon
750 ml/1⅓ pints/3 cups boiling water
350 ml/12 fl oz/1½ cups canned
    salt-free vegetable juice
225 g/½ lb/2 cups frozen peas
handful of finely chopped fresh parsley
3 tablespoons/3 tablespoons plus 3
    teaspoons cornflour
65 ml/2 fl oz/¼ cup water

Preheat the oven to 190°C/375°F.

Prepare the fresh vegetables by peeling and cutting them into cubes. The potato cubes should be twice the size of the other vegetables. In a large ovenproof dish, dissolve the Vecon in 250 ml/8 fl oz/1 cup of the boiling water. Add all the cubed vegetables. Cover with the remaining water and the vegetable juice. Cover, and cook for about 40 minutes.

When the vegetables are just tender, add the peas, parsley and combined cornflour and 65 ml/2 fl oz/¼ cup of water. Bring to the boil and cook for 5 minutes.

Serve with wholemeal bread.

Potato Hunza Pie

MAKES 8–10 SLICES

1.25 kg/2¾ lb potatoes, peeled and
    cubed
1 small bunch spinach, roughly chopped
90 g/3 oz/1 cup chopped spring onion
1 teaspoon ground nutmeg
pinch of cayenne pepper
6 sheets wholemeal filo pastry
2 tablespoons/2 tablespoons plus 2
    teaspoons sesame seeds or poppyseeds

Preheat the oven to 230°C/450°F.

Steam the potatoes until tender and drain. Steam the spinach until cooked and drain. Combine the potato, spinach, spring onion, nutmeg and cayenne pepper, and mix well.

Line a large, lightly greased pie dish with four sheets of the filo pastry and trim the edges. Fill with the spinach and potato mixture and spread evenly. Top with the two remaining sheets of filo pastry and trim the edges. Using a pastry brush, lightly wipe the top with water. Sprinkle with sesame seeds. Bake for 10 minutes, turn the heat down to 200°C/400°F and bake for a further 20 minutes.

Potato Bean Bake

xxxxxxxxxxxxxxxxxxxxxxxxxxxxxxxxxxxxxxxxxxxxxxxxxxxxxxxxxxxxxxxxxxxxxxxxxxxxxxxxxxxxxx

SERVES 4–6

1 onion, chopped
1 teaspoon crushed garlic
125 g/¼ lb/1¼ cups chopped celery
1 teaspoon curry powder
1 teaspoon garam masala
125 g/¼ lb/1¼ cup chopped carrot
125 g/¼ lb/1 cup frozen peas
a little water
350 ml/12 fl oz/1½ cups salt-free
*   tomato juice*
2 tablespoons/2 tablespoons plus 2
*   teaspoons salt-free tomato paste*
450 g/1 lb/2 cups red kidney beans,
*   cooked*
large handful finely chopped fresh parsley
750 g/1 lb 10 oz potatoes, peeled and
*   cut into thin rounds*
100 g/3½ oz/1 cup grated low-fat
*   grating cheese*
a little paprika

Preheat the oven to 200°C/400°F.

In a non-stick saucepan cook the onion, garlic, celery and spices until soft. Add the carrot and peas with a little water, and cover. Cook until the carrot is tender. Add 250 ml/ 8 fl oz/1 cup of the tomato juice, tomato paste, beans and parsley. Cover and remove from the heat.

Cook the potato until just tender – not too soft. Drain.

Place a layer of potato slices on the bottom of a rectangular casserole dish. Add the vegetable and bean mixture. Overlap the remaining potato slices on top. Pour the remaining tomato juice on top, and sprinkle with the cheese and paprika.

Cook for 30 minutes or until well browned on top.

Sweet-potato and Lentil Burgers

xxxxxxxxxxxxxxxxxxxxxxxxxxxxxxxxxxxxxxxxxxxxxxxxxxxxxxxxxxxxxxxxxxxxxxxxxxxxxxxxxxxxxx

MAKES 6

90 g/3 oz/½ cup brown lentils
100 g/3½ oz carrots, chopped
400 g/14 oz sweet potatoes, peeled and
*   chopped*
1 onion, chopped
2 teaspoons low-salt soy sauce
2 tablespoons/2 tablespoons plus 2
*   teaspoons finely chopped fresh parsley*
*   or chives*
black pepper to taste
60 g/2 oz/½ cup oat bran

Yoghurt Curry Dressing
250 ml/8 fl oz/1 cup non-fat or low-fat
*   yoghurt*
1 teaspoon curry powder
1 teaspoon ground cummin

Boil the lentils for 30–40 minutes, until soft. Drain.

Cook the carrot, sweet potato and onion together until soft. Drain and mash. Add the lentils, soy sauce, parsley and black pepper. Shape into six burgers and lightly coat with the oat bran.

Cook in a non-stick frying pan to brown on both sides.

To make the Yoghurt Curry Dressing, combine all the ingredients. Mix well and serve with the burgers. Store any leftover dressing in a covered container in the refrigerator.

Potato and Corn Croquettes

MAKES 6

*500 g / 1 lb 2 oz potatoes, peeled and
   cubed*
1 onion, chopped
2 teaspoons wholegrain mustard
200 g / 7 oz cooked corn kernels, puréed
1 egg white
90 g / 3 oz / 1 cup grated carrot
*2 tablespoons / 2 tablespoons plus 2
   teaspoons finely chopped fresh parsley*
*2 egg whites mixed with 1 tablespoon / 1
   tablespoon plus 1 teaspoon water*
*90 g / 3 oz / 1½ cups fresh wholemeal
   breadcrumbs or oat bran or a
   combination of both*

Boil or steam the potato until tender and then drain. Add the onion, mustard, corn, egg white, carrot and parsley. Mix together well. Form into six croquettes and refrigerate until firm.

Dip the croquettes in the egg white and water mixture and roll in the breadcrumbs. Grease a non-stick frying pan with a little light olive oil. Gently cook, turning to brown all sides, for approximately 15–20 minutes; or preheat the oven to 180°C/350°F, place the croquettes on a non-stick baking tray and cook for 30 minutes or until browned and crisp on all sides.

Potato and Spinach Pasties

MAKES 8

Pastry
125 g / ¼ lb / 1 cup wholemeal plain flour
*125 g / ¼ lb / 1 cup unbleached white
   plain flour*
*60 g / 2 oz / ½ cup wholemeal self-raising
   flour*
*3 tablespoons / 3 tablespoons plus 3
   teaspoons light olive oil*
*1 tablespoon / 1 tablespoon plus 1
   teaspoon lemon juice*
250 ml / 8 fl oz / 1 cup cold water
extra flour for kneading

Filling
*575 g / 1¼ lb potatoes, peeled and
   chopped*
1 onion, finely chopped
125 g / ¼ lb / 1 cup frozen peas
*100 g / 3½ oz / 1 cup spinach, finely
   chopped*
*1 tablespoon / 1 tablespoon plus 1
   teaspoon salt-free tomato paste*
*1 tablespoon / 1 tablespoon plus 1
   teaspoon low-salt soy sauce*
*1 tablespoon / 1 tablespoon plus 1
   teaspoon geska herb cheese or
   parmesan cheese*
1 egg white combined with a little water

To make the Pastry, sift the flours into a large bowl, and return the husks to the bowl. Make a well in the middle of the flour and add the oil and lemon juice. Work through the flour with your fingertips. Gradually add the water. Mix well until the mixture comes together to make a ball. Knead lightly on a floured board. Chill for about 30 minutes in the refrigerator.

While the pastry is chilling, preheat the oven to 180°C/350°F and prepare the Filling. Steam the potato until just tender. Run it under cold water and drain well. Add the onion and frozen peas. Steam the spinach until soft, then squeeze any moisture from it and add it to the potato mixture. Stir in the tomato paste, soy sauce and cheese.

Cut the pastry into eight equal portions. Roll out each portion into a circle. Divide the filling between the circles. Wipe around the edge of the pastry with the combined egg white and water. Fold the pastry over to make half-circles. Cut small air holes in the pastry for steam to escape. Place on a non-stick baking tray and cook for 30 minutes. (See colour plate opposite.)

Potato and Spinach Pasty (opposite page) plated with mixed vegetables.

Mexican Bean Tortilla (opposite page).

Mexican Bean Tortillas

SERVES 2

2 tortillas
a little Tabasco (optional)
575 g/1¼ lb/2 cups cooked red kidney
*   beans*
a little shredded lettuce
1 tomato, seeded and chopped
30 g/1 oz/¼ cup chopped spring onion
60 g/2 oz/¼ cup cooked corn kernels
2 radishes, finely sliced
2 tablespoons/2 tablespoons plus 2
*   teaspoons non-fat or low-fat yoghurt*

Quick and Easy Tomato Sauce
1 onion, finely chopped
1 teaspoon crushed garlic
425 g/15 oz canned salt-free tomatoes in
*   natural juice, roughly chopped*
125 ml/4 fl oz/½ cup salt-free tomato
*   paste*
½ teaspoon dried basil
½ teaspoon dried oregano
black pepper to taste

To make the Quick and Easy Tomato Sauce, sauté the onion and garlic in a saucepan over a low heat until the onion begins to soften. Add all the other ingredients. Simmer, uncovered, for 10 minutes.

Heat the tortillas in a hot oven until crisp. In a saucepan, heat 1 cup of the tomato sauce. Add a little Tabasco for a hotter taste if desired. Mash 185 g/6 oz/1 cup of the kidney beans and add to the tomato sauce. Spread this equally over the tortillas. Combine all the salad ingredients and add to the tortillas. Top with the remaining beans, and 1 tablespoon of yoghurt per tortilla. Serve immediately. (See colour plate opposite.)

Pumpkin Bean Bake

SERVES 2

2 small orange baby pumpkins
310 g/10½ oz canned red kidney beans,
*   rinsed*
250 ml/8 fl oz/1 cup Quick and Easy
*   Tomato Sauce (see* Mexican Bean
*   Tortillas this page)*
2 tablespoons/2 tablespoons plus 2
*   teaspoons finely chopped fresh parsley*
2 tablespoons/2 tablespoons plus 2
*   teaspoons finely chopped fresh chives*

Preheat the oven to 200°C/400°F.

Cut the tops off the pumpkins and put aside. Scoop out the seeds and discard. Cut away the pumpkin flesh to create a firm outer shell. Chop up the pumpkin flesh finely. Add this to the beans, Quick and Easy Tomato Sauce and herbs. Spoon the mixture back into the pumpkins, and place the lids on. Put the pumpkins in a shallow dish and cover.

Bake for 50 minutes or until the pumpkins are very tender.

Pumpkin Almond Pie

SERVES 8

Base
125 g/¼ lb/1 cup wheatgerm
*60 g/2 oz/1 cup fresh wholemeal
  breadcrumbs*

Filling
*500 g/1 lb 2 oz pumpkin, peeled and
  grated*
4 potatoes, peeled and grated
*125 g/¼ lb/2 cups fresh wholemeal
  breadcrumbs*
1 onion, grated
90 g/3 oz/1 cup finely chopped celery
¼ teaspoon ground nutmeg
¼ teaspoon cayenne pepper
4 egg whites
65 ml/2 fl oz/¼ cup skim milk

Topping
*60 g/2 oz/½ cup oat or barley or
  wheat bran*
60 g/2 oz/½ cup flaked almonds

Preheat the oven to 200°C/400°F.

To make the Base, line a 20-cm/8″ round cake tin with foil. Combine the wheatgerm and breadcrumbs and press down into the base of the cake tin.

To make the Filling, combine the Filling ingredients and mix well. Press this mixture firmly onto the base.

To make the Topping, mix the oat bran and almonds and sprinkle this over the filling. Cover with foil. Bake for 1½ hours. Remove the foil and cook for a further 10 minutes, until the almonds brown slightly. Serve hot or cold.

If you are serving the pie hot, let it stand for a few minutes before removing it from the foil and cake tin and transferring it to a serving plate. (See left colour plate between pages 56 and 57.)

Ratatouille

SERVES 4

125 ml/4 fl oz/½ cup stock or water
2 white onions, cut into wedges
2 cloves garlic, crushed
2 eggplants, coarsely chopped
2 zucchini, sliced
4 tomatoes, peeled and chopped
2 capsicums, chopped
6 green beans, chopped
1 stick celery, chopped
10 cauliflower florets
1 carrot, finely sliced
1 teaspoon dried basil
1 teaspoon celery seeds

Put the stock, onion and garlic into a large frying pan. Cover, and cook for 2 minutes over a gentle heat. Add the eggplant and zucchini, and cook for 5 minutes. Add the tomato and all the other vegetables. Sprinkle the basil and celery seed over the top. Move the ingredients around the frying pan for 10 minutes. Serve on a bed of brown rice or wholemeal toast.

Minestrone Stew

SERVES 8–10

125 g /¼ lb /⅔ cup haricot or red kidney beans
2 cloves garlic, crushed
1 leek, thoroughly washed and chopped
500 ml /16 fl oz /2 cups Vegetable Stock (see p. 14) or water
10 green beans, topped and tailed
100 g /3½ oz carrots, chopped
100 g /3½ oz celery, chopped
100 g /3½ oz zucchini, chopped
100 g /3½ oz potatoes, peeled and chopped
10 mushrooms, cut in half
1 teaspoon dried basil
1 teaspoon dried marjoram
425 g /15 oz canned whole tomatoes in natural juice, salt-free
3 tablespoons /3 tablespoons plus 3 teaspoons cornflour
65 ml /2 fl oz /¼ cup water
handful of finely chopped fresh parsley
2 tablespoons /2 tablespoons plus 2 teaspoons finely chopped fresh chives
wholemeal noodles or wholemeal toast for serving

Soak the beans overnight. Drain and cover with water. Bring to the boil, reduce heat and simmer for 1–1½ hours or until the beans are tender. Drain.

Place the garlic, leek and stock in a casserole dish or saucepan. Simmer for 10 minutes. Quarter the green beans and add them to the casserole dish with the remaining ingredients except the haricot beans, cornflour, water, parsley and chives. Cook until the vegetables are tender.

Mix the cornflour with the water. Add to the casserole dish. Bring to the boil and stir to thicken. Reduce the heat. Add the haricot beans, parsley and chopped chives.

Serve with the wholemeal noodles or wholemeal toast.

Spinach Roulade

SERVES 4

200 g /7 oz cooked and drained spinach
2 tablespoons /2 tablespoons plus 2 teaspoons unbleached white plain flour
1 tablespoon /1 tablespoon plus 1 teaspoon geska herb cheese or parmesan cheese
6 egg whites

Filling
200 g /7 oz /¾ cup low-fat cottage cheese
2 tablespoons /2 tablespoons plus 2 teaspoons finely chopped fresh chives
40 g /1½ oz /½ cup finely chopped red capsicum
2 tablespoons /2 tablespoons plus 2 teaspoons finely chopped carrot

Preheat the oven to 180°C /350°F.

Leave the spinach to cool. Place in a food processor or blender. Add the flour and cheese, and purée until smooth. Beat the egg whites until stiff peaks form. Gently fold in the spinach purée until well combined.

Line a small slice tray with non-stick baking paper. Pour the mixture into the tray and spread out evenly. Cook for 10–15 minutes. Remove from the oven and upturn the roulade onto a dry tea towel. Carefully roll up and leave to cool. Combine all the filling ingredients, and mix well. Spread evenly over the cooled roulade. Roll up and secure. Refrigerate until firm.

Spinach Triangles

XXXXXXXXXXXXXXXXXXXXXXXXXXXXXXXXXXXXXXXXXXXXXXXXXXX

SERVES 8

400 g/14 oz spinach
400 g/14 oz/1¾ cups low-fat ricotta
  cheese
1 teaspoon ground nutmeg
1 teaspoon geska herb cheese or
  parmesan cheese
3 sheets plain or wholemeal filo pastry
  per triangle
1 egg white
65 ml/2 fl oz/¼ cup water
sesame seeds or poppyseeds
a little oat bran (optional)

Preheat the oven to 180°C/350°F.

Chop the spinach roughly, and wash. Steam until soft. Do not wring dry. Leave to drain in a colander.

Combine the spinach with the ricotta cheese. Leave a little crumbly. Add nutmeg and geska herb cheese. Fold the filo into three. Fold over to make triangles. Mix the egg white and water together, and wipe over the pastry. Sprinkle with the sesame seeds. If using plain filo, sprinkle a little bran between each sheet. Cook for 20 minutes.

Tomato Cheese Quiche

XXXXXXXXXXXXXXXXXXXXXXXXXXXXXXXXXXXXXXXXXXXXXXXXXXX

SERVES 4 – 6

Base
185 g/6 oz/3 cups fresh wholemeal
  breadcrumbs
2 tablespoons/2 tablespoons plus 2
  teaspoons salt-free tomato juice

Filling
1 onion, chopped
a little water
425 g/15 oz canned whole tomatoes in
  natural juice, salt-free
½ teaspoon dried basil
½ teaspoon dried oregano
½ teaspoon ground coriander
400 g/14 oz/1¾ cups low-fat ricotta
  cheese
4 egg whites
2 large tomatoes, sliced
100 g/3½ oz/1 cup finely grated low-fat
  grating cheese
extra tomato slices for garnishing
freshly chopped parsley for garnishing

Preheat the oven to 180°C/350°F.

Combine the Base ingredients and press firmly into a 23-cm/9″ round lightly greased pie dish. Bake for 10–15 minutes or until lightly browned. Remove from the oven and leave to cool.

For the Filling, turn oven up to 230°C/450°F. Cook the onion in a little water until soft, approximately 2–3 minutes. Remove from the heat, add the tomatoes, basil, oregano, coriander and ricotta cheese. Purée in a food processor or blender until very smooth. Beat the egg whites until light and fluffy and gently fold into the tomato mixture.

Pour the mixture over the cooked breadcrumb base. Carefully cover the mixture with the tomato slices and spread the grated cheese evenly over the tomato. Cook at 230°C/450°F for 15 minutes and turn down to 190°C/375°F for a further 30 minutes.

Garnish top with the extra slices of tomato and fresh parsley. This quiche is delicious either hot or cold.

Curried Vegetables and Yoghurt Dip

SERVES 2

a selection of the following: broccoli, cauliflower, carrots, zucchini, squash, capsicum, Brussels sprouts, celery

Yoghurt Dip
125 ml/4 fl oz/½ cup non-fat or low-fat yoghurt
30 g/1 oz/¼ cup peeled, seeded and chopped cucumber
a little crushed garlic (optional)
pinch of dried dill

Curry Sauce
1 teaspoon light olive oil or 2 tablespoons water
½ onion, chopped
1 teaspoon crushed garlic
1 teaspoon crushed fresh ginger
1 teaspoon turmeric
1 teaspoon ground coriander
1 teaspoon garam masala
1 teaspoon ground cummin
1 tablespoon/1 tablespoon plus 1 teaspoon water
350 ml/12 fl oz/1½ cups skim milk
1 tablespoon/1 tablespoon plus 1 teaspoon cornflour

Cut the broccoli and cauliflower into florets and cut each floret into three thin slices. Carrots can be diagonally cut into thin slices. Cut zucchini into julienne strips. Slice squash thinly. Cut capsicums into thin strips. Cut Brussels sprouts in half. Cut celery in Chinese-style diagonals.

Steam the chosen vegetables until just tender.

To make the Yoghurt Dip, combine all the ingredients and refrigerate.

To make the Curry Sauce, place the oil, onion, garlic and spices in a saucepan. Stir over a low heat until the onion begins to soften. Add the water to make a paste. Stir for 1 minute. Mix a little of the milk with the cornflour to make a paste. Stir it through the remaining milk. Add to the curry paste, stirring continuously until the sauce simmers and thickens.

Add the vegetables to the sauce and coat well. Serve on a plate with brown rice and 65 ml/2 fl oz/¼ cup of Yoghurt Dip per person. (See colour plate opposite page 41.)

Vegetable Frittata

SERVES 6

500 g/1 lb 2 oz grated peeled potato
200 g/7 oz/2¼ cups grated carrot
200 g/7 oz/2¼ cups grated parsnip
200 g/7 oz/2¼ cups grated zucchini (juice squeezed out)
90 g/3 oz/1 cup finely sliced mushrooms (optional)
200 g/7 oz/2 cups grated low-fat grating cheese
60 g/2 oz/1 cup finely chopped mixed fresh herbs (e.g. parsley, chives, basil, marjoram, thyme, oregano)
6 egg whites
2 teaspoons turmeric
lots of black pepper

Wash the grated potato, removing the starch. Squeeze out any moisture. Combine the potato, carrot, parsnip, zucchini, mushroom, cheese and herbs. Mix well.

Lightly beat the egg whites and turmeric. Fold into the vegetable mixture, and add the black pepper.

Grease the base and sides of a heavy pan. Wipe out any excess oil. Press the vegetable mixture into the pan. Cover. Cook for 15 minutes. Place under the grill to brown the top.

Cut into triangle slices and serve with salad.

Vegetable and Orange Casserole

xxxxxxxxxxxxxxxxxxxxxxxxxxxxxxxxxxxxxxxxxxxxxxxxxxxxxxxxxxxxxxxxxxxxxxxxxxxxxxxxxxxxxxxxxxxxx

SERVES 6–8

4 large potatoes, peeled and cut into
  large cubes
2 carrots, cut into large chunks
1 parsnip, cut into chunks
185 g/6 oz/1 cup celery chunks
125 g/¼ lb/1 cup peas
185 g/6 oz/1 cup green beans
425 g/15 oz canned salt-free tomatoes,
  chopped and drained
1 green capsicum, cut into chunks
1 red capsicum, cut into chunks
500 ml/16 fl oz/2 cups unsweetened
  orange juice
1 tablespoon/1 tablespoon plus 1
  teaspoon finely grated orange rind
500 ml/16 fl oz/2 cups water or
  Vegetable Stock or Chicken Stock
  (see p. 14)
400 g/14 oz/2 cups grated swede
black pepper to taste
a little cornflour (optional)

Preheat the oven to 190°C/375°F.

Place all the ingredients in a large earthenware casserole dish. Cook, covered, for 2 hours. The casserole is ready to eat when the vegetables are tender and the liquid has reduced into a thick sauce. If a thicker sauce is preferred, dissolve a little cornflour in some cooled casserole liquid and then add this to the casserole.

Vegetable Spring Rolls

xxxxxxxxxxxxxxxxxxxxxxxxxxxxxxxxxxxxxxxxxxxxxxxxxxxxxxxxxxxxxxxxxxxxxxxxxxxxxxxxxxxxxxxxxxxxx

MAKES 8

1 egg white
2 tablespoons/2 tablespoons plus 2
  teaspoons cornflour
65 ml/2 fl oz/¼ cup water
1 teaspoon curry powder
8 sheets filo pastry

Filling

1 teaspoon finely grated fresh ginger
½ red capsicum, finely chopped
4 shallots, finely chopped
5 mushrooms, finely chopped
60 g/2 oz/1 cup fresh wholemeal
  breadcrumbs
400 g/14 oz cabbage, finely shredded
1 tablespoon/1 tablespoon plus 1
  teaspoon dry sherry
1 tablespoon/1 tablespoon plus 1
  teaspoon low-salt soy sauce

Preheat the oven to 190°C/375°F.

Combine all the filling ingredients and mix well with your hands.

Combine the egg white, cornflour, water and curry powder and make a thin paste.

To assemble, fold a filo sheet in half. Brush lightly with the cornflour mixture. Take a handful of filling and place it evenly across one corner of the filo sheet. Roll it up in an envelope shape, ensuring the edges have been brushed with the cornflour mixture. Place on a non-stick baking tray. Repeat with the remaining mixture.

Bake the spring rolls for 30–40 minutes.

Sweet-and-sour Vegetables

SERVES 6–8

2 tablespoons/2 tablespoons plus 2
    teaspoons salt-free tomato paste
2 tablespoons/2 tablespoons plus 2
    teaspoons low-salt soy sauce
1 teaspoon finely chopped fresh ginger
200 ml/7 fl oz/¾ cup unsweetened
    pineapple juice
65 ml/2 fl oz/¼ cup white wine vinegar
300 ml/10 fl oz/1¼ cups Vegetable
    Stock (see p. 14)
1 small onion, sliced into rings
200 g/7 oz carrots, diagonally cut and
    halved again
200 g/7 oz celery, diagonally cut
200 g/7 oz zucchini, cut into small
    chunks
200 g/7 oz mushrooms, sliced
1 red capsicum, chopped
1 green capsicum, chopped
425 g/15 oz canned unsweetened
    pineapple pieces
1 heaped tablespoon/1 heaped tablespoon
    plus 1 heaped teaspoon cornflour
6 spring onions, diagonally sliced, for
    garnishing

Add the tomato paste, soy sauce, ginger, pineapple juice and vinegar to a cold wok with 65 ml/2 fl oz/¼ cup of the Vegetable Stock. Slowly bring to the boil and simmer, covered, for 1 minute. Add the onion, carrot, celery and zucchini. Toss to combine the ingredients. Cook, covered, for 2 minutes.

Add the mushroom and capsicum. Toss to combine all the ingredients. Cook, covered for another 2 minutes.

Add the pineapple pieces and the remaining stock combined with the cornflour. Wait for the sauce to boil and cook, covered, for a further 3 minutes. Serve immediately, garnished with the spring onion. (See colour plate opposite page 72.)

Vegetarian Chili con Carne

SERVES 10–12

400 g/14 oz/2½ cups red kidney beans
12 large potatoes
2 small onions, chopped
2 cloves garlic, crushed
310 g/10½ oz carrots, chopped
400 g/14 oz green beans, sliced
2 small red capsicums, chopped
1 cup salt-free tomato juice
800 g/1¾ lb canned whole tomatoes in
    natural juice, salt-free
1–2 teaspoons chilli powder
1 large handful finely chopped parsley

Soak the beans overnight. Drain and cover with water. Bring to the boil, reduce heat and simmer for 1 hour or until the beans are tender. Drain, and reserve the cooking liquid.

While the beans are cooking, preheat the oven to 180°C/350°F, prick the potatoes all over and bake them.

Towards the end of the potatoes' cooking time, heat the onion and garlic in a little water in a large covered saucepan until soft and transparent (approximately 3 minutes). Add the vegetables and 125 ml/4 fl oz/½ cup of the reserved cooking liquid from the beans. Simmer, uncovered, until the vegetables begin to soften. Add the tomato juice, tomatoes and chilli powder. Cook gently for 20 minutes. Add the beans. Sprinkle parsley over the top and serve in a scooped-out baked potato. Mash the extra potato and pipe on top. Reheat in the oven if necessary.

Chinese Vegetable Combination

SERVES 4 – 6

2 teaspoons finely chopped fresh ginger
2 cloves garlic, crushed
1 tablespoon/1 tablespoon plus 1
    teaspoon low-salt soy sauce
2 tablespoons/2 tablespoons plus 2
    teaspoons Chinese wine or dry sherry
125 ml/4 fl oz/½ cup unsweetened
    orange juice
2 onions, quartered
3 sticks celery, diagonally sliced
225 g/½ lb green beans, diagonally
    sliced
225 g/½ lb carrots, diagonally sliced
125 g/¼ lb mushrooms, sliced
125 g/¼ lb snow peas, stringed, topped
    and tailed
225 g/½ lb canned baby corn, rinsed to
    remove salt
250 ml/8 fl oz/1 cup Vegetable Stock
    (see p. 14)
1 tablespoon/1 tablespoon plus 1
    teaspoon cornflour
200 g/7 oz bean shoots

Add the ginger, garlic, soy sauce, Chinese wine and orange juice to a cold wok. Slowly bring to the boil and simmer for 2 minutes.

Add the onion and celery. Toss to combine the ingredients and cook, covered, for 2 minutes.

Add the beans, carrot, mushroom and snow peas. Toss and cook for 3 minutes.

Add the corn and cook, covered, for 1 minute. Pour over the combined Vegetable Stock and cornflour. Return to the boil. Add the bean shoots. Cook, covered, for 1 minute. Serve immediately. (See colour plate opposite.)

Vegetable Omelette

SERVES 1

1 egg
1 extra egg white
125 ml/4 fl oz/½ cup of reduced-fat
    soymilk or skim milk
75 g/2½ oz/½ cup grated carrot
100 g/3½ oz/½ cup grated zucchini
    (juice squeezed out)
75 g/2½ oz/¼ cup finely chopped
    tomato
60 g/2 oz/½ cup grated low-fat grating
    cheese

Beat the egg and extra egg white with the soymilk until light and fluffy. Fold in the vegetables. Pour onto a hot, lightly greased, non-stick frying pan, ensuring that the vegetables are evenly distributed. Sprinkle the cheese over the top. Cook for a few minutes until the omelette begins to firm on the bottom then place under a grill until the top browns. Fold the omelette in half and remove from the frying pan. Serve with a salad.

Chinese Vegetable Combination (opposite page); Chinese Spring Rolls (page 73).

Pumpkin Almond Pie (page 50).

Steamed Whole Chicken (page 90); ingredients for Vegetable Stock and Chinese Chicken Stock (page 14).

Vegetable and Potato Pie (opposite page).

Vegetable and Potato Pie

SERVES 6–8

2 carrots, sliced
1 sweet potato (white or orange), peeled and cubed
1 zucchini, chopped
12 small Brussels sprouts
150 g/5 oz cauliflower florets
150 g/5 oz broccoli florets
100 g/3½ oz pumpkin, peeled and cubed
225 g/½ lb/2 cups peas

Gravy

1 onion, chopped
500 ml/16 fl oz/2 cups Vegetable Stock or Chicken Stock (see p. 14) or water
1 tablespoon/1 tablespoon plus 1 teaspoon salt-free tomato paste or Mango Chutney (see Chicken Burgers p. 89)
2 tablespoons/2 tablespoons plus 2 teaspoons cornflour
2 tablespoons/2 tablespoons plus 2 teaspoons water
handful of finely chopped fresh parsley

Topping

1 kg/2¼ lb/4 cups hot mashed potato
100 g/3½ oz/1 cup finely grated low-fat grating cheese (optional)

Preheat the oven to 230°C/450°F.

Place all the vegetables in the top of a steamer and steam for 10–12 minutes or until the vegetables are tender.

To make the Gravy, sauté the onion in 2 tablespoons/2 tablespoons plus 2 teaspoons of Vegetable Stock for 3 minutes in a covered saucepan. Add the remaining stock and tomato paste. Combine the cornflour and water to make a paste. Stir the cornflour mixture through the stock and bring to the boil Cook for 2–3 minutes, stirring, or until gravy thickens. Add the chopped parsley.

Place the vegetables in a casserole dish. Pour the gravy over the top. Cover with the potato combined with the cheese. Place the casserole dish in a baking dish containing water that reaches half-way up the side of the casserole dish. Bake, uncovered, for 30–40 minutes. (See colour plate opposite.)

Stuffed Zucchini

SERVES 6

3 large zucchini
60 g/2 oz/1 cup fresh wholemeal
 breadcrumbs
100 g/3½ oz/1 cup grated low-fat
 grating cheese

Chilli Beans

90 g/3 oz/¼ cup adzuki beans
425 g/15 oz canned whole tomatoes in
 natural juice, salt-free
2 small red chillies, finely chopped or
 (for a milder flavour) 1 capsicum,
 finely chopped
2 spring onions, finely chopped
1 clove garlic, crushed
¼ teaspoon ground cummin
¼ teaspoon dried oregano
2 tablespoons/2 tablespoons plus 2
 teaspoons salt-free tomato paste

To prepare the Chilli Beans, soak the beans overnight. Drain, and discard any beans that have not absorbed the water. Place in a clean saucepan and cover with water. Bring to the boil. Reduce the heat, cover, and simmer for 1–1½ hours or until the beans are tender. Drain and set aside.

Chop the tomatoes and put in the saucepan with the juice. Add the chilli, spring onion, garlic, cummin, oregano and tomato paste. Cook for 15 minutes, stirring occasionally.

Cut the zucchini in half lengthwise and scoop out the seeds and some flesh. Chop the flesh finely and add it to the tomato mixture. Cook for a further 5 minutes. Add the beans and keep hot.

Preheat the oven to 200°C/400°F.

Lightly steam the zucchini shells until just tender. Fill the zucchini with the bean mixture. Place in a non-stick casserole dish. Sprinkle the breadcrumbs and the cheese over the top. Bake for 15 minutes, and serve.

Zucchini Oat au Gratin

SERVES 4 – 6

2 onions, quartered and sliced
1 teaspoon crushed garlic
1 teaspoon light olive oil
100 g/3½ oz red capsicums, cubed
100 g/3½ oz green capsicums, cubed
1 tablespoon/1 tablespoon plus 1
 teaspoon water
400 g/14 oz zucchini, cut into rounds
425 g/15 oz canned whole tomatoes in
 natural juice, salt-free
60 g/2 oz/½ cup rolled oats
500 ml/16 fl oz/2 cups salt-free tomato
 juice
1 teaspoon dried marjoram
1 teaspoon dried thyme
black pepper to taste
100 g/3½ oz/1 cup grated low-fat
 grating cheese

Preheat the oven to 200°C/400°F.

In a saucepan, cook the onion and garlic in the oil over a low heat until the onion becomes tender. Add the capsicum and cover. Cook until the vegetables soften. Add the water and zucchini. Continue cooking until the zucchini is tender. Remove from the heat.

Chop the tomatoes roughly and place in a bowl with the juice. Add the oats, tomato juice, herbs, pepper and cheese.

Spoon the vegetables into a large, shallow casserole dish. Cover with the tomato sauce. Bake for 45 minutes, or until the top is well browned and the casserole bubbling. Serve with a salad.

Zucchini Moussaka

SERVES 6-8

575 g/1¼ lb zucchini, finely sliced
100 g/3½ oz/1 cup grated low-fat
    grating cheese

Tomato Sauce
1 onion, finely chopped
2 cloves garlic, crushed
2 tablespoons/2 tablespoons plus 2
    teaspoons water
225 g/½ lb/3 cups carrots, finely
    chopped
225 g/½ lb/3 cups mushrooms, finely
    chopped
3 bay leaves
1 teaspoon dried oregano
1 teaspoon dried basil
425 g/15 oz canned whole tomatoes in
    natural juice, salt-free
75 g/2½ oz/¼ cup salt-free tomato
    paste

White Sauce
500 ml/16 fl oz/2 cups reduced-fat
    soymilk or low-fat evaporated milk
30 g/1 oz/¼ cup cornflour
pinch of cayenne pepper
1 tablespoon/1 tablespoon plus 1
    teaspoon geska herb cheese

Preheat the oven to 190°C/375°F.

Boil or steam the zucchini until just tender and drain. Set aside.

To make the Tomato Sauce, cook the onion and garlic in the water until soft and transparent. Add the remaining ingredients except the tomato paste and simmer, covered, for 15 minutes. Remove the bay leaves and break up the tomatoes using a wooden spoon. Add the tomato paste. Turn the heat up and cook, uncovered, until the sauce thickens, stirring occasionally.

To make the White Sauce, place 200 ml/7 fl oz/¾ cup of the soymilk in a saucepan. Mix the reserved milk with the cornflour to make a paste. Bring the milk in the saucepan almost to a boil, and stir in the cayenne pepper and cheese. Add the cornflour paste and stir continuously until the sauce thickens.

Lightly grease an oblong, high-sided ovenproof dish. Place a layer of zucchini on the base of the dish. Cover the zucchini with a layer of Tomato Sauce. Repeat with alternate layers of zucchini and Tomato Sauce. Top with a layer of White Sauce. Sprinkle the grated cheese over the top. Bake for 20–30 minutes or until the cheese melts and is brown and bubbling. (See right colour plate between pages 72 and 73.)

Zucchini, Cheese and Oat-bran Pancakes

MAKES 8

150 g/5 oz/1 cup rolled oats
60 g/2 oz/½ cup oat bran
125 g/¼ lb/1 cup unbleached white
    plain flour
2 teaspoons baking powder
350 g/¾ lb/2 cups grated zucchini, juice
    squeezed out
30 g/1 oz/¼ cup grated low-fat grating
    cheese
250 ml/8 fl oz/1 cup evaporated skim
    milk
250 ml/8 fl oz/1 cup water
2 egg whites
black pepper to taste

In a large bowl combine the rolled oats and oat bran. Sift the flour and baking powder over the oats, and combine. Add the zucchini and cheese and mix well.

Combine the milk and water and stir through the flour and zucchini mixture.

Beat the egg whites until stiff and gently fold through the batter. Cook on a lightly greased, non-stick pancake pan until browned on both sides.

Serving suggestions
- Top with avocado, alfalfa sprouts and low-fat mayonnaise.
- Top with lettuce, tomato, cucumber slices, and tuna with horseradish mayonnaise (grate fresh horseradish into low-fat mayonnaise).
- Make White Sauce (see page 239) and add chicken, leftover fish, salmon or cooked vegetables, and use as a filling.

FISH
&
SEAFOOD

ish and seafood are an excellent source of protein. Recent studies have shown that with two or more meals of fish per week there is a lower prevalence of coronary heart disease, as well as other health benefits. It is believed that this is due to the presence of polyunsaturated Omega 3 fatty acids, eicosapentaenoic acid and docosahaxaenoic acid. Hormone-like compounds called prostaglandins are created by these fatty acids. They lower the level of triglyceride in the blood, reduce blood clotting, and enhance immune function.

Fish from sub-tropical and tropical waters are very low in fat content. Cold-water fish such as salmon, tuna, trout, sardines, herrings, pilchards, mackerel and eel have a higher fat content. The fats, however, are polyunsaturated, which are not as harmful to health as saturated fats.

The level of iron in seafood is about one-third that of red meat but it is high in iodine and provides an excellent source of selenium and fluoride. It contains some zinc and magnesium, and is a good source of niacin and vitamin B12, and a moderate source of thiamin, riboflavin and vitamin B6.

No longer is battered fish an acceptable part of a healthy diet. Fish is delicious steamed, lightly grilled, or sautéd with herbs and spices. Serve portions of no more than 100 g/3½ oz to maintain health benefits.

Do not over-cook fish. If it becomes dry it loses a lot of its flavour.

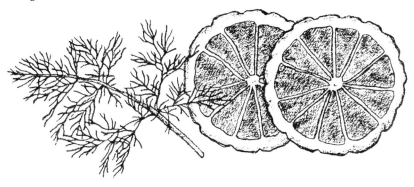

Barbecued Marinated Fish Fillets

Use any combination of garlic, ginger, unsweetened orange juice, dry white wine, dry sherry, mango chutney, Quick and Easy Tomato Sauce (see Mexican Bean Tortillas, page 49), lemon juice, lime juice and fresh herbs. Marinate the fish for at least 2 hours before barbecuing. The fish can be barbecued in foil or in a wire-frame fish holder.

Fish Parcel with Apple and Lemon

SERVES 2

2 × 100-g/3½-oz fish fillets (e.g. whiting, trout, John Dory)
1 Granny Smith apple, peeled
juice of ½ lemon
a little dry white wine
grated rind of 1 lemon
2 teaspoons capers
a little lemon grass or lemon thyme

Preheat the oven to 180°C/350°F.
Place the fillets on foil. Slice the apple into thin segments, arranging them equally over the fish. Squeeze the lemon juice over the top. Chop the lemon grass or thyme and add with the wine, lemon rind and capers. Wrap up securely. Cook in the oven or on a barbecue until the fish breaks away easily when a knife is inserted into its centre. Pour the remaining juices over the fish and serve immediately.

Fish and Asparagus Casserole

SERVES 4-6

500 g/1 lb 2 oz asparagus
200 g/7 oz broccoli, finely sliced
200 g/7 oz cauliflower, finely sliced
185 g/6 oz carrots, chopped
400 g/14 oz cooked fish fillets
8 spring onions
125 g/¼ lb frozen peas

Sauce
750 ml/1⅓ pints/3 cups skim milk
60 g/2 oz/½ cup cornflour
1 teaspoon dried oregano
1 teaspoon dried basil
140 g/4½ oz/½ cup salt-free tomato
  paste

Topping
60 g/2 oz/½ cup rice bran
30 g/1 oz/½ cup fresh wholemeal
  breadcrumbs
60 g/2 oz/¼ cup low-fat cheese, grated
large handful finely chopped fresh parsley

Preheat the oven to 180°C/350°F.
Lightly steam the asparagus, broccoli, cauliflower and carrot. Combine the fish and all the vegetables.
To make the Sauce, mix 250 ml/8 fl oz/1 cup of the milk with the cornflour, dried herbs and tomato paste. Return this to the remaining milk and heat in a small saucepan until the sauce thickens.
Place the fish and vegetables in a casserole dish. Pour the sauce on top.
Combine all the Topping ingredients and spread evenly over the casserole. Cook for 40 minutes.

Fish Cutlets with Asparagus

SERVES 4

4 fish cutlets
350 g/¾ lb canned asparagus spears
65 ml/2 fl oz/¼ cup dry white wine
black pepper to taste
small sprig rosemary
4 shallots, finely chopped
1 tablespoon/1 tablespoon plus 1
  teaspoon wholemeal plain flour
3 tablespoons/3 tablespoons plus 3
  teaspoons non-fat or *low-fat yoghurt*

Preheat the oven to 180°C/350°F.

Arrange the fish in a non-stick shallow ovenproof dish. Drain the liquid from the asparagus and put aside. Scatter the asparagus over the fish, and then add the wine. Sprinkle the fish with pepper and add the rosemary, cover with foil, and bake for about 25 minutes or until the fish is tender.

While the fish is cooking, stir-fry the chopped shallot in a small amount of the reserved asparagus liquid, add the flour and stir for a minute or two. Gradually stir in the remaining asparagus liquid and cook, stirring, until boiling.

Arrange the fish on a heated serving platter. Pour the liquid from the fish into the sauce, stir well, and then stir in the yoghurt. Gently reheat the sauce before pouring it over the fish.

Cucumber Fish with Mushrooms

SERVES 6

65 ml/2 fl oz/¼ cup lemon juice
6 fish fillets
1 cucumber, peeled
125 g/¼ lb/1 cup finely chopped leek
125 ml/4 fl oz/½ cup Vegetable Stock
  or Chicken Stock (see p. 14)
4 tomatoes, chopped
1 small green capsicum, cut into strips

Sauce
2 tablespoons/2 tablespoons plus 2
  teaspoons water
2 tablespoons/2 tablespoons plus 2
  teaspoons cornflour
2 tablespoons/2 tablespoons plus 2
  teaspoons finely chopped fresh parsley

Marinated Mushrooms
350 g/¾ lb/3 cups finely sliced
  mushroom
250 ml/8 fl oz/1 cup unsweetened
  orange juice
2 tablespoons/2 tablespoons plus 2
  teaspoons tarragon vinegar
handful of freshly chopped mixed herbs
  (e.g. parsley, chives, basil)

Pour almost all the lemon juice over the fish in a bowl and leave for 10 minutes. Cut the cucumber into four pieces. Using a sharp knife, carefully remove the seeds, leaving a hollow. Slice into rounds. Add the chopped leek and cucumber rounds to a small non-stick frying pan. Pour the stock over the top. Cover, and simmer for 10 minutes. Add the tomato and capsicum, cover, and cook for a further 5 minutes over a low heat. Remove the lid.

Place the fish fillets on top of the vegetables. Cover the frying pan and cook for 3 minutes.

Place the fish and vegetables on the serving plates, leaving some juice in the frying pan. Add the remaining lemon juice to the Sauce ingredients and make a paste. Add the paste to the remaining juice and slowly bring to the boil, stirring continuously. When the sauce thickens, remove from heat and spoon over the fish.

To make the Marinated Mushrooms, combine all the ingredients and marinate in the refrigerator for at least 2 hours.

Serve the fish with lightly steamed broccoli and Marinated Mushrooms.

Fish in Dill Sauce

SERVES 2

1 small onion, finely chopped
2 fillets sea perch
125 ml/4 fl oz/½ cup dry white wine
250 ml/8 fl oz/1 cup skim milk
2 tablespoons/2 tablespoons plus 2
    teaspoons cornflour
2 tablespoons/2 tablespoons plus 2
    teaspoons freshly chopped dill
slices of lemon and sprigs of dill for
    garnishing

Place the onion, fish and white wine in a small frying pan. Cook gently until the fish turns white and is cooked on both sides. Use a slotted spoon to remove it. Keep the fish warm.

Combine the milk and cornflour to make a paste. Stir this through the pan juices and bring to the boil, stirring continuously until the sauce thickens. Return the fish to the sauce. Sprinkle with chopped dill, and heat through.

Garnish with the lemon slices and dill sprigs and serve immediately.

Steamed Ginger Fish

SERVES 1

1 × 100-g/3½-oz fish fillet
1 teaspoon finely chopped fresh ginger
1 teaspoon grated lemon rind
juice of ½ lemon

To steam in the microwave, place the fish in a shallow glass casserole dish. Do not cover. Sprinkle the fish with the ginger and lemon rind, and squeeze the lemon juice over the top. Microwave on high for a few minutes or until the fish is tender.

To steam in a Chinese steamer, bring the water to the boil. Place the steamer on the saucepan. Arrange the fish in the steamer as for microwave cooking. Cover and steam until the fish is tender.

If you do not have a steamer, you can gently simmer the prepared fish in a little water or vegetable stock in a shallow saucepan with the lid on.

Hawaiian Fish Kebabs

SERVES 2

200 g/7 oz trevally fillets
4 kebab skewers
16 bite-sized pieces green capsicum
8 bite-sized pieces red capsicum
8 bite-sized pieces fresh pineapple
8 small mushrooms

Marinade
125 ml/4 fl oz/½ cup unsweetened
    pineapple juice
1 tablespoon/1 tablespoon plus 1
    teaspoon lemon juice
1 teaspoon wholegrain mustard
1 teaspoon finely grated lemon rind
a little cornflour (optional)

Cut the fish into 16 pieces, each piece about 2.5 cm/1" square. Thread the fish, capsicum, pineapple and mushrooms onto kebab sticks.

To make the Marinade, combine all the ingredients except the cornflour in a bowl.

Place the kebab sticks in the marinade and leave for 1 hour, turning frequently.

To cook the kebabs, cover them in the marinade and microwave for just a couple of minutes on both sides. Alternatively, barbecue them or cook them under a hot grill. They are cooked when the fish has turned very white.

When serving, the marinade can be thickened with a little cornflour to make a sauce to pour over the fish. (See colour plate opposite.)

Hawaiian Fish Kebabs (opposite page).

Fish Vegetable Bundle (opposite page).

Fish Vegetable Bundles

SERVES 6

575 g/1¼ lb/6 fish fillets

julienne strips of carrot, zucchini, green beans, cucumber, red and green capsicum (approximately 8–10 strips per fillet)

250 ml/8 fl oz/1 cup non-fat or low-fat yoghurt

60 g/2 oz/½ cup grated low-fat grating cheese

60 g/2 oz/1 cup fresh wholemeal breadcrumbs

2 tablespoons/2 tablespoons plus 2 teaspoons finely chopped fresh parsley

2 tablespoons/2 tablespoons plus 2 teaspoons finely chopped fresh chives

Preheat the oven to 180°C/350°F.

Roll the fish fillets so that they are flattened slightly. Place the combination of julienne vegetables in the centre of each fillet with the ends of the vegetables visible at both sides. Roll up. Place in a shallow, lightly greased ovenproof dish with seam side down. Pour over the yoghurt and sprinkle the cheese over the top.

Combine the breadcrumbs, parsley and chives. Sprinkle over the fish. Cover with foil. Bake for 20–30 minutes or until the fish is tender. Remove the foil for the last few minutes to brown and crisp the breadcrumbs. Serve with salad or steamed vegetables and small steamed potatoes. (See colour plate opposite.)

Jamaican Fish Rumba

SERVES 4

1 whole fish
2 bananas, sliced
6 apricots, sliced
1 tablespoon/1 tablespoon plus 1 teaspoon capers
250 ml/8 fl oz/1 cup unsweetened orange juice

Place the fish on a large piece of foil. Scatter the banana and apricot on top, add the capers and then pour over the orange juice. Seal the foil and barbecue the fish.

Lemon and Garlic Snapper

SERVES 4

1 whole snapper
juice of ½ lemon
3–4 cloves garlic, crushed
65 ml/2 fl oz/¼ cup non-fat or low-fat yoghurt
several lettuce leaves
a little freshly chopped dill
65 ml/2 fl oz/¼ cup dry white wine

Rub the outside and inside of the fish with the lemon juice. Mix together the garlic and yoghurt. Using a basting brush, wipe the mixture over the fish. Place the fish on the lettuce leaves on a piece of foil. Sprinkle the fresh dill on top and cover with the wine. Seal the foil and barbecue the fish.

Fish Mould with Lemon Sauce and Salad

SERVES 6

500 g/1 lb 2 oz fish fillets
500 g/1 lb 2 oz/2 cups mashed potato
2 Granny Smith apples, peeled and
grated
1 egg white
60 g/2 oz/½ cup finely chopped spring
onion (white part only)
1 tablespoon/1 tablespoon plus 1
teaspoon finely chopped fresh basil
2 tablespoons/2 tablespoons plus 2
teaspoons finely chopped fresh oregano
65 ml/2 fl oz/¼ cup non-fat or low-fat
yoghurt

Rice
575 g/1¼ lb/3 cups hot cooked brown
rice
60 g/2 oz/1 cup freshly chopped parsley

Salad
24 cherry tomatoes
2 odourless onions, peeled and cut into
thin wedges
1 cucumber, halved lengthwise, seeded
and finely sliced
250 ml/8 fl oz/1 cup Herb Vinaigrette
(see p. 141)

Sauce
125 ml/4 fl oz/½ cup lemon juice
125 ml/4 fl oz/½ cup unsweetened
orange juice
1 tablespoon/1 tablespoon plus 1
teaspoon apple juice concentrate
2 tablespoons/2 tablespoons plus 2
teaspoons arrowroot

Preheat the oven to 180°C/350°F.

To cook the fish, chop the fish fillets into small pieces. Combine with the potato, apple, egg white, spring onion, herbs and yoghurt. Lightly grease a mould (preferably a fish-shaped mould). Spoon the mixture into the mould and pack down firmly. Place in a baking dish containing water and cover with foil. Cook for 30 minutes.

Combine the rice and parsley.

To make the Salad, combine all the ingredients.

To make the Sauce, combine all the sauce ingredients in a saucepan and stir over heat until the sauce boils and thickens. Pour over the fish. Serve the fish with the rice and salad.

Lemon Fish with Fresh Mango

SERVES 2

2 fish fillets
juice of ½ lemon
125 ml/4 fl oz/½ cup dry white wine
sprig of lemon thyme
a little grated lemon rind
1 mango

Marinate the fish in the lemon juice, white wine, thyme and lemon rind. The fish can be barbecued, steamed in a Chinese bamboo steamer, microwaved or grilled. Cut the mango into thin slivers. Top the cooked fish with the mango, and serve.

Note
If you are grilling the fish, the mango can be grilled on top of it.

Fish in Mango Sauce

SERVES 4

8 × 65-g whiting fillets
250 ml/8 fl oz/1 cup Chicken Stock
  (see p. 14)
black pepper to taste
juice of ½ lemon

Sauce
250 ml/8 fl oz/1 cup dry white wine
125 ml/4 fl oz/½ cup non-fat or low-
  fat yoghurt
1 mango, peeled and sliced
black pepper to taste.

Poach the fillets in the stock in a frying pan. While poaching, season each fillet with black pepper and a squeeze of lemon juice. Poach for no more than 3 minutes on each side. Remove carefully to a warm platter.

To make the Sauce, use the same pan that the fish has been poached in. Remove any leftover stock. Pour in the white wine and yoghurt and keep the heat on high for the liquid to reduce. Add the mango as the sauce reduces. The mango only takes a couple of minutes to cook, so stir occasionally to prevent sticking. The sauce takes approximately 4 minutes to cook and will turn a golden brown colour.

Place the fish fillets on serving plates and spoon a small amount of sauce over them.

Fish Mornay

SERVES 6

Base
310 g/10½ oz/2 cups cooked brown rice
60 g/2 oz/½ cup finely chopped spinach
60 g/2 oz/½ cup finely chopped leek
2 tablespoons/2 tablespoons plus 2
  teaspoons water

Filling
2 tablespoons/2 tablespoons plus 2
  teaspoons wholemeal plain flour
200 ml/7 fl oz/¾ cup skim milk
65 ml/2 fl oz/¼ cup dry white wine
125 ml/4 fl oz/½ cup low-fat
  evaporated skim milk
60 g/2 oz/½ cup finely grated low-fat
  grating cheese
500 g/1 lb 2 oz cooked fish fillets,
  broken into small pieces
1 large apple, grated
125 g/¼ lb/1 cup finely chopped spring
  onion

Topping
30 g/1 oz/½ cup fresh wholemeal
  breadcrumbs
large handful finely chopped celery leaves

Preheat the oven to 180°C/350°F.

To make the Base, combine the ingredients and spoon into a lightly greased baking dish.

To make the Filling, place the flour in a saucepan. Stir over low heat for a few seconds. Pour in the skim milk and stir briskly, until quite smooth. Add the wine, gently bring to the boil and cook until the sauce thickens. Add the evaporated skim milk and cheese, and stir until the cheese melts. Combine the fish, grated apple and spring onions, and add to the sauce. Pour the filling over the base.

To make the Topping, combine the breadcrumbs and celery, and sprinkle over the filling. Bake, uncovered, for 30 minutes.

Fish Fillets in Orange Sauce

SERVES 4

4 fish fillets, bones removed
black pepper to taste
125 ml/4 fl oz/½ cup unsweetened
    orange juice
125 ml/4 fl oz/½ cup dry sherry
65 ml/2 fl oz/¼ cup low-fat yoghurt
1 orange, segmented

Season the fish fillets (try whiting, bream or garfish) with black pepper. Place the orange juice and sherry in a frying pan. Bring to the boil and add the fish. Reduce the heat to a gentle simmer. Poach the fish, turning once, until tender. Remove the fish and place on a warm platter.

Increase the heat under the frying pan and add the yoghurt. Boil until slightly thickened. Add the orange segments and heat through. Pour a little orange sauce and some orange segments over each fillet on the platter, and serve.

Spicy Fish Crumble

SERVES 5

1 clove garlic, finely chopped
60 g/2 oz/½ cup finely chopped spring
    onion
75 g/2½ oz/½ cup finely chopped celery
2 tablespoons/2 tablespoons plus 2
    teaspoons finely chopped fresh parsley
5 fillets blue grenadier
225 g/½ lb/1 cup canned whole
    tomatoes in natural juice, puréed
125 ml/4 fl oz/½ cup low-fat yoghurt
2 teaspoons low-salt soy sauce
2 teaspoons white wine vinegar
½–1 teaspoon curry powder
½ teaspoon dried tarragon
½ teaspoon dried basil

Topping
60 g/2 oz/1 cup fresh breadcrumbs
½ teaspoon dried basil
1 stick celery, finely chopped
60 g/2 oz/½ cup grated low-fat grating
    cheese

Place the garlic, spring onion and celery on the base of an oblong casserole dish. Sprinkle with the parsley. Place the fish fillets on top of the parsley. Mix together the tomato purée, yoghurt, soy sauce, vinegar, curry powder, tarragon and basil. Pour over the fish. Cover, and stand for approximately 1 hour.

When ready to cook, preheat the oven to 180°C/350°F.

Mix the Topping ingredients together. Spread over the top of the fish. Bake for 35–40 minutes. Serve with a selection of steamed vegetables or brown rice and tossed salad.

Whole Fish with Shallots

SERVES 4

1 whole fish
juice of ½ lemon
60 g/2 oz low-fat grating cheese
2 shallots, chopped
large handful freshly chopped parsley
250 ml/8 fl oz/1 cup unsweetened apple
    juice

Cut five slits across the fish and gently ease them open. Squeeze the lemon juice into each slit. Cut the cheese into thin strips and push the strips into each slit. Add the chopped shallots. Sprinkle the parsley over the top of the fish and then pour over the apple juice. Seal the foil and cook the fish on the barbecue.

Fish and Spinach Rolls

SERVES 6

12 large spinach or silver beet leaves
  (white part removed)
400 g/14 oz fish fillets
juice of ½ lemon
2 carrots, grated
40 g/1½ oz/¼ cup finely chopped leek
  or 90 g/3 oz/½ cup chopped spring
  onion
90 g/3 oz/½ cup finely sliced canned
  water chestnuts
½ teaspoon fresh ginger juice (press
  ginger through a garlic crusher) and
  pulp
2 teaspoon finely grated lemon rind
100 g/3½ oz/½ cup cooked brown rice
  or grated apple

Sauce
125 ml/4 fl oz/½ cup salt-free tomato
  juice
200 ml/7 fl oz/¾ cup unsweetened
  orange juice
handful of chopped parsley
1 tablespoon/1 tablespoon plus 1
  teaspoon cornflour

Wash the spinach leaves thoroughly under hot water. Mince the fish fillets in a food processor. Add all the other ingredients, except those for the Sauce, and mix well. Place two leaves on top of each other and add some filling. Repeat until all the leaves are used. Divide filling equally between leaves. Roll up the leaves and place side by side in a large steamer. Cook, with the lid on, for 35 minutes.

To make the Sauce, combine all the ingredients and mix thoroughly. Simmer until the sauce thickens. Pour over the rolls and serve with a baked potato and tossed salad.

Fish Parcels with Thyme and Lemon

SERVES 2

1 lemon, finely sliced
2 fish fillets
125 ml/4 fl oz/½ cup dry white wine
1 teaspoon freshly chopped thyme

Cut out two large square pieces of foil. Place two slices of lemon on each piece of foil. Place a fillet of fish on top. Add more lemon. Pour the wine over the fish and sprinkle them liberally with thyme.

Fold up the foil to completely seal. Either cook on a hot barbecue or steam in water. On the barbecue the fish will take about 5–10 minutes to cook, depending on their size and the heat. If steaming, put 2 cm/¾" of water in the base of a saucepan and bring to a simmer. Put the foil parcels in the water, cover the pan and leave the fish to steam for 10–15 minutes. Open the foil and serve immediately.

Fish Parcels with Tomato and Basil

SERVES 1

*1 fish fillet (e.g. sea perch, blue
  grenadier, trevally, gemfish)*
½ tomato, sliced
2 spring onions, chopped
black pepper to taste
*a little freshly chopped basil or ¼–½
  teaspoon dried basil*

Cut out a large square piece of foil. Place two slices of tomato on the centre of the foil. Place the fish on top. Add more slices of tomato. Sprinkle with the chopped spring onion, black pepper and basil. Fold up the foil to completely seal, and place on a hot barbecue for about 10 minutes.

Alternatively, place 2 cm/¾" of water in the base of a saucepan and bring to a simmer. Place the foil parcels in the water, cover the pan and leave the fish to steam for 10–15 minutes. Open the foil and serve immediately.

Fish and Chips

SERVES 4

65 ml/2 fl oz/¼ cup lemon juice
4 fish fillets
125 g/¼ lb/1 cup wholemeal plain flour
2 egg whites, lightly beaten
*60 g/2 oz/1 cup fresh wholemeal
  breadcrumbs*
4 large potatoes
a little garlic powder
a little onion powder
*a little cayene pepper or grated geska
  herb cheese*

Squeeze the lemon juice over the fish. Dip the fish in the flour and shake off any excess flour. Dip the fish in the lightly beaten egg white and press down into the breadcrumbs until both sides are evenly coated. Shake off any excess breadcrumbs. Refrigerate the fish for at least 2 hours prior to cooking.

Before cooking the fish, prepare the chips. Preheat the oven to 230°C/450°F and cut peeled or unpeeled potatoes into chips. Place on a non-stick baking tray. Cook for 15 minutes or until browned.

Add flavour by sprinkling the garlic powder, onion powder, cayenne pepper or cheese on top.

Potato can be quickly sealed in plastic bags to freeze to be used as required.

Cook the fish in a lightly greased non-stick frying pan until both sides are golden brown (approximately 3 minutes on each side) or place in a lightly floured oven bag, seal and cook at 200°C/400°F for 15–20 minutes.

Fish cooks quickly, so do not over-cook. It is cooked when an inserted knife flakes the flesh easily.

Variation
■ To help fish retain moisture and to add flavour, fish fillets can be marinated in fruit juices with fresh herbs, garlic, ginger, tomato paste, white wine, non-fat or low-fat yoghurt and spices. Try your own combinations. Take the fish from the marinade and place it in the breadcrumbs, and cook as above.

Gemfish Pockets

SERVES 2

2 fillets gemfish
200 g/7 oz asparagus, steamed and
   lightly puréed

Sauce
250 ml/8 fl oz/1 cup skim milk
2 tablespoons/2 tablespoons plus 2
   teaspoons cornflour
1 teaspoon wholegrain mustard
¼ teaspoon dry mustard
¼ teaspoon ground ginger

Cut a deep pocket in each fillet. Fill the pockets with the asparagus purée. If you have puréed the asparagus to a smooth paste you may need to secure the pockets with toothpicks. Wrap the fish in foil, place in a steamer and cover. Steam the fish pockets until the fish is cooked through, approximately 10–15 minutes.

To make the Sauce, mix a little milk in a saucepan with the cornflour to make a paste. Add the remaining ingredients, and stir well. Slowly bring to the boil, stirring until the sauce thickens. Turn the heat down. Cook for a further couple of minutes, and then pour over the cooked fish just before serving.

Sea Perch and Zucchini Balls

SERVES 4–6

Fish Balls
500 g/1 lb 2 oz sea perch fillets
½ onion, chopped
150 g/5 oz/¾ cup grated zucchini, juice
   squeezed out
1 teaspoon lemon juice
1 egg white
30 g/1 oz/½ cup fresh wholemeal
   breadcrumbs

Marinade
65 ml/2 fl oz/¼ cup apple juice
   concentrate
2 teaspoons finely chopped fresh ginger
250 ml/8 fl oz/1 cup unsweetened
   orange juice
200 ml/7 fl oz/¾ cup dry sherry
1 tablespoon/1 tablespoon plus 1
   teaspoon low-salt soy sauce
thin strips orange rind
3 tablespoons/3 tablespoons plus 3
   teaspoons cornflour
2 tablespoons/2 tablespoons plus 2
   teaspoons water

Place the fish in a food processor and mince. Remove the mince to a bowl, add all the remaining Fish Ball ingredients and mix well using your hands. Shape into eight or twelve balls.

Mix all the Marinade ingredients together except the cornflour and water. Put the fish balls in the marinade and marinate for at least 4–6 hours, turning twice.

When ready to cook, preheat the oven to 180°C/350°F.

Place the fish balls in a shallow casserole dish with the marinade liquid and cook for approximately 30–35 minutes or until the fish is tender. Remove the fish balls, set aside and cover.

Place the Marinade ingredients, except for the cornflour and water, in a small saucepan. Mix the cornflour and water to a paste. Stir this into the marinade as it comes to the boil, and continue to stir until thickened. Pour the sauce over the fish balls.

Curry Salmon Patties

MAKES 4

350 g/¾ lb potatoes, peeled
150 g/5 oz carrots
200 g/7 oz canned red salmon
juice of ½ small lemon
30 g/1 oz/¼ cup grated low-fat grating
    cheese
½–1 teaspoon curry powder
2 tablespoons/2 tablespoons plus
    2 teaspoons finely chopped fresh
    parsley
2 tablespoons/2 tablespoons plus
    2 teaspoons finely chopped spring
    onion (green part only)
1 egg white with 2 tablespoons/2
    tablespoons plus 2 teaspoons water
    (beaten together)
40 g/1½ oz/¾ cup fresh wholemeal
    breadcrumbs and 30 g/1 oz/¼ cup
    oat bran

Preheat the oven to 180°C/350°F.

Cover the potatoes and carrots with water and cook until just tender. Drain and mash well. Add the salmon, lemon juice, cheese, curry powder, parsley and spring onion, and mix well.

Form into patties; two small ones or one large one per person. Dip each patty into the combined egg white and water, and roll in the combined breadcrumbs and oat bran. Lightly grease a non-stick frying pan and brown the patties on both sides for just a few minutes.

Place the patties on a baking tray lined with non-stick baking paper and finish cooking in the oven for approximately 15–20 minutes. (See colour plate opposite.)

Salmon Bake

SERVES 6–8

Base
150 g/5 oz/1 cup cooked brown rice
400 g/14 oz broccoli, cooked and puréed

Filling
1 onion, finely chopped
2 tablespoons/2 tablespoons plus
    2 teaspoons water
500 ml/16 fl oz/2 cups reduced-fat
    soymilk
30 g/1 oz/¼ cup cornflour
425 g/15 oz canned red salmon
1 teaspoon hot English mustard
1 red capsicum, finely chopped
1 green capsicum, finely chopped
a little water

Topping
6 slices wholemeal bread
125 g/¼ lb/1¼ cups low-fat grating
    cheese, grated
handful of finely chopped fresh parsley

Preheat the oven to 190°C/375°F.

To make the Base, combine the rice and broccoli and mix well. Spoon into a shallow, lightly greased ovenproof dish.

To make the Filling, cook the onion for 3 minutes in the water. Add 435 ml/14 fl oz/1¾ cups soymilk. Blend the reserved milk with the cornflour to make a paste. Add to the heated soymilk, stirring until it thickens. Cook gently for 2 minutes, stirring continuously. Add the salmon and mustard, and mix well. Remove from the heat.

Cook the capsicum in a little water for 2 minutes until soft. Drain. Add to the salmon mixture, and pour it on the base.

To make Topping, make the bread slices into breadcrumbs, add the cheese and parsley, and mix well. Spoon over the top of the salmon. Cook for 20–30 minutes, until the top browns. (See right colour plate overleaf.)

*C*urry Salmon Patty *(opposite page) and*
Sweet-and-sour Vegetables (page 55).

*Tuna Potato Roulade (page 76) with
Spicy Tomato Sauce (page 238).*

Top to bottom: Tuna and Vegetable Pie (page 78); Zucchini Moussaka (page 59); Salmon Bake (page 72).

Chinese Whole Fish (opposite page).

Chinese Whole Fish

SERVES 4–6

1.5 kg/3½ lb/1 whole fish
65 ml/2 fl oz/¼ cup lemon juice
1.5 litres/2½ pints/6 cups Chicken
  Stock (see p. 14)
1 onion, chopped
1 stick celery, chopped
1 carrot, cut into strips
1 teaspoon finely chopped fresh ginger
2 cloves garlic, crushed
sprigs of coriander

Garnish

1 carrot, cut into matchstick strips
2–3 spring onions, diagonally sliced
125 ml/4 fl oz/½ cup white wine
  vinegar
65 ml/2 fl oz/¼ cup unsweetened
  orange juice

Clean and scale the fish. Rub the fish inside and out with the lemon juice. Place the Chicken Stock in a wok or large, deep frying pan. Add the vegetables, ginger and garlic. Arrange a rack using chopsticks or place an upturned bowl in the base of the wok. Bring to the boil over a low heat and place the fish on the rack. Steam for 20–30 minutes or until cooked.

Place the fish on a heated serving dish. Bring the remaining stock to a rapid boil until reduced slightly. Spoon over the fish.

Mix the Garnish ingredients together and soak for 1 hour. Drain the carrot and spring onion, and sprinkle over the fish. Serve immediately. This dish may also be served cold. After cooking, cool, then refrigerate. Serve well chilled. (See colour plate opposite.)

Chinese Spring Rolls

MAKES 10

575 g/1¼ lb shredded cabbage
1 red capsicum, chopped
8 spring onions, finely chopped
125 g/¼ lb mushrooms, finely chopped
8 water chestnuts, chopped
500 g/1 lb 2 oz cooked prawns, chopped
1 teaspoon finely chopped fresh ginger
2 tablespoons/2 tablespoons plus
  2 teaspoons dry sherry
1 tablespoon/1 tablespoon plus
  1 teaspoon low-salt soy sauce
1 tablespoon/1 tablespoon plus
  1 teaspoon apple juice concentrate
1 tablespoon/1 tablespoon plus
  1 teaspoon cornflour
65 ml/2 fl oz/¼ cup water
2 teaspoons extra low-salt soy sauce
2 tablespoons/2 tablespoons plus
  2 teaspoons extra water
20 sheets wholemeal filo pastry

Preheat the oven to 200°C/400°F.

Combine the cabbage, capsicum, spring onion, mushroom, water chestnuts, prawns, ginger, sherry, soy sauce and apple juice concentrate and, using your hands, mix well. Let stand for 30 minutes, and toss frequently. Place the ingredients in a strainer to allow excess liquid to drain away. Use two sheets of filo pastry per roll. Fold in half. Turn the filo pastry sheet around so that a corner faces you. Spread the ingredients across the pastry. Turn the corner over the filling, and wipe all the remaining edges with the cornflour mixed with the water. Fold over the edges and roll up into a long roll. Repeat with the remaining ingredients to make 10 rolls.

Place on a non-stick baking tray. Wipe the tops with the extra soy sauce and water. Do not soak the pastry. Cook for 20 minutes. Serve immediately. (See colour plate opposite page 56.)

Spinach Pancakes with Lobster Filling

MAKES 8

Pancakes

225 g/½ lb/2 cups wholemeal plain flour
30 g/1 oz/¼ cup finely chopped spinach
30 g/1 oz/¼ cup skim milk powder
625 ml/1 pint/2½ cups water
2 egg whites

Sauce

500 ml/16 fl oz/2 cups skim milk
3 tablespoons/3 tablespoons plus 3 teaspoons cornflour
1 tablespoon/1 tablespoon plus 1 teaspoon salt-free tomato paste
2 teaspoons Dijon mustard
2 tablespoons/2 tablespoons plus 2 teaspoons grated low-fat grating cheese
black pepper or *squeeze of lemon juice (optional)*

Filling

90 g/3 oz lobster meat per pancake

To make the pancakes, combine all the ingredients in a food processor or blender and blend until smooth. Leave to stand for 30 minutes before using. Lightly grease a non-stick pancake pan or frying pan, pour small amounts of batter on to the pan and spread evenly. Cook for 3 minutes on one side or until air bubbles appear. Turn over and cook for 2 minutes. Keep warm.

To make the Sauce, slowly bring 450 ml/15 fl oz/1¾ cups of skim milk to the boil. Combine ¼ cup skim milk and the cornflour, tomato paste and Dijon mustard, and mix well. Add the boiling milk and stir thoroughly until thickened (add more cornflour if you desire a thicker sauce). Add the cheese and pepper.

Fill the pancakes with the lobster and pour the sauce over the top before rolling.

Mussels in Chilli Tomato Sauce

SERVES 4

1 onion, finely chopped
2 cloves garlic, crushed
1–2 sweet chillies, sliced
2 tablespoons/2 tablespoons plus 2 teaspoons water
850 g/2 lb ripe tomatoes, chopped
125 ml/4 fl oz/½ cup Chicken Stock (see p.14)
65 ml/2 fl oz/¼ cup dry white wine or vermouth
½ teaspoon dried oregano or dried basil
2 tablespoons/2 tablespoons plus 2 teaspoons salt-free tomato paste
black pepper to taste
575 g/1¼ lb mussels
fresh basil leaves for garnishing

Cook the onion, garlic and chilli in the water. Add the tomato, Chicken Stock, wine, oregano and tomato paste. Bring to the boil and simmer for 20 minutes or until the tomato breaks down to make a thick sauce. Purée the sauce or push through a sieve, and return the sauce to a clean saucepan. Bring the sauce to the boil. Add the cleaned mussels (see below), cover and simmer. Mussels are cooked in 5–7 minutes or when the majority of mussels are opened. Garnish with fresh basil leaves and serve immediately.

Storing and Cleaning Mussels

Live mussels should be covered with cold water until you are ready to cook them. If standing overnight, add a handful of oatmeal to the pot to feed the mussels: this will keep them alive. Throw away any mussels that float to the top, are broken, are open prior to cooking, or will not close when you tap them sharply. Scrape away the barnacles and the beard and hold under running water to remove sand or mud before cooking. After cooking, discard any mussels that do not open.

Prawn Curry

SERVES 4

a little light olive oil
1 large onion, chopped
400 g/14 oz ripe tomatoes, quartered
1 tablespoon/1 tablespoon plus
    1 teaspoon Vindaloo curry paste
1 teaspoon finely chopped fresh ginger
450 g/1 lb green prawns, peeled and
    deveined
1 tablespoon/1 tablespoon plus
    1 teaspoon lemon juice
65 ml/2 fl oz/¼ cup non-fat or low-fat
    yoghurt
200 g/7 oz extra ripe tomatoes,
    quartered
finely chopped fresh parsley

Wipe the base of a non-stick frying pan with the oil and remove any excess oil. Gently cook the onion, tomato, Vindaloo Curry Paste and ginger with the lid on. The tomato will break down to make a sauce. Add the prawns. Cover, and cook gently until the prawns are just tender. Add the lemon juice and yoghurt. Stir continuously until the sauce boils and thickens. Add the extra tomato, and heat through just before serving. Sprinkle with parsley. Serve with steamed brown rice.

Curried Scallop and Potato Pie

SERVES 4 – 6

150 g/5 oz/1 cup sliced celery
125 g/¼ lb/1 cup peas
200 g/7 oz/1¼ cups carrots, cut into
    chunks
400 g/14 oz scallops, cleaned
850 g/2 lb potatoes, peeled
2 bay leaves
a little skim milk

Curry Sauce
60 g/2 oz/½ cup finely chopped onion
1 teaspoon crushed garlic
2 tablespoons/2 tablespoons plus 2
    teaspoons water
2 teaspoons curry powder
1 teaspoon ground cummin
2 teaspoons pink peppercorns
60 g/2 oz/½ cup cornflour
750 ml/1⅓ pints/3 cups skim milk

To make the Curry Sauce, combine the onion, garlic, water, curry powder, cummin and peppercorns in a small saucepan and cook over a gentle heat with the lid on until the onion is quite soft.

Combine the cornflour with a little of the milk to make a paste. Stir in the remaining milk. Pour this over the cooked onion and spices. Slowly bring to the boil, stirring continuously until the sauce thickens. Cover and set aside.

Steam the celery, peas and carrot until just tender, and drain. While the vegetables are cooking, place the scallops in a dish and cover with boiling water. Place a lid on the dish and allow the scallops to stand until they just change colour, approximately 1½–2 minutes. Drain well. Add the vegetables and scallops to the sauce and place in a deep casserole dish.

Cook the potatoes and bay leaves in water until the potatoes are tender. Drain, remove leaves and mash the potatoes with a little skim milk until smooth. For an attractive topping, spoon the potato into a piping bag and pipe decoratively over the top of the scallop and vegetable mixture.

When ready to cook, preheat the oven to 180°C/350°F and bake for 40 minutes or until the pie bubbles and the potato is lightly browned on top.

Tuna Curry Slice

SERVES 6

Base
125 g/ ¼ lb/2 cups fresh wholemeal
    breadcrumbs

Filling
400 g/14 oz canned tuna
150 g/5 oz/1 cup finely sliced celery
1 large apple, grated
handful of finely chopped fresh chives
2 tablespoons/2 tablespoons plus
    2 teaspoons wholemeal plain flour
125 ml/4 fl oz/½ cup skim milk
125 ml/4 fl oz/½ cup unsweetened
    apple juice
3 egg whites
2–3 teaspoons curry powder
500 g/1 lb 2 oz/2 cups mashed potato
2 tablespoons/2 tablespoons plus
    2 teaspoons finely grated low-fat
    grating cheese

Preheat the oven to 180°C/350°F.

To make the Base, toast the breadcrumbs until brown and crisp. Lightly grease a 20-cm × 30-cm/8″ × 12″, deep, rectangular baking dish and line with foil. Press the breadcrumbs onto the base of the dish while still hot. Set aside.

To make the Filling, combine the tuna, celery, apple and chives, and spread over the base. Heat the flour in a saucepan for a few seconds. Add the milk and stir briskly. Add the apple juice and stir until the sauce thickens. Beat the egg whites lightly. Remove the sauce from the heat and stir the egg white through it. Add the curry powder to taste. Cook for 2 minutes. Pour over the tuna mixture. Combine the potato with the cheese, and spread evenly over the top. Press down with a fork. Cook for 30-40 minutes or until the top is browned.

Tuna Potato Roulade

SERVES 6 – 8

1 kg/2¼ lb potatoes, peeled
30 g/1 oz/¼ cup chopped spring onion
    (green part only)
185 g/6 oz/3 cups fresh wholemeal
    breadcrumbs
1 egg white
a little wholemeal plain flour

Filling
200 g/7 oz canned tuna
125 g/¼ lb/1 cup chopped spring onion
    (green part only)
1 Granny Smith apple, peeled and
    quartered
10 mushrooms, washed
1 tablespoon/1 tablespoon plus
    1 teaspoon lemon juice

Preheat oven to 230°C/450°F.

Steam the potatoes lightly until tender, and then drain and mash. Fold in the spring onion, breadcrumbs and egg white and mix well. Place a sheet of foil on a baking tray (approximately 30 cm × 35 cm/12″ × 14″). Lightly grease the foil and sprinkle the wholemeal plain flour over the top. While the potato is still warm, spoon it onto the foil. Flatten it with the palm of your hand so that it is approximately 1 cm thick.

Combine the Filling mixture in a food processor or blender and, using the stop–start button, lightly blend. Spoon the mixture onto the potato along one edge of the longer side of foil. Press down firmly. With the aid of the foil, roll up to form the roulade. (If the filling starts to fall, just keep pressing it back into position with your hand.) Use a knife or spatula to flatten the edge, making an even finish.

Carefully place the roll on a lightly greased baking tray. Cook for 30 minutes, turn the oven down to 200°C/400°F and cook for a further 30 minutes.

Serve with salad or lightly steamed julienne of fresh vegetables. (See left colour plate between pages 72 and 73.)

Tuna and Vegetable Casserole

SERVES 6

425 g/15 oz canned tuna, drained
8 spring onions
500 g/1 lb 2 oz zucchini, cut into
  chunks
125 g/¼ lb/1 cup finely sliced broccoli
125 g/¼ lb/1 cup finely sliced
  cauliflower
150 g/5 oz/1 cup finely chopped carrot
75 g/2½ oz/½ cup finely chopped red
  capsicum
75 g/2½ oz/½ cup finely chopped green
  capsicum

Sauce
750 ml/1⅓ pints/3 cups skim milk
60 g/2 oz/½ cup cornflour
1 teaspoon dried oregano
1 teaspoon dried basil
140 g/4½ oz/½ cup salt-free tomato
  paste

Topping
60 g/2 oz/½ cup oat bran
30 g/1 oz/½ cup fresh wholemeal or rye
  breadcrumbs
60 g/2 oz/½ cup grated low-fat grating
  cheese
large handful finely chopped fresh parsley

Preheat the oven to 180°C/350°F.

Combine the tuna and spring onions in a casserole dish. Steam the vegetables until just tender, and then drain. Add to the dish.

To make the Sauce, combine 250 ml/8 fl oz/1 cup of milk with the cornflour, herbs and tomato paste, and mix well. Return this to the remaining milk and heat in a small saucepan until the sauce thickens.

Pour the sauce over the combined tuna and vegetables in the casserole dish. Combine all the Topping ingredients and spread evenly over the casserole. Bake for 40 minutes or until bubbling and the top is golden brown.

This is an excellent casserole to prepare a day ahead; just cover and refrigerate. It will need a little more time in the oven if it goes straight from the refrigerator to the oven. (See right colour plate between pages 72 and 73.)

Variation
- 125 g/¼ lb/1 cup frozen peas can be used instead of the red and green capsicum.

Tuna and Vegetable Croquettes

MAKES 12 (6 SERVINGS)

425 g/15 oz canned tuna
310 g/10½ oz/1 cup corn kernels
500 g/1 lb 2 oz potatoes, mashed
juice of 1 small lemon
100 g/3½ oz/¾ cup grated carrot
100 g/3½ oz/½ cup grated zucchini
  (juice squeezed out)
125 g/¼ lb/1 cup finely chopped onion
3 egg whites
1 teaspoon dried dill
1 teaspoon freshly chopped basil or ¼
  teaspoon dried basil
black pepper to taste
60 g/2 oz/½ cup oat bran

Preheat the oven to 180°C/350°F.

Drain the tuna and corn. Combine all the ingredients, except the oat bran, and mix well using your hands. Form into small croquettes and roll lightly in the oat bran. Refrigerate until firm.

Lightly grease a non-stick frying pan and cook croquettes until light brown, a few minutes on each side. Complete the cooking by placing the croquettes on a lined baking tray and cooking for a further 15–20 minutes in the oven.

Tuna and Vegetable Pie

xxxxxxxxxxxxxxxxxxxxxxxxxxxxxxxxxxxxxxxxxxxxxxxxxxxxxxxxxxxxxxxxxxxxxxxxxxxxx

SERVES 6

Crust
6 slices wholemeal bread

Filling
1 onion, finely chopped
1 tablespoon/1 tablespoon plus
* 1 teaspoon water*
350 ml/12 fl oz/1½ cups low-fat
* evaporated milk or reduced-fat*
* soymilk*
1 tablespoon/1 tablespoon plus
* 1 teaspoon salt-free tomato paste*
200 g/7 oz canned tuna
150 g/5 oz/1 cup grated carrot
150 g/5 oz/1 cup finely chopped celery
1 small green capsicum, finely chopped
handful of finely chopped fresh parsley
2 tablespoons/2 tablespoons plus
* 2 teaspoons finely chopped fresh chives*
30 g/1 oz/¼ cup cornflour
125 ml/4 fl oz/½ cup water

Preheat the oven to 200°C/400°F.

Crumble the bread into fine breadcrumbs. Lightly grease a small pie dish. Reserve 40 g/1½ oz/¾ cup breadcrumbs for the topping. Place the breadcrumbs in the pie dish and spread over the base and sides evenly. Firm down with your fingers and the palm of your hand. Bake for 10 minutes. Remove from the oven. Turn the oven up to 230°C/450°F.

While the pie crust is cooking, cook the onion in the water in a large saucepan for 3 minutes or until transparent. Add the milk and simmer for 2 minutes. Stir in the tomato paste. Add the tuna, carrot, celery and capsicum. Simmer, covered, for 5 minutes. Add the parsley and chives.

Mix the cornflour with 125 ml/4 fl oz/½ cup of water to make a thin paste. Stir this through the tuna mixture and cook for 2 minutes, stirring continuously. Cool slightly. Pour into the pie crust. Sprinkle with the remaining breadcrumbs. Cook at 230°C/450°F for 10 minutes. Turn the oven down to 200°C/400°F and cook for a further 20 minutes.

Serve with tossed salad or lightly steamed vegetables.

POULTRY

*C*hicken is one of the most popular meats. Its white, tender flesh lends itself to nearly every spice and sauce that the clever cook can imagine. It appears on most national menus. You can easily recognise where recipes originate by the spices, sauce and cooking method used. Many of these traditional recipes can still be included in a low-fat diet, with only some slight adaptations and variations to ingredients.

The majority of fat in chicken is found just under the skin, in large pockets and in the skin itself. The fat and skin should be removed before cooking. Because chicken is such a versatile meat it can be steamed, poached, grilled, baked, barbecued, and cooked in a casserole. Serve portions of 100 g/3½ oz to maintain a low-fat, low-cholesterol diet.

Skinless turkey is much lower in fat and cholesterol than chicken meat. It is a drier meat and therefore needs more basting during cooking. You can add a moist, flavoursome stuffing to the centre of the turkey to stop it drying out during cooking.

Other poultry, such as duck and goose, is much higher in fat and cholesterol and is best avoided on a low-fat, low-cholesterol diet.

Chicken, Artichoke and Leek Casserole

SERVES 6

1 × 1.5-kg/3½-lb chicken (all skin and
  fat removed)
2 teaspoons crushed garlic
1 large leek, thoroughly washed and cut
  into rounds
1 large carrot, cut into thin rounds
a little water
10 large mushrooms
1 tablespoon/1 tablespoon plus
  1 teaspoon low-salt soy sauce
1 teaspoon light olive oil
250 ml/8 fl oz/1 cup dry white wine
¼ teaspoon dried rosemary
2 tablespoons/2 tablespoons plus
  2 teaspoons cornflour
250 ml/8 fl oz/1 cup low-fat evaporated
  milk
425 g/15 oz canned artichoke hearts,
  drained

Preheat the oven to 180°C/350°F.

Cut the chicken into large pieces. Rub the garlic over the base of a non-stick frying pan. Heat the pan and brown the chicken pieces on both sides. Do not have the pan too hot. Remove the chicken pieces and place in a casserole dish.

Cook the leek and carrot in a little water until the carrot has softened slightly. Drain and add to the casserole dish.

Place the mushrooms, soy sauce and oil in the pan. Cover, and cook until the mushrooms are soft. Check frequently to see that the mushrooms are not sticking to the pan. (If they are, turn the heat down.) Add the cooked mushrooms to the casserole dish. Pour in the wine and add the rosemary. Cover, and cook in the oven for 40–45 minutes. Remove from the oven.

Combine the cornflour and a little of the milk to make a paste. Add this to the remaining milk and stir through the casserole until the sauce thickens. Continue cooking in the oven for another 15–20 minutes.

Rinse the artichoke hearts thoroughly in cold water to remove any salt. Cut them in half and add to the casserole. Leave the casserole standing, covered, for 5 minutes before serving, to allow the artichokes to heat through. Serve with brown rice or salad. (See colour plate opposite.)

Chicken, Apricot and Pistachio Terrine

SERVES 4–6

1.5 kg/3½ lb chicken breasts (all skin
  and fat removed)
2 egg whites
100 g/3½ oz/½ cup dried apricots
125 g/¼ lb/¾ cup pistachio nuts
black pepper to taste
large handful finely chopped fresh herbs
  (e.g. chives, parsley, thyme, basil)
water or unsweetened orange juice or dry
  white wine
½–1 teaspoon agar powder or 2
  teaspoons gelatine

Preheat the oven to 180°C/350°F.

Mince 800 g/1¾ lb of the chicken fillets and combine with the egg whites. Chop the apricots. Shell the pistachios, and chop. Add the chopped apricot and nuts, black pepper and herbs to the chicken mixture, and set aside.

With a rolling pin, flatten the remaining chicken breasts by rolling between two layers of plastic wrap. Lightly grease a glass terrine dish. Line the terrine with the flattened chicken breasts. Spoon in the minced chicken filling and press down. Cover with a sheet of greaseproof paper and then foil. Tie with string. Place in a baking dish containing water and cook for 1 hour. Remove from the oven and pour any juices into a jug. Place a heavy weight on top of the chicken while it cools.

Skim any fat from the juices and make up to 250 ml/ 8 fl oz/1 cup of liquid using water, orange juice or white wine. Add the agar powder to the liquid and bring to the boil. Simmer for 2 minutes. Pour down the sides of the cold terrine. This will set and keep the chicken terrine from drying out. It will also give the terrine a neater presentation. Refrigerate. Turn out and cut into slices.

Chicken, Artichoke and Leek Casserole
(opposite page).

Chicken and Fruit Curry (opposite page).

Grilled Chicken and Apricot Kebabs

SERVES 6

575 g/1¼ lb chicken breasts (all skin
    and fat removed)
5 apricots, cut into quarters
1 large onion, quartered
¼ pineapple, cut into 12 cubes
6 kebab skewers

Marinade
250 ml/8 fl oz/1 cup unsweetened
    orange juice
1 teaspoon finely chopped fresh ginger
1 tablespoon/1 tablespoon plus
    1 teaspoon apple juice concentrate
1 tablespoon/1 tablespoon plus
    1 teaspoon dry sherry
2 teaspoons finely grated lemon rind

Cut the chicken into large bite-sized pieces. Marinate all the ingredients for at least 2 hours before grilling. Divide the ingredients evenly between the 6 skewers. Spoon over a little of the Marinade during cooking.

Note
To prevent wooden skewers from burning, soak them in cold water for 2 hours before using.

Chicken and Fruit Curry

SERVES 4–6

400 g/14 oz chicken breasts (all skin
    and fat removed)
2 cloves garlic, crushed
1 large onion, chopped
1 tablespoon curry powder
500 ml/16 fl oz/2 cups Chicken Stock
    (see p. 14)
2 bay leaves
425 g/15 oz canned unsweetened apricot
    halves, drained
425 g/15 oz canned unsweetened
    pineapple pieces, drained
6 water chestnuts, finely sliced
250 ml/8 fl oz/1 cup reduced-fat
    soymilk
1 heaped tablespoon/1 heaped tablespoon
    plus 1 heaped teaspoon cornflour

Cut the chicken into 2-cm/¾″ chunks and stir fry in a hot, non-stick frying pan to seal and lightly brown the meat. This will take approximately 3 minutes. Remove the chicken from the pan. Add the garlic, onion and curry powder. Toss continuously until the onion is transparent, approximately 2–3 minutes.

Add the chicken stock and bay leaves and bring to the boil. Add the chicken and simmer for 20 minutes or until the chicken is tender. Add the apricot, pineapple and water chestnut. Combine the soymilk and cornflour to make a paste. Add, stirring continuously until the sauce boils and thickens. Serve with brown rice. (See colour plate opposite.)

Chicken and Carrot Loaf

SERVES 6–8

750 g/1½ lb chicken breasts (all skin and fat removed), minced
60 g/2 oz/1 cup freshly chopped parsley
3–4 carrots, grated
1 small onion, chopped
30 g/1 oz/½ cup fresh wholemeal breadcrumbs
black pepper to taste
300 ml/10 fl oz/1¼ cups low-fat yoghurt with a squeeze of lemon juice

Preheat the oven to 180°C/350°F.

Combine the chicken, half the parsley, 225 g/½ lb/ 1½ cups of carrot, the onion, breadcrumbs, pepper and yoghurt in a large bowl, and mix well. Press a third of the mixture into a deep 23-cm × 13-cm/9″ × 5″ glass terrine dish. Sprinkle the remaining carrot over the top and press down firmly. Add another third of the chicken mixture, press down well, and sprinkle the remaining parsley over the top. Top with the remaining chicken mixture and press firmly down. Cover with foil and bake, in a dish containing water, for 1 hour or until golden brown. Leave to cool in the terrine dish.

Gently ease a metal spatula around the sides of the chicken loaf, turn onto a plate and chill well before serving. Serve with salad and fresh wholemeal rolls. This is an excellent loaf for a picnic. (See left colour plate between pages 88 and 89.)

Chicken and Ginger Zucchini Balls

MAKES 16–20

400 g/14 oz chicken breasts (all skin and fat removed)
2 Granny Smith apples, peeled and grated
1 onion, chopped
2 zucchini, grated
1 teaspoon finely grated fresh ginger
1 teaspoon finely grated lemon rind
60 g/2 oz/1 cup fresh wholemeal breadcrumbs

Preheat the oven to 200°C/400°F.

Combine the chicken, apple and onion in a food processor or blender. Blend until smooth. Add the zucchini, ginger and lemon rind, and mix well. Roll a dessertspoonful of mixture into a ball. Roll the ball in the breadcrumbs. Repeat until all the mixture is used.

Place on a lightly greased oven tray and cook for 30–40 minutes or until lightly browned. Serve with a selection of salads.

Creamy Lemon and Mint Chicken

SERVES 4

1 clove garlic
400 g/14 oz chicken breasts (all skin and fat removed)

Sauce
2 tablespoons/2 tablespoons plus 2 teaspoons lemon juice
500 ml/16 fl oz/2 cups skim milk
handful of finely chopped fresh mint or 1 tablespoon/1 tablespoon plus 1 teaspoon dried mint
3 tablespoons/3 tablespoons plus 3 teaspoons cornflour

Rub the garlic over the base of a non-stick frying pan. Heat the pan until very hot, and cook the chicken on both sides. Remove the chicken and keep warm. Turn the heat down.

To make the Sauce, put the lemon juice, all but 65 ml/ 2 fl oz/¼ cup of milk and the mint in the pan. Mix the cornflour with the remaining milk to make a paste. Stir into the mixture. The sauce will begin to curdle, but continue stirring briskly. As the sauce boils and thickens the curd will be absorbed back into it and you should see only a fine white fleck through the sauce. Turn the heat down, add the chicken, and heat through. Serve with a green vegetable such as broccoli or zucchini.

Chicken with Apple and Prunes

SERVES 4

4 chicken breasts (all skin and fat
    removed)
500 ml/16 fl oz/2 cups Chicken Stock
    (see p. 14)
250 ml/8 fl oz/1 cup unsweetened
    orange juice
30 g/1 oz/¼ cup cornflour
1 tablespoon/1 tablespoon plus
    1 teaspoon lemon juice
finely grated rind of 1 lemon
1 tablespoon/1 tablespoon plus
    1 teaspoon apple juice concentrate
1 teaspoon finely chopped fresh parsley
2 cooking apples, peeled and cored
12 moist prunes
250 ml/8 fl oz/1 cup water

Cook the chicken breasts in 250 ml/8 fl oz/1 cup of the Chicken Stock in a saucepan until they are just tender. Remove the chicken. Mix a little of the orange juice with the cornflour to make a paste and stir into the stock in the pan. Add the remaining stock, lemon juice and rind, apple juice concentrate and parsley. Bring to the boil. Simmer until the sauce thickens, and then return the chicken to the pan.

Cut each apple into 6 rings and cook with the prunes in the water until the apple rings are just tender but still holding their shape. Drain well.

Serve one chicken breast, three apple slices and three prunes per person, and spoon the lemon sauce from the pan over the top.

Mango Curry Chicken Salad

SERVES 4

1 mango
250 ml/8 fl oz/1 cup non-fat or low-fat
    yoghurt
½ teaspoon curry powder
½ teaspoon ground cummin
400 g/14 oz cooked chicken (all skin
    and fat removed), broken into pieces
lettuce
fresh mango slices or fresh peach slices
extra kiwi fruit slices
alfalfa sprouts
freshly chopped chives

Peel the mango and remove the flesh from the stone. Push through a sieve. Add the yoghurt and spices, and mix well. Add the chicken pieces and coat well. Refrigerate for at least 2 hours before serving.

Make a bed of lettuce and add the chicken salad. Arrange the extra mango, kiwi fruit and alfalfa sprouts around the salad. Sprinkle the chives over the top.

Hot Chicken Terrine

SERVES 10 – 12

1 kg/2¼ lb chicken breasts (all skin and
    fat removed), minced
185 g/6 oz/3 cups fresh wholemeal
    breadcrumbs
4 Granny Smith apples, grated
90 g/3 oz/¾ cup chopped spring onion
2 teaspoons finely grated lemon rind
1 egg white

Preheat the oven to 200°C/400°F.

Mix all the ingredients thoroughly with your hands. Press firmly into a large foil-lined terrine dish. Cook for 1½ hours in a baking dish containing water. Turn out onto a serving dish. Serve with Blueberry Sauce (see page 236) or a gravy of your choice and vegetables. (See left colour plate between pages 208 and 209.)

Creamy Chicken Marsala

SERVES 4

4 chicken breasts
250 ml/8 fl oz/1 cup skim milk
1 large clove garlic, bruised
2 tablespoons/2 tablespoons plus
   2 teaspoons finely chopped spring
   onion or chives
2 tablespoons/2 tablespoons plus
   2 teaspoons Marsala
1 tablespoon/1 tablespoon plus
   1 teaspoon Chicken Stock (see p. 14)
1–2 teaspoons cornflour
black pepper to taste

Remove all skin and fat from the chicken breasts. Cook the chicken in a very hot frying pan for 2–3 minutes on both sides until tender. Remove from the pan and keep warm. In a separate saucepan, add the milk, garlic, spring onion and Marsala. Gently heat until just simmering. Combine the Chicken Stock and cornflour and add to the pan, stirring continuously until the sauce thickens. Do not boil. Season with black pepper. Add the warm chicken breasts (you can cut each breast into three pieces for easier serving), and let stand for a few minutes to heat through. Remove the garlic before serving. Serve with a salad.

Barbecued Marinated Chicken

Marinade 1
200 ml/7 fl oz/¾ cup dry white wine
1 onion, finely chopped
1 clove garlic, crushed
1 teaspoon dried marjoram
½ teaspoon dried thyme
1 teaspoon apple juice concentrate
black pepper to taste

Each of the following marinades is enough for 1 chicken. Remove all the skin and fat from the chicken, cut into pieces and marinate for 2 hours before cooking. Cut flesh away and thread onto skewers, alternating chicken with a selection of vegetables and fruit. Baby onions, baby mushrooms, fresh pineapple, capsicum, prunes, figs, dates, cherry tomatoes and baby squash all make tasty accompaniments. Cook quickly on the barbecue until the chicken is done.

Marinade 2
2 tablespoons/2 tablespoons plus 2
   teaspoons low-salt soy sauce
2 tablespoons/2 tablespoons plus 2
   teaspoons salt-free tomato paste
1 teaspoon finely chopped fresh ginger
1 teaspoon apple juice concentrate
a little dry white wine

Marinade 5
125 ml/4 fl oz/½ cup dry red wine
1 tablespoon/1 tablespoon plus
   1 teaspoon lemon or lime juice
125 ml/4 fl oz/½ cup French Dressing
   (see p. 140)
1 tablespoon/1 tablespoon plus
   1 teaspoon finely chopped fresh basil
   leaves

Marinade 3
200 ml/7 fl oz/¾ cup dry white wine or
   apple cider
1 onion, finely chopped
1–2 teaspoons finely chopped fresh ginger
1 tablespoon/1 tablespoon plus 1
   teaspoon lemon rind
2 teaspoons apple juice concentrate

Marinade 6
125 ml/4 fl oz/½ cup dry red wine
1 teaspoon crushed dried chilli
1 teaspoon dried tarragon
1 tablespoon/1 tablespoon plus
   1 teaspoon apple juice concentrate

Marinade 4
3 cloves garlic, crushed
1 red chilli, finely chopped
2 stalks lemon grass (tender part only),
   finely chopped
250 ml/8 fl oz/1 cup Chicken Stock
   (see p. 14) or dry white wine

Marinade 7
250 ml/8 fl oz/1 cup unsweetened
   pineapple juice
1 onion, finely chopped
2 tablespoons/2 tablespoons plus
   2 teaspoons preserved ginger, finely
   chopped
65 ml/2 fl oz/¼ cup dry sherry

Chicken Breasts in Filo Pastry

SERVES 4–6

6 chicken breasts (all skin and fat removed)
2 large apples, grated
60 g/2 oz/½ cup roughly chopped walnuts or raw almonds
125 ml/4 fl oz/½ cup non-fat or low-fat yoghurt
2 tablespoons/2 tablespoons plus 2 teaspoons Date and Apple Chutney (see p. 235)
100 g/3½ oz/½ cup sultanas
black pepper to taste
12 sheets filo pastry
extra yoghurt

Preheat the oven to 200°C/400°F.

Put the chicken between sheets of plastic on a wooden board. Roll out with a wooden rolling pin or beat out with a wooden meat mallet until fairly thin.

Combine the apple, walnuts, yoghurt, chutney, sultanas and black pepper. Spread this mixture over the flattened chicken, and fold up into neat parcels.

Brush 2 sheets of filo pastry with the extra yoghurt. Fold in half and brush once more. Place 1 chicken roll on the end of the pastry sheet. Fold the sides of the pastry sheet up over the chicken to form a parcel. Continue with the remaining chicken and filo.

Place the chicken parcels on a baking tray with the seam side down and bake for 30 minutes, until the pastry is golden brown and the chicken is tender. The parcels can be prepared ahead and kept, covered with plastic wrap, in the refrigerator.

Chicken Chasseur

SERVES 6–8

1 kg/2¼ lb chicken drumsticks and wings (all skin and fat removed)
2 cloves garlic, crushed
400 g/14 oz mushrooms
2 tablespoons/2 tablespoons plus 2 teaspoons low-salt soy sauce
250 ml/8 fl oz/1 cup dry white wine
425 g/15 oz canned whole tomatoes in natural juice, puréed
2 tablespoons/2 tablespoons plus 2 teaspoons salt-free tomato paste
¼ teaspoon dried tarragon
575 g/1¼ lb carrots, cut into chunks
30 g/1 oz/¼ cup chopped spring onion
2 tablespoons/2 tablespoons plus 2 teaspoons finely chopped fresh parsley
brown rice or mashed potato or wholemeal noodles for serving

Sauce
1 onion, finely sliced
75 g/2½ oz/½ cup grated parsnip
40 g/1½ oz/⅓ cup cornflour
750 ml/1⅓ pints/3 cups Chicken Stock (see p. 14)

Preheat the oven to 200°C/400°F.

In a frying pan, stir-fry the chicken to seal the meat and slightly brown. Do in three lots. Remove the chicken and set aside.

To make the Sauce, stir-fry the onion and parsnip until the onion is transparent, approximately 3 minutes. Add the combined cornflour and stock. Bring to the boil, reduce the heat and simmer for 10 minutes. Remove the sauce from the pan and set aside.

Wash the pan and stir-fry the garlic and mushrooms in soy sauce until the mushrooms are soft. Add the wine and boil until the liquid has reduced by half. Add the combined puréed tomato, tomato paste and tarragon. Stir to combine.

Add the sauce to the mushroom mixture, then add the chicken and carrot. Mix through before removing to a casserole dish. Cover. Bake in the oven for 40 minutes or until the chicken and carrot are tender.

When the casserole is cooked, top with the spring onion and parsley and serve with brown rice, mashed potato or wholemeal noodles. (See right colour plate between pages 88 and 89.)

Chicken with Chinese Vegetables

SERVES 4

400 g/14 oz chicken breasts (all skin
   and fat removed)
30 g/1 oz Chinese dried mushrooms
225 g/½ lb canned bamboo shoots
   (rinsed)
1 teaspoon crushed ginger
200 ml/7 fl oz/¾ cup Chicken Stock
   (see p. 14)
1 tablespoon/1 tablespoon plus
   1 teaspoon dry sherry
2 teaspoons apple juice concentrate
225 g/½ lb/2 cups finely sliced broccoli
100 g/3½ oz/1 cup diagonally sliced
   celery
2 tablespoons/2 tablespoons plus
   2 teaspoons extra Chicken Stock
1 teaspoon cornflour

Chop the chicken into bite-sized pieces. Cover the dried mushrooms with hot water and stand for 15 minutes, until the mushrooms are soft. Drain and finely slice the mushrooms. Slice the bamboo shoots.

Place the chicken, mushroom, bamboo shoot, ginger, Chicken Stock, sherry and apple juice concentrate in a wok. Simmer with the lid on until the chicken is just tender. Add the broccoli and celery, cover, and simmer until the vegetables are just tender. Combine the extra stock and cornflour. Add to the wok and bring to the boil. Stir continuously and cook for 1 minute. Serve immediately.

Chicken Sesame Drumsticks

SERVES 12

12 chicken drumsticks (skin removed)

Sauce
3 tablespoons/3 tablespoons plus
   3 teaspoons cornflour
2 tablespoons/2 tablespoons plus
   2 teaspoons water
65 ml/2 fl oz/¼ cup apple juice
   concentrate
2 teaspoons finely chopped fresh ginger
250 ml/8 fl oz/1 cup unsweetened
   orange juice
200 ml/7 fl oz/¾ cup dry sherry
1 tablespoon/1 tablespoon plus
   1 teaspoon low-salt soy sauce
2 tablespoons/2 tablespoons plus
   2 teaspoons toasted sesame seeds

Preheat the oven to 180°C/350°F.

Mix the cornflour and water together to make a paste. Add to the remaining Sauce ingredients and pour over the drumsticks. Cover and cook for 20 minutes or until the chicken is tender Boil the sauce to reduce and thicken if desired. Serve the chicken with brown rice.

Chicken Kedgeree

SERVES 8 – 10

185 g/6 oz/1 cup brown rice
310 g/10½ oz/2 cups basmati rice water
3 onions, sliced
3 sweet chillies, finely chopped
1 tablespoon/1 tablespoon plus 1 teaspoon cummin seeds
2 tablespoons/2 tablespoons plus 2 teaspoons freshly grated ginger
2 teaspoons turmeric
1 teaspoon ground coriander
1 teaspoon ground cinnamon
850 g/2 lb cooked chicken breasts (all skin and fat removed), cut into cubes
8 hard-boiled eggs, quartered (yolks removed)
large handful coarsely chopped fresh parsley
large handful coarsely chopped fresh chives or basil
black pepper to taste

Wash the rice and cover with water. Bring to the boil. Turn the heat down to a gentle simmer and cook until the rice is tender. Drain. Wipe the base of a non-stick frying pan with oil and wipe out any excess oil. Sauté the onion, chilli, cummin and ginger until the onion is soft. Add the turmeric, coriander and cinnamon and the cooked rice. Heat through. Add the chicken, egg, parsley and chives. Toss gently to warm through. Season with pepper.

Malay Chicken with Coconut Milk

SERVES 6

250 ml/8 fl oz/1 cup skim milk
1 tablespoon/1 tablespoon plus 1 teaspoon shredded coconut
2 teaspoons chilli paste (1 teaspoon for a milder curry)
1 sweet chilli, sliced
1 tablespoon/1 tablespoon plus 1 teaspoon Vindaloo curry paste
1 teaspoon turmeric
1 teaspoon ground cummin
1–2 cloves garlic, crushed
2 Spanish onions, finely chopped
575 g/1¼ lb chicken breasts (all skin and fat removed)
1 tablespoon/1 tablespoon plus 1 teaspoon low-salt tomato paste
2 teaspoons cornflour
2 tablespoons/2 tablespoons plus 2 teaspoons water

Place the skim milk and coconut in a saucepan. Bring to the boil. Turn off the heat, and stand for 1 hour.

Combine the chilli paste, sweet chilli, Vindaloo curry paste, turmeric, cummin, garlic, onion and chicken in a large pan. Cook gently, continuously stirring, for 5 minutes. Add the coconut milk. Turn the heat down to lowest temperature. Cover, and cook for 10–15 minutes or until the chicken is very tender. Combine the tomato paste, cornflour and water, and stir through the chicken mixture. Cook for a further 2 minutes. Serve with brown rice, yoghurt and Indian Rice Crisps (see Lamb Curry, page 109).

Chicken Casserole with Snow Peas

SERVES 4

400 g/14 oz chicken breasts
½ teaspoon ground cummin
½ teaspoon ground coriander
500 ml/16 fl oz/2 cups Chicken Stock (see p. 14)
200 g/7 oz carrots
200 g/7 oz zucchini
100 g/3½ oz celery
2 tablespoons/2 tablespoons plus 2 teaspoons cornflour
2 tablespoons/2 tablespoons plus 2 teaspoons water
100 g/3½ oz snow peas
5 spring onions

Remove all skin and fat from the chicken breasts. Cut the chicken into bite-sized pieces. Heat a large non-stick frying pan to moderately hot and add the chicken. Keep tossing to seal the meat. This will take approximately 3 minutes. Add the spices and continue to toss. Add the Chicken Stock and bring to the boil. Reduce the heat to simmer and cook for 10–15 minutes.

Cut the carrots and zucchini into rounds and then quarter. Slice the celery diagonally. Add to the meat, cover, and simmer for a further 10 minutes. Add the combined cornflour and water. Top and tail the snow peas, slice the spring onions diagonally and add to pan. Cook for 5–8 minutes, stirring continuously.

Serve on a bed of wholemeal spaghetti or brown rice. (See colour plate opposite.)

Roast Chicken

Oven Roast Method

oranges
onions
1 chicken
250 ml/8 fl oz/1 cup unsweetened orange juice
250 ml/8 fl oz/1 cup water
sprig of herb of your choice or cloves of garlic or piece fresh ginger
a little cornflour

Alternative Cooking Liquids

250 ml/8 fl oz/1 cup white wine
250 ml/8 fl oz/1 cup apple cider
or
125 ml/4 fl oz/½ cup sherry
350 ml/12 fl oz/1½ cups water
or
250 ml/8 fl oz/1 cup vermouth
250 ml/8 fl oz/1 cup water

Oven Bag Method

3 cloves garlic or 1 lemon, cut in half
2 tablespoons/2 tablespoons plus 2 teaspoons unbleached white plain flour
1 teaspoon dried basil
1 teaspoon dried oregano
1 chicken
freshly ground black pepper

Most of the fat in chicken lies under the skin in large fat pockets and within the skin. It is best to remove all these fat pockets before cooking, because the fat tends to be absorbed into the meat during the cooking process. You can leave the skin on during the cooking so the meat does not dry out and then remove the skin before eating.

To roast chicken using the Oven Roast Method, cut up some oranges and onions (leave the skins on) and place in the base of a baking dish. Place the chicken on top. Combine the orange juice and water and pour over the chicken.

For extra flavour add a sprig of your favourite fresh herb, for example, thyme, rosemary or oregano, or some cloves of garlic or a piece of fresh ginger.

The chicken can be placed in the liquid or just above on a wire rack. Cook at 180°C/350°F for 20–25 minutes per 500 g/1 lb 2 oz. Baste the chicken frequently during the cooking. Juices can be strained and defatted to make a delicious gravy. Simply add a little cornflour to thicken.

■ ■ ■

To roast chicken using the Oven Bag Method, remove all the skin and fat from the chicken. Rub the chicken all over with 1 clove of garlic and insert 2 cloves in the cavity (if using lemon, rub one half all over the chicken and insert the other half in the cavity). Combine the flour, basil, oregano and ground black pepper. Place this in the oven bag. Add the chicken and coat well with the seasoning ingredients. Tie up the bag.

Cook at 200°C/400°F for 20 minutes per 500 g/1 lb 2 oz.

*Chicken Casserole with Snow Peas
(opposite page).*

Chicken and Carrot Loaf (page 82).

Sweet-and-sour Chicken (page 91); Chicken Chasseur (page 85) plated with brown rice.

Chicken Burger (opposite page) served with Tabouleh Rice (page 126).

Chicken Burgers

MAKES 4

200 g/7 oz chicken breasts
1 Granny Smith apple, peeled and grated
60 g/2 oz/½ cup grated low-fat grating
  cheese
60 g/2 oz/1 cup fresh wholemeal
  breadcrumbs
2 tablespoons/2 tablespoons plus
  2 teaspoons finely chopped fresh chives
2 tablespoons/2 tablespoons plus
  2 teaspoons finely chopped fresh
  parsley
4 wholemeal burger buns or 8 wholemeal
  pita breads
a little shredded lettuce
a little sliced cucumber
a little grated carrot
alfalfa sprouts

Mango Chutney
1 onion, chopped
1 teaspoon finely chopped fresh ginger
65 ml/2 fl oz/¼ cup Chicken Stock
  (see p. 14) or water
flesh of 2 mangoes
2 Granny Smith apples
250 ml/8 fl oz/1 cup unsweetened
  orange juice
75 ml/3 fl oz/⅓ cup brown rice vinegar
½ teaspoon chilli powder
½ teaspoon ground cummin
rind of 1 orange
125 ml/4 fl oz/½ cup apple juice
  concentrate

Mince the chicken (after discarding all the skin and fat), add the apple, cheese, breadcrumbs and herbs and mix well. Form into four balls and flatten. Cook in a non-stick frying pan for 2 minutes on both sides. Serve in a wholemeal burger bun or between 2 wholemeal pita breads. Add the shredded lettuce, sliced cucumber, grated carrot and alfalfa sprouts.

To make the Mango Chutney, simmer the onion and ginger in stock for 5 minutes. Peel and grate the apple and add it, with all the other ingredients, to the stock. (The brown rice vinegar is macrobiotic and is available from health-food shops.) Cover and bring to the boil. Remove the lid and cook for 1 hour. Stir frequently to prevent the chutney sticking to the base of the saucepan. Cool, pour into sterilised jars and keep refrigerated. Add some chutney to the filling in each of the chicken burgers or place a spoonful on top. (See colour plates opposite and left between pages 104 and 105.)

Variations
- If doubling the recipe, do not double the quantity of cheese. Add 30 g/1 oz/¼ cup of extra cheese for 200 g/7 oz of extra chicken.
- When mangoes are out of season you can substitute canned unsweetened peaches. Drain before using.

Tamarind Chicken

SERVES 4

2 tablespoons/2 tablespoons plus
  2 teaspoons tamarind paste
250 ml/8 fl oz/1 cup boiling water
400 g/14 oz chicken breasts
1 teaspoon chilli powder
1 tablespoon/1 tablespoon plus
  1 teaspoon apple juice concentrate
rind of 1 lemon
juice of ½ small lemon

Tamarind is the semi-dried flesh from the seed pods of the tamarind tree. It makes a strongly flavoured acidulating liquid for tenderising meats and for adding a sourish tang.

Soak the tamarind paste in the boiling water for 1 hour. Strain the liquid and use the liquid only. Discard the skin and fat from the chicken. Combine the tamarind liquid, chilli powder, apple juice concentrate, lemon rind and lemon juice. Pour over the chicken. Marinate for at least 1 hour. Barbecue or steam the chicken. Keep hot. Pour the marinade juices into a small saucepan. Bring to the boil and reduce by half. Arrange the cooked chicken on a bed of brown rice and pour the sauce over the top.

Chicken Niçoise

SERVES 6

4 small zucchini, cut into rounds
1 red capsicum, cut into strips
1 red chilli, finely chopped
2 large Spanish onions, sliced
6 large tomatoes, roughly chopped
12 black olives
black pepper to taste
sprig of oregano
6 chicken breasts
lemon slices
a little water

Sauté the zucchini, capsicum, chilli, onion and tomato until the tomato begins to break down and make a sauce. Turn the heat down to its lowest. Add the olives, pepper and sprig of oregano. Cover, and cook for 10 minutes. Remove the oregano. Set aside.

To cook the chicken, discard all the skin and fat first and then poach, covered with some slices of lemon, in a little water in the bottom of a saucepan. Turn the chicken over half-way through cooking. Keep the heat very low.

You can cut the breasts into pieces or keep them whole and add to sauce. Heat through before serving. Serve with baby boiled potatoes and green beans.

Provençale Chicken

SERVES 4–6

4 pieces chicken
plain flour
black pepper
ground cinnamon
3 cloves garlic
8 small onions, peeled and left whole
1 green capsicum, cut into strips
200 g/7 oz baby mushrooms, washed
425 g/15 oz canned whole tomatoes in
   natural juice, salt-free
65 ml/2 fl oz/¼ cup dry white wine
140 g/4½ oz/½ cup tomato paste
1 sprig fresh thyme
3 bay leaves
black pepper to taste

Preheat the oven to 160°C/325°F.

Remove all the skin and fat from the chicken. Mix the flour, pepper and cinnamon together. Roll the chicken pieces in it. Brown the chicken on both sides in a hot non-stick frying pan. Combine all the ingredients in a casserole dish and cook slowly for 1½ hours or until the chicken is very tender.

Serve with pasta or brown rice and salad.

Steamed Whole Chicken

SERVES 4–6

1 × 1.5-kg/3½-lb chicken
½ lemon
65 ml/2 fl oz/¼ cup unsweetened
   orange juice or apple juice or dry
   white wine
350 ml/12 fl oz/1½ cups water
sprigs of parsley
1 stick celery with leaves, chopped
½ carrot, chopped
black pepper to taste

Remove all skin and fat from the chicken. Place the chicken in a saucepan that just accommodates it (so that legs and wings do not come adrift in the cooking process). Place the lemon in the chicken cavity and pour the orange juice and water over the top. Place the parsley, celery and carrot around the chicken and season with black pepper. Bring to the boil. Turn the heat down and simmer, with the lid on, for 30 minutes. Test with a skewer to see if chicken is cooked, and remove from the stock. Cover the chicken to prevent drying. Serve hot, or cool, refrigerate and use when required. (See right colour plate between pages 56 and 57.)

Chicken Roll with Mustard Sauce

SERVES 6

575 g/1¼ lb chicken breasts (all skin and fat removed), minced
1 teaspoon finely chopped fresh ginger
1 teaspoon Dijon mustard
75 g/2½ oz/¼ cup salt-free tomato paste
100 g/3½ oz/¾ cup rolled oats
100 g/3½ oz broccoli florets, halved
1 long strip carrot

Mustard Sauce
250 ml/8 fl oz/1 cup unsweetened orange juice
125 ml/4 fl oz/½ cup dry sherry
2 teaspoons wholegrain mustard
2 tablespoons/2 tablespoons plus 2 teaspoons apple juice concentrate
2 tablespoons/2 tablespoons plus 2 teaspoons cornflour
3 tablespoons/3 tablespoons plus 3 teaspoons water or cooking liquid from chicken

Combine the minced chicken, ginger, Dijon mustard, tomato paste and rolled oats in a bowl, and mix well.

Steam the broccoli and carrot until just tender. Take half the chicken mixture and flatten it out on the bench in a log shape. Top with broccoli and carrot running down the centre of the log. Top with the remaining chicken. Press the ends and sides firmly together.

Place the chicken log in a frying pan or large shallow saucepan and add enough water to come halfway up the side of the chicken. Bring to the boil and simmer for 15 minutes. Turn the log carefully and simmer for a further 15 minutes. Remove from the water. Stand for 5 minutes before slicing into 12 rounds.

To make the Mustard Sauce, mix all the ingredients together thoroughly and bring to the boil. Simmer and stir until the sauce thickens. Pour the sauce over the chicken roll just before serving. Accompany with steamed vegetables.

Sweet-and-sour Chicken

SERVES 6

500 g/1 lb 2 oz chicken breasts (all skin and fat removed)
1 red capsicum
1 green capsicum
2 carrots
2 zucchini
6 spring onions
3 sticks celery
125 g/¼ lb fresh pineapple, chopped

Sauce
250 ml/8 fl oz/1 cup unsweetened apple juice
1 teaspoon finely chopped fresh ginger
2 teaspoons low-salt soy sauce
1 tablespoon/1 tablespoon plus 1 teaspoon salt-free tomato paste
1 clove garlic, crushed (optional)

Cut the chicken into 2-cm/¾" chunks. Cut the vegetables into even-sized pieces.

Combine all the Sauce ingredients in a wok or large, shallow saucepan. Bring to the boil and simmer gently. Add the chicken. Cook for 15–20 minutes or until tender.

Remove the chicken and turn up the heat. Add all the vegetables and cook for 2 minutes, tossing continuously through the sauce. Add the chicken and pineapple. Place the lid on the wok or saucepan and cook for a further minute. (See right colour plate between pages 88 and 89.)

Roast Turkey Breast

xxxxxxxxxxxxxxxxxxxxxxxxxxxxxxxxxxxxxxxxxxxxxxxxxxxxxxxxxxxxxxxxxxxxxxxxxxxxxxxx

SERVES 10

1 clove garlic

*2 tablespoons/2 tablespoons plus
  2 teaspoons finely chopped onion*

*1½ tablespoons/1½ tablespoons plus
  1½ teaspoons unsweetened orange
  juice*

*60 g/2 oz/1 cup fresh wholemeal
  breadcrumbs*

6 mushrooms, finely sliced

2 spring onions, finely chopped

¼ teaspoon dried sage

½ teaspoon dried marjoram

*1 × 1-kg/2¼-lb turkey breast (all skin
  and fat removed)*

2 carrots, cut into thin rounds

350 ml/12 fl oz/1½ cups water

Gravy

*1 tablespoon/1 tablespoon plus
  1 teaspoon salt-free tomato paste*

*2 tablespoons/2 tablespoons plus
  2 teaspoons cornflour*

a little water

Crunchy Baked Mushrooms

20 mushrooms

*310 g/10½ oz/1¼ cups low-fat cottage
  cheese*

*30 g/1 oz/½ cup fresh wholemeal
  breadcrumbs*

Preheat the oven to 180°C/350°F.

Cook the garlic and onion in the orange juice for 3 minutes, until the onion is soft. Add to the breadcrumbs, mushroom, spring onion and herbs, and mix well.

Cut a pocket into the turkey breast. Fill the pocket with the prepared mixture. Secure with skewers.

Line the base of a baking dish with the carrot. Add the water. Place the turkey breast on top and cover with foil. Cook for 1 hour. Baste the turkey every 15 minutes.

Remove the turkey from the baking dish and turn up the oven to 200°C/400°F. To make the Gravy, place the juices and carrot in a food processor or blender. Add the tomato paste. Blend until smooth. Pour into a saucepan and slowly bring to the boil. Make a paste with the cornflour and the water. Stir into the gravy to thicken. Spoon over the turkey slices. Keep warm.

To prepare the Crunchy Baked Mushrooms, peel and remove the stems of the mushrooms. Top each mushroom with a little cottage cheese and sprinkle generously with the breadcrumbs. Cook for 10 minutes or until well browned. Serve with the roast turkey breast.

Turkey Breast with Orange Curry Sauce

xxxxxxxxxxxxxxxxxxxxxxxxxxxxxxxxxxxxxxxxxxxxxxxxxxxxxxxxxxxxxxxxxxxxxxxxxxxxxxxx

SERVES 10 – 12

*1 × 1-kg/2¼-lb turkey breast (all skin
  and fat removed)*

1 onion, sliced

2 Granny Smith apples, peeled and sliced

2 teaspoons finely grated orange rind

1 teaspoon dried sage

1 teaspoon dried thyme

*250 ml/8 fl oz/1 cup dry white wine or
  water*

Preheat the oven to 190°C/375°F.

Lightly pound the turkey breast. Place the onion and apple slices on the bottom of a shallow baking dish. Place the turkey breast on top of the onion and apple. Sprinkle with the orange rind, sage and thyme, and pour the white wine over the top. Cover and cook for 2 hours. The turkey is cooked when you insert a fine skewer through it and the juices run clear.

Let the turkey stand for a few minutes before slicing. Use an electric knife to cut into 10 or 12 portions, and keep hot. Serve with Orange Curry Sauce (see page 237).

MEAT

The consumption of red meat has shown a decline since the 1930s. This has been due to the influence of cultures in which grains, pasta and vegetables play a major role, the trend towards lighter, healthier meals, and a larger following for vegetarianism.

Red meat contains high amounts of saturated fats and cholesterol, but if all the visible fat is removed and small portions are eaten, red meat contributes to a well-balanced diet. It is an excellent source of protein, iron, zinc and niacin, and an important source of essential vitamin B12.

The quality and tenderness of your meat depends on the cut, the sex and age of the animal and the way it has been handled before and after killing.

Always store your meat in the coldest part of the refrigerator, preferably where air can circulate around it. To freeze the meat, seal it in airtight plastic bags and defrost it slowly in the refrigerator.

Look for the better cuts of meat, in which fat is visible on the outside and can be removed easily, rather than those in which fat is marbled throughout the meat.

To maintain a low-fat, low-cholesterol meal, portions should be kept to 100 g/3½ oz. Do not cook meat in extra fat, oil or butter. The following cooking methods are recommended: dry stir-frying in a very hot pan to seal and brown the meat before further cooking; grilling; stewing; cooking in a casserole; barbecuing; and steaming (only suitable for the more tender cuts of meat).

Gravy Beef Ramekins

SERVES 4

1 onion, chopped
1 carrot, grated
1 stick celery, chopped
400 g/14 oz gravy beef
1 litre/1¾ pints/4 cups water
60 g/2 oz/½ cup frozen peas
225 g/½ lb/¾ cup corn kernels, cooked
black pepper to taste
2–3 tablespoons cornflour
1 tablespoon/1 tablespoon plus
   1 teaspoon extra water
handful of finely chopped fresh chives
1.5 kg/3½ lb/6 cups mashed potato

Simmer the onion, carrot, celery and gravy beef (all fat and sinew removed) in the 1 litre/1¾ pints/4 cups of water for approximately 3 hours or until the gravy beef is tender. Mix in a food processor or blender to break up the meat, but do not purée to a pulp. Add the peas, corn and pepper.

Mix the cornflour with 1 tablespoon/1 tablespoon plus 1 teaspoon of water to make a paste. Stir through the meat mixture and cook until thickened. Add the chives.

Preheat the oven to 200°C/400°F.

Spoon the mixture into four large individual ramekins. Top with mashed potato. Cook until the potato has browned and the mixture is bubbling.

Serve with salad.

Beef and Banana Kebabs

SERVES 6

1 tablespoon/1 tablespoon plus
   1 teaspoon low-salt soy sauce
1 tablespoon/1 tablespoon plus
   1 teaspoon finely chopped fresh ginger
125 ml/4 fl oz/½ cup Date and Apple
   Chutney (see p. 235)
575 g/1¼ lb rump steak
4 bananas, cut into 2.5-cm/1″ cubes

Mix the soy sauce, ginger and Date and Apple Chutney together. Trim all fat and sinew from the steak and cut the meat into 2.5-cm/1″ cubes. Thread the meat and banana onto 12 skewers. Using a pastry brush, brush the kebabs with the chutney mixture. Leave to stand for 2 hours. Grill the kebabs. Brush any extra chutney mixture over the kebabs while they are cooking.

Serve with a salad.

Beef and Beans

SERVES 6

400 g/14 oz lean minced beef
1 large onion, chopped
2 cloves garlic, crushed
a little water
2 sticks celery, finely chopped
2 small green capsicums, chopped
400 g/14 oz green beans
2 tablespoons/2 tablespoons plus
   2 teaspoons low-salt soy sauce
1 tablespoon/1 tablespoon plus
   1 teaspoon toasted sesame seeds
225 g/½ lb/1 cup canned whole
   tomatoes in natural juice, puréed
125 ml/4 fl oz/½ cup water

Cook the meat, onion and garlic in a little water in a large saucepan for 10–15 minutes, stirring occasionally to break up the meat. Keep covered. Add the remaining ingredients and simmer, uncovered for 15 minutes.

Serve on wholemeal toast, brown rice, wholemeal pasta or cooked beans and lentils.

Cabbage Rolls with Tomato Sauce

MAKES 12

1 onion, chopped
½ teaspoon finely chopped fresh ginger
½ teaspoon ground cummin
¼ teaspoon ground coriander
2 tablespoons/2 tablespoons plus
*   2 teaspoons water*
575 g/1¼ lb lean minced beef
225 g/½ lb/1½ cups grated carrot
100 g/3½ oz/½ cup grated zucchini
310 g/10½ oz/2 cups cooked brown rice
18 large cabbage leaves (choose green
*   cabbage with thin, soft leaves)*
freshly chopped parsley for garnishing

Tomato Sauce
425 g/15 oz canned whole tomatoes in
*   natural juice, salt-free*
75 g/2½ oz/¼ cup salt-free tomato
*   paste*
65 ml/2 fl oz/¼ cup water or *dry white*
*   wine* or *Vegetable Stock (see p. 14)*
1 large clove garlic
½ teaspoon ground cummin

Preheat the oven to 200°C/400°F.

Cook the onion, ginger and spices in the water until the onion is soft. Add the meat and break up. Cover, and simmer for 15–20 minutes. Continue to break the meat up as it cooks, making sure it is well browned and cooked through. Remove from the heat. Add all the other ingredients except the cabbage leaves and parsley, and mix well. Cool.

Place the cabbage leaves in boiling water in a large saucepan and cook for approximately 5 minutes, until soft. Drain. Do five leaves at a time if your saucepan is not very large. Divide the mixture evenly between the cabbage leaves. Roll up securely, making sure the filling cannot ooze out from the sides.

To make the Tomato Sauce, purée all the ingredients. Pour half the sauce into the bottom of a large shallow baking dish. Place the cabbage rolls, seam side down, on top of the sauce and pack tightly together. Pour the remaining sauce over the top. Cover, and bake for 30 minutes. Remove the lid and cook for a further 15 minutes.

Serve with a boiled or baked potato and an orange vegetable such as pumpkin or carrot, or with a tossed salad. Garnish with the parsley.

Variations
- The cabbage rolls can be steamed in a steamer for approximately 30–40 minutes. The Tomato Sauce can be cooked in a saucepan for 20 minutes or until thickened, and then poured over the steamed cabbage rolls.
- Make other sauces, such as a White Sauce (see page 239) with reduced-fat soymilk and 60 g/2 oz/½ cup of grated low-fat grating cheese, to serve over steamed cabbage rolls.
- Sprinkle 60 g/2 oz/1 cup of fresh wholemeal breadcrumbs over the top of the cabbage rolls after 30 minutes of cooking time. Cook for a further 15 minutes.
- Sprinkle 60 g/2 oz/½ cup of grated low-fat grating cheese over the rolls 10 minutes before they are cooked. The cheese should be just melted, not well browned.

Beef and Capsicum

xxxxxxxxxxxxxxxxxxxxxxxxxxxxxxxxxxxxxxxxxxxxxxxxxxxxxxxxxxxxxxxxxxxxxxxxxx

SERVES 6

500 g/1 lb 2 oz beef
1 large onion, cut into 8 pieces
1 green capsicum, cut into chunks
1 red capsicum, cut into chunks
2 sticks celery, diagonally sliced

Sauce
1 teaspoon finely chopped fresh ginger
1 tablespoon/1 tablespoon plus
   1 teaspoon salt-free tomato paste
1 tablespoon/1 tablespoon plus
   1 teaspoon low-salt soy sauce
½ teaspoon dried basil
½ teaspoon dried oregano
500 ml/16 fl oz/2 cups Beef Stock (see
   p. 15) or water
2 tablespoons/2 tablespoons plus
   2 teaspoons cornflour

Trim all fat and sinew from the beef (use eye fillet, preferably). Slice the meat into strips and stir-fry in a non-stick frying pan, in three lots, to seal and lightly brown. Remove the meat from the pan. Add the onion, capsicum and celery and toss. Cook for 2 minutes. Return meat to the pan.

To make the Sauce, combine all the ingredients. Pour over the meat in the pan. Bring to the boil and then reduce the heat. Simmer with the lid on for 20–30 minutes. Stir occasionally so the meat does not stick to the base of the pan.

Serve with hot mashed potato or brown rice. (See colour plate opposite.)

Beef Burgers with the Lot

xxxxxxxxxxxxxxxxxxxxxxxxxxxxxxxxxxxxxxxxxxxxxxxxxxxxxxxxxxxxxxxxxxxxxxxxxx

MAKES 10

10 wholemeal burger buns or
   20 wholemeal pita breads
shredded lettuce
onion rings
slices of tomato
grated carrot
red and green capsicum rings
bean sprouts

Beef Burgers
500 g/1 lb 2 oz lean minced beef
200 g/7 oz/1¼ cups grated carrot
185 g/6 oz/1 cup grated zucchini
1 large Granny Smith apple, peeled and
   grated
400 g/14 oz potatoes, peeled and grated
60 g/2 oz/1 cup fresh wholemeal
   breadcrumbs
2 tablespoons/2 tablespoons plus
   2 teaspoons wholemeal plain flour
handful of finely chopped fresh parsley
½ teaspoon ground nutmeg
½ teaspoon dried mixed herbs

To make the Beef Burgers, combine all the ingredients and mix with your hands. Shape into balls of equal size. Flatten down. Place in a lightly greased non-stick frying pan and cook on moderate heat for approximately 6 minutes. Carefully turn over and cook for a further 4–5 minutes. Remove from the pan and rest on absorbent paper for a few minutes.

Serve in wholemeal burger buns or between wholemeal pita breads. Add the shredded lettuce, onion rings, tomato slices, grated carrot, red and green capsicum rings, and bean sprouts. Top with some Spicy Tomato Sauce (see page 238). (See left colour plate between pages 104 and 105.)

Beef and Capsicum (opposite page).

Beef and Vegetable Casserole (opposite page).

Beef and Vegetable Casserole

XXXXXXXXXXXXXXXXXXXXXXXXXXXXXXXXXXXXXXXXXXXXXXXXXXXXXXXXXXXXXXXXXXXXXXX

SERVES 6

2 tablespoons/2 tablespoons plus
    2 teaspoons salt-free tomato paste
2 tablespoons/2 tablespoons plus
    2 teaspoons low-salt soy sauce
1 tablespoon/1 tablespoon plus
    1 teaspoon apple juice concentrate
½ teaspoon ground cinnamon
1 teaspoon ground nutmeg
575 g/1¼ lb blade steak (all fat and
    sinew removed), cut into bite-sized
    chunks
2 teaspoons crushed garlic
2 onions, quartered and sliced
225 g/½ lb carrots, cut into rounds
225 g/½ lb parsnips, cut into rounds
225 g/½ lb swedes, cut into chunks
225 g/½ lb zucchini, cut into rounds
1 red capsicum, cut into chunks
a little water
200 ml/7 fl oz/¾ cup dry red wine
250 ml/8 fl oz/1 cup water
2 tablespoons/2 tablespoons plus
    2 teaspoons cornflour
125 g/¼ lb/1 cup frozen peas

Mix together the tomato paste, soy sauce, apple juice concentrate, cinnamon and nutmeg, and marinate the steak in this marinade for at least 1 hour before cooking. Turn the meat frequently through the marinade.

When ready to cook, preheat the oven to 200°C/400°F. Drain the meat. Heat a wok until very hot and cook the meat in three batches, turning quickly to brown on both sides. Transfer the meat to a large casserole dish and clean the wok.

Cook the garlic, onion, carrot, parsnip, swede, zucchini and capsicum in a little water in the wok until they just begin to soften. Remove from the stove and place the vegetables in the casserole dish. Add the wine and 65 ml/2 fl oz/¼ cup of the water. Cover, and cook for 1½–2 hours, or until the meat is tender.

Combine the cornflour with the remaining water and add to the casserole. Stir to thicken. Add the peas and cook for a further 15 minutes.

Serve with brown rice and pappadams. (See colour plate opposite.)

Caraway Beef

XXXXXXXXXXXXXXXXXXXXXXXXXXXXXXXXXXXXXXXXXXXXXXXXXXXXXXXXXXXXXXXXXXXXXXX

SERVES 6

1 teaspoon light olive oil
1 onion, chopped
1 teaspoon caraway seeds
575 g/1¼ lb lean minced beef
575 g/1¼ lb canned champignons
500 ml/16 fl oz/2 cups reduced-fat
    soymilk or skim milk
30 g/1 oz/¼ cup cornflour
black pepper to taste

Pour the oil into a large saucepan and cook the onion and caraway seeds over a gentle heat until soft. Add the meat. Use a wooden spoon to break up the meat as it cooks. Cook for 10 minutes or until all the meat has changed colour. Add the champignons and cover. Cook for a further 20 minutes over a very low heat. Combine the soymilk and cornflour to make a paste and add to the meat. Stir until the sauce thickens. Add the black pepper to taste.

Serve with brown rice or noodles, and a salad.

Family Meatloaf

xxxxxxxxxxxxxxxxxxxxxxxxxxxxxxxxxxxxxxxxxxxxxxxxxxxxxxxxxxxxxxxxxxxxxxxxxxxxxxxxxx

SERVES 6

1 onion, finely chopped
1 teaspoon finely chopped garlic
100 g/3½ oz/¾ cup finely sliced
   mushroom
500 g/1 lb 2 oz lean minced beef
100 g/3½ oz/¾ cup grated zucchini
   (juice squeezed out)
100 g/3½ oz/¾ cup grated carrot
60 g/2 oz/½ cup frozen peas
2 Granny Smith apples, peeled and
   grated (juice squeezed out)
1 egg white
125 g/¼ lb/1 cup rolled oats
1 teaspoon dried basil
½ teaspoon dried oregano
½ teaspoon ground cummin or dried
   thyme
large handful finely chopped fresh parsley
black pepper to taste

Topping
3 tablespoons/3 tablespoons plus
   3 teaspoons salt-free tomato paste
200 g/7 oz/2 cups grated low-fat
   grating cheese
60 g/2 oz/½ cup rolled oats

Preheat the oven to 180°C/350°F.

In a saucepan, cook the onion, garlic and mushroom until just soft (you may need to add a teaspoon of water to prevent sticking).

Place all the remaining meatloaf ingredients in a large bowl. Add the cooked ingredients from the saucepan and mix well using your hands. Press the mixture firmly into a lightly greased meatloaf dish.

To make the Topping, spoon the tomato paste over the meatloaf. Combine the cheese with the oats, and sprinkle over the meatloaf. Cover the dish and cook for 1 hour in a baking dish containing water. Uncover, and cook for a further 10 minutes to brown the top.

Peachy Beef Strips

xxxxxxxxxxxxxxxxxxxxxxxxxxxxxxxxxxxxxxxxxxxxxxxxxxxxxxxxxxxxxxxxxxxxxxxxxxxxxxxxxx

SERVES 4

2 onions, quartered and sliced
1 teaspoon crushed garlic
1 teaspoon light olive oil
400 g/14 oz beef fillet (all fat and
   sinew removed), cut into thin strips
1 teaspoon ground cummin
1 teaspoon curry powder
½ teaspoon ground cinnamon
250 ml/8 fl oz/1 cup unsweetened peach
   juice
250 ml/8 fl oz/1 cup water
310 g/10½ oz/1 cup canned
   unsweetened peach pieces, drained
2 zucchini, diagonally sliced and lightly
   steamed

In a wok or non-stick frying pan cook the onion and garlic in the oil until the onion just begins to turn in colour. Add the beef strips and toss until all the meat has browned. Add the spices and continue cooking for about 2 minutes. Add the peach juice and water. Cover, and cook until the meat is tender and the sauce has reduced and thickened. Add the peach pieces and zucchini. Heat through before serving.

Beef Stroganoff

SERVES 6

500 g/1 lb 2 oz rump steak (all fat and sinew removed), cut into bite-sized chunks
2 onions, chopped
225 g/½ lb carrots, cut into thin rounds and then quartered
575 g/1¼ lb mushrooms, finely sliced
1 tablespoon/1 tablespoon plus 1 teaspoon Vecon (natural vegetable stock available at health-food shops)
250 ml/8 fl oz/1 cup boiling water
250 ml/8 fl oz/1 cup dry red wine
2 tablespoons/2 tablespoons plus 2 teaspoons salt-free tomato paste
black pepper to taste
250 ml/8 fl oz/1 cup reduced-fat soymilk
1 heaped tablespoon/1 heaped tablespoon plus 1 heaped teaspoon cornflour

Preheat the oven to 200°C/400°F.

In a large non-stick frying pan stir-fry the meat to seal and lightly brown. Remove the meat from the pan. Stir-fry the onion until transparent, approximately 2–3 minutes. Add the carrot and mushroom, and toss to combine. Dissolve the Vecon in the boiling water, and add to the pan. Simmer for 3 minutes. Return the meat to the pan. Add the red wine and tomato paste and season with black pepper.

Transfer to an ovenproof casserole dish and cook, covered, for 1¼ hours. Combine the soymilk and cornflour. Remove the casserole from the heat and allow to cool slightly. Stir through the soymilk and cornflour until the sauce becomes thick and creamy.

Serve with mashed or baked potatoes.

Hot Thai Beef

SERVES 6

575 g/1¼ lb eye fillet steak (all fat and sinew removed), cut into thin strips
1 large onion, finely chopped
1 tablespoon/1 tablespoon plus 1 teaspoon Thai spice (less for a milder flavour)
a little light olive oil
2 cloves garlic
2 tablespoons/2 tablespoons plus 2 teaspoons salt-free tomato paste
250 ml/8 fl oz/1 cup water or Chicken Stock (see p. 14)
1 tablespoon/1 tablespoon plus 1 teaspoon cornflour
310 g/10½ oz mushrooms, finely sliced
310 g/10½ oz broccoli, finely sliced

Combine the meat, onion, and Thai spice. Toss the meat to coat well with the spice. Cover, and stand for 1–2 hours.

Wipe the base of a non-stick frying pan with the oil and remove any excess oil. Wipe the garlic cloves over the base of the pan, and remove. Heat the pan. Cook the meat and onion for 5 minutes or until the meat is lightly browned.

Combine the tomato paste, water and cornflour to make a smooth liquid. Pour over the meat and onion and add the mushroom. Simmer for 10–15 minutes or until the meat is tender. Add the broccoli and cook until the broccoli is just tender.

Serve with brown rice or spiral noodles. You may also like to serve this dish with some non-fat or low-fat yoghurt and freshly chopped tomatoes.

Note
Thai spice is available at most supermarkets or you can make your own using a combination of the following: dried onion, ground coriander, dried red capsicum, ground cummin, dried ginger, black pepper, anise, lemon grass, turmeric, dried garlic and ground cloves.

Veal with Capsicum in Vermouth Sauce

SERVES 4

450 g/1 lb veal (all fat and sinew
    removed)
1 tablespoon/1 tablespoon plus
    1 teaspoon finely chopped fresh ginger
250 ml/8 fl oz/1 cup vermouth
1 tablespoon/1 tablespoon plus
    1 teaspoon low-salt soy sauce
2 red capsicums, cut into strips
1 green capsicum, cut into strips
1 tablespoon/1 tablespoon plus
    1 teaspoon cornflour
1 tablespoon water
6 spring onions, diagonally sliced

Cut the veal into bite-sized pieces. Brown quickly in a very hot non-stick frying pan with the ginger. Turn the heat down and add the vermouth, soy sauce and capsicum. Cook gently, covered, for 1 hour or until the meat is tender. Combine the cornflour and water, and add to the meat and capsicum. Stir continuously until the sauce thickens.

Garnish with spring onion just prior to serving. Serve with soyaroni noodles or brown rice and a tossed salad.

Chilli Veal and Vegetable Dumplings

MAKES 12

a little water

Dough
350 g/¾ lb/3 cups unbleached white
    plain flour
1 tablespoon/1 tablespoon plus
    1 teaspoon baking powder
1 tablespoon/1 tablespoon plus
    1 teaspoon lemon juice
125 ml/4 fl oz/½ cup non-fat or low-
    fat yoghurt
250 ml/8 fl oz/1 cup reduced-fat
    evaporated skim milk

Filling
575 g/1¼ lb lean minced veal
100 g/3½ oz/¾ cup grated carrot
150 g/5 oz/¾ cup grated zucchini (juice
    squeezed out)
100 g/3½ oz/¾ cup finely chopped
    green beans
100 g/3½ oz/¾ cup finely chopped
    mushroom
1 teaspoon finely chopped fresh ginger
1 tablespoon/1 tablespoon plus
    1 teaspoon chilli paste
1 teaspoon ground coriander or
    1 tablespoon/1 tablespoon plus
    1 teaspoon freshly chopped coriander

To make the Dough, sift the flour and baking powder into a bowl. Combine the lemon juice, yoghurt and milk. Stir this into the flour with a fork until all the mixture comes together to create a scone-like dough. Knead lightly on a floured board. Cut into twelve portions. Roll each portion out to make a thin circle, approximately 10 cm/4".

Combine all the Filling ingredients. Place an equal amount on each circle of dough. Brush the edge lightly with water. Press the edges of dough together. Take the two ends of each dumpling and fold under to make a neat parcel. Cut twelve squares of non-stick baking paper. Place each dumpling on a square of paper in a Chinese double bamboo steamer. Steam for 20 minutes.

Veal in Herb and Mushroom Sauce

SERVES 6

575 g/1¼ lb veal (all fat and sinew removed)
1 tablespoon/1 tablespoon plus 1 teaspoon dried tarragon
1 tablespoon/1 tablespoon plus 1 teaspoon dried basil
1 tablespoon/1 tablespoon plus 1 teaspoon parmesan cheese
2 tablespoons/2 tablespoons plus 2 teaspoons unbleached white plain flour
a little light olive oil
2 cloves garlic
250 ml/8 fl oz/1 cup water or Chicken Stock (see p. 14) or Beef Stock (see p. 15)
65 ml/2 fl oz/¼ cup medium-dry sherry
1 teaspoon finely grated lemon rind
200 g/7 oz baby mushrooms, finely sliced

Veal is a bland-tasting meat and in this recipe is complemented by strong flavours of both tarragon and basil.

Cut the veal into eighteen equal portions (three portions per serve). Place between two pieces of plastic wrap and lightly pound with a meat mallet to a 2.5-cm/1″ thickness. Coat the veal with the combined tarragon, basil, parmesan cheese and white flour.

Wipe the base of a non-stick saucepan with the oil and remove any excess oil. Wipe the garlic cloves over the base of the pan and leave in the pan. Heat the pan and add the veal. Do not have the heat too high. Just brown lightly on both sides and remove from the pan. Add any left-over flour and herb mixture and stir over a very low heat. Add the water, sherry and lemon rind, and stir thoroughly until well combined. Add the meat and mushroom to the pan and simmer for 20–30 minutes or until the meat is tender. During cooking, spoon the sauce over the veal and turn the veal over.

Serve with green beans and julienne of carrots.

Hungarian Veal

SERVES 6

500 g/1 lb 2 oz veal (all fat and sinew removed)
2 tablespoons unbleached white plain flour
2 teaspoons paprika
425 g/15 oz canned whole tomatoes in natural juice, salt-free
250 ml/8 fl oz/1 cup dry red wine
250 ml/8 fl oz/1 cup water
black pepper to taste
2 sweet potatoes, peeled and cubed
freshly chopped parsley for garnishing

Cut the meat into large chunks. Combine the flour and paprika, and toss the meat in it. Cook the meat on both sides, quickly, in a very hot non-stick frying pan. Add any left-over flour and paprika, the tomatoes, wine, water and pepper. Cook gently for 30 minutes. Add the sweet potato. Cook for a further 30 minutes or until the meat and vegetables are tender.

Garnish with the parsley. Serve with mashed potato and a green salad.

Veal Marsala

SERVES 4

450 g/1 lb veal steaks (all fat and sinew removed)
black pepper to taste
a little unbleached white plain flour
1 tablespoon/1 tablespoon plus 1 teaspoon finely chopped onion
125 ml/4 fl oz/½ cup Marsala
grated rind of 1 orange
125 ml/4 fl oz/½ cup freshly squeezed orange juice
125 ml/4 fl oz/½ cup Chicken Stock (see p. 14) or water
1 tablespoon cornflour
freshly chopped parsley for garnishing

Pound the steaks out thinly. Combine the black pepper with the flour, and coat the veal. Cook in a hot non-stick frying pan for 2–3 minutes on both sides until lightly brown. Set aside. Add the onion to the pan and cook gently, moving it over the base of the pan. Add the Marsala and orange rind. Boil for 2 minutes, stirring continuously. Add the orange juice. Add a little of the Chicken Stock to the cornflour to make a paste. Stir this into the remaining stock. Add this to the simmering sauce with the par-cooked veal steaks. Turn the heat down to its lowest. Cover, and cook for a further 8–10 minutes.

Garnish with the parsley, and serve with hot mashed potatoes.

Veal Chops Paprika

SERVES 4

2 teaspoons paprika
4 veal chops or steaks (all fat and sinew removed)
1 small onion, chopped
1 tablespoon/1 tablespoon plus 1 teaspoon water
1 tablespoon/1 tablespoon plus 1 teaspoon salt-free tomato paste
65 ml/2 fl oz/¼ cup extra water
black pepper to taste
1 teaspoon cornflour
65 ml/2 fl oz/¼ cup reduced-fat evaporated milk
freshly chopped parsley for garnishing

Rub the paprika into the chops. Cook in a hot non-stick frying pan until browned on both sides. Lift out and keep warm. In a saucepan, cook the onion gently with the water until soft. Add the tomato paste, extra water and black pepper. Stir until the mixture begins to simmer. Combine the cornflour with the milk and add, stirring continuously. Return the chops to the frying pan, reheat and pour the sauce over the meat.

Garnish with the parsley, and serve with potatoes and salad.

Roast Veal

Oven Bag Method

*2 tablespoons/2 tablespoons plus
   2 teaspoons wholemeal plain flour*
veal roast
black pepper to taste
2 cloves garlic
2 small brown onions (skins left on)
1 tablespoon mixed fresh herbs

Oven Roast Method

2 onions, chopped
1 large carrot, chopped
2 sticks celery, chopped
piece of parsnip
veal roast
250 ml/8 fl oz/1 cup water or stock
*a little vermouth or dry sherry or dry red
   wine (optional)*
black pepper to taste
*sprig of herb (e.g. thyme, sage,
   marjoram)*
a little cornflour (optional)
extra black pepper

Veal is a very lean meat so you need to baste it frequently during the cooking, or cook it in an oven bag so that it does not dry out. Veal should always be cooked right through.

To cook veal using the Oven Bag Method, place the flour in the bag with the veal, black pepper, garlic, onions and herbs. Cook for 20 minutes per 500 g/1 lb 2 oz at 200°C/400°F.

■   ■   ■

To cook veal using the Oven Roast Method, place the onion, carrot, celery and parsnip in the base of baking dish. Place the veal among the vegetables. Add the water. You can add the vermouth for extra flavour. Add the black pepper and a sprig of fresh herb. Cook at 180°C/350°F for 25 minutes per 500 g/1 lb 2 oz, basting frequently with the juices. When the meat is cooked, this juice can be strained and thickened with a little cornflour to make a gravy. Season with black pepper.

Veal Tomachilli

SERVES 4

*450 g/1 lb veal steaks (all fat and sinew
   removed)*
a little unbleached white plain flour
1 small onion, chopped
2 cloves garlic, crushed
200 g/7 oz mushrooms, finely sliced
1 sweet red chilli, seeded and chopped
*425 g/15 oz canned whole tomatoes in
   natural juice*
350 ml/12 fl oz/1½ cups dry white wine
*1 teaspoon dried basil or 2 tablespoons/
   2 tablespoons plus 2 teaspoons freshly
   chopped basil*
*2 tablespoons/2 tablespoons plus
   2 teaspoons salt-free tomato paste*
freshly ground black pepper to taste

Pound the steaks out thinly. Flour them lightly and cook in a hot non-stick frying pan for 2 minutes on both sides until lightly brown. Set aside. Clean the pan. Add all the remaining ingredients. Bring to the boil. Turn the heat down and simmer for 15–20 minutes. Add the veal steaks and cover with the sauce. Cook for a further 10 minutes.

Serve with pasta and a green salad.

Osso Bucco

‹‹

SERVES 6

4 veal shanks or knuckles
a little unbleached white plain flour
black pepper to taste
2 cloves garlic, bruised
2 large onions, quartered
2 carrots, chopped
1 green capsicum, seeded and chopped
425 g/15 oz canned whole tomatoes in
    natural juice, salt-free
250 ml/8 fl oz/1 cup dry red wine
250 ml/8 fl oz/1 cup Beef Stock (see
    p. 15)
140 g/4½ oz/½ cup salt-free tomato
    paste
2 bay leaves
1 teaspoon dried basil
1 teaspoon dried thyme
a little cornflour (optional)
grated rind of 1 lemon for garnishing
freshly chopped parsley for garnishing

Preheat the oven to 180°C/350°F.

Ask the butcher to cut the shanks into 5-cm/2″ pieces. Season the flour with pepper, and coat the shanks with the flour. Brown the shanks on both sides in a non-stick frying pan and place in a large casserole dish. Place all the remaining ingredients, except the cornflour, lemon rind and parsley, into the dish. Cover, and cook, stirring occasionally, for 1½ hours or until the veal is tender. For a thicker gravy you can add a little cornflour. Garnish with lemon rind and parsley before serving.

Serve with wholemeal toast and salad.

Zucchini Meatloaf

‹‹

SERVES 10 – 12

400 g/14 oz zucchini, grated
500 g/1 lb 2 oz lean minced beef
1 onion, finely chopped
100 g/3½ oz/¾ cup finely chopped red
    capsicum
125 g/¼ lb/2 cups fresh wholemeal
    breadcrumbs
1 egg white
2 tablespoons/2 tablespoons plus
    2 teaspoons salt-free tomato paste
1 tablespoon/1 tablespoon plus
    1 teaspoon finely chopped fresh
    tarragon or parsley
1 tablespoon/1 tablespoon plus
    1 teaspoon finely chopped fresh basil
black pepper to taste
30 g/1 oz/¼ cup grated low-fat grating
    cheese

Preheat the oven to 180°C/350°F.

Combine all the ingredients except the cheese. Using your hands mix all the ingredients thoroughly. Press the mixture into a foil-lined terrine dish. Press down firmly and cover with foil. Place the terrine dish in a large baking dish containing water that reaches at least 2 cm/¾″ up the side of the terrine dish. Cook for 1¼ hours.

Drain off any liquid and unmould the terrine onto a foil-lined baking tray. Sprinkle the cheese over the top. Return to the oven to cook for a further 10 minutes. Let stand for 10 minutes before slicing if serving hot, or cool and refrigerate.

Serve as a luncheon loaf with salads or use in sandwiches or on wholemeal biscuits. (See colour plate opposite.)

Zucchini Meatloaf (opposite page).

Beef Burger with the Lot (page 96);
Chicken Burger (page 89).

*Mexican Meat Balls (page 110); Lamb Roast
with Vegetables (page 111).*

*B*eef and Carrot Hotpot *(opposite page)*.

Beef and Carrot Hotpot

SERVES 5

500 g/1 lb 2 oz beef (all fat and sinew removed)
1 large onion, chopped
2 cloves garlic, crushed
250 ml/8 fl oz/1 cup dry red wine
½–1 teaspoon ground nutmeg
2 tablespoons/2 tablespoons plus 2 teaspoons salt-free tomato paste
500 ml/16 fl oz/2 cups Beef Stock (see p. 15) or water
500 g/1 lb 2 oz carrots, cut into chunks
3 bay leaves
2 tablespoons/2 tablespoons plus 2 teaspoons finely chopped fresh parsley

Preheat the oven to 190°C/375°F.

Cut the meat into small pieces and then stir-fry, in two lots in a large non-stick frying pan, to seal and lightly brown. Remove from the pan. Stir-fry the onion and garlic until the onion is transparent, approximately 2–3 minutes. Return the meat to the pan. Add the red wine and nutmeg, and cook for 5 minutes. Add the tomato paste and stock. Pour into a casserole dish. Add the carrot and bay leaves. Toss well, cover and bake for 1¾ hours or until the meat is tender. Add the parsley before serving.

Serve with hot mashed potato, brown rice or wholemeal noodles. (See colour plate opposite.)

Meat Pie

SERVES 4

1 quantity Scone Dough (see Asparagus and Cheese Pizza Wheel, p. 173)
a little oat bran
500 ml/16 fl oz/2 cups Bolognese Sauce (see Spaghetti Bolognese, p. 119)
125 g/¼ lb/1 cup frozen peas
a little skim milk

Preheat the oven to 200°C/400°F.

Cut Scone Dough into two pieces – one slightly bigger than the other. Roll out the bigger piece to fit the base and sides of a deep 20-cm/8″ round cake tin. Lightly oil the sides of the tin and sprinkle with oat bran. Line with the dough.

Combine the Bolognese Sauce and peas and spoon over the Scone Dough. Roll out remaining dough and place on top of the pie. Trim the edges. Brush the edges and top with skim milk. Cut slits in the top of the pie.

Cook in preheated oven for 20 minutes, then turn heat down to 160°C/325°F and cook a further 10 minutes.

Serve with a salad.

Pork, Apple and Prune Casserole

SERVES 4

60 g/2 oz/½ cup oat bran
1 tablespoon/1 tablespoon plus
    1 teaspoon grated parmesan cheese
black pepper to taste
400 g/14 oz pork butterfly steaks (all
    fat and sinew removed), cut into 4
    portions
1 large onion, sliced into rings
2 large cooking apples, peeled, cored and
    sliced into rings
16 moist prunes
250 ml/8 fl oz/1 cup unsweetened apple
    juice
2 sprigs rosemary

Preheat the oven to 200°C/400°F.

Mix the oat bran, cheese and pepper on a plate. Press the pork pieces into the mixture until well coated. Shake off the excess.

Arrange the onion rings on the base of a casserole dish. Place the coated pork pieces on top of the onion. Top with the apple slices, prunes, apple juice and rosemary. Cover the casserole dish. Bake for 40–50 minutes, or until all the liquid has reduced to make a thick sauce.

Serve with brown rice and salad.

Pork and Apple Curry

SERVES 4–6

2 onions, quartered and sliced
1 teaspoon light olive oil
500 g/1 lb 2 oz pork fillet (all fat and
    sinew removed), cut into bite-sized
    chunks
3 Granny Smith apples, peeled and
    quartered
1–2 teaspoons curry powder
1 teaspoon ground coriander
½ teaspoon ground cinnamon
500 ml/16 fl oz/2 cups water
2 tablespoons/2 tablespoons plus
    2 teaspoons cornflour
2 tablespoons/2 tablespoons plus
    2 teaspoons extra water

Cook the onion in the oil over a gentle heat until soft. Add the pork. Toss frequently until all the pork pieces have changed colour, approximately 8–10 minutes.

Cut each apple quarter into six pieces and add to the pork with the spices. Cook a further few minutes. Add the 500 ml/16 fl oz/2 cups of water. Turn the heat down, cover, and simmer for about 30–40 minutes, or until the pork is tender.

Make a paste with the cornflour and 2 tablespoons/2 tablespoons plus 2 teaspoons of water. Stir through the pork mixture and stir until thickened.

Serve with brown rice or noodles, and salad.

Mustard Pork Medallions

SERVES 4

2 teaspoons crushed garlic
2 tablespoons wholegrain mustard
1–2 teaspoons hot English mustard
4 × 100-g/3½-oz pork medallions (all
    fat and sinew removed)

Combine the garlic and mustards. Spread evenly over the pork and stand for 2 hours before cooking. Grill or barbecue the pork. This pork takes very little cooking and will dry out if over-cooked.

Serve with a salad.

Pork Satay

SERVES 6

575 g/1¼ lb pork fillets (all fat and sinew removed), cut into 2.5-cm/ 1″ cubes

Marinade
1 teaspoon ground coriander
1 teaspoon cummin seeds
1 small onion, finely chopped
2 tablespoons/2 tablespoons plus 2 teaspoons low-salt soy sauce
2 teaspoons apple juice concentrate
60 ml/2 fl oz/¼ cup lemon juice
1 teaspoon finely chopped fresh ginger (optional)
1 teaspoon cornflour

Thread the pork evenly onto 12 skewers. Marinate the pork in the Marinade ingredients for at least 1 hour, or overnight. Grill or barbecue, regularly basting with the Marinade. Heat any remaining Marinade and serve over the kebabs when cooked.

Serve with brown rice and salad.

Steamed Pork Spring Rolls

SERVES 4

400 g/14 oz lean minced pork
100 g/3½ oz/¾ cup finely chopped carrot
100 g/3½ oz/¾ cup finely chopped leek
1 tablespoon/1 tablespoon plus 1 teaspoon finely chopped fresh ginger
1 tablespoon/1 tablespoon plus 1 teaspoon low-salt soy sauce
1 teaspoon grated lemon rind
8 sheets filo pastry
8 long thin strips of leek
extra low-salt soy sauce and finely chopped ginger

Combine the pork, carrot, leek, ginger, soy sauce and lemon rind. Mix well and stand for 2 hours. Divide the mixture into eight equal portions. Take a piece of filo pastry and fold in half. Place the mixture in the centre of the pastry and make a small rectangular parcel by folding the pastry over to have the same amount of pastry on both sides. Tie the parcel with a strip of leek. Repeat with remaining mixture. Place on a square piece of non-stick baking paper in a Chinese bamboo steamer. Steam for 10–15 minutes.

Combine the extra soy sauce and ginger to make a dipping sauce. Serve with salad.

Stuffed Pork Fillet with Cheese Sauce

SERVES 1

1 × 125-g/¼-lb pork fillet (all fat and
   sinew removed)
12 spinach leaves, steamed
2 tablespoons/2 tablespoons plus
   2 teaspoons low-fat ricotta cheese
pinch of ground nutmeg
1 tablespoon/1 tablespoon plus
   1 teaspoon oat bran
1 tablespoon/1 tablespoon plus
   1 teaspoon wholemeal plain flour
1 teaspoon grated geska herb cheese or
   parmesan cheese
black pepper to taste

Sauce
125 ml/4 fl oz/½ cup skim milk or low-
   fat evaporated skim milk or reduced-
   fat soymilk
1 bay leaf
1 teaspoon grated parmesan cheese
black pepper to taste
2 teaspoons cornflour

Preheat the oven to 200°C/400°F.

Cut the fillet to open out flat. Cover with the spinach leaves, spread the ricotta cheese on top and sprinkle with nutmeg. Roll up and secure with a steel skewer.

Combine the oat bran, flour, cheese and pepper, and place in an oven bag. Place the meat in the bag and toss to coat with the oat-bran mixture. Discard any loose oat-bran mixture, tie up the oven bag and place it on a baking tray. Cook for 20–30 minutes.

To make the Sauce, combine all the ingredients in a saucepan and mix well. Over a moderate heat, stir until the sauce thickens. Remove the bay leaf.

To serve, pour the sauce on a plate, cut the pork fillet into three portions and place on the sauce. Serve with steamed broccoli and baby carrots.

Lamb and Basil Balls with Basil Sauce

SERVES 4

450 g/1 lb lean very finely minced lamb
1 small onion, finely chopped
1 tablespoon finely chopped fresh basil
1 teaspoon low-salt soy sauce
1 egg white
2 teaspoons cornflour
black pepper to taste

Sauce
4 shallots, finely chopped
250 ml/8 fl oz/1 cup dry white wine
500 ml/16 fl oz/2 cups skim milk
30 g/1 oz/¼ cup cornflour
handful of fresh basil leaves

Combine the lamb, onion, basil, soy sauce, egg white, cornflour and black pepper, and mix well. Roll into balls the size of a golf ball. Place in the top of a steamer and steam for 10–15 minutes.

While the meat balls are steaming, make the Sauce. Cook the chopped shallot and wine until reduced by half. Mix the cornflour with a little milk to make a paste. Blend this into the remaining milk. Stir into the reduced wine, and add the basil. Cook until the sauce boils and thickens. Pour over the warm meat balls.

Serve with noodles and a salad.

Lamb Curry

SERVES 10

1 kg/2¼ lb lamb (all fat and sinew removed)
1 large onion, chopped
1 teaspoon finely chopped fresh ginger
150 g/5 oz/1 cup finely chopped carrot
150 g/5 oz/1 cup finely chopped beans
150 g/5 oz/1 cup finely chopped celery
150 g/5 oz/1 cup finely chopped green capsicum
200 g/7 oz/1 cup sultanas

Sauce
750 ml/1⅓ pints/3 cups Lamb Shank Stock (see p. 15) or water
3 tablespoons/3 tablespoons plus 3 teaspoons salt-free tomato paste
3 tablespoons/3 tablespoons plus 3 teaspoons cornflour
2 teaspoons curry powder
½ teaspoon ground cummin
rind of ½ lemon, cut into thin strips

Indian Rice Crisps
185 g/6 oz/1½ cups rice flour
40 g/1½ oz/¼ cup wholemeal self-raising flour
100 g/3½ oz/1 cup grated low-fat grating cheese
1 teaspoon ground cummin
1 teaspoon caraway seeds
250 ml/8 fl oz/1 cup skim milk

Preheat the oven to 190°C/375°F.

Mince the lamb. In a large wok or very large non-stick saucepan, stir-fry the lamb, in three lots, to seal and lightly brown. Remove from the pan and set aside. Stir-fry the onion and ginger until the onion is transparent, approximately 2–3 minutes. Add the vegetables and sultanas, tossing to combine. Add the meat.

To make the Sauce, combine the ingredients and add to the pan. Transfer the contents of the pan to a casserole dish. Cook for 1 hour.

Before making the Indian Rice Crisps, preheat the oven to 200°C/400°F. Mix all ingredients together to make a soft dough. Spoon the dough into a piping bag with a large serrated nozzle. Squeeze out twisted shapes onto a greased baking tray (the mixture will make about 24 crisps). Bake for 10–12 minutes. Serve hot. They are delicious served with curries, soups or as a snack. Store leftover crisps in an airtight container.

Indian Lamb Steaks

xxxxxxxxxxxxxxxxxxxxxxxxxxxxxxxxxxxxxxxxxxxxxxxxxxxxxxxxxxxxxxxxxxxxxxxxxxxxxxxxxxxxxxxxx

SERVES 4

4 lamb steaks (all fat and sinew
   removed)
a little unbleached white plain flour
2 onions, chopped
2 potatoes, peeled and cubed
1 parsnip, cubed
2 teaspoons crushed garlic
2 teaspoons finely chopped fresh ginger
1 teaspoon ground cummin
1 teaspoon ground coriander
1 teaspoon curry powder
750 ml/1⅓ pints/3 cups water or stock
a little cornflour (optional)
black pepper to taste

Coat the lamb steaks with the flour. Shake off the excess. Brown the lamb on both sides in a hot non-stick frying pan. Remove from the pan. Add the onion, potato, parsnip, garlic, ginger, spices and water, and bring to a simmer. Add the lamb. Turn the heat down to its lowest temperature. Cook for 1½–2 hours or until the lamb is very tender. It will make its own thickened sauce, but you could add a little cornflour if you desire a thicker consistency. Season with black pepper.

Serve with green beans and sweet potato.

Mexican Meat Balls

xxxxxxxxxxxxxxxxxxxxxxxxxxxxxxxxxxxxxxxxxxxxxxxxxxxxxxxxxxxxxxxxxxxxxxxxxxxxxxxxxxxxxxxxx

SERVES 6

400 g/14 oz lamb (all fat and sinew
   removed)
1 onion, finely chopped
125 g/¼ lb/2 cups fresh wholemeal
   breadcrumbs
450 ml/15 fl oz/1¾ cups water
350 g/¾ lb/3 cups peas
12 small sweet potatoes

Sauce
1 onion, chopped
2 cloves garlic, crushed (optional)
½ teaspoon finely chopped fresh ginger
250 ml/8 fl oz/1 cup stock (liquid in
   which meat balls are cooked)
425 g/15 oz canned salt-free tomatoes in
   natural juice, puréed
75 g/2½ oz/¼ cup salt-free tomato
   paste
2 tablespoons/2 tablespoons plus
   2 teaspoons low-salt soy sauce
1 large red capsicum
4 spring onions
2 sticks celery

Mince the lamb and mix with the onion and breadcrumbs. Roll the mixture into small balls (approximately 20). Place in a shallow saucepan. Cover with the water and bring to the boil. Cover, and turn the heat down to simmer. Cook for 30 minutes. Remove the meatballs and retain the stock.

Preheat the oven to 200°C/400°F.

To make the Sauce, place the onion, garlic and ginger in a saucepan. Add a little stock and cook for 3 minutes. Add the tomato, tomato paste, remaining stock and soy sauce. Cook for 10 minutes. Cut the capsicum in half. Remove the seeds and cut into long strips. Cut the spring onions and celery into small diagonal pieces.

Place the meat balls in a casserole dish and add the capsicum, onion and celery. Add the sauce. Cover the casserole. Bake for 30 minutes.

Serve with two sweet potatoes and 60 g/2 oz/½ cup of green peas per person. To cook the sweet potatoes, peel and cut into cubes. Simmer until just tender. (See right colour plate between pages 104 and 105.)

Potted Lamb

SERVES 4–6

500 g/1 lb 2 oz cooked lamb from
    Lamb Shank Stock (see p. 15)
2 Granny Smith apples, peeled and
    chopped
500 ml/16 fl oz/2 cups Lamb Shank
    Stock (see p. 15)
3 teaspoons gelatine
½ teaspoon ground nutmeg
1 teaspoon dried basil
1 tablespoon/1 tablespoon plus
    1 teaspoon finely chopped fresh
    parsley

Remove all fat and sinew from the lamb. Chop the lamb and place in deep ceramic or china bowl. Cook the apple in the stock for 2 minutes. Add the gelatine and stir to dissolve. Remove from the heat. Add the nutmeg and herbs. Pour over the meat. Set aside to cool, and then refrigerate.

Serve the meat, allowing two slices per person, with salads.

Lamb Roast with Vegetables

SERVES 4

1-kg/2¼-lb boned piece of shoulder lamb
    (all fat and sinew removed)
a little wholemeal plain flour seasoned
    with black pepper

Stuffing
125 g/¼ lb/2 cups fresh wholemeal
    breadcrumbs
10 dried apricots, finely chopped
1 apple, peeled and grated
handful of finely chopped fresh parsley
½ teaspoon dried sage

Gravy
2 tablespoons/2 tablespoons plus
    2 teaspoons salt-free tomato paste
water
2 tablespoons/2 tablespoons plus
    2 teaspoons cornflour
2 tablespoons/2 tablespoons plus
    2 teaspoons extra water

Preheat the oven to 200°C/400°F.

To make the Stuffing, combine all the ingredients, mix well and fill the meat cavity. Secure the ends with fine skewers. Roll the meat in the seasoned wholemeal flour, and shake off the excess. Place in an oven bag and cook for 50 minutes.

When cooked, pour the excess juice into a saucepan and remove the fat. Add the tomato paste and enough water to make 250 ml/8 fl oz/1 cup of liquid. Bring to a simmer. Combine the cornflour with the extra water to make a paste. Add to the pan, and stir until thick.

Serve with any of the following vegetables: potatoes, pumpkin, peas, Brussels sprouts, cauliflower, carrots, beans, spinach, parsnip, corn, zucchini, cabbage, sweet potatoes, yellow squash, broccoli, tomatoes and capsicums. The vegetables can be steamed or baked. To bake vegetables, place on a non-stick baking tray or place in an oven bag. Follow the cooking instructions on the oven-bag packet. (See right colour plate between pages 104 and 105.)

Spicy Lamb and Rice

SERVES 10 – 12

310 g/10½ oz/2 cups brown rice
1 kg/2¼ lb lamb (all fat and sinew removed)
2 onions, finely chopped
a little water
½–1 teaspoon ground coriander
½ teaspoon ground ginger
½–1 teaspoon ground cummin
250 ml/8 fl oz/1 cup Beef Stock (see p. 15) or Vegetable Stock (see p. 14)
2 green capsicums, cut into small pieces
2 carrots, cut into small pieces
2 sticks celery, cut into small pieces
425 g/15 oz/2 cups sultanas
10–12 crisp lettuce cups or par-baked eggplant shells for serving

Cook the rice in boiling water until tender, drain, and set aside. Mince the lamb.

In a large saucepan cook the onion in the water for 3 minutes or until soft. Add the meat and spices. Simmer, covered, for 30 minutes.

Break the meat up into small pieces as it cooks so that it retains its minced texture. Add the stock as necessary so the meat does not dry out. This is a dry dish so avoid adding too much liquid. Add the vegetables and sultanas and cook, covered, for 10 minutes. Fold through the rice.

Serve in the lettuce cups or par-baked eggplant shells. (See colour plate opposite.)

Note

If using eggplant shells rather than lettuce cups, scoop the seeds out of the desired number of eggplant halves, leaving a lining of flesh. Bake in a moderate oven for about 15 minutes until the flesh has softened and started to colour. Keep warm until the Spicy Lamb and Rice is ready.

Lamb Kebabs

SERVES 4

450 g/1 lb lamb steaks (all fat and sinew removed), cut into cubes
8 small onions

Marinade
200 ml/7 fl oz/¾ cup dry white wine
1 onion, finely chopped
1 clove garlic, crushed
1 teaspoon dried basil
1 tablespoon/1 tablespoon plus 1 teaspoon dried mint
1 teaspoon apple juice concentrate
black pepper to taste

Combine the Marinade ingredients. Thread the meat and whole onions evenly onto 4 skewers. Pour the Marinade over the meat, and stand for 2 hours. Grill the kebabs, basting frequently with the Marinade. Serve on a bed of brown rice with salad.

Spicy Lamb and Rice (opposite page).

Lamb Risotto in Butternut Boats
(opposite page).

Lamb Risotto in Butternut Boats

SERVES 2

1 butternut pumpkin
1 clove garlic, crushed
2 tablespoons/2 tablespoons plus
    2 teaspoons finely chopped onion
2 tablespoons/2 tablespoons plus
    2 teaspoons finely chopped red
    capsicum
185 g/6 oz lean minced lamb
a little water
½–1 teaspoon ground cummin
150 g/5 oz/1 cup grated carrot
2 large tomatoes, peeled, seeded and
    chopped
150 g/5 oz/1 cup cooked brown rice
60 g/2 oz/1 cup fresh wholemeal
    breadcrumbs
2 tablespoons/2 tablespoons plus
    2 teaspoons grated low-fat grating
    cheese

Preheat the oven to 200°C/400°F.

Cut the pumpkin in half lengthwise. Scoop out the seeds and the pumpkin flesh to leave a deep cavity. Place the garlic, onion, capsicum and lamb in a small saucepan. Add a little water. Cook on a low heat for 20 minutes or until the meat is tender. Turn frequently. Add the cummin, grated carrot and tomato. Cover, and cook over a gentle heat for a further 5 minutes. Add more liquid if necessary (however, the mixture should be fairly dry). Remove from the heat and fold in the rice.

Spoon equal quantities of mixture into the two pumpkin halves. Top with the breadcrumbs and sprinkle equal quantities of the cheese over the top. Place in an oven bag, or on a baking tray and cover with foil. Cook in the oven for 40–45 minutes or until the top is browned. (See colour plate opposite.)

Savoury Lamb Mince

SERVES 4

1 clove garlic, crushed
1 large onion, finely chopped
225 g/½ lb lean minced lamb
2 tablespoons/2 tablespoons plus
    2 teaspoons water
150 g/5 oz/1 cup finely chopped celery
150 g/5 oz/1 cup grated carrot
100 g/3½ oz/½ cup sultanas or raisins
125 g/¼ lb/1 cup oat bran
black pepper to taste
140 g/4½ oz/½ cup salt-free tomato
    paste
425 g/15 oz canned whole tomatoes in
    natural juice, salt-free
250 ml/8 fl oz/1 cup Chicken Stock
    (see p.14) or water

Stir-fry the garlic, onion and meat in the water. Add all the other ingredients and gently simmer, covered, for 30 minutes.

Serve on wholemeal toast or with rice.

PASTA
&
RICE DISHES

Pasta has become the staple food of many countries but is perhaps best known for its place in Italian cuisine. It is made from just a few simple ingredients, including flour or semolina and water. Eggs are often added for a firmer texture and more colour. Salt is usually not added in the manufacturing process, so it is an ideal food for those on a low-salt diet.

To keep your fat and cholesterol intake low, choose the egg-free varieties, which can also be flavoured and coloured with spinach or tomato purée.

Contrary to popular belief, pasta is not fattening. Traditional oil-based or cream-based sauces are the culprits. Follow the guidelines for simple low-fat sauté alternatives, as suggested here, and you will enjoy a meal high in complex carbohydrate and low in kilojoules.

Like pasta, rice is an excellent source of complex carbohydrate. Use brown rice in preference to white rice because it still contains the outer layer of bran and has twice as much dietary fibre. It can be used to complement a main meal or, with the addition of vegetables and meats, it can become a wholesome well-balanced meal in itself.

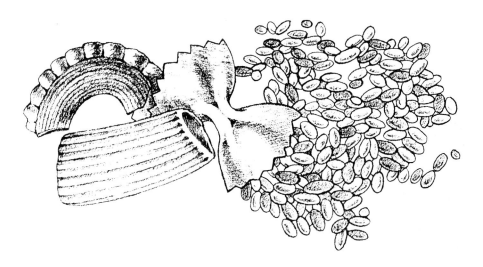

Fish and Spinach Cannelloni

SERVES 6

1 kg/2¼ lb fish fillets (e.g. sea perch, whiting, flake)
12 sheets wholemeal lasagne

Spinach and Ricotta Filling
200 g/7 oz spinach
200 g/7 oz/¾ cup ricotta cheese
½ teaspoon ground nutmeg
½ teaspoon grated geska herb cheese

Tomato Sauce
1 onion, chopped
2 cloves garlic, crushed
a little water
850 g/2 lb canned whole tomatoes in natural juice, salt-free
140 g/4½ oz/½ cup salt-free tomato paste
½ teaspoon freshly chopped basil
½ teaspoon dried oregano

Preheat the oven to 180°C/350°F.

Prepare the fish by removing any skin and bones, and then cut into 12 pieces. Put each piece between plastic and gently roll out to approximately the shape of the lasagne.

Cook the sheets of lasagne in boiling water until just tender. Remove and drain.

To make the Spinach and Ricotta Filling, cook the spinach, drain well and finely chop. Combine with all the other filling ingredients.

To make the Tomato Sauce, cook the onion and garlic with a little water in a saucepan until soft. Purée the tomatoes and juice, tomato paste and herbs, and add to the onion and garlic. Slowly bring to the boil. Turn down and simmer for 5 minutes.

To assemble the cannelloni, top a sheet of cooked lasagne with one piece of rolled-out fish. Place a dessertspoon of the Spinach and Ricotta Filling across one end of the fish, and roll up to encase the fish and filling. Repeat to make 12 cannelloni. Place in a large casserole dish and pour the Tomato Sauce on top. Cover with lid or foil. Bake for 45–55 minutes.

Serve two cannelloni per person, with a salad.

Lima Bean Cannelloni

SERVES 4

310 g/10½ oz canned lima beans, drained
200 g/7 oz cooked and well-drained spinach
60 g/2 oz/½ cup grated low-fat grating cheese
¼ teaspoon ground nutmeg
1 egg white
12 cannelloni shells

Tomato Sauce
1 small onion, chopped
1 teaspoon crushed garlic
1 teaspoon light olive oil or water
6 large mushrooms, finely sliced
125 ml/4 fl oz/½ cup dry red wine
425 g/15 oz canned whole tomatoes in natural juice, salt-free
2 tablespoons/2 tablespoons plus 2 teaspoons salt-free tomato paste

Rinse the lima beans under cold water to remove salt. Chop the spinach and add to the beans. Add the cheese, nutmeg and egg white to the bean mixture. Mix together and spoon into the 12 cannelloni shells. Cover.

To make the Tomato Sauce, cook the onion and garlic in the oil until the onion is soft. Add the sliced mushroom. Continue cooking until the mushroom is soft. Add the red wine. Chop the tomatoes and add with the juice. Mix in the tomato paste. Stir frequently and simmer for 20 minutes.

While the sauce is cooking, preheat the oven to 180°/350°F. Place the filled cannelloni shells in a lightly greased baking dish. Pour the sauce over the top. Cover and bake for 30 minutes.

Serve with a salad.

Spinach and Cottage Cheese Cannelloni

SERVES 4

200 g/7 oz/¾ cup low-fat cottage cheese

1 teaspoon grated geska herb cheese or parmesan cheese

2 tablespoons/2 tablespoons plus 2 teaspoons freshly chopped chives

150 g/5 oz/½ cup cooked, well-drained spinach

pinch of ground nutmeg

1 egg white

8 cannelloni shells

Tomato Sauce

½ onion, chopped

1 teaspoon crushed garlic

425 g/15 oz canned whole tomatoes in natural juice, salt-free

125 ml/4 fl oz/½ cup dry white wine

140 g/4½ oz salt-free tomato paste

1 tablespoon/1 tablespoon plus 1 teaspoon freshly chopped basil or ½ teaspoon dried basil

1 tablespoon/1 tablespoon plus 1 teaspoon freshly chopped chives

Preheat the oven to 180°C/350°F.

Combine all the cannelloni filling ingredients. Mix well and spoon into the shells.

To make the Tomato Sauce, sauté the onion and garlic over a low heat until the onion begins to soften. Break up the tomatoes and add with the wine and remaining ingredients. Simmer, uncovered, for 20 minutes. Place the cannelloni in a shallow casserole dish and pour the sauce over the top. Cover, and cook in the oven for 30 minutes.

Portions of this dish can be frozen and reheated in the microwave oven.

Chicken Macaroni

SERVES 6

750 g/1½ lbs/3 cups cooked wholemeal
   macaroni
500 g/1 lb 2 oz/2 cups chopped cooked
   chicken
425 g/15 oz canned whole tomatoes in
   natural juice, chopped
150 g/5 oz/1 cup chopped celery
150 g/5 oz/1 cup chopped green
   capsicum
150 g/5 oz/1 cup grated carrot
handful freshly chopped chives
handful freshly chopped parsley
1 teaspoon grated fresh ginger (optional)
black pepper to taste
250 ml/8 fl oz/1 cup Chicken Stock
   or Vegetable Stock (see p. 14)

Preheat the oven to 180°C/350°F.

Combine all the ingredients in an ovenproof baking dish. Cover, and cook for 30–40 minutes or until well heated through. (See left colour plate between pages 120 and 121.)

Macaroni with Vegetables and Cheese

SERVES 6–8

150 g/5 oz/1 cup wholemeal macaroni
   or soyaroni noodles
225 g/½ lb carrots, chopped
225 g/½ lb zucchini, chopped
4 sticks celery, chopped
500 ml/16 fl oz/2 cups Vegetable
   Stock (see p.14) or water
500 ml/16 fl oz/2 cups skim milk
90 g/3 oz/¾ cup cornflour
large handful finely chopped fresh parsley
100 g/3½ oz/1 cup grated low-fat
   grating cheese

Preheat the oven to 200°C/400°F.

Cook the macaroni in boiling water until tender. Drain. Cook the vegetables in the stock until tender. Drain and reserve liquid. Cool the stock slightly. Add 350 ml/12 fl oz/ 1½ cups of skim milk and bring to just under the boil. Combine 125 ml/4 fl oz/½ cup of the skim milk with the cornflour and stir to make a paste. Stir through the remaining skim milk and stock, stirring continuously until the stock thickens.

Add the parsley and cheese. Combine the vegetables and macaroni in an ovenproof dish. Pour the cheese sauce over the top. Cook for 15–20 minutes or until the top begins to brown.

Macaroni Cheese

SERVES 4

450 g/1 lb/3 cups wholemeal macaroni
   or soyaroni noodles or vegetable
   noodles
60 g/2 oz/½ cup grated low-fat grating
   cheese
handful of finely chopped fresh herbs
   (e.g. parsley, chives, basil)

Cook the macaroni, following the instructions on the packet. Sprinkle with the low-fat grating cheese and toss through the fresh herbs.

Spaghetti Bolognese

SERVES 4 – 6

500 g / 1 lb 2 oz semolina spaghetti

Bolognese Sauce
2 onions, chopped
1 teaspoon crushed garlic
750 g / 1½ lbs lean minced beef
1 teaspoon dried basil
1 teaspoon dried oregano
½ teaspoon dried thyme
125 g / ¼ lb / 1 cup rolled oats
250 ml / 8 fl oz / 1 cup dry red wine
850 g / 2 lb canned whole tomatoes in
  natural juices, salt-free
140 g / 4½ oz / ½ cup salt-free tomato
  paste

I always cook more of the Bolognese Sauce than I need for six servings, because the leftovers can be used in so many other quick and easy meals. Refrigerate or freeze until required.

To make the Bolognese Sauce, place the onion and garlic in a large non-stick saucepan and cook gently until soft. Add the meat a little at a time. Use a wooden spoon to break up the meat as it browns. Turn the meat frequently until it has browned (do not have the heat up too high or the meat and onions will burn rather than brown).

Add the herbs and rolled oats. Cook for 2 minutes, stirring frequently. Add the wine. Chop the tomatoes and add, with the juice, to the saucepan. Add the tomato paste. Bring to the boil. Turn the heat down to a simmer. Stir frequently to avoid sticking and cook, uncovered, for 20–30 minutes, or until the sauce is thick and a rich red colour.

To cook the spaghetti, follow the instructions on the packet. Serve the spaghetti in bowls topped with the sauce.

To Use Left-over Bolognese Sauce
- Serve on hot toast as a lunchtime snack.
- Serve in hot baked potatoes.
- Scoop out the inside of suitable vegetables (for example, eggplant, baby pumpkins, zucchini) and steam or bake the vegetables until just tender. Fill the vegetables with sauce and top with some grated low-fat grating cheese. Return the vegetables to the oven and bake until the sauce has heated through and the cheese is browned. Serve with a salad.
- Use as a topping for pizza.
- Use as a filling for wholemeal lasagne.

Spaghetti and Spinach Sauce

SERVES 6

575 g / 1¼ lb wholemeal spaghetti

Spinach Sauce
2 bunches spinach
2 cloves garlic, crushed
60 g / 2 oz / ¼ cup pine nuts
2 teaspoons freshly chopped basil or ½
  teaspoon dried basil
handful of freshly chopped parsley
black pepper to taste

Wash the spinach and place the leaves in water in a saucepan. Cover, and bring to the boil. Reduce the heat and simmer for 5 minutes. Reserve a little of the cooking liquid. Put the spinach in a food processor or blender with the garlic, pine nuts, basil and parsley. Blend until smooth, adding a little of the spinach cooking liquid if necessary. Season with black pepper.

To cook the spaghetti, follow the instructions on the packet.

Place the spaghetti on serving plates and spoon the Spinach Sauce on top.

Seafood Fettuccine

SERVES 4

400 g/14 oz fettuccine
1 onion, chopped
1 large clove garlic, crushed
65 ml/2 fl oz/¼ cup dry white wine
400 g/14 oz fish fillets or *combination of fish and shellfish*
100 g/3½ oz fresh spinach, torn into small pieces
625 ml/1 pint/2½ cups skim milk
30 g/1 oz/¼ cup cornflour
2 teaspoons wholegrain mustard
½ teaspoon dry mustard

Drop the fettuccine into a saucepan of rapidly boiling water. Cook until tender and drain.

While the fettuccine is cooking place the onion and garlic in a saucepan over low heat and cover. Cook for 2–3 minutes. Add the wine and bring to the boil. Chop the fish into bite-sized pieces and add to the saucepan. Turn the heat down a little. Cover, and cook the fish until just tender. Add the spinach and cover.

In a bowl mix a little of the skim milk with the cornflour to make a paste. Add the mustards and remaining skim milk. Pour this into the saucepan with the fish, and gently stir continuously until the sauce boils and thickens.

Place equal portions of fettuccine on four plates and top with the seafood and spinach sauce. Serve immediately. (See colour plate opposite.)

Spaghetti with Spinach and Herbs

SERVES 4–6

500 g/1 lb 2 oz wholemeal spaghetti
100 g/3½ oz/1 cup cooked and well-drained spinach
a little water
60 g/2 oz/1 cup mixed finely chopped fresh herbs (e.g. parsley, chives, oregano, basil)
150 g/5 oz/1 cup finely sliced celery
65 ml/2 fl oz/¼ cup lemon juice
60 g/2 oz/⅓ cup currants
75 g/2½ oz/1 cup alfalfa sprouts or *mung bean sprouts*

Cook the spaghetti in boiling water. Finely chop the spinach. Mix all the remaining ingredients together and add to the cooked spaghetti. Toss gently and serve. (See right colour plate overleaf.)

*Seafood Fettuccine (opposite page) with
mussels in their shells.*

Chicken Macaroni (page 118); Tomato Sorbet (page 35).

*Spaghetti with Spinach and Herbs
(page 120).*

*Spaghetti with Tomato and Vegetables
(opposite page).*

Spaghetti with Tomato and Vegetables

SERVES 6

575 g/1¼ lb wholemeal spaghetti
handful of freshly chopped parsley or
grated low-fat grating cheese for
garnishing

Sauce
1 large onion, chopped
1 green capsicum
1 red capsicum
2 sticks celery, finely chopped
150 g/5 oz/1 cup finely chopped green
beans
150 g/5 oz/1 cup finely chopped carrot
425 g/15 oz canned whole tomatoes in
natural juice, puréed
75 g/2½ oz/¼ cup salt-free tomato
paste
250 ml/8 oz/1 cup water
½ teaspoon dried basil
½ teaspoon dried oregano
2 bay leaves

To make the Sauce, cook the onion in a very lightly greased saucepan, stirring, until just transparent, approximately 2–3 minutes. Finely chop the capsicums and add to the saucepan. Add the remaining sauce ingredients. Bring to the boil. Reduce the heat and simmer for 30–40 minutes.

Boil 2 litres/3½ pints/8 cups of water while making the Sauce. Add the wholemeal spaghetti and cook until tender.

Pour the Sauce over the cooked spaghetti. Sprinkle with the finely chopped parsley or low-fat grating cheese, or a combination of both. (See colour plate opposite.)

Spaghetti and Meat Balls

SERVES 6

575 g/1¼ lb wholemeal spaghetti

Meat Balls
225 g/½ lb lean minced beef or *veal*
1 onion, finely chopped
60 g/2 oz/1 cup fresh wholemeal
breadcrumbs
1 Granny Smith apple, peeled and grated

Tomato Sauce
1 onion, chopped
1 small green capsicum, chopped
1 small red capsicum, chopped
a little water
425 g/15 oz canned whole tomatoes in
natural juice, salt-free
250 ml/8 fl oz/1 cup water
2 tablespoons/2 tablespoons plus 2
teaspoons salt-free tomato paste
½ teaspoon dried basil
½ teaspoon dried oregano
handful of finely chopped fresh parsley

To make the Meat Balls, combine all the meat-ball ingredients and roll into very small balls. Place in a shallow saucepan in approximately 2.5 cm/1″ of water. Bring to the boil, turn the heat down and simmer, covered, for about 8 minutes. Remove from the saucepan and drain.

To make the Tomato Sauce, cook the onion and capsicum in a little water until soft, approximately 3 minutes. Purée the tomatoes and add to the saucepan with the water. Bring to the boil. Add the tomato paste, basil and oregano. Cook for 20 minutes. The sauce should boil and thicken and slightly reduce. Add the meat balls to the sauce, and heat through.

Boil 2 litres/3½ pints/8 cups of water while making the sauce. Add the wholemeal spaghetti and cook until tender. Serve the sauce and meat balls over the spaghetti and sprinkle with the fresh parsley.

Chicken and Eggplant Lasagne

SERVES 6

2 onions, chopped

2 teaspoons light olive oil or 2
  tablespoons water

575 g/1¼ lb chicken fillets (all skin and
  fat removed), cubed

750 ml/1⅓ pints/3 cups skim milk or
  reduced-fat soymilk

1 teaspoon dried dill

1 teaspoon dried basil

60 g/2 oz/½ cup cornflour

200 g/7 oz eggplant, cubed

200 g/7 oz red capsicums, chopped

200 g/7 oz broccoli florets, sliced

200 g/7 oz zucchini, sliced

200 g/7 oz instant wholemeal lasagne

Cheese Sauce

2 tablespoons/2 tablespoons plus 2
  teaspoons cornflour

250 ml/8 fl oz/1 cup skim milk or
  reduced-fat soymilk

black pepper to taste

100 g/3½ oz/1 cup grated low-fat
  grating cheese

Topping

2 tablespoons/2 tablespoons plus 2
  teaspoons oat bran

1 tablespoon/1 tablespoon plus 1
  teaspoon grated geska herb cheese or
  parmesan cheese

In a large saucepan cook the onion over a gentle heat in half the oil or water. Add the chicken. Toss frequently and cook, covered, for 10 minutes. Add 625 ml/1 pint/2½ cups of the skim milk, and the herbs. Mix together the cornflour and remaining skim milk. Stir through the chicken, and stir until the sauce thickens.

While the chicken is cooking, in another saucepan cook the eggplant with the remaining oil or water (the oil gives the vegetables a roasted flavour, especially the eggplant). When the eggplant has softened, add the other vegetables. Toss frequently and cook, covered, until all the vegetables are tender. Add the vegetables to the chicken in the saucepan.

To make the Cheese Sauce, blend the cornflour with a little of the skim milk, and return to the remaining skim milk. Add the black pepper. Cook, and stir the sauce until it thickens. Take off the heat and add the grated cheese.

Preheat the oven to 180°C/350°F and assemble the lasagne. Place a layer of lasagne on the base of the lasagne dish. Top with the chicken and vegetable mixture, another layer of lasagne, another layer of chicken and vegetable mixture, and cover with lasagne. Spoon the cheese sauce over the top and sprinkle with the Topping of combined oat bran and cheese.

Cook for 30 minutes.

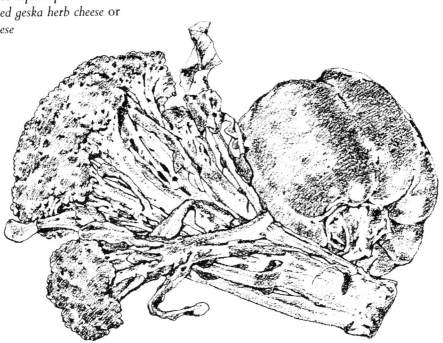

Seafood and Vegetable Lasagne

SERVES 12

1 small onion, finely chopped
500 ml/16 fl oz/2 cups dry white wine
1 teaspoon pink peppercorns
1 large carrot
2 sticks of celery with leaves
1 kg/2¼ lb seafood marinara mixture, drained
1 litre/1¾ pints/4 cups skim milk
60 g/2 oz/½ cup cornflour
1 teaspoon dried tarragon
200 g/7 oz broccoli, finely sliced
200 g/7 oz zucchini, cut into julienne strips
200 g/7 oz carrots, cut into julienne strips
200 g/7 oz red and green capsicums, cut into julienne strips
oat bran or *wholemeal breadcrumbs*
24 sheets instant lasagne

Cheese Sauce

350 ml/12 fl oz/1½ cups skim milk
30 g/1 oz/¼ cup cornflour
black pepper to taste
100 g/3½ oz/1 cup grated low-fat grating cheese

Combine the onion, wine, peppercorns, the whole carrot and celery in a large frying pan and bring to the boil. Turn the heat down and gently simmer, covered, for 10 minutes. Remove the carrot and celery, and return to the boil. Add the seafood and cover. Seafood cooks very quickly, so turn it once or twice and keep covered so it steams in the stock.

Combine enough skim milk with the cornflour to make a paste, add to remaining skim milk and stir well. Add the tarragon. When the fish is cooked, turn the heat down a little and slowly and gently stir in the skim milk mixture. Stir constantly as the mixture returns to the boil and thickens. Allow to stand, covered.

Blanch the broccoli, zucchini, carrot and capsicum in rapidly boiling water until just tender. Quickly remove and plunge into cold water. Drain well.

To make the Cheese Sauce, combine enough skim milk with the cornflour to make a paste. Return this to the remaining skim milk and stir well. Add the pepper. Slowly bring to the boil, stirring constantly until the sauce thickens. Turn off the heat. Add half the grated cheese and stir through.

Lightly grease a large, rectangular, deep-sided lasagne dish, and sprinkle the base with oat bran. Place a layer of lasagne over the base. Top with broccoli and one-third of the seafood mixture, then another layer of lasagne. Next, top with a layer of carrot and another third of the seafood mixture, then another layer of lasagne. Next, top with a layer of zucchini and the remaining third of the seafood mixture. Add a final layer of lasagne and spread the capsicum evenly over the top. Cover with the Cheese Sauce and sprinkle with the remaining grated cheese.

When ready to cook, preheat the oven to 180°C/350°F. If cooking immediately, the lasagne will take 40 minutes. If prepared a day ahead of time and refrigerated, the lasagne should be covered with foil and cooked for 45 minutes – remove the foil for the last 15 minutes.

If reheating a slice of lasagne in the microwave, always reheat on MEDIUM, so that the seafood does not dry up.

Vegetable Lasagne

SERVES 6–8

24 sheets spinach lasagne
125 ml/4 fl oz/½ cup lemon juice
310 g/10½ oz fresh spinach leaves or
  silver beet leaves
100 g/3½ oz/1 cup grated low-fat
  grating cheese

Vegetable Sauce

2 cloves garlic, crushed
2 small onions, finely chopped
a little water
75 g/2½ oz/½ cup finely sliced celery
150 g/5 oz/1 cup finely chopped green
  beans
185 g/6 oz/1 cup finely chopped
  zucchini
150 g/5 oz/1 cup finely chopped carrot
150 g/5 oz/1 cup finely chopped red
  capsicum
60 g/2 oz/½ cup finely sliced mushroom
1 teaspoon dried oregano
1 teaspoon dried rosemary
1 teaspoon dried basil
350 ml/12 fl oz/1½ cups water or dry
  white wine
850 g/2 lb canned whole tomatoes in
  natural juice
140 g/4½ oz/½ cup salt-free tomato
  paste

White Sauce

500 ml/16 fl oz/2 cups reduced-fat
  soymilk
2 bay leaves
30 g/1 oz/¼ cup cornflour

Preheat the oven to 180°C/350°F.

Drop the sheets of lasagne one at a time into a large saucepan of boiling water. Add the lemon juice to the boiling water. As the lasagne sheets cook remove and drop into chilled water. Leave there until required. Drain well before using.

To make the Vegetable Sauce, cook the garlic and onion gently with a little water, covered, for 3 minutes. Add the remaining ingredients except the tomatoes and tomato paste. Cover, and cook for 10 minutes. Add the tomatoes and their juice. Simmer, uncovered, for 20 minutes. Add the tomato paste and cook for a further 10 minutes. Stir occasionally so that the vegetables do not stick to the bottom of the saucepan. Remove from the heat.

Place the spinach leaves in a saucepan with boiling water and cook for 2 minutes. Drain well.

To make the White Sauce, place 450 ml/15 fl oz/1¾ cups of soymilk and the bay leaves in a saucepan. Slowly bring to the boil. Mix the remaining soymilk with the cornflour to make a paste. Stir through the milk briskly before it comes to the boil. Stir all the time while the sauce thickens, approximately 2 minutes.

Place a layer of lasagne in the bottom of a large lasagne dish. Top with some Vegetable Sauce and then a layer of lasagne. Cover with half the remaining Vegetable Sauce, top with the spinach and half the White Sauce, and top with another layer of lasagne. Cover with the remaining Vegetable Sauce and top with lasagne. Spread the remaining White Sauce evenly over the top layer of lasagne, and sprinkle with the grated cheese. Cook for 40 minutes.

Variation

■ The spinach (and the lemon juice) can be omitted, if desired, and wholemeal pita breads can be used instead of the lasagne sheets. Simply cut the pita breads into rectangles to fit the dish you are using and layer them as you would the lasagne. (See left colour plate between pages 136 and 137.)

Eggplant and Mushroom Lasagne

SERVES 6–8

450 g/1 lb eggplant, chopped
1 small onion, chopped
1 teaspoon light olive oil
225 g/½ lb/2 cups sliced mushroom
500 g/1 lb 2 oz grated carrot
850 g/2 lb canned whole tomatoes in
*   natural juice, salt-free*
125 ml/4 fl oz/½ cup water or dry
*   white wine*
1 teaspoon dried dill
1 teaspoon dried basil
1 teaspoon ground cummin
black pepper to taste
140 g/4½ oz/½ cup salt-free tomato
*   paste*
½ red capsicum, chopped
½ green capsicum, chopped
225 g/½ lb instant wholemeal lasagne
125 g/¼ lb/1¼ cups grated low-fat
*   grating cheese*
125 g/¼ lb/1 cup rolled oats
a little paprika

Cook the eggplant and onion in the oil until the eggplant softens and begins to brown. Add the mushroom. Cover, and continue cooking until the mushroom has softened and changed colour. Stir frequently. Add the carrot, tomatoes and juice, water, herbs and spices. Simmer, covered, for 20 minutes. Add the tomato paste and capsicum, and cook for a further 10 minutes.

Preheat the oven to 200°C/400°F.

Place a layer of lasagne on the base of a shallow casserole dish. Spoon one-third of the sauce over the top. Repeat with another layer of lasagne and another third of the sauce. Finally add another layer of lasagne and the remaining sauce.

Combine cheese, rolled oats and paprika and spread evenly over the top of the dish. Bake for 30–40 minutes, or until the top is browned. Serve with a salad.

Egg Combination Rice

SERVES 6

3 eggs
200 ml/7 fl oz/¾ cup reduced-fat
*   soymilk*
1 onion, chopped
1 clove garlic, crushed
½ teaspoon finely chopped fresh ginger
150 g/5 oz/1 cup finely chopped red
*   capsicum*
150 g/5 oz/1 cup finely chopped green
*   capsicum*
150 g/5 oz/1 cup finely chopped carrot
150 g/5 oz/¾ cup finely chopped
*   zucchini (juice squeezed out)*
1 tablespoon/1 tablespoon plus 1
*   teaspoon water*
pinch of ground cummin
pinch of ground coriander
pinch of chilli powder
1 tablespoon/1 tablespoon plus 1
*   teaspoon low-salt soy sauce*
575 g/1¼ lb cooked brown rice

Beat the eggs and soymilk until light and fluffy. Pour into a large, hot, lightly greased, non-stick frying pan. Cook and then turn over to cook the other side. The egg is cooked when firm and a yellow colour. Do not allow to brown. Remove from the pan and chop up into small pieces. Clean away the egg from the pan.

Add the onion, garlic, ginger, vegetables and water to the pan. Toss well and add the spices and soy sauce. Cook for 3 minutes. Turn the heat up high. Add the rice, a cup at a time, and mix to combine evenly. Keep turning, using an egg lifter so the rice does not stick to the bottom of the pan. Add the chopped egg and mix through the rice. Serve when the rice is heated through.

Note
If any member of the family has high cholesterol, it may be best to avoid using egg yolks.

Rice Mould

SERVES 8 – 10

150 g/5 oz/3 cups brown rice
125 g/¼ lb/1 cup peas
150 g/5 oz/1 cup grated carrot
75 g/2½ oz/½ cup finely chopped green
   capsicum
75 g/2½ oz/½ cup finely chopped red
   capsicum
75 g/2½ oz/1 cup alfalfa sprouts
125 g/¼ lb/1 cup finely chopped spring
   onion
150 g/5 oz/1 cup finely chopped celery
75 g/2½ oz/½ cup peeled, seeded and
   chopped cucumber
large handful freshly chopped herbs
2 tablespoons/2 tablespoons plus 2
   teaspoons Garlic Vinaigrette (see
   p. 141)
150 g/5 oz/½ cup cooked puréed apple
¼ teaspoon cayenne pepper

Cook the rice in boiling water for 20 minutes. Add the peas and cook for a further 5 minutes. Drain. Set aside to cool slightly.

Combine all the other ingredients and mix well while the rice is still warm. Lightly grease a deep mould and firmly press the rice mixture into it. Press down firmly around the top. Cover with foil and refrigerate for at least 4 hours before serving.

Serve a slice of Rice Mould on a bed of lettuce with chunks of fresh pineapple and cherry tomatoes. (See right colour plate between pages 136 and 137.)

Saffron Rice

SERVES 2

625 ml/1 pint/2½ cups Chicken Stock
   (see p. 14)
pinch of saffron
185 g/6 oz/1 cup long-grain brown rice
1 teaspoon grated lemon rind
¼–½ teaspoon ground cinnamon

Bring the Chicken Stock to the boil and simmer. Add the saffron. Simmer for 3 minutes. Add the rice. Cover, and cook until the rice is soft but still slightly chewy. It should have absorbed the colour and flavour of the saffron. Add the lemon rind and cinnamon, mix well and serve.

Tabouleh Rice

SERVES 6

310 g/10½ oz/2 cups cooked brown rice
4 tomatoes, peeled, seeded and finely
   chopped
4 spring onions, finely chopped
60 g/2 oz/1 cup finely chopped fresh
   parsley
60 g/2 oz/1 cup finely chopped fresh
   coriander
large handful finely chopped fresh mint
200 ml/7 fl oz/¾ cup Garlic
   Vinaigrette (see p. 141)

Combine all the ingredients. Mix well, chill and serve. (See colour plate opposite page 89.)

Chilli Rice

SERVES 4

4 egg whites
125 ml/4 fl oz/½ cup low-fat soymilk
150 g/5 oz/1 cup finely chopped celery
60 g/2 oz/½ cup finely chopped spring onion
1 small green capsicum, cut into strips
1 small red capsicum, cut into strips
½ teaspoon dried basil
½ teaspoon ground ginger
½ teaspoon turmeric
½–1 teaspoon chilli powder
125 ml/4 fl oz/½ cup stock
575 g/1¼ lb/4 cups cooked brown rice

Beat the egg whites and soymilk. Very lightly grease a non-stick frying pan. Heat the pan until moderately hot. Pour in the egg mixture and cook until it sets. Turn and cook the other side. Remove from the heat and slice thinly. Add the celery, spring onion, capsicum, basil, spices and stock to the pan. Cook on high for 2 minutes or until all the moisture is absorbed. Add the rice. Remove from the heat, and toss the rice until just warm. Add the sliced egg, and serve.

Sweet Rice

SERVES 8

575 g/1¼ lb/4 cups cooked chilled brown rice
100 g/3½ oz/½ cup dried apricots, finely chopped
60 g/2 oz/⅓ cup currants
60 g/2 oz/¼ cup raisins, finely chopped
60 g/2 oz/¼ cup dried apples, finely chopped
1 carrot, chopped
2 sticks celery, chopped
1 tablespoon/1 tablespoon plus 1 teaspoon sunflower seeds
1 tablespoon/1 tablespoon plus 1 teaspoon sesame seeds, toasted
2 teaspoons grated orange rind
65 ml/2 fl oz/¼ cup unsweetened orange juice

Combine all the ingredients and serve immediately. (See colour plate opposite page 136.)

Lemon Rice

SERVES 4

575 g/1¼ lb/4 cups cooked brown rice
60 g/2 oz/1 cup mixed finely chopped fresh herbs
2 tablespoons/2 tablespoons plus 2 teaspoons tarragon vinegar
2 teaspoons lemon juice
2 teaspoons grated lemon rind

Combine all the ingredients, mix well and refrigerate until chilled. Serve as a salad.

Risotto with Prawns

SERVES 4

1 onion, chopped
1 teaspoon crushed garlic
1 teaspoon finely chopped fresh ginger
½ teaspoon ground cummin
¼ teaspoon chilli powder
½ teaspoon ground coriander
1 teaspoon light olive oil
1 green capsicum, finely sliced
125 g / ¼ lb / 1 cup frozen peas
225 g / ½ lb / 1 cup long-grain brown rice,
   cooked
500 g / 1 lb 2 oz shelled, deveined and
   cooked prawns
12 cherry tomatoes
freshly chopped coriander for garnishing

Cook the onion, garlic, ginger, cummin, chilli powder and coriander powder in the oil in a large saucepan until the onion begins to soften and turn transparent. Add the capsicum and peas, and toss until the vegetables are soft. Add the rice, prawns and tomatoes. Toss to combine with the vegetables. Cover for just a few minutes to heat evenly.

Serve garnished with the freshly chopped coriander. (See colour plate opposite.)

Vegetable Fried Rice

SERVES 5

a little water
2 egg whites
310 g / 10½ oz / 2 cups cooked, chilled
   brown rice
1 small capsicum, finely chopped
1 onion or 6 spring onions, chopped
125 g / ¼ lb / 1 cup finely sliced mushroom
1 carrot, grated
75 g / 2½ oz / 1 cup fresh bean shoots
90 g / 3 oz / 1 cup finely shredded cabbage
black pepper to taste
¼ teaspoon chilli powder
handful of freshly chopped parsley

Moisten the base of a non-stick frying pan or wok with a little water. Slowly cook the egg whites until set and then chop. Return to the pan and add the rice, vegetables and spices. Cook on a low heat for 10 minutes. Keep moving the ingredients so they do not stick. Stir the parsley through the rice just prior to serving. (See colour plate overleaf.)

Carrot and Cummin Rice

SERVES 4

575 g / 1¼ lb / 4 cups cooked brown rice
310 g / 10½ oz / 2 cups grated carrot
60 g / 2 oz / ⅓ cup currants
60 g / 2 oz / ½ cup finely chopped spring
   onion
½–1 teaspoon ground cummin
½–1 teaspoon ground ginger
65 ml / 2 fl oz / ¼ cup unsweetened
   pineapple juice

Combine all the ingredients, mix well and refrigerate until chilled. Serve as a salad.

Risotto with Prawns (opposite page).

Vegetable Fried Rice (page 128).

SALADS & DRESSINGS

A perfect salad is the combination of super-fresh ingredients delicately flavoured with herbs or a little salad dressing of your making.

Wash all your ingredients thoroughly and shake or pat dry. Before using them, seal in airtight bags or containers in the refrigerator to make them crisp.

Raw foods are an essential part of a healthy diet and, ideally, should accompany all main meals. You can create a well-balanced, whole meal with the addition of a variety of salad ingredients such as lettuce greens, carrot, capsicum, broccoli, tomato, avocado, celery and Spanish onion.

By regularly eating salads you will increase the vitamins, water content and natural fibre content of your diet and help maintain and control your weight.

Simple Summer Greens

lettuce
lemon juice
white wine vinegar
finely chopped fresh herbs

Choose one variety of lettuce or combine different varieties and break into small pieces in a bowl. Add a little lemon juice, a little white wine vinegar and some finely chopped fresh herbs. Toss and serve.

Salad Greens with Sun-dried Tomatoes

SERVES 4

2 handfuls mixed lettuce
1 avocado, roughly chopped
handful of snow peas or sugar peas,
*   topped and tailed*
100 g/3½ oz sun-dried tomatoes,
*   drained and chopped*
2 tablespoons/2 tablespoons plus 2
*   teaspoons pumpkin kernels*
1 tablespoon/1 tablespoon plus 1
*   teaspoon pine nuts*
a little French Dressing *(see p. 140)*

Scatter the lettuce on a platter, and add the avocado and snow peas. Top with the chopped sun-dried tomatoes, pumpkin kernels and pine nuts. Add a little French Dressing.

Variation
■ To make the salad into a main meal, add some cubes of tofu. The blandness of the tofu goes well with the sun-dried tomatoes and the nutty texture of the pumpkin kernels and pine nuts.

Apple Salad

SERVES 6

2 green apples
2 red apples
1 small red capsicum
1 small green capsicum
2 sticks celery
125 ml/4 fl oz/½ cup unsweetened
*   apple juice*
2 tablespoons/2 tablespoons plus 2
*   teaspoons lemon juice*
1 tablespoon/1 tablespoon plus 1
*   teaspoon cider vinegar*
2 tablespoons/2 tablespoons plus 2
*   teaspoons pine nuts, roasted*
2 tablespoons/2 tablespoons plus 2
*   teaspoons finely chopped fresh mint,*
*   for garnishing*
2 tablespoons/2 tablespoons plus 2
*   teaspoons finely chopped fresh chives,*
*   for garnishing*
alfalfa sprouts

Core the apples and cut into thin wedges. Chop the capsicums. Cut the celery into thin slices. Mix the apple juice, lemon juice and vinegar, and combine with the fruit, vegetables and pine nuts. Garnish with the mint and chives. Serve with alfalfa sprouts.

Banana and Celery Salad

SERVES 4

1 lettuce
4 bananas (not too ripe)
65 ml/2 fl oz/¼ cup lemon juice mixed
    with 125 ml/4 fl oz/½ cup water
4 sticks celery, cut into chunks
large handful freshly chopped chives
250 ml/8 fl oz/1 cup non-fat or low-fat
    yoghurt
black pepper to taste

Set aside 4 crisp lettuce cups. Shred the remaining lettuce finely. Peel the bananas and slice diagonally. Soak in the lemon juice and water for 5 minutes. Drain and towel dry. Combine the banana, shredded lettuce and celery in a bowl. Mix the chives in the yoghurt and add the black pepper. Add this mixture to the lettuce, banana and celery, and toss well. Spoon equal amounts of mixture into each lettuce leaf, and serve.

Beetroot Mould

SERVES 4

6 beetroot, cooked, peeled, cooled and
    roughly chopped
a little beetroot juice or dry white wine
    (if necessary)
2 teaspoons gelatine
2 tablespoons/2 tablespoons plus 2
    teaspoons boiling water
2 tablespoons/2 tablespoons plus 2
    teaspoons lemon juice
250 ml/8 fl oz/1 cup non-fat or low-fat
    yoghurt
large handful finely chopped fresh parsley
orange slices for garnishing

Purée the beetroot in a food processor or blender. If it is too dry, add a little beetroot juice. Set aside. Dissolve the gelatine in the boiling water and add the lemon juice. Stir the gelatine mixture through the beetroot purée and fold the yoghurt and parsley through. Pour into a mould and refrigerate until set. Garnish with the orange slices.

Cucumber Salad Mould

SERVES 2–4

½ cucumber, peeled and seeded
1 orange
½ lemon
½ small onion
2 sprigs parsley
water (if necessary)
2 teaspoons gelatine
2 tablespoons/2 tablespoons plus 2
    teaspoons boiling water
200 g/7 oz/1½ cups mixed grated
    vegetables (e.g. carrot, cucumber,
    radish, green and red capsicum)
black pepper to taste
cucumber slices for garnishing

Juice the cucumber, orange, lemon, onion and parsley. Make up to 300 ml/10 fl oz/1¼ cups with water if necessary. Dissolve the gelatine in the boiling water. Stir into the juice and add the grated vegetables. Season with black pepper. Pour into a ring mould and refrigerate to set. Remove from the mould, garnish with the cucumber slices, and serve.

Mushroom Salad

xxxxxxxxxxxxxxxxxxxxxxxxxxxxxxxxxxxxxxxxxxxxxxxxxxxxxxxxxxxxxxxxxxxxxxxxxxxxx

SERVES 4–6

500 g/1 lb 2 oz baby mushrooms
2 teaspoons light olive oil
3 cloves garlic, crushed
1 teaspoon curry powder
1 teaspoon ground cummin
1 teaspoon ground coriander
1 teaspoon turmeric
100 g/3½ oz/½ cup pine nuts, toasted
2 tablespoons/2 tablespoons plus 2
    teaspoons sesame seeds, toasted

Wash the mushrooms and pat dry. Cut off the stems and leave the mushrooms whole. Pour the oil into a non-stick frying pan. Add the garlic and spices, and coat the base of the pan with them. Keep the heat low. Place the mushrooms in the pan and toss well to coat with the spices. Cover, and gently cook for 10 minutes. Remove the lid. Cook until any liquid is absorbed. Place in a serving bowl and add the pine nuts and sesame seeds. Serve hot or cold.

Orange and Nasturtium Salad

xxxxxxxxxxxxxxxxxxxxxxxxxxxxxxxxxxxxxxxxxxxxxxxxxxxxxxxxxxxxxxxxxxxxxxxxxxxxx

SERVES 4–6

6 oranges
a few nasturtium leaves
1 large Spanish onion, chopped
12 black olives, stoned and chopped
a few nasturtium flowers
a little white wine vinegar

Peel the oranges and slice into rounds. For a peppery flavour, chop up some of the nasturtium leaves. Combine all the ingredients in a salad bowl. Add a little wine vinegar, and decorate with nasturtium flowers. Don't forget to eat the nasturtium flowers – they are very tasty!

Minty Potato Salad

xxxxxxxxxxxxxxxxxxxxxxxxxxxxxxxxxxxxxxxxxxxxxxxxxxxxxxxxxxxxxxxxxxxxxxxxxxxxx

SERVES 4–6

1 kg/2¼ lb new potatoes, washed
large handful finely chopped fresh mint
black pepper to taste
Mayonnaise (see p. 138)

Cook the potatoes in their skins until just tender, peel and roughly chop. Add the mint and black pepper, and cool. Fold the mayonnaise through the potato, chill, and serve.

Potatoes in Spicy Tomato Dressing

xxxxxxxxxxxxxxxxxxxxxxxxxxxxxxxxxxxxxxxxxxxxxxxxxxxxxxxxxxxxxxxxxxxxxxxxxxxxx

SERVES 10–12

40 small new potatoes
1 quantity Spicy Tomato Dressing
    (see p. 144)

Wash the potatoes and peel if necessary. Lightly steam until just tender, rinse in cold water and drain thoroughly. Place in a serving bowl. Pour the Spicy Tomato Dressing over the top. Cover and refrigerate.

Potato Salad with Tahini and Yoghurt

SERVES 6

5–6 large potatoes
1 quantity Tahini and Yoghurt
    Dressing *(see p. 143)*

Parboil the potatoes and cut into large pieces. Pour Dressing over the potato just before serving.

Spinach and Water Chestnut Salad

SERVES 1

100 g/3½ oz/1 cup shredded spinach
100 g/3½ oz/1 cup shredded lettuce
90 g/3 oz cooked chicken fillet, roughly chopped
30 g/1 oz/¼ cup sliced water chestnuts
2 tablespoons/2 tablespoons plus 2 teaspoons chopped chives
1 slice wholemeal bread, cubed
1 tablespoon/1 tablespoon plus 1 teaspoon garlic powder
2 tablespoons/2 tablespoons plus 2 teaspoons vinaigrette of your choice

Preheat the oven to 200°C/400°F.

Toss the spinach and lettuce together. Add the chicken and sliced water chestnuts, and sprinkle the chives over the top. Toss the bread cubes with the garlic powder. Shake off the excess garlic powder, and place on a non-stick baking tray. Cook in the oven for 10 minutes or until well browned. Add the vinaigrette to the salad and lightly toss. Add the garlic bread cubes and serve.

Spicy Sprout Salad

SERVES 12

225 g/½ lb/1 cup sultanas
250 ml/8 fl oz/1 cup unsweetened orange juice
½–1 teaspoon ground cummin
4 sticks celery, finely sliced
150 g/5 oz/2 cups mung bean sprouts
150 g/5 oz/2 cups lentil sprouts

Soak the sultanas in the orange juice with the cummin for at least 2 hours, or overnight. Combine all the ingredients, mix well, and serve.

Tabouleh Salad

SERVES 2–4

60 g/2 oz/⅓ cup burghul
2 tomatoes
3 spring onions, finely chopped
large handful finely chopped fresh parsley
large handful finely chopped fresh coriander
a little Cucumber Dressing *(see p. 139)*
crisp lettuce leaves for serving

Soak the burghul in lukewarm water for 10 minutes. Drain, and spread out to dry on absorbent paper. Peel, seed and finely chop the tomatoes. Combine all the ingredients except the Cucumber Dressing and lettuce leaves in a bowl and mix gently. Be careful not to make a mush. Add a little Cucumber Dressing, and serve on a bed of lettuce leaves.

Tomato and Fresh Basil Salad

SERVES 4–6

225 g / ½ lb cherry tomatoes
225 g / ½ lb yellow pear-shaped tomatoes
small bunch fresh basil, roughly chopped
black pepper to taste
a little parmesan cheese

Cut the tomatoes in half. Combine the tomatoes and basil on a large platter. Season with pepper and sprinkle the parmesan cheese on top.

Variation
■ Add some red and green capsicum strips that have been parboiled in a little water or stock. Drain and cool before adding to the salad.

Tomato and Chilli Salad

SERVES 4–6

4 large tomatoes
4 spring onions, finely chopped
a little finely chopped fresh parsley
a little finely chopped fresh chilli
black pepper to taste

Cut the tomatoes in half and squeeze out the seeds. Chop the tomato roughly. Add the spring onion, parsley, chilli and black pepper to taste. Let the salad stand for 1 hour to allow flavours to develop before serving.

Tomato, Fennel and Parsley Salad

SERVES 2–4

2 bunches spring onions, chopped
125 g / ¼ lb fennel, chopped
400 g / 14 oz tomatoes, peeled, seeded
   and chopped
40 g / 1½ oz / ¾ cup coarsely chopped
   fresh parsley
large handful coarsely chopped fresh mint
2 tablespoons / 2 tablespoons plus 2
   teaspoons lemon juice
black pepper to taste

Combine all the ingredients, toss gently, and serve.

Tuna Salad

SERVES 1

1 tomato
60 g / 2 oz / ½ cup cooked peas
2 teaspoons finely chopped fresh mint
3 baby carrots, peeled if necessary
juice of ½ lemon
90 g / 3 oz canned tuna, drained
2 tablespoons / 2 tablespoons plus 2
   teaspoons finely chopped spring onion
3 lettuce leaves
4 rings green capsicum

Slice the top off the tomato. Scoop out the seeds and flesh and discard. Combine the peas and mint and spoon into the tomato case. Refrigerate.

Drop the carrots into boiling water. Cook for 3 minutes. Drain and plunge into cold water. Drain.

Squeeze the lemon juice over the tuna and then add the spring onion.

Place the lettuce leaves on a dinner plate and position the tomato on top, to one side. Place the carrots side by side on the leaves, place the capsicum rings alongside them, and top with the tuna.

Fruity Coleslaw

xxxxxxxxxxxxxxxxxxxxxxxxxxxxxxxxxxxxxxxxxxxxxxxxxxxxxxxxxxxxxxxxxxxxx

SERVES 6–8

575 g/1¼ lb/6 cups finely shredded
*   white cabbage*
2 oranges, peeled and segmented
60 g/2 oz/¼ cup dried apricots, cut into
*   thin strips*
60 g/2 oz/¼ cup dried peaches, cut into
*   thin strips*
30 g/1 oz/¼ cup finely sliced spring
*   onion*
40 g/1½ oz/¼ cup finely sliced celery
15 g/½ oz/⅓ cup shredded coconut
*   (optional)*
350 g/¾ lb fresh pineapple pieces or
*   canned unsweetened pineapple pieces*
2 teaspoons grated orange rind
2 teaspoons grated lemon rind

Orange Dressing
250 ml/8 fl oz/1 cup unsweetened
*   orange juice*
2 teaspoons arrowroot or cornflour
1–2 teaspoons white wine vinegar

Combine all the ingredients except the Orange Dressing in a large salad bowl.

To make the Orange Dressing, combine all the ingredients in a small saucepan. Bring to the boil and stir until the sauce thickens. Cool and refrigerate.

Pour the dressing over the top of the salad and toss well. Leave to stand in the refrigerator for at least 1 hour before serving. Serve chilled.

Vegetable Coleslaw

xxxxxxxxxxxxxxxxxxxxxxxxxxxxxxxxxxxxxxxxxxxxxxxxxxxxxxxxxxxxxxxxxxxxx

SERVES 6–8

280 g/10 oz/3 cups finely shredded
*   green cabbage and 280 g/10 oz/3*
*   cups finely shredded red cabbage or*
*   575 g/1¼ lb/6 cups finely shredded*
*   green cabbage*
75 g/2½ oz/½ cup grated carrot
100 g/3½ oz/½ cup grated zucchini
*   (juice squeezed out)*
40 g/1½ oz/¼ cup finely sliced celery
30 g/1 oz/¼ cup finely sliced spring
*   onion*
125 g/¼ lb/½ cup cooked corn kernels
40 g/1½ oz/¼ cup finely sliced red
*   capsicum*
40 g/1½ oz/¼ cup finely sliced green
*   capsicum*
large handful finely chopped fresh parsley
*   (optional)*
pinch of cayenne pepper
250 ml/8 fl oz/1 cup Mayonnaise
*   (see p. 138)*

Combine all the vegetables and the cayenne pepper in a large salad bowl. Pour the Mayonnaise over the top, toss well, and refrigerate. Leave to stand in the refrigerator for at least 1 hour before serving and serve chilled.

Hawaiian Coleslaw

SERVES 4 – 6

400 g/14 oz/4 cups finely shredded
  green cabbage
1 small green capsicum, cut into strips
1 small red capsicum, cut into strips
75 g/2½ oz/½ cup finely chopped
  carrot
350 g/¾ lb fresh pineapple chunks
125 ml/4 fl oz/½ cup Mayonnaise
  (see p. 138)
65 ml/2 fl oz/¼ cup unsweetened
  pineapple juice

Combine all the vegetables and fruit in a salad bowl. Combine the Mayonnaise and pineapple juice, and pour it over the vegetables and fruit. Toss well, and chill for at least 1 hour before serving. (See colour plate opposite.)

Variation
- If fresh pineapple is unavailable, unsweetened canned pineapple chunks can be used.

Orange, Cucumber and Mint Salad

SERVES 6 – 8

3 oranges
1 small cucumber
125 ml/4 fl oz/½ cup cider vinegar
2 tablespoons/2 tablespoons plus 2
  teaspoons freshly chopped mint
a bed of lettuce leaves or alfalfa sprouts

Remove the rind and pith from the oranges and cut into thin rounds. Peel the cucumber and cut into thin rounds. Place alternate layers of orange and cucumber in a bowl. Pour the vinegar over the top and sprinkle with the mint. Cover and chill. Serve on the lettuce leaves or alfalfa sprouts. (See colour plate opposite.)

Vegetarian Salad

SERVES 1

75 g/2½ oz/½ cup grated carrot
6 green beans, cooked
30 g/1 oz/¼ cup finely grated low-fat
  grating cheese
6 slices tomato
30 g/1 oz/½ cup alfalfa sprouts or
  mung sprouts or lentil sprouts
1 small piece cucumber, cut into strips
75 g/2½ oz/½ cup grated beetroot
1 small Jonathan apple, cored and cut
  into thin wedges

Parsley Rice Mould
2 tablespoons/2 tablespoons plus 2
  teaspoons finely chopped spring onion
2 tablespoons/2 tablespoons plus 2
  teaspoons finely chopped parsley
30 g/1 oz/¼ cup cooked brown rice

Although a lot of salads in this section would suit a vegetarian palate, I like the simplicity of this salad, and its presentation.

To prepare the Parsley Rice Mould, fold the spring onion and parsley through the rice. Press into a small mould and cool if the rice is still hot. Refrigerate for at least 2 hours before removing from the mould.

Carefully unmould the rice onto the centre of a round platter and surround with the vegetables, cheese and apple.

Hawaiian Coleslaw and Orange, Cucumber and Mint Salad (opposite page); Sweet Rice (page 127).

Vegetable Lasagne (page 124).

Rice Mould (page 126).

Cantaloup and Prawn Salad and Spinach and
Sprout Salad (opposite page).

Cantaloup and Prawn Salad

SERVES 1

½ cantaloup, well chilled
3 mignonette lettuce leaves
90 g/3 oz small prawns, shelled and
    deveined
40 g/1½ oz/¼ cup grated cucumber
40 g/1½ oz/¼ cup grated apple
2 tablespoons/2 tablespoons plus 2
    teaspoons lemon juice
2 teaspoons finely chopped fresh dill
½ small red capsicum, cut into strips
2 tablespoons/2 tablespoons plus 2
    teaspoons Mayonnaise (see p. 138)
2 teaspoons salt-free tomato paste

Remove the seeds from the cantaloup, and peel. Wash and dry the lettuce. Cut out a U-shape on one side of the cantaloup, (so the filling can fall out onto the lettuce). Combine the prawns, cucumber, apple, lemon juice and dill. Refrigerate for 1 hour.

Add the capsicum to the mixture and toss. Place the lettuce on a dinner plate. Sit the cantaloup on the lettuce and spoon the filling into its centre. Let some filling fall out onto the lettuce. Combine the Mayonnaise and tomato paste and spoon over the top before serving. (See colour plate opposite.)

Spinach and Sprout Salad

SERVES 1

2 spinach leaves
2 lettuce leaves
4 slices tomato
4 slices peeled cucumber
30 g/1 oz/½ cup bean shoots
30 g/1 oz/½ cup alfalfa sprouts
30 g/1 oz/½ cup lentil sprouts
65 ml/2 fl oz/¼ cup Spicy Tomato
    Dressing (see p. 144)

Wash and shake dry the spinach and lettuce leaves. Shred finely together and arrange on a dinner plate. Top with the tomato, cucumber, bean shoots and sprouts. Add the Spicy Tomato Dressing and toss. Serve. (See colour plate opposite.)

Vegetable Rice Salad

SERVES 6

1 carrot, chopped
2 small sticks celery, chopped
1 small green capsicum, chopped
1 small red capsicum, chopped
60 g/2 oz/¼ cup cooked corn kernels
30 g/1 oz/¼ cup cooked peas
450 g/1 lb/3 cups cooked chilled brown
    rice
2 tablespoons/2 tablespoons plus 2
    teaspoons finely chopped fresh parsley
2 tablespoons/2 tablespoons plus 2
    teaspoons finely chopped fresh mint
6 tomatoes (optional)

Combine the vegetables in a container of iced water for 10 minutes. Drain well. Combine all the ingredients except the tomatoes and toss well.

For a special treat, remove the tops of the tomatoes. Scoop out the inside flesh, stuff with the rice mixture, and serve.

Tossed Vegetable Salad

SERVES 4–6

200 g / 7 oz mixed lettuce leaves
2 sticks celery, cut into chunks
1 small green capsicum, cut into chunks
1 small red capsicum, cut into chunks
2 small carrots, cut into strips
1 zucchini, cut into rounds
100 g / 3½ oz cherry tomatoes, cut in half
100 g / 3½ oz snow peas, topped and tailed
dressing of your choice

Wash the lettuce leaves and shake dry. Store the lettuce in a plastic bag in the crisper compartment of the refrigerator or wrap in a tea towel until required.

To crisp the vegetables, soak in iced water for at least 10 minutes. Drain and store as for lettuce until required.

Toss all the ingredients together and add the dressing of your choice just before serving.

Variation
- Add 500 g / 1 lb 2 oz of tofu cut into 2.5-cm / 1″ squares.

Waldorf Salad

SERVES 2–4

2 red apples, cut into chunks
3 sticks celery, cut into chunks
½ cup walnuts
a little Cucumber Dressing *(see p. 139)*

Combine the apple, celery and walnuts. Add a little Cucumber Dressing, toss gently, and serve.

Mayonnaise

MAKES 350 ML / 12 FL OZ / 1½ CUPS

200 ml / 7 fl oz / ¾ cup low-fat evaporated skim milk
65 ml / 2 fl oz / ¼ cup apple juice concentrate
2 teaspoons Dijon mustard
125 ml / 4 fl oz / ½ cup white wine vinegar

Place all the ingredients in a jar, seal, and shake well. Refrigerate, and use as required. Shake well before each use.

Dill Mayonnaise

MAKES 350 ML / 12 FL OZ / 1½ CUPS

2 teaspoons finely chopped fresh dill
200 ml / 7 fl oz / ¾ cup reduced-fat soymilk
65 ml / 2 fl oz / ¼ cup apple juice concentrate
2 teaspoons Dijon mustard
125 ml / 4 fl oz / ½ cup white wine vinegar

Place all the ingredients in a screw-top jar, seal, and shake well. Refrigerate, and use as required. Shake well before each use.

Soymilk Mayonnaise

MAKES 350 ML / 12 FL OZ / 1½ CUPS

200 ml / 7 fl oz / ¾ cup reduced-fat soymilk
65 ml / 2 fl oz / ¼ cup apple juice concentrate
2 teaspoons Dijon mustard
125 ml / 4 fl oz / ½ cup white wine vinegar

Place all the ingredients in a jar, seal, and shake well. Refrigerate, and use as required. Shake well before each use.

Creamy Cottage Cheese Dressing

MAKES 250 ML / 8 FL OZ / 1 CUP

200 g / 7 oz / 2 cups low-fat cottage cheese
1 tablespoon / 1 tablespoon plus 1 teaspoon apple juice concentrate
1 tablespoon / 1 tablespoon plus 1 teaspoon Tarragon Vinegar (see p. 144)
65 ml / 2 fl oz / ¼ cup unsweetened apple juice or *unsweetened pineapple juice*

Combine all the ingredients in a food processor or blender and process until thick and creamy. Place in a jar, seal, and refrigerate.

Cucumber Dressing

MAKES 300 ML / 10 FL OZ / 1¼ CUPS

½ small cucumber
250 ml / 8 fl oz / 1 cup low-fat yoghurt
2 tablespoons / 2 tablespoons plus 2 teaspoons freshly chopped parsley
2 tablespoons / 2 tablespoons plus 2 teaspoons freshly chopped chives
1 tablespoon / 1 tablespoon plus 1 teaspoon lemon juice
1 tablespoon / 1 tablespoon plus 1 teaspoon white wine vinegar

Peel, seed and grate the cucumber and combine all the ingredients. Mix well. Place in a jar, seal, and refrigerate.

Creamy Cucumber Dressing

MAKES 250 ML / 8 FL OZ / 1 CUP

125 ml / 4 fl oz / ½ cup low-fat yoghurt
¼ teaspoon dried dill
4 teaspoons lemon juice
75 g / 2½ oz / ½ cup coarsely grated cucumber
black pepper to taste

Combine all the ingredients and mix well. Place in a jar, seal, and refrigerate. This dressing can also be used as a dip to serve with a platter of raw vegetables.

Curry Dressing

MAKES 125 ML / 4 FL OZ / ½ CUP

125 ml/4 fl oz/½ cup non-fat or low-
fat yoghurt
1 teaspoon curry powder
1 teaspoon salt-free tomato paste
1 tablespoon/1 tablespoon plus 1
teaspoon unsweetened orange juice

Combine all the ingredients and mix well. Place in a jar, seal, and refrigerate.

French Dressing

MAKES 250 ML / 8 FL OZ / 1 CUP

2 tablespoons/2 tablespoons plus 2
teaspoons freshly chopped basil or 1
teaspoon dried basil
½ teaspoon black pepper
75 ml/3 fl oz/⅓ cup lemon juice
2 tablespoons/2 tablespoons plus 2
teaspoons freshly chopped parsley
2 teaspoons grated lemon rind
175 ml/6 fl oz/⅔ cup white wine
vinegar

Place all the ingredients in a jar and seal. Shake well and refrigerate.

French Dressing with Cholesterol-free Oil

MAKES 350 ML / 12 FL OZ / 1½ CUPS

250 ml/8 fl oz/1 cup light cold-pressed
olive oil
65 ml/2 fl oz/¼ cup lemon juice
1 tablespoon/1 tablespoon plus 1
teaspoon wholegrain mustard
a little grated lemon rind
a little grated orange rind
2 cloves garlic, crushed (optional)

Place all the ingredients in a screw-top jar, shake well and refrigerate. The lemon and orange rind infuses a subtle flavour as the dressing stands over a period of time. Shake well before use.

Spicy Fruit Dressing

MAKES 125 ML / 4 FL OZ / ½ CUP

125 ml/4 fl oz/½ cup non-fat or
low-fat yoghurt
¼ teaspoon ground allspice
¼ teaspoon ground nutmeg
1 tablespoon/1 tablespoon plus 1
teaspoon unsweetened orange juice

Combine all the ingredients and mix well. Place in a jar, seal, and refrigerate.

Garlic Dressing

MAKES 450 ML / 15 FL OZ / 1¾ CUPS

250 ml/8 fl oz/1 cup white wine vinegar
125 ml/4 fl oz/½ cup water
juice of 1 lemon
½ cucumber, peeled and seeded
2–3 cloves garlic
black pepper to taste

Combine all the ingredients in a food processor or blender and blend for 1 minute. Place in a jar, seal, and refrigerate.

Garlic Vinaigrette

MAKES 350 ML / 12 FL OZ / 1½ CUPS

200 ml/7 fl oz/¾ cup unsweetened
  apple juice
125 ml/4 fl oz/½ cup white wine
  vinegar
2 tablespoons/2 tablespoons plus 2
  teaspoons lemon juice
2 teaspoons grated lemon rind
4 small cloves garlic, halved

Combine all the ingredients and mix well. Store in a jar, seal, and refrigerate. Shake every now and then and remove the garlic before using, or remove and crush and then return to the vinaigrette.

Hazelnut or Walnut Dressing

MAKES 200 ML / 7 FL OZ / ¾ CUP

125 ml/4 fl oz/½ cup light cold-pressed
  olive oil
2 tablespoons/2 tablespoons plus 2
  teaspoons lemon juice
1 tablespoon/1 tablespoon plus 1 teaspoon
  finely chopped hazelnuts or walnuts

Combine all the ingredients and mix well. The dressing is best if left in the refrigerator for 7 days before using. Shake well before use.

Allow about a tablespoon per person.

Herb Vinaigrette

MAKES 350 ML / 12 FL OZ / 1½ CUPS

200 ml/7 fl oz/¾ cup unsweetened
  orange juice
125 ml/4 fl oz/½ cup white wine
  vinegar
2 tablespoons/2 tablespoons plus 2
  teaspoons finely chopped fresh oregano
2 tablespoons/2 tablespoons plus 2
  teaspoons finely chopped fresh chives
2 tablespoons/2 tablespoons plus 2
  teaspoons finely chopped fresh parsley

Combine all the ingredients and mix well. Place in a jar, seal, and refrigerate.

Mixed Herb Dressing

MAKES 625 ML/1 PINT/2½ CUPS

250 ml/8 fl oz/1 cup Herb Vinegar
  (*see* Tarragon Vinegar, p. 144)
250 ml/8 fl oz/1 cup unsweetened apple
  juice
juice of 1 lemon
½ cucumber, peeled and seeded
2 tablespoons/2 tablespoons plus 2
  teaspoons mixed freshly chopped herbs

Combine all the ingredients except the herbs in a food processor or blender and blend for 1 minute. Add the herbs and mix but do not blend. Place in jars, seal, and refrigerate.

Island Dressing

MAKES 300 ML/10 FL OZ/1¼ CUPS

125 ml/4 fl oz/½ cup low-fat yoghurt
125 g/¼ lb/½ cup low-fat ricotta cheese
juice of 1 lemon
100 g/3½ oz/⅓ cup salt-free tomato
  paste
3 drops Tabasco
3 teaspoons chopped green capsicum
a little finely chopped fresh parsley
a little finely chopped fresh chives

Place all the ingredients except the parsley and chives in a food processor or blender and blend until smooth. Fold the parsley and chives through the dressing. Store in a jar, seal, and refrigerate.

Mustard Dressing

MAKES 250 ML/8 FL OZ/1 CUP

1 teaspoon dry mustard
250 ml/8 fl oz/1 cup low-fat yoghurt
1 tablespoon/1 tablespoon plus 1
  teaspoon Dijon mustard
1 tablespoon/1 tablespoon plus 1 teaspoon
  Tarragon Vinegar (*see* p. 144)

Mix the dry mustard with a small amount of the yoghurt until well blended. Add this to the other ingredients and mix well. Place in a jar, seal, and refrigerate.

Sesame Dressing

MAKES 200 ML/7 FL OZ/¾ CUP

125 ml/4 fl oz/½ cup light cold-pressed
  olive oil
2 tablespoons/2 tablespoons plus 2
  teaspoons lemon juice
1 tablespoon/1 tablespoon plus 1
  teaspoon sesame seeds

Combine all the ingredients and mix well. The dressing is best left in the refrigerator for 7 days before using. Shake well before use.
  Allow about a tablespoon per person.

Fruity Orange Dressing

MAKES 450 ML / 15 FL OZ / 1¾ CUPS

250 ml / 8 fl oz / 1 cup unsweetened
*   orange juice*
125 ml / 4 fl oz / ½ cup white wine
*   vinegar*
½ cucumber, peeled and seeded
2 cloves garlic
1 tablespoon / 1 tablespoon plus 1
*   teaspoon grated lemon rind*
1 tablespoon / 1 tablespoon plus 1
*   teaspoon grated orange rind*
2 tablespoons / 2 tablespoons plus 2
*   teaspoons freshly chopped herbs*
*   (e.g. parsley, basil, chives, thyme)*

Combine all the ingredients except the lemon and orange rind and fresh herbs. Blend in a food processor or blender for 1 minute. Add the other ingredients but do not blend. Place in a jar, seal, shake well and refrigerate.

Tahini Dressing

MAKES 250 ML / 8 FL OZ / 1 CUP

125 g / ¼ lb / ½ cup firm, non-oily tahini
2 tablespoons / 2 tablespoons plus 2
*   teaspoons lemon juice*
1 tablespoon / 1 tablespoon plus 1
*   teaspoon horseradish paste*
a little crushed garlic (optional)
a little water

Combine all the ingredients in a food processor or blender. Thin to the desired consistency with water.
   Allow about a tablespoon per person.

Tahini and Yoghurt Dressing

MAKES 250 ML / 8 FL OZ / 1 CUP

3 tablespoons / 3 tablespoons plus 3
*   teaspoons firm, non-oily tahini*
65 ml / 2 fl oz / ¼ cup lemon juice
1 teaspoon ground coriander
1 teaspoon curry powder
2 cloves garlic, crushed
125 ml / 4 fl oz / ½ cup low-fat yoghurt
a little finely chopped red chilli
*   (optional)*

Mix all ingredients together. This dressing is delicious when served with potatoes as a salad.

Tarragon Vinegar

MAKES 1.25 LITRES / 2¼ PINTS / 5 CUPS

60 g/2 oz/1 cup fresh tarragon leaves, washed
1.25 litres/2¼ pints/5 cups white wine vinegar
extra tarragon sprigs

Place the tarragon leaves in screw-top jars and pour the vinegar over the top. Cover, and leave to stand in the refrigerator for 2–3 weeks. Shake frequently. Strain, and pour into sterilised jars. Place a sprig of tarragon in each jar, and seal. Use as required.

Variations
- To make Herb Vinegar, substitute the tarragon leaves with 1 tablespoon/1 tablespoon plus 1 teaspoon each of freshly chopped chives, marjoram, basil and parsley.
- To make Lemon Vinegar or Orange Vinegar, substitute the finely peeled rind of 2 lemons or 2 oranges for the tarragon leaves.

Spicy Tomato Dressing

MAKES 625 ML / 1 PINT / 2½ CUPS

250 ml/8 fl oz/1 cup salt-free tomato juice
250 ml/8 fl oz/1 cup unsweetened orange juice
finely grated rind of 1 orange
65 ml/2 fl oz/¼ cup white wine vinegar
2 small cloves garlic
½ teaspoon dried oregano
½ teaspoon dried basil
dash of cayenne pepper
3 teaspoons arrowroot
1 tablespoon/1 tablespoon plus 1 teaspoon water

Combine all the ingredients except the arrowroot and water in a saucepan and slowly bring to the boil. Mix the arrowroot with the water, add to the saucepan and stir until thick. Simmer for 2 minutes. Cool, store in jars, seal, and refrigerate. Remove the garlic before using.

Vinaigrette Dressing

MAKES 350 ML / 12 FL OZ / 1½ CUPS

200 ml/7 fl oz/¾ cup unsweetened apple juice
125 ml/4 fl oz/½ cup white wine vinegar
1 teaspoon dry mustard
sprig of rosemary
6 black peppercorns
2 teaspoons grated orange rind
1 tablespoon/1 tablespoon plus 1 teaspoon lemon juice
1 tablespoon/1 tablespoon plus 1 teaspoon apple juice concentrate

Combine all the ingredients and mix well. Store in a jar, seal, and refrigerate. Shake every now and then, and remove the peppercorns before using.

VEGETABLES & VEGETABLE DISHES

Vegetables are full of nutrients, low in fats and high in fibre. An essential part of a well-balanced diet, vegetables help build a healthy immune system and assist in the prevention of disease.

Most of us have a vegetable that we love to hate: Brussels sprouts for some, parsnip, cauliflower or cabbage for others. But with simple variation in the cooking method, or the addition of herbs or a delicately flavoured sauce, such tastes can change!

To maximise the nutritional value and flavour of all vegetables, it is best to steam, parboil or stir-fry them in a little water or stock. (Avoid over-cooking vegetables. They should never be soft and colourless: this indicates too long in the pot and most of the nutrients will be in the cooking water rather than in the vegetables.) You needn't miss out on roast vegetables, either: try dry-roasting them – they're just as delicious as those cooked traditionally and are much better for you.

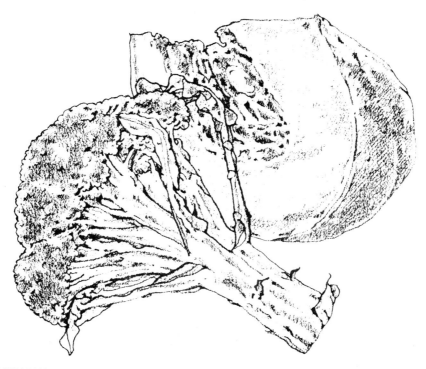

ASPARAGUS

Nutritional Information
Asparagus is a good source of vitamins C and E, iron, potassium, phosphorus and calcium.

Buying and Storing
Asparagus is available in spring and summer. Select bright-green asparagus with a thick base and tightly compressed full heads, which should snap cleanly from the base. Store in an airtight container in the refrigerator for only 2 to 3 days, and wash just before using.

Preparing and Cooking
Snap off the heads from the woody base. Trim the scales down the stem and wash in cold water. Cook the asparagus loosely or tie in bundles. Steam, or simmer in a little water or stock, until the asparagus is just tender. If serving cold, as soon as it is cooked plunge the asparagus into iced water to retain its colour. Never over-cook asparagus; it should be bright green and tender but still firm.

Asparagus with Soy and Ginger

SERVES 4–6

1 kg/2¼ lb asparagus
3 tablespoons/3 tablespoons plus
 3 teaspoons low-salt soy sauce
1 tablespoon/1 tablespoon plus
 1 teaspoon finely chopped fresh ginger

Serve as an entrée or vegetable accompaniment. Cook the asparagus until just tender. Drain and place on individual serving plates or on a large serving platter. Combine the soy sauce with the ginger, spoon over the asparagus while hot, and serve.

Asparagus with Yoghurt and Horseradish

SERVES 4–6

1 kg/2¼ lb asparagus
125 ml/4 fl oz/½ cup low-fat yoghurt
1 tablespoon/1 tablespoon plus
 1 teaspoon horseradish paste
1 tablespoon/1 tablespoon plus
 1 teaspoon toasted sesame seeds

Serve as an entrée or vegetable accompaniment. Cook the asparagus until just tender. Drain and place on individual serving plates or on a large serving platter. Combine the yoghurt with the horseradish paste, spoon over the asparagus while hot, and sprinkle with sesame seeds.

BEANS, GREEN

Nutritional Information
Green beans are a good source of vitamin C and a moderate source of vitamin A, iron, fibre, phosphorus, potassium and thiamin.

Buying and Storing
Green beans are available all year round. Select young firm beans without blemishes. Fresh beans will snap easily when broken. Store in an airtight container in the refrigerator for only 4 to 5 days, and wash just before using.

Preparing and Cooking
Top and tail and string the beans. Leave whole or cut into short lengths, or slice thinly using a special bean slicer. Cook in boiling water until just tender. Drain and serve immediately.

Beans with Basil

SERVES 4 – 6

handful of freshly chopped basil
1 kg/2¼ lb green beans, cooked
black pepper to taste

Serve as a vegetable accompaniment. Toss the basil with the cooked beans, add the black pepper, and serve.

Beans with Bean Shoots

SERVES 4 – 6

400 g/14 oz green beans
75 ml/3 fl oz/⅓ cup Chicken Stock (see p. 14)
3 sticks celery, diagonally sliced
500 g/1 lb 2 oz bean shoots
1 teaspoon finely chopped fresh dill
black pepper to taste

Slice the green beans diagonally. Heat a wok and add the Chicken Stock. As it bubbles furiously, add all the ingredients except the bean shoots. Keep the ingredients moving while they cook for 2 minutes. Add the bean shoots and cook for a further minute. Serve immediately.

Ginger Garlic Beans

SERVES 2 – 4

500 g/1 lb 2 oz green beans
1 clove garlic
2.5 cm/1" piece fresh ginger
squeeze of lemon juice
65 ml/2 fl oz/¼ cup water

Finely chop the ginger and toss it with the beans, garlic, ginger and lemon juice. Add the water. Heat a wok or large non-stick frying pan. Place the vegetables in the wok and cook for 3 to 4 minutes, stirring constantly. Serve immediately.

BEETROOT

Nutritional Information
Raw beetroot is a good source of vitamin C and potassium, and a moderate source of vitamin A.
Buying and Storing
Beetroot is available all year round. Select deep-red, firm and well-shaped beetroot. The smaller the beetroot, generally the sweeter the flavour. Remove the tops and store in an airtight container in the refrigerator for only 4 to 5 days.
Preparing and Cooking
Cut off the tops, leaving about 2.5 cm/1" of stem to avoid 'bleeding' when cooking. Clean the beetroot well and cover with boiling water. Cook until tender (insert a fine skewer to test). When cool enough to handle, remove the skin and stems. Slice or chop as desired. Serve as a hot or cold vegetable.

Beetroot tops can be cooked in the same way as spinach or silver beet and served as a vegetable to accompany a main meal; or you can tear the leaves and add to a tossed salad.

Stuffed Baked Beetroot

SERVES 4

4 beetroots
400 g/14 oz/2 cups grated apple (juice
    squeezed out)
60 g/2 oz grated onion
75 g/2½ oz/½ cup chopped celery
75 g/2½ oz/½ cup chopped capsicum
125 g/¼ lb/2 cups fresh wholemeal
    breadcrumbs
1 tablespoon/1 tablespoon plus
    1 teaspoon lemon juice
black pepper to taste

Preheat the oven to 200°C/400°F.
    Peel the beetroots. Cut away the tops and make a hollow through each beetroot using an apple corer. Mix all the ingredients and fill the hollow in each beetroot. Wrap the beetroots in foil and bake for 1 hour or until the beetroots are tender, in a baking dish containing water.

Sweet Cinnamon Beetroot

SERVES 4

8 baby beetroots
250 ml/8 fl oz/1 cup unsweetened
    orange juice
2 tablespoons/2 tablespoons plus
    2 teaspoons finely grated orange rind
1–2 teaspoons ground cinnamon
125 ml/4 fl oz/½ cup water

Wash the beetroots and place in a saucepan. Cover with the orange juice and add the rind and cinnamon. If there is not enough liquid, add the water. Gently simmer for 1 hour or until the beetroots are tender. Add more water if necessary during the cooking. Peel and serve immediately.

Beetroot in Orange Sauce

SERVES 4

250 ml/8 fl oz/1 cup unsweetened
    orange juice
2 tablespoons/2 tablespoons plus
    2 teaspoons tarragon vinegar
2 tablespoons/2 tablespoons plus
    2 teaspoons fine strips orange rind
1 tablespoon/1 tablespoon plus
    1 teaspoon cornflour
65 ml/2 fl oz/¼ cup dry white wine
4 beetroots, cooked and peeled

Place the orange juice, vinegar and orange rind in a saucepan and bring to the boil. Mix the cornflour with the white wine and add to the orange liquid. Simmer gently until thickened. Scoop into the beetroots with a melon baller to make small balls. Add the beetroot balls to the orange sauce, heat through and serve immediately.

Variation
■ Instead of making beetroot balls, add whole baby beetroots to the orange sauce. (See colour plate opposite page 160.)

BROCCOLI

Nutritional Information
Broccoli is a good source of vitamins A, C and E, and folic acid. It is a moderate source of fibre, calcium and iron.

Buying and Storing

Broccoli is available all year round. Select compact dark-green or purplish-green heads free from any yellowing, with tender stalks. Store, unwashed, in an airtight container in the refrigerator for only 1 to 2 days.

Preparing and Cooking

Wash thoroughly before cooking. Trim the stems and break into equal-sized florets. Broccoli needs to be cooked gently for a short time, to retain its bright-green colour and subtle flavour. Boiling reduces the vegetable's vitamin C by two-thirds. Serve immediately. If using cold, refresh in iced water and drain.

Broccoli with Mustard Sauce

SERVES 2–4

250 ml/8 fl oz/1 cup White Sauce *(see p. 239)*
1 teaspoon hot English mustard
1 teaspoon wholegrain mustard
500 g/1 lb 2 oz broccoli florets, cooked

Make the White Sauce and add, a teaspoon at a time, the two mustards combined until the desired taste is achieved. Pour over the cooked broccoli before serving.

BRUSSELS SPROUTS

Nutritional Information

Brussels sprouts are a good source of vitamins A and C. They are a moderate source of fibre, phosphorus, iron and folic acid.

Buying and Storing

Brussels sprouts are available all year round but are best in winter. Select bright-green, firm and compact sprouts. Avoid any yellowing or wilted leaves, which is a sign of old age and poor quality. The smaller ones have the best flavour. Store in an airtight container in the refrigerator for up to 7 days.

Preparing and Cooking

Thoroughly wash before cooking, remove any loose bottom leaves and trim the stem. Score the stem with a cross to allow heat to penetrate. Gently boil or steam until just tender. Add some finely chopped fresh ginger to the cooking water for a refreshing flavour. Do not over-cook, or the vegetable develops a sulphur smell and becomes unpalatable.

Serving Suggestions

■ Toss in some finely chopped fresh herbs such as oregano, chives, parsley, basil and dill.
■ Add a pinch of spice such as ground cummin, nutmeg, allspice, ginger or coriander.
■ Sprinkle with toasted sesame seeds.
■ Sprinkle with poppyseeds.

CABBAGE

Nutritional Information

Cabbage is a good source of vitamins C (especially when raw) and A, calcium, phosphorus, potassium and iron. Small amounts of vitamins B and K are present in green cabbage. Green and red cabbage are more nutritious than white.

Buying and Storing

Cabbage is available all year round but there are more varieties to choose from in winter. Select from different varieties (round smooth head, pointed head, savoy, red and Chinese) and choose firm, crisp cabbage, vibrant in colour, with a clear sweet smell. The leaves should break away with a snap. Store in an airtight container in the refrigerator for up to 7 days.

Preparing and Cooking

Remove the outer hard or discoloured leaves. Cut the portions to be cooked and leave whole or slice thinly. Boil or steam the cabbage, but do not over-cook. You can add some thinly sliced Granny Smith apples to the saucepan for a combination of sweet apple and cabbage. When cooked, sprinkle with caraway seeds. Another cooking idea is to add a piece of fresh ginger to the saucepan and remove before serving.

Serving Suggestions

- Cover the cabbage with White Sauce (see page 239) mixed with a little curry powder or freshly chopped dill.
- Pour a mixture of low-salt soy sauce and crushed garlic over the cabbage before serving.

CAPSICUMS

Nutritional Information

Capsicums are a good source of vitamins A and C, potassium, phosphorus, calcium, niacin and iron.

Buying and Storing

Capsicums are available all year round. Select well-shaped, vibrant-coloured, firm capsicums without blemishes. Store in an airtight container in the refrigerator for up to 12 days.

Preparing and Cooking

Wash the capsicums, slice in half lengthwise and remove the seeds. Capsicums can be stuffed and then baked in the oven, or cut into rings, strips, chunky pieces or dice and steamed or grilled.

Roasted Capsicum

SERVES 4–6

2 red capsicums
2 green capsicums
2 yellow capsicums
a little balsamic vinegar
black pepper to taste

Serve as a vegetable accompaniment. Cut the capsicums in half lengthwise and remove the seeds. Place outside uppermost on a baking tray and cook under a grill until the outside skin of the capsicum turns black. Remove from the oven and stand, covered, for 10 minutes to cool. Peel off the skin and cut the capsicum into long strips. Place on a platter and pour the balsamic vinegar over the top. Season with black pepper.

Capsicums in Sherry

SERVES 4–6

2 red capsicums
2 yellow capsicums
125 ml/4 fl oz/½ cup dry sherry
a little freshly chopped thyme

Cut the capsicums in half lengthwise and remove the seeds. Cut into long strips. Place in a shallow saucepan, add the sherry, and cover. Cook the capsicum gently until soft. Sprinkle the thyme over the capsicum before serving.

CARROTS

Nutritional Information
Carrots are a good source of vitamin A (high in beta-carotene) and a moderate source of vitamin C, fibre, phosphorus, calcium and potassium.
Buying and Storing
Carrots are available all year round but are best in spring. Select brightly coloured, firm carrots. Store in an airtight container in the refrigerator for up to 7 days.
Preparing and Cooking
Wash the carrots with a scrubbing brush. Do not peel, as most nutrients are just beneath the surface. Remove the green tops and leave whole, cut into rings or julienne strips or dice. Lightly boil or steam until just tender.

Carrots with Cummin and Pine Nuts

SERVES 4 – 6

500 g/1 lb 2 oz carrots, cut into rings
1 teaspoon ground cummin
2 tablespoons/2 tablespoons plus
  2 teaspoons toasted pine nuts

Cook the carrot rings until tender. Add the cummin and toasted pine nuts, and serve hot.

Note
Toast pine nuts in a non-stick frying pan, taking care to keep the pan moving over the heat while the nuts colour.

Whole Carrots with Honey and Nutmeg

SERVES 2 – 4

500 g/1 lb 2 oz baby carrots
2 teaspoons honey or *apple juice*
  concentrate
dash of ground nutmeg

Cook the carrots until tender. Drizzle the honey over the top and add the nutmeg. Serve hot.

Whole Carrots with Honey and Sesame

SERVES 4 – 6

500 g/1 lb 2 oz baby carrots
1 teaspoon honey
1 tablespoon/1 tablespoon plus
  1 teaspoon freshly squeezed orange
  juice
1 tablespoon/1 tablespoon plus
  1 teaspoon toasted sesame seeds

Cook the carrots until tender. Drizzle the honey over the top. Add the orange juice and toasted sesame seeds, and serve hot.

Lemon Mint Carrots

SERVES 4 – 6

500 g/1 lb 2 oz carrots
175 ml/6 fl oz/⅔ cup Chicken Stock
  (see p. 14)
1 tablespoon/1 tablespoon plus
  1 teaspoon finely chopped fresh mint
juice of ½ lemon

Cut the carrots into julienne strips. Simmer the carrot strips gently in the Chicken Stock and then drain. Squeeze the lemon juice and sprinkle the mint over the top. Stand for 5 minutes before serving.

Whole Carrots with Peas and Mint

SERVES 4 – 6

500 g/1 lb 2 oz baby carrots
350 g/¾ lb/3 cups peas
2 tablespoons/2 tablespoons plus
  2 teaspoons finely chopped fresh mint
2 tablespoons/2 tablespoons plus
  2 teaspoons freshly squeezed orange
  juice

Cook the whole baby carrots until tender. Cook the peas until tender. Combine the vegetables and add the mint and orange juice. Serve hot.

CAULIFLOWER

Nutritional Information
Cauliflower is a good source of vitamin C (especially when raw) and folic acid. It is a moderate source of iron, fibre, calcium and phosphorus.

Buying and Storing
Cauliflower is available all year round but is best in winter. The 'curd' of the cauliflower should be firm with compact white or creamy white heads. Loose, open-flowered clusters are a sign that the vegetable is over-mature. Remove the outer green leaves and store in an airtight container in the refrigerator for up to 6 days.

Preparing and Cooking
Wash thoroughly to remove insects and grubs. Lightly boil or steam the cauliflower whole or break into equal-sized florets. The vegetable is excellent raw combined with other salad ingredients.

Cauliflower with Soy and Ginger

SERVES 4 – 6

500 g/1 lb 2 oz cauliflower
2 tablespoons/2 tablespoons plus
  2 teaspoons low-salt soy sauce
2 teaspoons finely chopped fresh ginger

Cut the cauliflower into florets and steam them. Drain, add the soy sauce and the ginger, and serve hot.

Cauliflorets

SERVES 4–6

500 g/1 lb 2 oz cauliflower
large handful finely chopped fresh mint
125 ml/4 fl oz/½ cup white wine
  vinegar
125 ml/4 fl oz/½ cup unsweetened
  orange juice
black pepper to taste

Cut the cauliflower into florets, steam and drain. Combine all the other ingredients in a bowl and add the florets. Toss lightly (be careful not to break up the florets). Refrigerate for at least 2 hours. Drain and serve on a serving dish. (See colour plate opposite page 160.)

Cauliflower in Sesame Sauce

SERVES 4–6

500 g/1 lb 2 oz cauliflower
500 ml/16 fl oz/2 cups White Sauce
  (see p. 239)
60 g/2 oz/¼ cup sesame seeds

Preheat the oven to 200°C/400°F.

Cut the cauliflower into florets, lightly steam, and drain. Make the White Sauce. Toast the sesame seeds under the grill. Place the cauliflower pieces in a serving dish, cover with the White Sauce and sprinkle the sesame seeds over the top. Cook in the oven for 10 minutes, and serve.

Variation

- Substitute 30 g/1 oz/½ cup of toasted shredded coconut for the sesame seeds.

CELERY

Nutritional Information
Celery is a moderate source of vitamins A and C, calcium, phosphorus, sodium, potassium and fibre.
Buying and Storing
Celery is available all year round. Select a compact bunch of celery with good green colouring. It may be a lighter green towards the centre. The stalks should snap cleanly and crisply when broken, indicating peak freshness. Store, without washing, in an airtight container in the refrigerator for up to 10 days.
Preparing and Cooking
Remove the leaves (keep and add to soups or vegetable juices) and strings. Wash the celery and cut into diagonal slices (as for Chinese cooking), long strips or dice. The vegetable is excellent served raw or lightly steamed with White Sauce (see page 239).

CORN

Nutritional Information
Corn is a good source of vitamin C, fibre, phosphorus, folic acid, thiamin and niacin. It has a higher protein and vitamin B content than most vegetables.
Buying and Storing
Corn is available all year round but is best in autumn and summer. Select corn with the fresh green

husk still attached. The silk threads under the husk layer should feel damp and the corn kernels when pricked should squirt out a whitish milk. When you remove the husks the sugar content in corn changes to starch, resulting in a poorer taste; so remove them just before cooking. Store in an airtight container in the refrigerator for only 2 days.

Preparing and Cooking
Before cooking, remove the husks and silk threads. Place the corn in iced water 1 hour before cooking. Drain and add to a saucepan of boiling water. Cook the corn until just tender, and serve immediately.

Corn Fritters

SERVES 6

575 g/1¼ lb/2 cups cooked corn
1 onion, finely chopped
3 egg whites
65 ml/2 fl oz/¼ cup skim milk
125 g/¼ lb/1 cup wholemeal plain flour
½ teaspoon paprika
1 teaspoon baking powder
black pepper to taste

Combine all the ingredients. Drop spoonfuls into a non-stick frying pan. Cook for 3 minutes and turn over to brown the other side. Serve with chicken drumsticks and salad.

Corn and Potato Bake

SERVES 4

125 g/¼ lb/2 cups fresh wholemeal
    breadcrumbs
4 large potatoes, peeled, parboiled and
    sliced
500 g/1 lb 2 oz/2 cups low-fat ricotta
    cheese
black pepper to taste
1.25 kg/2¾ lb/4 cups cooked corn
60 g/2 oz/½ cup grated low-fat grating
    cheese

Preheat the oven to 200°C/400°F.
   Spread 60 g/2 oz/1 cup of the breadcrumbs over the base of an ovenproof dish. Top with a layer of potato. Combine the ricotta cheese, black pepper and corn, and mix well. Spread a small amount over the potato. Top with another layer of potato and continue with alternate layers of corn mixture and potato until they are used up. Combine the grated cheese and remaining breadcrumbs and spread over the top of the casserole. Bake for 30–40 minutes or until golden brown.

EGGPLANT

Nutritional Information
Eggplant is a good source of vitamin C and a moderate source of potassium, iron, niacin and folic acid.

Buying and Storing
Eggplant is available all year round. Select firm eggplant of a rich purple–black colour. The soft wrinkled ones are usually bitter and not so tasty. Store in an airtight container in the refrigerator for up to 7 days.

Preparing and Cooking
Eggplant can be baked whole in the oven, or sliced or finely chopped and cooked in a frying pan. As soon as it is cut, eggplant begins to discolour, so do not leave it standing. To remove bitterness

fro... ...stand for 30 minutes. Rinse the salt
off ... ...you can simply parboil slices in boiling
wat... ...greased non-stick frying pan until brown
on ...

If ... ...slice it in half lengthwise when cooled and
scoo... ...and a sauce and refill the eggplant shell. Top
with ... ...cheese and return it to the oven. Bake until it
is ho...

Vari...

- Cook slices of eggpla... ...ith White Sauce (see page 239) to which you have added a little curry powder.
- Cook slices of eggplant as abo... ...e hot, topped with grated low-fat grating cheese, fresh herbs such as parsley, chives and b... ...d a dash of paprika.
- Serve ratatouille in a baked eggplant s... ...l, top with breadcrumbs and grated low-fat grating cheese, and bake until the cheese is brown.

LEEKS

Nutritional Information
Leeks are a good source of vitamin C, iron and fibre.

Buying and Storing
Leeks are available in winter. Small leeks are full of flavour. Look for green tops without yellowing and a firm white base. Trim the tops off and store in an airtight container in the refrigerator for up to 5 days.

Preparing and Cooking
Layers of the bulb collect soil in the growing process, so wash under cold running water thoroughly before cooking. Leeks can be poached whole in a little wine or stock and served with a white sauce, or sliced into rounds or chopped and used in soups, casseroles or quiches.

Leek Casserole

SERVES 4

6 leeks, thoroughly washed
200 g/7 oz/2 cups celery, cut into chunks
225 g/½ lb/2 cups carrot, cut into chunks
225 g/½ lb/2 cups potato, peeled and cut into chunks
1.5 litres/2½ pints/6 cups Chicken Stock (see p. 14)
425 g/15 oz canned whole tomatoes in natural juice, salt-free
black pepper to taste or 4 black peppercorns
large handful of freshly chopped parsley
a little cornflour (optional)

Trim the roots from the leeks and discard most of the green tops. Split the leeks in half lengthwise then cut into chunks. Add the leek, celery, carrot and potato to the Chicken Stock. Simmer for 20 minutes or until the vegetables are tender. Place in a casserole dish. Add the tomatoes and juice, pepper and parsley. Cover, and cook for 30 minutes. If desired, thicken with a little cornflour mixed with some of the cooled liquid.

ONIONS

Nutritional Information

Onions are a good source of vitamin C.

Buying and Storing

Onions fall into one of two categories: dry and green. Dry onions are left in the ground to mature; this produces a vegetable suitable for storing. The varieties included in this category are the white, brown, Spanish red and yellow, red globe and pickling onions. The green onion is an immature onion that has been removed from the ground when the top is green and before the bulb has formed (for example, spring onions). Onions are available all year round but are best in summer and autumn.

When buying dry onions select those that are firm and have dry, crisp skins. Do not buy onions that have sprouted; they are already beginning to lose their goodness and flavour. Keep onions in a cool dry place away from other vegetables. Look for firm, plump spring onions; these should be kept in the refrigerator.

Preparing and Cooking

Whole onions can be baked, roasted, barbecued or steamed with or without skins. They can be sliced or chopped and cooked gently until tender. For a richer stock, leave brown skins on onions when you add them.

Braised Onions

SERVES 4–6

4–6 onions, sliced
125 ml/4 fl oz/½ cup sherry or Beef
  Stock (see p. 15)
finely chopped fresh parsley
1 bay leaf
finely chopped fresh thyme
sprigs of thyme for garnishing

Place the onion in a shallow saucepan and cook gently over a low heat until transparent (as the onion contains its own oil, there is no need to add oil or butter – simply add a little water if it begins to stick). Add the sherry, parsley, bay leaf and thyme. Cover, and cook over the lowest heat for 20 minutes. Remove the bay leaf before serving. Serve garnished with the sprigs of thyme.

PARSNIPS

Nutritional Information

Parsnips are a good source of vitamin C and a moderate source of vitamin E, calcium, phosphorus and thiamin.

Buying and Storing

Parsnips are available all year but are best in winter. Select small firm parsnips for the best flavour. Large ones tend to be woody at the core. Store in an airtight container in the refrigerator for up to 10 days.

Preparing and Cooking

Wash the parsnips with a scrubbing brush. Do not peel, as most nutrients are just beneath the surface. Parsnips combine well with the flavour of carrot. They can be lightly boiled, steamed or baked.

Variations

■ Cut julienne strips of parsnip and carrot and cook together until tender. Drain and add a pinch of ground nutmeg.

■ Chop parsnip and cook until just tender. Drain. Squeeze the juice of half a lemon on top just before serving.

■ Toss cooked rounds of parsnip in poppyseeds before serving.

PEAS

×××

Nutritional Information
Peas are a good source of vitamin A and C, phosphorus, iron, potassium, thiamin and fibre. They are a moderate source of calcium and folic acid.

Buying and Storing
Peas are available in spring, summer and autumn. Select bright-green well-filled pods. The best way to determine their freshness is to taste them. The peas should be free of wrinkles and blemishes and taste sweet. Yellowing of the pod indicates over-maturity. Store peas in their pods in an airtight container in the refrigerator for up to 4 days.

Preparing and Cooking
Shell the peas, place in boiling water and cook for 5 minutes or until tender (they need minimum cooking). You can add some fresh mint leaves to the water for extra flavour.

Chilli Peas

×××

SERVES 4 – 6

2 teaspoons finely chopped chilli
2 teaspoons finely chopped fresh ginger
500 g / 1 lb 2 oz cooked peas

Cook the chilli in a lightly greased non-stick frying pan until soft. Add the ginger and the cooked peas. Toss until the peas are heated through.

Peas and Corn

×××

SERVES 4 – 6

225 g / ½ lb / 2 cups cooked peas
225 g / ½ lb / 2 cups cooked corn kernels
handful of finely chopped fresh chives
handful of finely chopped fresh basil

Combine the peas and corn kernels, season with the chives and basil, and serve.

Mint Peas

×××

SERVES 4

125 ml / 4 fl oz / ½ cup Chicken Stock
 (see p. 14)
several lettuce leaves
500 g / 1 lb 2 oz / 4 cups peas
125 g / ¼ lb / 1 cup chopped shallots
handful of freshly chopped mint

Pour the Chicken Stock into a shallow saucepan. Place enough lettuce leaves on the base of the saucepan to hold the peas so that they do not actually come into contact with the stock. Add the peas, shallots and mint. Cover, and cook over a medium heat, shaking occasionally, until the peas are tender.

POTATOES

Nutritional Information
Potatoes are a good source of vitamins A and C, phosphorus, iron, thiamin, niacin, potassium, and fibre if the skin is eaten.

Buying and Storing
There are several varieties of potato that are available at different times throughout the year, the most popular being the Pontiac and the Robinson. Select firm, well-shaped potatoes free of blemishes and sprouts. Green potatoes have a bitter taste and if eaten in large amounts can cause illness. Do not wash potatoes before storing. Keep in a cool, dark place. Old potatoes can be kept for several months; new potatoes for several weeks.

Preparing and Cooking
Scrub the potatoes with a soft brush and leave the skin on to retain nutrients and fibre, or keep peelings as thin as possible. Do not soak potatoes. Lightly boil, steam, or dry-bake in a hot oven.

Baked Peeled Potatoes

SERVES 4

4 large or 8 small potatoes

Preheat the oven to 230°C/450°F.

Wash and peel the potatoes. With a sharp knife, cut 10 diagonal slits across the top of each large potato, 5 across each small one. Place the potatoes on a non-stick baking tray and bake for 40 minutes or until the potatoes are crisp and lightly browned. Serve immediately. (See left colour plate between pages 208 and 209.)

Baked Potatoes with Bolognese Sauce

SERVES 4

4 large unpeeled potatoes, washed
*500 ml/16 fl oz/2 cups Bolognese Sauce
(see* Spaghetti Bolognese, *p. 119)*
*100 g/3½ oz/1 cup low-fat cottage
cheese*

Preheat the oven to 200°C/400°F.

Place the potatoes on the oven rack and bake until the outside is crunchy and the centre is soft, approximately 1 hour.

Remove the potatoes from the oven, open at the top and fill with Bolognese Sauce (an ideal way to use up the left-over sauce from spaghetti). Top with the cottage cheese. Serve with a salad.

Baked Potatoes with Cheese and Beans

SERVES 4

4 large unpeeled potatoes, washed
*125 g/¼ lb/1 cup finely chopped spring
onion*
*310 g/10½ oz/1 cup any combination of
beans (e.g. kidney beans, butter beans,
garbanzo beans, lima beans), cooked*
*125 g/¼ lb/1 cup grated low-fat grating
cheese*

Preheat the oven to 200°C/400°F.

Place the potatoes on the oven rack and bake until the outside is crunchy and the centre is soft, approximately 1 hour.

Remove the potatoes from the oven, open at the top and fill with the spring onion and bean mixture. Top with the grated cheese and serve with a salad.

Baked Potatoes with Cheesy Capsicum

SERVES 4

4 large unpeeled potatoes, washed
225 g / ½ lb / 1 cup low-fat cottage cheese
125 g / ¼ lb / 1 cup grated low-fat grating cheese
75 g / 2½ oz / ½ cup chopped green capsicum
75 g / 2½ oz / ½ cup chopped red capsicum

Preheat the oven to 200°C/400°F.

Place the potatoes on the oven rack and bake until the outside is crunchy and the centre is soft, approximately 1 hour.

Remove the potatoes from the oven, cut open at the top and fill with a mixture of the cheeses and capsicum. Serve with a salad.

Baked Potatoes with Mushroom Sauce

SERVES 4

4 large unpeeled potatoes, washed
250 ml / 8 fl oz / 1 cup Mushroom Sauce *(see p. 237)*
60 g / 2 oz / 1 cup fresh wholemeal breadcrumbs

Preheat the oven to 200°C/400°F.

Place the potatoes on the oven rack and bake until the outside is crunchy and the centre is soft, approximately 1 hour.

Remove the potatoes from the oven and cut open at the top. Scoop out the potato and chop roughly. Combine with the Mushroom Sauce and fill the potatoes with the mixture. Top with the breadcrumbs. Serve with a salad.

Baked Potatoes with Salmon Dip

SERVES 4

4 large unpeeled potatoes, washed
alfalfa sprouts

Salmon Dip
425 g / 15 oz well-drained salmon
200 g / 7 oz / ¾ cup low-fat cottage cheese
3 tablespoons / 3 tablespoons plus 3 teaspoons salt-free tomato paste
1 tablespoon / 1 tablespoon plus 1 teaspoon lemon juice
black pepper to taste
3 shallots, finely chopped (optional)

Preheat the oven to 200°C/400°F.

Place the potatoes on the oven rack and bake until the outside is crunchy and the centre is soft, approximately 1 hour.

Combine all the Salmon Dip ingredients, except the shallots, in a food processor or blender, and blend until smooth. Fold in the chopped shallots.

Remove the potatoes from the oven and cut open at the top. Scoop out the potato and chop roughly. Combine with the dip and fill the potatoes with the mixture. Top with alfalfa sprouts and serve.

This dip is also good served with vegetable crudités, in sandwiches, or, with lots of grated vegetables, as a filling for lettuce cups.

Filled Baked Potatoes

SERVES 4

4 large potatoes

Ricotta Cheese and Chive Filling
2 tablespoons/2 tablespoons plus
  2 teaspoons low-fat ricotta cheese
2 teaspoons finely chopped fresh chives
black pepper to taste
1 egg white

Tomato Filling
2 teaspoons tomato purée
½ teaspoon dried basil
¼ teaspoon black pepper
1 tomato, skinned, seeded and chopped
1 egg white

Shrimp Filling
30 g/1 oz shelled shrimps
4 spring onions, finely chopped
½ teaspoon grated lemon rind
½ teaspoon finely chopped parsley
¼ teaspoon cayenne pepper
1 egg white

Preheat the oven to 200°C/400°F.

Bake the potatoes in their jackets until tender when pierced with a skewer. Slice the top off each potato and scoop out the inside, but leave a firm casing to be filled. Be careful not to pierce the skin. Combine the potato flesh from the potatoes with the filling of your choice and pack into the empty casings. Return the potatoes to the oven and bake for 10–15 minutes or until the tops are golden brown. (See colour plate opposite.)

Apple Filling
30 g/1 oz/¼ cup finely grated low-fat
  grating cheese
1 small apple, grated (juice squeezed out)
¼ teaspoon Dijon mustard

Celery and Walnut Filling
2 tablespoons/2 tablespoons plus
  2 teaspoons low-fat ricotta cheese
40 g/1½ oz/¼ cup finely chopped celery
2 tablespoons/2 tablespoons plus
  2 teaspoons finely chopped walnuts
black pepper to taste

Jacket Potatoes

SERVES 4

4 large potatoes
freshly ground black pepper
125 g/¼ lb/½ cup low-fat cottage
  cheese
handful of freshly chopped chives

Preheat the oven to 230°C/450°F.

Scrub the potatoes clean, leaving the skins on. Prick each potato in several places with a skewer and place in a piece of foil. Grind the pepper over the top and secure the foil tightly. Cook for 40 minutes or until the potatoes are soft. Remove from the foil. Squeeze an opening in the top of each potato. Mix the cottage cheese and chives and fill the openings.

Cauliflorets (page 153); Beetroot in Orange Sauce (page 148); baked tomatoes (page 164); Filled Baked Potatoes (opposite page); Zucchini Boats (page 166).

Vegetarian Chili con Carne (page 266).

Baked Potatoes with Salmon Horseradish

SERVES 4

4 large unpeeled potatoes, washed
alfalfa sprouts

Salmon Horseradish
125 g/¼ lb canned red salmon
2 tablespoons/2 tablespoons plus
*   2 teaspoons non-fat or low-fat*
*   yoghurt*
2 tablespoons/2 tablespoons plus
*   2 teaspoons horseradish paste*
squeeze of lemon juice

Preheat the oven to 200°C/400°F.

Place the potatoes on the oven rack and bake until the outside is crunchy and the centre is soft, approximately 1 hour.

In a bowl combine all the ingredients for the Salmon Horseradish. Mix thoroughly.

Remove the potatoes from the oven and cut open at the top. Scoop out the potato and chop roughly. Combine with the dip and fill the potatoes with the mixture. Top with alfalfa sprouts and serve.

Baked Potatoes with Waldorf Salad

SERVES 4

4 large unpeeled potatoes, washed
75 g/2½ oz chopped celery
75 g/2½ oz chopped apple
60 g/2 oz/½ cup chopped walnuts
2 tablespoons/2 tablespoons plus
*   2 teaspoons Soymilk Mayonnaise*
*   (see p. 139)*
225 g/½ lb/1 cup low-fat cottage cheese
100 g/3½ oz/1 cup grated low-fat
*   grating cheese*

Preheat the oven to 200°C/400°F.

Place the potatoes on the oven rack and bake until the outside is crunchy and the centre is soft, approximately 1 hour.

In a bowl combine the celery, apple and walnuts and mix together with a little Soymilk Mayonnaise.

Remove the potatoes from the oven, open at the top and fill with the fruit and nut mixture. Top with the cottage cheese and grating cheese, and serve with a salad.

Creamy Mashed Potato

SERVES 4

6 potatoes, peeled
200 ml/7 fl oz/¾ cup skim milk
black pepper to taste
2 tablespoons/2 tablespoons plus
*   2 teaspoons chopped chives*
1 tablespoon/1 tablespoon plus
*   1 teaspoon roughly chopped walnuts*
*   (optional)*

Steam the potatoes until just tender. Drain and place in a food processor or blender. Add the skim milk and blend to the desired consistency. Add more skim milk if necessary. Add the black pepper and chives. If you wish, add the chopped walnuts for a nutty flavour.

Scalloped Potatoes

SERVES 4

*4 large potatoes, parboiled and sliced
    into rounds*
*1 tablespoon/1 tablespoon plus
    1 teaspoon wholemeal plain flour*
freshly ground black pepper
250 ml/8 fl oz/1 cup warm milk
*100 g/3½ oz/1 cup grated low-fat
    grating cheese*
a little ground nutmeg

Preheat the oven to 230°C/450°F.

Place a layer of potato in a shallow casserole dish. Sprinkle with a little flour and grind some pepper on top. Continue the layers until all the potato and flour are used. Cover with the milk. Top with the cheese. Bake until the cheese has browned. Sprinkle the nutmeg over the top before serving.

PUMPKIN

Nutritional Information
Pumpkin is a good source of vitamin A and a moderate source of vitamin C, folic and pantothenic acid.

Buying and Storing
Most varieties of pumpkin are available all year round. Popular varieties include the butternut, golden nugget, Queensland blue, Windsor black and the blue Max. Select firm, unblemished pumpkins. Store whole pumpkins in a cool, dark place, and cut pumpkins in an airtight container in the refrigerator for up to 7 days.

Preparing and Cooking
Pumpkin can be cooked in various ways. It is delicious if lightly boiled, mashed and seasoned with freshly ground black pepper or nutmeg and freshly chopped chives. Before steaming pumpkin remove the skin and seeds; the skin can be left on if you are using the dry-roasting method. Pumpkins can also be baked whole and the soft flesh scooped out of the hard shell after cooking.

Pumpkin au Gratin

SERVES 4

*500 g/1 lb 2 oz pumpkin, peeled and
    sliced*
freshly ground black pepper
dash of ground nutmeg
¼ teaspoon ground cloves
3 egg whites
65 ml/2 fl oz/¼ cup skim milk
*65 ml/2 fl oz/¼ cup non-fat or low-fat
    yoghurt*
*60 g/2 oz/½ cup finely grated low-fat
    grating cheese*

Preheat the oven to 230°C/450°F.

Boil the pumpkin until tender and drain. Combine with the pepper, nutmeg and cloves. Place in an ovenproof casserole dish. Beat the egg whites, skim milk, yoghurt and half the grated cheese. Pour over the pumpkin. Sprinkle the remaining cheese over the top. Bake for 15–20 minutes.

SANDWICHES, PIZZAS, PITAS & SAVOURY SNACKS

One of the simplest, healthiest meals I can think of is a sandwich made with two slices of wholegrain or oat-bran bread and lots of salad ingredients.

Most people are amazed when they realise the equivalent kilojoule value of one sausage roll is two rather large rounds of salad sandwiches. Even though the kilojoule value of the sausage roll is high, most people would not feel satisfied with only one.

There are lots of interesting healthy breads available today. Look for the salt-free or low-salt varieties and those that are low in fats.

There are also alternatives to traditional breads, such as pita breads. For healthy snacks, make savoury muffins (see Breads, Cereals, Muffins & Scones, page 211) or pizza bases with wholesome ingredients.

Mushroom Mini Pies

xxxxxxxxxxxxxxxxxxxxxxxxxxxxxxxxxxxxxxxxxxxxxxxxxxxxxxxxxxxxxxxxxxxxxxxxxxxxx

MAKES 6

6 slices wholemeal bread
125 g/¼ lb/1 cup finely chopped
  mushrooms
150 g/5 oz/¾ cup finely grated zucchini
125 g/¼ lb/1 cup tomatoes, skinned and
  finely chopped
2 tablespoons/2 tablespoons plus
  2 teaspoons finely chopped fresh
  parsley
1 teaspoon dried oregano
1 teaspoon dried basil
3 egg whites
125 ml/4 fl oz/½ cup non-fat or low-
  fat yoghurt
125 g/¼ lb/1 cup grated low-fat grating
  cheese

Preheat the oven to 200°C/400°F.

Lightly grease six small pie plates. Roll the bread slices out flat using a rolling pin. Use scissors to cut out circles to fit in the pie plates. Press into the plates and trim the edges with the scissors.

Combine the mushroom, zucchini, tomato and herbs.

Beat the egg whites and add the yoghurt. Fold the cheese into the egg mixture and add the mushroom mixture. Spoon into the pie plates. Use the bread scraps to make breadcrumbs and sprinkle on top.

Cook for 15 minutes and then turn the oven down to 180°C/350°F and cook for a further 15 minutes. Serve hot or cold. (See colour plate opposite.)

Alfalfa, Celery, Walnut and Fish Pita

xxxxxxxxxxxxxxxxxxxxxxxxxxxxxxxxxxxxxxxxxxxxxxxxxxxxxxxxxxxxxxxxxxxxxxxxxxxxx

FILLS ½ PITA

60 g/2 oz/¼ cup cooked flaked fish
  fillet, chilled
handful of alfalfa sprouts
2 tablespoons/2 tablespoons plus
  2 teaspoons sliced celery
2–3 walnuts, roughly chopped
½ small wholemeal pita bread
dressing of your choice

Combine all the ingredients, except the pita bread, and add a little dressing of your choice. Spoon the mixture into the pocket of the pita.

Beetroot and Mushroom Pita

xxxxxxxxxxxxxxxxxxxxxxxxxxxxxxxxxxxxxxxxxxxxxxxxxxxxxxxxxxxxxxxxxxxxxxxxxxxxx

FILLS ½ PITA

40 g/1½ oz/¼ cup grated beetroot
  (juice squeezed out)
30 g/1 oz/¼ cup shredded lettuce
2–3 mushrooms, sliced
2–3 slices cucumber
½ small wholemeal pita bread
a little freshly chopped dill
black pepper to taste

Combine all the vegetables and spoon into the pocket of the pita. Sprinkle the dill and pepper on top of the mixture.

Mushroom Mini Pie (opposite page).

Top to bottom: Mushroom Pizza, Hawaiian Pizza and Vegetarian Pizza (page 172).

Health sandwich (pages 170–171).

*Pita pockets (pages 168–70) with vegetables
and poached meat balls.*

Carrot, Apple and Pecan Nut Pita

FILLS ½ PITA

40 g/1½ oz/¼ cup grated carrot
30 g/1 oz/¼ cup grated low-fat grating
  cheese
60 g/2 oz/¼ cup finely chopped apple
2–3 pecan nuts, roughly chopped
black pepper to taste
½ small wholemeal pita bread

Combine all the ingredients, except the pita bread, and spoon into the pocket of the pita.

Chicken and Cucumber Pita

FILLS ½ PITA

60 g/2 oz/¼ cup chopped cooked
  chicken
30 g/1 oz/¼ cup shredded lettuce
2 tablespoons/2 tablespoons plus
  2 teaspoons chopped cucumber
1 tablespoon/1 tablespoon plus
  1 teaspoon chopped spring onion
½ small wholemeal pita bread

Remove all the skin and fat from the chicken before cooking. Combine all the ingredients, except the pita bread, and spoon into the pocket of the pita.

Chilli Bean Salad on Pita

SERVES 6

6 small wholemeal pita breads
½ lettuce, shredded
6–8 tomatoes
1 quantity Chilli Beans (see Stuffed
  Zucchini, *p. 58)*
thin strips carrot for garnishing
alfalfa sprouts for garnishing

Top the pita breads with shredded lettuce. Cut the tomatoes into quarters, remove the seeds and cut each quarter into four thin strips. Make a circle of strips around the outside edge of the pita breads. Top with hot or cold Chilli Beans. Garnish with the carrot and alfalfa sprouts.

Sardine Pita

FILLS 1 PITA

1 small wholemeal pita bread
75 g/2½ oz sardines, drained
squeeze of lemon juice
60 g/2 oz/½ cup shredded lettuce
8 slices cucumber
40 g/1½ oz/¼ cup grated carrot
alfalfa sprouts for garnishing

Split the pita bread into two rounds. Squeeze the lemon juice over the sardines. Spread the sardines over one piece of the pita. Top with the remaining ingredients and then cover with the other half of the pita.

Zucchini, Carrot and Mushroom Pita

FILLS ½ PITA

60 g/2 oz/¼ cup grated zucchini (juice
  squeezed out)
40 g/1½ oz/¼ cup grated carrot
30 g/1 oz/¼ cup finely sliced mushroom
a little freshly chopped basil
a little freshly chopped parsley
a few sesame seeds
½ small wholemeal pita bread

Combine all the ingredients, except the pita bread, and spoon into the pocket of the pita.

Cottage Cheese and Banana Sandwich

SERVES 1

125 g/¼ lb/½ cup low-fat cottage
  cheese
1 tablespoon/1 tablespoon plus
  1 teaspoon mashed banana
60 g/2 oz/¼ cup sultanas or chopped
  dates or chopped figs
2 slices wholemeal bread

Combine the cheese, banana and sultanas and place between the slices of bread.

Cucumber and Salmon Sandwich

SERVES 1

30 g/1 oz/¼ cup shredded lettuce
2 slices wholemeal bread
1 slice Salmon and Ricotta Terrine
  (see p. 37)
6 slices cucumber
3 slices onion (optional)
alfalfa sprouts

Place the lettuce on a slice of bread. Add the slice of Salmon and Ricotta Terrine. Top with the cucumber, onion and alfalfa sprouts, and cover with the other slice of bread.

Curried Chicken and Celery Sandwich

SERVES 1

30 g/1 oz/¼ cup shredded lettuce
125 g/¼ lb chopped cooked chicken (all
  skin and fat removed)
1 tablespoon/1 tablespoon plus
  1 teaspoon finely chopped celery
1 tablespoon/1 tablespoon plus
  1 teaspoon finely chopped apple
a little Curry Dressing (see p. 140)

Place some of the lettuce on a slice of bread. Combine the chicken, celery, apple and Curry Dressing in a bowl and toss well. Spread on top of the lettuce. Top with more lettuce and cover with the other slice of bread.

Currant, Carrot and Parsley Sandwich

SERVES 1

1 tablespoon/1 tablespoon plus
  1 teaspoon currants
75 g/2½ oz/½ cup grated carrot
1 tablespoon/1 tablespoon plus
  1 teaspoon finely chopped fresh
  parsley
65 ml/2 fl oz/¼ cup unsweetened
  orange juice
30 g/1 oz/¼ cup shredded lettuce
2 slices wholemeal bread
black pepper to taste
finely chopped spring onion

Marinate the currants, carrot and parsley in the orange juice for 1 hour. Drain well. Place some of the lettuce on a slice of bread. Add the carrot filling, season with pepper, top with spring onion and more lettuce, and cover with the other slice of bread.

Tomato, Onion and Sprout Sandwich

SERVES 1

30 g/1 oz/¼ cup shredded lettuce
2 slices wholemeal bread
4 slices tomato
4 slices Spanish red onion
1 tablespoon/1 tablespoon plus
  1 teaspoon finely chopped fresh basil
  or chives
1 tablespoon/1 tablespoon plus
  1 teaspoon alfalfa sprouts
black pepper to taste

Place the lettuce on a slice of bread. Top with some of the tomato, some of the onion, more tomato and more onion. Sprinkle with the herbs. Add the alfalfa sprouts, season with pepper and top with the other slice of bread.

Vegetable Combination Sandwich

SERVES 1

30 g/1 oz/¼ cup shredded lettuce
2 slices wholemeal bread
40 g/1½ oz/¼ cup grated carrot
40 g/1½ oz/¼ cup grated beetroot
  (juice squeezed out)
60 g/2 oz/¼ cup grated zucchini (juice
  squeezed out)
30 g/1 oz/¼ cup grated Spanish red onion
30 g/1 oz/¼ cup grated low-fat grating
  cheese
black pepper to taste

Place some of the lettuce on a slice of bread. Place the grated vegetables and cheese in a bowl and mix well. Spread on top of the lettuce, and season with pepper. Top with more lettuce and cover with the other slice of bread.

Pizza Party

xxxxxxxxxxxxxxxxxxxxxxxxxxxxxxxxxxxxxxxxxxxxxxxxxxxxxxxxxxxxxxxxxxxxxxxxxxxxxxxxxxxxxxxxxxxxx

SERVES 15–20

1 quantity Pizza Sauce (see Marinara
Oat-bran Pizza, *p. 174)*
5 large pita breads

Hawaiian Pizza

1 green capsicum, cut into strips
1 red capsicum, cut into strips
425 g/15 oz canned or fresh
unsweetened pineapple chunks, crushed
and well drained
125 g/¼ lb/1 cup finely grated low-fat
grating cheese

Mushroom Pizza

8 mushrooms, finely chopped
125 g/¼ lb/1 cup finely grated low-fat
grating cheese

Vegetarian Pizza

200 g/7 oz/2 cups finely grated low-fat
grating cheese
200 g/7 oz carrots, cut into thin rounds
and lightly cooked until just soft
200 g/7 oz zucchini, cut into thin
rounds and lightly cooked until just
soft
1 tomato, finely sliced

Preheat the oven to 200°C/400°F. Cover the pita breads with the following toppings.

The Hawaiian Pizza recipe makes two pizzas. Divide the ingredients equally between two bases. Spread 250 ml/8 fl oz/1 cup Pizza Sauce over each base. Add the capsicum and pineapple, and top with the cheese. Bake for 10–15 minutes.

For the Mushroom Pizza, spread 250 ml/8 fl oz/1 cup Pizza Sauce over the base. Sprinkle the mushroom on top and cover with the cheese. Bake for 10–15 minutes.

The Vegetarian Pizza recipe makes two pizzas. Divide the ingredients equally between two bases. Spread 250 ml/8 fl oz/1 cup Pizza Sauce over each base. Sprinkle the cheese over the sauce. Arrange the carrot and zucchini over the cheese. Top with the tomato. Bake for 10–15 minutes.

Serve the pizzas with a large tossed salad. (See left colour plate between pages 168 and 169.)

Artichoke and Leek Pizza Slice

xxxxxxxxxxxxxxxxxxxxxxxxxxxxxxxxxxxxxxxxxxxxxxxxxxxxxxxxxxxxxxxxxxxxxxxxxxxxxxxxxxxxxxxxxxxxx

SERVES 4–6

1 quantity Scone Dough (see Asparagus
and Cheese Pizza Wheel, *p. 173)*
200 ml/7 fl oz/¾ cup Pizza Sauce (see
Marinara Oat-bran Pizza, *p. 174)*
425 g/15 oz canned artichoke hearts,
well drained
1 leek, thoroughly washed, sliced,
steamed and well drained
125 g/¼ lb/1 cup grated low-fat grating
cheese

Preheat the oven to 230°C/450°F.

Roll out the Scone Dough into a circle or a rectangle. Place on a non-stick baking tray. Spread with the Pizza Sauce. Slice the artichoke hearts and place on top of the pizza with the sliced leek. Sprinkle the cheese on top of the artichoke and leek. Bake the pizza for 20 minutes. Serve with soup or salad. (See colour plate opposite page 16.)

Asparagus and Cheese Pizza Wheel

SERVES 4–6

Scone Dough
185 g/6 oz/1½ cups unbleached white plain flour
60 g/2 oz/½ cup oat bran
3 teaspoons baking powder
1 tablespoon/1 tablespoon plus 1 teaspoon lemon juice
1 tablespoon/1 tablespoon plus 1 teaspoon non-fat or low-fat yoghurt
175 ml/6 fl oz/⅔ cup skim milk

Filling
350 g/¾ lb canned asparagus spears
125 g/¼ lb/1 cup grated low-fat grating cheese
a little cayenne pepper

Preheat the oven to 200°C/400°F.

Sift the flour, oat bran and baking powder into a bowl. Combine the lemon juice and yoghurt and add to the flour mixture. Rub in with your fingers. Add the milk and work into a firm dough. Place on a lightly floured bench and knead well. Roll out to a rectangular shape, approximately 28 cm × 23 cm/11″ × 9″. Use a sharp knife to cut away any uneven edges.

Drain the asparagus well, mash then spread evenly over the dough. Sprinkle half the cheese over the asparagus. Carefully roll up to make a long log.

Using a very sharp knife, cut the log into eight pieces. Line a baking tray with non-stick baking paper and place the circles flat on it, starting at the centre and working outwards so that the circles as a whole form a circular shape. The circles should almost touch. Sprinkle the remaining cheese and a little cayenne pepper on top. Bake for 20 minutes or until well browned. Serve with soup or a salad.

Cottage Cheese and Salmon Pizza

SERVES 4

1 quantity Scone Dough (see Asparagus and Cheese Pizza Wheel, this page)
425 g/15 oz canned red salmon
1 zucchini
125 g/¼ lb/½ cup grated low-fat cottage cheese
1 tablespoon/1 tablespoon plus 1 teaspoon grated horseradish
1 tablespoon/1 tablespoon plus 1 teaspoon finely chopped fresh chives
100 g/3½ oz/1 cup grated low-fat grating cheese

Preheat the oven to 230°C/450°F.

Roll the dough out to a round or rectangular shape. Place on a baking tray.

Drain the salmon well. Grate the zucchini and squeeze out the juice. Mix the salmon and zucchini with the cottage cheese, horseradish and chives. Spread over the dough. Sprinkle the cheese over the top.

Bake for 15–20 minutes or until the base looks crisp and the top is lightly browned.

Eggplant and Potato Pizza

SERVES 4–6

1 teaspoon light olive oil
1 small eggplant, cut into thin rounds
1 large potato, peeled
1 quantity Scone Dough (see Asparagus and Cheese Pizza Wheel, this page)
200 ml/7 fl oz/¾ cup Pizza Sauce (see Marinara Oat-bran Pizza, p. 174)
125 g /¼ lb/1 cup grated low-fat grating cheese

Preheat the oven to 180°C/350°F.

Lightly grease a baking tray with the oil. Lay the rounds of eggplant on the tray. Bake until the eggplant changes colour and softens. Remove from the oven and allow to cool.

Cut the potato into thin rounds and lightly steam them until just tender but still firm. Drain and cool.

Increase the oven temperature to 230°C/450°F. Roll out the Scone Dough to the required shape. Place on a non-stick baking tray. Spread with the Pizza Sauce. Top with overlapping eggplant and potato. Sprinkle the cheese on top of the vegetables, and bake for 20 minutes. Serve with a salad.

Marinara Oat-bran Pizza

SERVES 3 - 4

½ quantity Basic Oat-bran Bread
  dough *(see p. 212)*
*60 g/2 oz/½ cup grated low-fat grating
  cheese (optional)*

Pizza Sauce
3 onions, chopped
2 cloves garlic, crushed
*850 g/2 lb canned whole tomatoes in
  natural juice, puréed*
*280 g/10 oz/1 cup salt-free tomato
  paste*
½ teaspoon dried basil
1 teaspoon dried oregano

Marinara Topping
800 g/1¾ lb marinara mixture
*1 tablespoon/1 tablespoon plus
  1 teaspoon capers*
30 g/1 oz/¼ cup chopped spring onion
*125 g/¼ lb/1 cup grated low-fat grating
  cheese*

Prepare the Basic Oat-bran Bread dough. If you want a very crisp pizza base, omit the calcium ascorbate in the Basic Oat-bran Bread recipe, and add 60 g/2 oz/½ cup of low-fat grating cheese when you add the oil and apple juice concentrate.

Preheat the oven to 200°C/400°F.

Roll out the dough to the size of a pizza tray, on a well-floured board. Grease a tray and wipe off the excess oil. Carefully put the rolled-out dough onto the pizza tray and press it out to the sides.

Place the base, covered with a tea towel, in a warm place for no more than 10 minutes.

To make the Pizza Sauce, cook the onion and garlic in a little water until soft. Add the remaining ingredients and boil for 5 minutes. Set aside to cool and then use as desired. This recipe makes about 1.25 litres/2¼ pints/5 cups of sauce so you will not need it all for the pizza. The sauce stores well in an airtight jar in the refrigerator and can also be frozen.

Spread 250 ml/8 fl oz/1 cup of Pizza Sauce over the base. Then add the Marinara Topping – first the seafood, then a sprinkling of capers and spring onion and lastly the grated cheese. Bake for 20 minutes.

Sardine and Mushroom Oat-bran Pizza

SERVES 6 - 8

½ quantity Basic Oat-bran Bread
  dough *(see p. 212)*
*60 g/2 oz/½ cup grated low-fat grating
  cheese (optional)*
*250 ml/8 fl oz/1 cup Pizza Sauce (see
  Marinara Oat-bran Pizza, this page)*
225 g/½ lb canned sardines
juice of 1 lemon
1 onion
*225 g/½ lb/2 cups finely sliced
  mushroom*
*large handful of finely chopped fresh
  chives*
*125 g/¼ lb/1 cup extra grated low-fat
  grating cheese*
black pepper to taste

Prepare the Basic Oat-bran Bread dough. If you want a very crisp pizza base, omit the calcium ascorbate in the Basic Oat-bran Bread recipe and add 60 g/2 oz/½ cup of grated low-fat grating cheese when you add the oil and apple juice concentrate.

Preheat the oven to 200°C/400°F.

Roll out the Basic Oat-bran Bread dough into a pizza shape. Place on a baking tray, cover with a tea towel and stand in a warm place for no more than 10 minutes.

Spread the Pizza Sauce over the base. Drain the oil from the sardines and squeeze the lemon juice over them. Break up the sardines and distribute over the sauce. Slice the onion into rings and spread over the top of the sardines. Add the mushroom and chives, and sprinkle the cheese and pepper on top. Bake for 20 minutes.

DESSERTS
&
ICE CREAMS

Eating healthily on a low-fat diet does not mean excluding desserts. You will be surprised to find how easy it is to present stunning desserts that not only look good but taste great as well.

Most of the desserts have been designed around a fruit in season. There is no need to add lots of sugar. Fruits are naturally sweet, but their sweetness can be enhanced by adding the juice of other fruits or by using a sugar alternative such as apple juice concentrate.

To garnish a dessert you can add non-fat or low-fat yoghurt flavoured with vanilla essence. A low-fat alternative to cream can be made using low-fat ricotta cheese, fruit juice and vanilla essence and you will find here many recipes to show you how to make your own delicious ice creams.

Fruit Custard Tart

SERVES 6–8

*450 g/1 lb/3 cups chopped fresh fruits
(banana, kiwi fruit, strawberries,
apricots, peaches, pears) or drained
and chopped unsweetened canned
fruits*

Pastry
125 g/¼ lb/1 cup wholemeal plain flour
125 g/¼ lb/1 cup rolled oats
*65 ml/2 fl oz/¼ cup cold-pressed
grapeseed oil*
*2 tablespoons/2 tablespoons plus
2 teaspoons apple juice concentrate*
*2 tablespoons/2 tablespoons plus
2 teaspoons (more if necessary)
unsweetened orange juice or lemon
juice*

Custard
500 ml/16 fl oz/2 cups skim milk
60 g/2 oz/½ cup cornflour
1 teaspoon vanilla essence
*1 tablespoon/1 tablespoon plus
1 teaspoon grated orange rind*
*2 tablespoons/2 tablespoons plus
2 teaspoons apple juice concentrate*
*250 ml/8 fl oz/1 cup non-fat or low-fat
yoghurt*

Glaze
*1 tablespoon/1 tablespoon plus
1 teaspoon sugar-free raspberry jam*
250 ml/8 fl oz/1 cup water
1 teaspoon agar powder

Preheat the oven to 200°C/400°F.

To make the Pastry, combine all the ingredients in a food processor or blender. Blend until the pastry binds together. Knead lightly. Roll the pastry out to fit a fluted pie dish. Place the pastry in the dish and trim the edges. Bake for 10–15 minutes. Remove from the dish and cool.

To make the Custard, bring 350 ml/12 fl oz/1½ cups of the milk to just below boiling point in a saucepan. Combine the rest of the milk with the cornflour, vanilla essence and orange rind to make a paste. Add this to the hot milk and stir briskly until thick. Cook for 2 minutes, stirring continuously. Remove from the heat. Add the apple juice concentrate, mix well, and then add the yoghurt. Pour into the cooled pastry shell, and add the chopped fruits.

To make the Glaze, place all the ingredients in a saucepan and bring to the boil, stirring continuously. Simmer, uncovered, for 6 minutes. Cool slightly and brush over the fruits. Cool before serving. (See colour plate opposite.)

Banquet of Berries

SERVES 10–12

½ large watermelon
310 g/10½ oz strawberries
200 g/7 oz/1½ cups boysenberries
200 g/7 oz/1½ cups raspberries
200 g/7 oz/1½ cups blackberries
200 g/7 oz/1½ cups loganberries
250 ml/8 fl oz/1 cup dry white wine

Using a melon baller, scoop out as many perfect watermelon balls as possible until all the watermelon flesh is used. Remove the seeds from the balls. Leave some red flesh around the inside of the watermelon, clean away any rough areas and remove all the seeds.

If all the berries are not available at the time, then double the quantity of the ones you have. Rinse the berries and drain. Combine with the watermelon balls and fill the watermelon shell. Pour the wine over the top and refrigerate before serving. (See left colour plate overleaf.)

Fruit Custard Tart (opposite page).

Banquet of Berries (page 176);
Citrus Cantaloup (page 181).

Apple Baked with Fruit Filling (page 177).

*Apple and Pear Strudel (opposite page) with Home-made Vanilla Ice Cream
(page 199) and Whipped Ricotta Cream (page 190).*

Apple and Date Cake

SERVES 8

125 g/¼ lb/1 cup wheatgerm
75 g/2½ oz/¼ cup freshly grated
coconut
30 g/1 oz/¼ cup raw almonds or 60 g/
2 oz/¼ cup sesame seeds
8 Granny Smith apples, peeled and sliced
60 g/2 oz/¼ cup dates, stoned and
roughly chopped
1 teaspoon finely grated lemon rind
250 ml/8 fl oz/1 cup unsweetened
orange juice
90 g/3 oz/¾ cup toasted muesli

Preheat the oven to 180°C/350°F.

Blend the wheatgerm, coconut and almonds in a food processor or blender for 2 minutes. Line a 20-cm/8″ round cake tin with foil. Press the wheatgerm mixture evenly over the base of the cake tin. Refrigerate until required.

Place the apple and chopped date in a saucepan with the lemon rind and orange juice, and gently cook until most of the moisture has been absorbed or the apple is tender. Pour off any excess liquid. Leave to cool just slightly.

Spoon the warm apple mixture over the wheatgerm and smooth down. Sprinkle the toasted muesli over the top of the apple evenly and press down with the palm of your hand.

Bake 30–40 minutes. Leave to cool, and then refrigerate for at least 2 hours (the longer it is refrigerated, the easier it will be to remove it from the tin). (See left colour plate between pages 184 and 185.)

Apples Baked with Fruit Filling

SERVES 4

4 Granny Smith apples, cored
60 g/2 oz/¼ cup mixed dried fruit
½ teaspoon ground cinnamon
½ teaspoon mixed spice
finely grated rind of 1 orange
250 ml/8 fl oz/1 cup unsweetened
orange juice

Peel the top half of each apple. Combine the dried fruit, spices and orange rind. Fill the apples with this mixture. Place in a saucepan in which the apples can stand up. Pour the orange juice over the top. Cover, and simmer gently for 10–15 minutes or until the apples are just tender. Serve with low-fat cream, non-fat or low-fat yoghurt or Custard (see page 182). (See right colour plate between pages 176 and 177.)

Apple and Pear Strudel

SERVES 6

3 pears, peeled and finely sliced
2 apples, peeled and finely sliced
1 egg white
1 tablespoon/1 tablespoon plus 1
teaspoon apple juice concentrate
2 tablespoons/2 tablespoons plus 2
teaspoons oat bran
2 tablespoons/2 tablespoons plus 2
teaspoons water
8 sheets filo pastry
150 g/5 oz dates, stoned and chopped
grated rind of 1 lemon
6 teaspoons lemon juice
a little ground cinnamon

Preheat the oven to 180°C/350°F.

In separate saucepans, lightly cook the pear and apple so that they remain firm and retain their shape.

Combine the egg white, apple juice concentrate and water. Place the filo pastry, layer on layer, on non-stick baking paper on a baking tray. Brush in between every second sheet of filo with some of the egg-white mixture, and sprinkle with a little of the oat bran.

In the centre of the pastry, leaving the edges uncovered to fold over later, make a layer of pear pieces. Top with half the chopped dates. Add a layer of apple slices and the remaining chopped dates. Top with the lemon rind and juice.

Brush the ends of the pastry with some of the egg-white mixture and fold over the fruit mixture. Brush the sides with the egg-white mixture and bring them up to almost touch, but leave a little of the fruit mixture exposed. Brush egg-white mixture all over the strudel. Sprinkle with the remaining oat bran and sprinkle the cinnamon over the top. Bake for 15–20 minutes. (See colour plate opposite.)

Apple Oat Crumble

SERVES 6

6–8 apples, peeled, cored and quartered
250 ml/8 fl oz/1 cup unsweetened
    orange and pineapple juice or orange
    juice
water
1 tablespoon/1 tablespoon plus
    1 teaspoon cornflour
a little extra water
grated rind of 1 lemon

Crumble Topping
125 g/¼ lb/¾ cup rolled oats
10 almonds
4 egg whites
1 teaspoon vanilla essence
2 tablespoons/2 tablespoons plus
    2 teaspoons apple juice concentrate

Preheat the oven to 180°C/350°F.

Cook the apples in the orange and pineapple juice in a saucepan until tender. Drain the fruit and reserve the liquid in the saucepan. Top up with water to make 250 ml/8 fl oz/1 cup of liquid. Blend the cornflour with a little water and add to the liquid in the saucepan. Add the lemon rind. Cook until the sauce thickens, stirring continuously. Place the apples in a baking dish and pour the sauce over the top. Leave to cool and set.

To make the Crumble Topping, blend the rolled oats and almonds to a breadcrumb texture in a food processor or blender. Beat the egg whites in a bowl until thick and stiff. Add the vanilla essence and apple juice concentrate. Fold in the oat and almond mixture. Spread evenly over the set apple.

Bake for 20 minutes. Serve with Home-made Vanilla Ice Cream (see page 199), or non-fat or low-fat yoghurt.

Apple Snow

SERVES 4

4 Granny Smith apples
1 teaspoon lemon juice
1 teaspoon grated lemon rind

Place the unpeeled apples in the freezer for at least 8 hours. Remove and let stand for 10 minutes. Carefully peel and core, and cut into chunks. Toss in the lemon juice and rind. Place in a food processor or blender and blend until light and fluffy.

Serve in cups with spoons, or mix with kiwi fruit. Alternatively, cut a pear in half and remove the core and some of the flesh. Brush lemon juice over the pear and freeze for 1 hour. Scoop the Apple Snow onto the pear. Garnish with blueberries, kiwi fruit or fresh strawberries, and serve.

Banana Custard

SERVES 6–8

3–4 bananas
1 tablespoon/1 tablespoon plus
    1 teaspoon lemon juice

Custard
1 litre/1¾ pints/4 cups skim milk
125 g/¼ lb/1 cup cornflour
2 teaspoons vanilla essence
1 tablespoon/1 tablespoon plus
    1 teaspoon grated orange rind
125 ml/4 fl oz/½ cup apple juice
    concentrate
250 ml/8 fl oz/1 cup non-fat or low-fat
    yoghurt

To make the Custard, bring 750 ml/1⅓ pints/3 cups of the milk to just below boiling. Combine the remaining cup of milk, the cornflour, vanilla essence and orange rind to make a paste. Add to the hot milk and stir briskly until thick. Cook for 2 minutes, stirring continuously. Remove from the heat. Add the apple juice concentrate and mix well. Add the yoghurt and mix well.

Cut the bananas into thin rounds and brush with the lemon juice. Line a shallow baking dish with foil or plastic wrap (for easy removal). Overlap the banana pieces on the base of the dish. Pour the custard over the top. Refrigerate for at least 3 hours or until set. Turn out and cut into squares. Top with low-fat cream.

Banana Mousse

SERVES 6

2 frozen bananas, peeled and chopped
65 ml/2 fl oz/¼ cup lemon juice
750 ml/1⅓ pints/3 cups low-fat
  evaporated milk, well chilled
2 teaspoons vanilla essence
2 tablespoons/2 tablespoons plus
  2 teaspoons gelatine
65 ml/2 fl oz/¼ cup boiling water
3 egg whites
½–1 teaspoon ground nutmeg
1–2 teaspoons rum (optional)

Purée the banana in a food processor or blender. Add the lemon juice. Beat the milk until thick and creamy, and then fold through the banana mixture. Add the vanilla essence. Dissolve the gelatine in the boiling water, and fold through the banana mixture. Beat the egg whites until stiff, and then fold through the mixture with the nutmeg. Pour into a mould or individual glass goblets. For special occasions add the rum.

Serve with Whipped Ricotta Cream (see Pancake Toppings, page 190) and slices of fresh banana.

Banana Date Steamed Pudding

SERVES 6–8

225 g/½ lb/1 cup dates, stoned
225 g/½ lb/1 cup sultanas
1 teaspoon vanilla essence
2 small bananas, mashed
125 g/¼ lb/1 cup wholemeal plain flour
1 teaspoon bicarbonate of soda
1 teaspoon baking powder
1 teaspoon ground cinnamon
1 teaspoon ground nutmeg
2 egg whites

Place the dates and sultanas in a food processor or blender and mince finely. Add the vanilla and banana, and mix well.

Sift the flour, bicarbonate of soda, baking powder and spices, and fold through the fruit mixture. Beat the egg whites until stiff. Fold through the fruit mixture. Pour into a lightly greased pudding basin, and seal.

Place in a saucepan and fill with boiling water to 2.5 cm/ 1″ from the top of the pudding basin. Keep just boiling for 1½–1¾ hours. Serve with Whipped Ricotta Cream (see Pancake Toppings, page 190) or Light Custard (see page 182).

Banana Split

SERVES 1

1 banana
1 large scoop Home-made Vanilla Ice
  Cream (see p. 199)
4 dates, stoned and chopped
2 walnuts, chopped

Cut the banana in half lengthwise. Top with the ice cream and chopped date and walnut.

Creamy Banana Whip

SERVES 2

2 frozen bananas
a little vanilla essence (optional)

Carefully cut the frozen banana into four pieces (mind your fingers). Cut away the peel and discard. Place the banana in a food processor or blender and blend until thick and creamy. Add a dash of vanilla essence if desired. Scoop out and serve with freshly sliced fruit or berries in season.

Blueberry Yoghurt Swirl

SERVES 1 – 2

250 ml/8 fl oz/1 cup non-fat or low-fat
*   yoghurt*
handful of fresh blueberries

Blueberry Sauce
450 ml/15 fl oz/1¾ cups unsweetened
*   pear juice*
1 tablespoon/1 tablespoon plus
*   1 teaspoon lemon juice*
75 ml/3 fl oz/⅓ cup apple juice
*   concentrate*
2 teaspoons agar powder
450 g/1 lb/3 cups fresh blueberries

To make the Blueberry Sauce, combine the pear juice, lemon juice, apple juice concentrate and agar powder in a small saucepan. Bring to the boil. Boil for 5 minutes, stirring continuously. Add the blueberries, and boil for 10 minutes.

Place 125 ml/4 fl oz/½ cup of the Blueberry Sauce in the bottom of a tall glass. Add the yoghurt. Using a long-handled spoon, swirl the sauce through the yoghurt. Top with the fresh blueberries and serve chilled.

Extra Blueberry Sauce can be poured into sterilised jars and kept refrigerated. Use on pancakes, in muffins and on toast.

Bread Pudding

SERVES 4 – 6

4 large slices wholemeal bread
4 heaped tablespoons sugar-free raspberry
*   jam or plum jam*
125 g/¼ lb/¾ cup currants
250 ml/8 fl oz/1 cup skim milk
1 tablespoon/1 tablespoon plus
*   1 teaspoon cornflour*
1 tablespoon/1 tablespoon plus
*   1 teaspoon apple juice concentrate*
2 teaspoons vanilla essence
2 egg whites

Preheat the oven to 180°C/350°F.

Lightly grease a deep rectangular baking dish or cake tin. The dish should accommodate two slices of bread placed side by side. Spread the jam on two slices of bread. Place the bread on the base of the dish. Sprinkle with half the currants. Top with the remaining bread slices and currants.

Combine a little of the milk with the cornflour to make a paste and stir into the remaining milk. Add the apple juice concentrate and vanilla essence. Beat the egg whites until firm and fold into the milk mixture. Pour this over the bread.

Cook for 30 minutes. Serve with Custard (see page 182).

Cantaloup Berry Baskets

SERVES 3

1 cantaloup
450 g/1 lb/3 cups mixed berries in
*   season (combination of boysenberries,*
*   blueberries, raspberries, loganberries,*
*   blackberries, strawberries), washed*
*   and drained*

Cut the cantaloup into quarters. From three of the quarters remove the seeds and scoop out the flesh to make a basket-like hollow. Using a sharp knife, carefully remove the inner flesh from the remaining quarter, leaving the skin with a layer of orange flesh approximately 1 cm/½″ thick. Cut the removed flesh into pieces and put aside for a snack.

Cut the shell of the fourth quarter into three long strips, which will become the basket handles. Using toothpicks, attach these to both ends of the other three quarters of the cantaloup. Fill the baskets with the berries.

Serve with Home-made Vanilla Ice Cream (see page 199), or non-fat or low-fat yoghurt.

Citus Cantaloup

SERVES 4

2 cantaloup
1 extra cantaloup or *250 ml/8 fl oz/1*
*   cup unsweetened orange juice*
2 oranges
2 grapefruit

Using a zig-zag knife cut 2 cantaloup in half (or try cutting a zig-zag pattern after you have halved the melons). Remove the seeds.

Peel the remaining cantaloup, cut in half, and remove the seeds. Feed portions of the flesh into a juicer (if you do not have a juicer substitute 250 ml/8 fl oz/1 cup of unsweetened orange juice).

Peel the oranges and grapefruit, and remove all the pith. Segment the fruit by cutting on both sides of the membrane and remove each segment. Place the segments in a bowl. Add the juice and refrigerate for at least 1 hour. Refrigerate the cantaloup halves too.

Place the cantaloup halves on a serving plate and fill with the fruit segments and the juice. (See left colour plate between pages 176 and 177.)

Carob Mousse

SERVES 6

1 litre/1¾ pints/4 cups skim milk
125 g/¼ lb/1 cup cornflour
2 teaspoons vanilla essence
30 g/1 oz/¼ cup carob powder
65 ml/2 fl oz/¼ cup boiling water
1 tablespoon/1 tablespoon plus
*   1 teaspoon grated orange rind*
½ teaspoon orange essence
250 ml/8 fl oz/1 cup non-fat or *low-fat*
*   yoghurt*
4 egg whites
310 g/10½ oz strawberries

Pour 750 ml/1⅓ pints/3 cups of the milk in a large saucepan and bring to just below boiling.

Add the remaining milk to the cornflour and mix to a smooth paste. Add the vanilla essence.

Combine the carob powder with the boiling water and mix to a paste to dissolve the powder. Add the orange rind and orange essence.

Combine the cornflour mixture and the carob mixture. Add to the heating milk and stir continuously until the sauce thickens. Remove from the heat and fold through the yoghurt.

Beat the egg whites until stiff peaks form. Gently fold through the mixture. Pour into a mould or individual glasses. Refrigerate for at least 2 hours.

Serve topped with fresh strawberries.

Cold Christmas Pudding

xxxxxxxxxxxxxxxxxxxxxxxxxxxxxxxxxxxxxxxxxxxxxxxxxxxxxxxxxxxxxxxxxxxxxxxxxx

SERVES 10 – 12

100 g/3½ oz/½ cup sultanas
100 g/3½ oz/½ cup dried apricots,
  finely chopped
100 g/3½ oz/½ cup prunes, stoned and
  chopped
100 g/3½ oz/½ cup currants
250 ml/8 fl oz/1 cup unsweetened
  orange juice
1 teaspoon mixed spice
2 tablespoons/2 tablespoons plus
  2 teaspoons dry sherry
425 g/15 oz sliced cooked apple, chilled
1 tablespoon/1 tablespoon plus
  1 teaspoon lemon juice
125 ml/4 fl oz/½ cup unsweetened
  apple juice
2 tablespoons/2 tablespoons plus
  2 teaspoons gelatine
65 ml/2 fl oz/¼ cup boiling water

Combine the fruit, orange juice, mixed spice and sherry in a saucepan. Slowly bring to the boil. Simmer for 3 minutes. Remove from the heat. Fold the apple through.

Combine the lemon juice and apple juice. Dissolve the gelatine in the boiling water and add to the apple and lemon juice. Pour into the fruit mixture, and mix well. Spoon into a 1.5-litre/2½-pint/6-cup pudding mould.

Cover, and refrigerate overnight or for longer. Use a sharp knife to slice into portions. (See left colour plate between pages 208 and 209.)

Light Custard

xxxxxxxxxxxxxxxxxxxxxxxxxxxxxxxxxxxxxxxxxxxxxxxxxxxxxxxxxxxxxxxxxxxxxxxxxx

SERVES 4

500 ml/16 fl oz/2 cups skim milk
2 tablespoons/2 tablespoons plus 2
  teaspoons unsweetened orange juice
1 tablespoon/1 tablespoon plus 1
  teaspoon vanilla essence
3 tablespoons/3 tablespoons plus 3
  teaspoons arrowroot

Combine all the ingredients in a small saucepan and mix well. Bring to the boil slowly, stirring continuously, until the custard thickens.

Custard

xxxxxxxxxxxxxxxxxxxxxxxxxxxxxxxxxxxxxxxxxxxxxxxxxxxxxxxxxxxxxxxxxxxxxxxxxx

SERVES 4

500 ml/16 fl oz/2 cups skim milk
30 g/1 oz/¼ cup cornflour
1 teaspoon vanilla essence
2 teaspoons grated orange rind
3 tablespoons/3 tablespoons plus
  3 teaspoons apple juice concentrate

In a saucepan, blend a little of the skim milk with the cornflour to make a paste. Stir in the remaining milk, vanilla essence and orange rind (the rind will give the liquid a lovely orange colour). Bring slowly to the boil, stirring continuously until the custard begins to thicken. Cook over a low heat for a further couple of minutes. Remove from the heat. Stir in the apple juice concentrate.

If you prefer a thinner custard, use a little more skim milk.

Serve the custard with stewed or fresh fruits, or the dessert of your choice. If custard is left to go cold it sets like a blancmange and can also be served as a cold dessert with Blueberry Sauce (see page 236) or Raspberry Sauce (see page 238).

Steamed Fruit Pudding

SERVES 4 – 6

60 g / 2 oz / ⅓ cup currants
200 g / 7 oz / 1 cup dried apricots
90 g / 3 oz / ½ cup mixed peel
½ teaspoon ground cinnamon
⅛ teaspoon ground nutmeg
⅛ teaspoon ground cloves
125 ml / 4 fl oz / ½ cup unsweetened
  orange juice
125 g / ¼ lb / 1 cup wholemeal self-raising
  flour
65 ml / 2 fl oz / ¼ cup skim milk
1 egg white, beaten

Line a pudding basin with foil. Place the fruits, spices and orange juice in a saucepan and let simmer for 5 minutes. Allow to cool but not get cold. Sift the flour and return the husks to the flour. Add to the fruit mixture, add the milk and beaten egg white and stir well. Pour into the pudding basin and cover tightly. Place in a large saucepan with boiling water. Steam the pudding for 1–1½ hours. Do not let the saucepan boil dry. The water in the saucepan should be boiling constantly. Serve hot with Light Custard (page 182).

When cold the pudding can be refrigerated for 24 hours. Cut into cake slices and serve with coffee after a light chilled dessert, or use as a fruit cake for morning or afternoon tea. (See left colour plate between pages 184 and 185.)

Lemon Parfait

SERVES 4 – 6

1 teaspoon gelatine
2 tablespoons / 2 tablespoons plus
  2 teaspoons boiling water
250 ml / 8 fl oz / 1 cup low-fat evaporated
  milk, well chilled
250 ml / 8 fl oz / 1 cup Lemon Filling (see
  Lemon Meringue Pie, p. 192)
green and purple grapes for garnishing
4–6 fresh mint leaves

Dissolve the gelatine in the boiling water and set aside to cool. Beat the milk until thick and at least doubled in size. Beat in the Lemon Filling (if it has been refrigerated you will need to heat it slightly to soften the texture and ensure easier combining). Add the gelatine, pour into parfait glasses and refrigerate. Garnish with green and purple grapes and a mint leaf.

Peach Yoghurt Mousse

SERVES 4 – 6

850 g / 2 lb canned unsweetened peaches
  in natural juice, drained
2 tablespoons / 2 tablespoons plus
  2 teaspoons apple juice concentrate
½ teaspoon orange essence
1 tablespoon / 1 tablespoon plus
  1 teaspoon gelatine
3 tablespoons / 3 tablespoons plus
  3 teaspoons boiling water
500 ml / 16 fl oz / 2 cups non-fat or low-
  fat yoghurt

Blend the peaches, apple juice concentrate and orange essence in a food processor or blender. Dissolve the gelatine in the boiling water and add to the peach mixture. Fold in the yoghurt. Pour into a wet mould and refrigerate until set. Serve with your favourite seasonal fruit.

Raspberry and Pear Summer Pudding

SERVES 6

800 g / 1¾ lb / 5½ cups raspberries (fresh
    or frozen, not canned)
250 ml / 8 fl oz / 1 cup water
2 teaspoons agar powder
1 pear, peeled and finely sliced
1 teaspoon grated lemon rind
10–12 slices wholemeal bread (crusts
    removed)
sliced fresh fruit for decorating

Place the raspberries, half of the water and the agar powder in a saucepan and bring to the boil. Simmer for 3 minutes. Remove from the heat. In the remaining water, cook the pear and the lemon rind until the pear is soft. Drain well.

Line a pudding basin with the bread slices. Overlap the slices so there are no gaps. Pour half the raspberry mixture over the top. Cover with the bread slices (again, slightly overlapping) and press down firmly. Place a layer of pear slices over the bread. Pour the remaining raspberries over the pears and top with more bread. Cover with plastic wrap. Place a plate and a heavy weight on top of the pudding. Refrigerate for at least 4–6 hours.

Turn the pudding out onto a plate. Cut into slices and decorate with sliced fresh fruit. Serve with Home-made Vanilla Ice Cream (see page 199) or Whipped Ricotta Cream (see Pancake Toppings, page 190). (See colour plate opposite.)

Strawberry Custard Tarts

MAKES 8

310 g / 10½ oz / 2 cups strawberries,
    washed and hulled

Pastry
125 g / ¼ lb / 1 cup wholemeal plain flour
125 g / ¼ lb / 1 cup rolled oats
65 ml / 2 fl oz / ¼ cup cold-pressed
    grapeseed oil
2 tablespoons / 2 tablespoons plus
    2 teaspoons apple juice concentrate
3 tablespoons / 3 tablespoons plus
    3 teaspoons unsweetened orange juice

Custard
500 ml / 16 fl oz / 2 cups skim milk
60 g / 2 oz / ½ cup cornflour
1 teaspoon vanilla essence
1 tablespoon / 1 tablespoon plus
    1 teaspoon grated orange rind
2 tablespoons / 2 tablespoons plus
    2 teaspoons apple juice concentrate
    (more if necessary)
125 ml / 4 fl oz / ½ cup non-fat or low-
    fat yoghurt

Preheat the oven to 200°C / 400°F.

Lightly grease eight small 8-cm × 2.5-cm / 3″ × 1″ tart pastry moulds. Combine all the Pastry ingredients in a food processor or blender. Blend until the pastry binds together. Cut the pastry into eight equal pieces and roll out to fit the moulds. Trim the edges and place on a baking tray. Bake for 10 minutes. Cool.

To make the Custard, bring 350 ml / 12 fl oz / 1½ cups of the milk to just below boiling point in a saucepan. Combine the rest of the milk with the cornflour, vanilla essence and orange rind to make a paste. Add to the milk in the saucepan and stir briskly until thick. Cook for 2 minutes, stirring continuously. Remove from the heat. Add the apple juice concentrate and mix well. Add the yoghurt and mix well. Cool slightly.

Pour the custard into the pastry shells. You should have approximately 65 ml / 2 fl oz / ¼ cup of custard left over for children who love to lick the bowl. Refrigerate. Cover the top of the tarts with the strawberries. (See right colour plate overleaf.)

Raspberry and Pear Summer Pudding
(opposite page).

*Baked Pineapple (page 186); Apple and Date Cake (page 177);
Steamed Fruit Pudding (page 183).*

Strawberry Custard Tart (page 184).

Jellied Fruit Salad (opposite page).

Apple Mint Jelly

SERVES 4

1 teaspoon agar powder
500 ml/16 fl oz/2 cups unsweetened apple juice
1–2 teaspoons finely chopped fresh mint or spearmint

Boil the agar powder with half the apple juice for 3 minutes or until the agar powder has dissolved. Stir briskly into the remaining cold apple juice. Stir continuously for 3 minutes. Stir the mint through the mixture and refrigerate until set.

Berry Summer Jelly Pudding

SERVES 8

800 g/1¾ lb mixed berries in season (combination of strawberries, blueberries, raspberries, red currants, cherries), washed
1 litre/1¾ pints/4 cups water
4 teaspoons agar powder
65 ml/2 fl oz/¼ cup apple juice concentrate

Remove any stems from the berries. Cut the strawberries in half. Remove the pips from the cherries and cut in half.

Place the water, agar powder and apple juice concentrate in a saucepan and bring to the boil. Simmer for 3–5 minutes or until the agar powder is dissolved.

Turn up the heat and add the berries. Stir carefully. Bring nearly to the boil. The fruits will begin to bleed their colours into the liquid and just begin to break open. Do not overcook.

Remove from the heat and pour into a round pudding basin. Refrigerate until set.

Cut into wedges to serve.

Fruit Cocktail Jelly

SERVES 4

1 teaspoon agar powder
500 ml/16 fl oz/2 cups unsweetened fruit juice cocktail (combination of orange, apple, mango and passionfruit juices)
1 tablespoon/1 tablespoon plus 1 teaspoon passionfruit pulp

Boil the agar powder with 250 ml/8 fl oz/1 cup of the fruit juice for 3 minutes or until the powder is thoroughly dissolved. Stir briskly into the remaining cold juice. Stir continuously for 3 minutes. Stir in the passionfruit pulp. Refrigerate until set.

Jellied Fruit Salad

SERVES 6–8

575 g/1¼ lb fresh fruit (strawberries, peaches, oranges, grapefruit, passionfruit, pineapple), chopped
500 ml/16 fl oz/2 cups chilled water
2 tablespoons/2 tablespoons plus 2 teaspoons apple juice concentrate
2 teaspoons agar powder

Place all the fruit on a plate and reserve the fruit juices.

Place the water and apple juice concentrate and agar powder in a saucepan and slowly bring to the boil. Simmer, stirring until the powder has dissolved. Cool slightly and then add the fruit juices and the fruit. Pour into a mould and refrigerate for at least 2–3 hours before serving. (See colour plate opposite.)

Mango and Peach Jelly Log

SERVES 6 – 8

2 mangoes, peeled
6 yellow peaches, peeled
2 passionfruit
250 ml/8 fl oz/1 cup water
1 tablespoon/1 tablespoon plus
    1 teaspoon apple juice concentrate
2 teaspoons agar powder
250 ml/8 fl oz/1 cup freshly squeezed
    orange juice, strained

Chop the fruit into bite-sized pieces and add the passionfruit pulp.

Combine the water, apple juice concentrate and agar powder in a saucepan. Slowly bring to the boil, stirring continuously until the powder dissolves. Remove from the heat and add the orange juice. Pour over the fruit immediately and spoon into a long glass terrine dish. Refrigerate until firm, and then cut into slices.

The log keeps well if covered and refrigerated.

Wine Jelly

SERVES 2

250 ml/8 fl oz/1 cup dry white wine
2 teaspoons gelatine
1 teaspoon lemon juice
150 g/5 oz/1 cup sliced fresh fruit (kiwi
    fruit, strawberries, nectarines, peaches,
    grapes, stoned cherries)

Combine the wine, gelatine and lemon juice in a heatproof dish and place in a saucepan containing boiling water. Stir until the gelatine is dissolved. Set aside to cool.

Place the fruit in the bottom of two small wine glasses. Pour a small amount of the gelatine mixture into the glasses and refrigerate until set. When firm, top with the remaining gelatine mixture, and refrigerate again.

Papaw in Passionfruit Sauce

SERVES 2 – 4

1 large papaw
125 ml/4 fl oz/½ cup unsweetened
    orange juice
3 large passionfruit

Peel the papaw and remove the seeds. Cut into chunky bite-sized pieces and place in a serving bowl. Combine the orange juice and passionfruit pulp and pour over the papaw. Coat well before chilling. This refreshing dessert should be served well chilled.

Baked Pineapple

SERVES 4

1 pineapple
1 teaspoon ground cinnamon
200 ml/7 fl oz/¾ cup unsweetened
    orange juice
2 tablespoons/2 tablespoons plus
    2 teaspoons grated orange rind

Preheat the oven to 190°C/375°F.

Cut the pineapple in half lengthwise right through the green top. Cut each half lengthwise into two. Cut along the top of each quarter to remove the tough core, which should come away easily in one long strip.

Wrap a piece of foil around the green top so it does not become brown while baking.

Place the pineapple pieces, skin side down, on a foil-lined baking tray. Cut wedges into each piece. Sprinkle the cinnamon over the pineapple. Bake for 10 minutes or until the pineapple is just warmed through.

Heat the orange juice and rind and pour over the pineapple just before serving. (See left colour plate between pages 184 and 185.)

Pineapple Pie

SERVES 8

150 g/5 oz/1¼ cups oat bran
185 g/6 oz/1½ cups unbleached white
   plain flour
1 teaspoon baking powder (optional)
2 teaspoons grated lemon rind
75 ml/3 fl oz/⅓ cup cold-pressed
   grapeseed oil
2 tablespoons/2 tablespoons plus
   2 teaspoons apple juice concentrate
65 ml/2 fl oz/¼ cup lemon juice
65 ml/2 fl oz/¼ cup water

Filling
500 ml/16 fl oz/2 cups unsweetened
   orange juice
1 tablespoon/1 tablespoon plus
   1 teaspoon orange-flavoured liqueur
   (e.g. Galliano, Grand Marnier)
1 tablespoon/1 tablespoon plus
   1 teaspoon grated orange rind or
   lemon rind
575 g/1¼ lb fresh pineapple pieces
30 g/1 oz/¼ cup cornflour

Preheat the oven to 200°C/400°F.

Combine the oat bran, flour, baking powder (this addition makes a 'cakier' pastry) and lemon rind in a bowl, and mix well.

Combine the oil, apple juice concentrate and lemon juice, add to the flour mixture, and work through. Add the water or enough to make a firm dough. Knead and roll out to fit a fluted pie dish. Bake for 12–15 minutes. Remove and cool.

To make the Filling, combine 350 ml/12 fl oz/1½ cups of the orange juice with the liqueur and orange rind in a saucepan. As the liquid begins to simmer, add the pineapple pieces. Blend the cornflour with the remaining juice and add. Stir until the sauce thickens. Cool slightly before pouring into the cooled pie shell. Refrigerate for at least 4–6 hours before serving.

Pumpkin Dessert Pie

SERVES 8 – 10

90 g/3 oz/½ cup raw almonds
60 g/2 oz/¼ cup raisins
125 g/¼ lb/1 cup wheat flakes or rolled
   oats
1½ teaspoons ground cinnamon
1 tablespoon/1 tablespoon plus
   1 teaspoon unsweetened apple juice
500 g/1 lb 2 oz cooked pumpkin
2 tablespoons/2 tablespoons plus
   2 teaspoons apple juice concentrate
2 teaspoons finely grated orange rind
125 ml/4 fl oz/½ cup low-fat soymilk
1 tablespoon/1 tablespoon plus
   1 teaspoon vanilla essence
100 g/3½ oz/½ cup currants or finely
   chopped dried apricots
4 egg whites
125 ml/4 fl oz/½ cup whipped low-fat
   cream
a little ground nutmeg

Preheat the oven to 180°C/350°F.

Combine the almonds, raisins, wheat flakes, cinnamon and apple juice in a food processor or blender and blend until the mixture just begins to stick together. Line a 23-cm/9″ round pie dish with foil and press the mixture very thinly over the base and sides.

Place the pumpkin, apple juice concentrate, orange rind, soymilk and vanilla essence in a food processor or blender and blend until smooth. Fold the currants through the mixture. Beat the egg whites until quite stiff and fold through. Pour into the pie base and bake for 50 minutes. Serve chilled, topped with the whipped low-fat cream and the nutmeg.

Raspberry Soufflé

xxxxxxxxxxxxxxxxxxxxxxxxxxxxxxxxxxxxxxxxxxxxxxxxxxxxxxxxxxxxxxxxx

SERVES 6

150 g/5 oz/1 cup raspberries (fresh or
   frozen, not canned) or combination of
   raspberries and blueberries
2 teaspoons apple juice concentrate
250 ml/8 fl oz/1 cup low-fat evaporated
   milk, well chilled
1 teaspoon vanilla essence
1 tablespoon/1 tablespoon plus
   1 teaspoon gelatine
65 ml/2 fl oz/¼ cup boiling water
extra fresh raspberries

Place the raspberries in a saucepan with the apple juice concentrate. Gently heat until the berries are soft. Cool slightly.

Beat the milk until doubled in size and quite thick. Add the berries and continue to beat. Add the vanilla essence.

Dissolve the gelatine in the boiling water. Add to the milk mixture while still beating.

Pour into a small soufflé dish (the height can be extended by wrapping foil around the top of the dish). Refrigerate for at least 2 hours or until set. Serve with fresh berries.

Strawberry and Passionfruit Pavlova

xxxxxxxxxxxxxxxxxxxxxxxxxxxxxxxxxxxxxxxxxxxxxxxxxxxxxxxxxxxxxxxxx

SERVES 12

10 dried apricots
125 ml/4 fl oz/½ cup unsweetened
   orange juice
350 ml/12 fl oz/1½ cups low-fat
   evaporated milk, well chilled
1 teaspoon vanilla essence
1 tablespoon/1 tablespoon plus
   1 teaspoon apple juice concentrate
1 teaspoon white wine vinegar
1 tablespoon/1 tablespoon plus
   1 teaspoon gelatine
125 ml/4 fl oz/½ cup boiling water
500 ml/16 fl oz/2 cups low-fat whipped
   cream
450 g/1 lb/3 cups strawberries, washed
   and hulled
65 ml/2 fl oz/¼ cup passionfruit pulp

Variation
1 litre/1¾ pints/4 cups unsweetened
   apple juice
1 tablespoon/1 tablespoon plus 1
   teaspoon agar powder
2 tablespoons/2 tablespoons plus
   2 teaspoons apple juice concentrate
2 teaspoons vanilla essence
350 ml/12 fl oz/1½ cups non-fat or
   low-fat yoghurt
450 g/1 lb/3 cups strawberries, washed
   and hulled
sliced kiwi fruit or mixed berries in
   season or sliced pineapple

This is a delicious alternative to the traditional pavlova.

Simmer the apricots in the orange juice for 10 minutes or until soft. Purée. Beat the milk until thick and at least doubled in size. Add the apricot purée, vanilla essence, apple juice concentrate and vinegar. Dissolve the gelatine in the boiling water and fold into the mixture. Pour into a round, spring-form cheesecake tin. Refrigerate until firm. Top with the cream, strawberries and passionfruit pulp.

Variation
■ Pour the apple juice into a saucepan and add the agar powder. Simmer and stir until the powder has dissolved. Add the apple juice concentrate and vanilla essence. Allow to cool slightly. Place in a food processor or blender and blend until frothy. Add the yoghurt and blend for a further 2 minutes. Pour into a flat mould and refrigerate. Top with strawberries and sliced kiwi fruit or mixed berries, such as raspberries, blueberries and loganberries, or sliced pineapple.

Strawberries in Orange

SERVES 6–8

575 g/1¼ lb/3½ cups strawberries,
   washed and hulled
250 ml/8 fl oz/1 cup unsweetened
   orange juice
1 tablespoon/1 tablespoon plus
   1 teaspoon brandy (optional)

Purée one-quarter of the strawberries with the orange juice and brandy in a food processor or blender. Pour the purée over the remaining strawberries and chill. Serve plain or with non-fat or low-fat yoghurt.

Watermelon Basket with Fresh Fruits

SERVES 15 – 20

1 large watermelon
any combination of the following fruits to
   fill 1 large empty watermelon:
   strawberries, pineapple, apples,
   bananas, grapes, pears, melons,
   oranges, plums, nectarines, mandarins,
   peaches, kiwi fruit and passionfruit
   pulp

Cut two segments out of the top half of the watermelon to produce a basket with a handle. Scoop out the flesh, leaving just a hint of red on the inside of the watermelon. Chop up some of the watermelon flesh and remove the pips. Make up the fresh fruit salad by cutting the fruits into chunks. Add the chopped watermelon to the fruit salad. Store any left-over watermelon flesh in the freezer to make watermelon juice or mush. Fill the watermelon basket with the fruits, and chill.

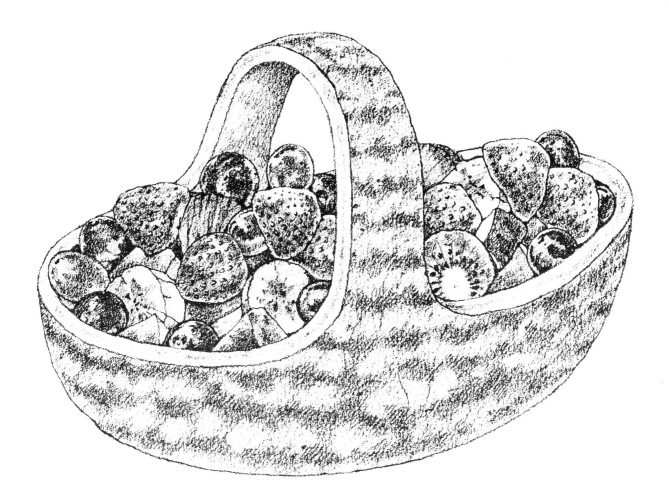

Pancake Toppings

SERVES 4–6

Cherry Topping
250 ml/8 fl oz/1 cup unsweetened
    orange juice
125 ml/4 fl oz/½ cup apple juice
    concentrate
½ teaspoon orange essence
grated rind of 1 lemon
1 tablespoon/1 tablespoon plus
    1 teaspoon lemon juice
1 teaspoon agar powder
500 g/1 lb 2 oz stoned cherries

Blueberry Topping
500 ml/16 fl oz/2 cups unsweetened
    pear juice
75 ml/3 fl oz/⅓ cup apple juice
    concentrate
450 g/1 lb blueberries (fresh or frozen,
    not canned)
1 tablespoon/1 tablespoon plus
    1 teaspoon lemon juice
30 g/1 oz/¼ cup cornflour

Lemon Topping
200 ml/7 fl oz/¾ cup lemon juice
125 ml/4 fl oz/½ cup apple juice
    concentrate
½ teaspoon orange essence
grated rind of 1 orange (optional)
300 ml/10 fl oz/1¼ cups water
30 g/1 oz/¼ cup cornflour

Banana Topping
350 ml/12 fl oz/1½ cups unsweetened
    orange or pear or apple juice
1–2 teaspoons cornflour
4 bananas
1 tablespoon/1 tablespoon plus
    1 teaspoon lemon juice
1 tablespoon/1 tablespoon plus
    1 teaspoon apple juice concentrate

Fruit and Yoghurt Topping
fresh fruit of your choice
non-fat or low-fat yoghurt

Whipped Ricotta Cream
225 g/½ lb/1 cup low-fat ricotta cheese
1–2 teaspoons vanilla essence
125 ml/4 fl oz/½ cup unsweetened pear
    or apple or apricot juice

To make the Cherry Topping, place all the ingredients except the cherries in a saucepan. Bring to the boil and simmer for 10–15 minutes. Add the cherries and cook for a further 5 minutes. Remove from the heat and cool slightly. The mixture will become jelly-like in texture as it cools. Pour over the pancakes and top with Whipped Ricotta Cream (see below).

To make the Blueberry Topping, mix 65 ml/2 fl oz/ ¼ cup of the pear juice with the cornflour to make a paste. Combine the other ingredients in a small saucepan and slowly bring to the boil. Add the cornflour and stir continuously until the sauce thickens. Remove from the heat and cool slightly. Pour over the pancakes. (See left colour plate between pages 192 and 193.)

To make the Lemon Topping, combine the lemon juice, apple juice concentrate, orange essence and rind and 1 cup of the water in a small saucepan. Combine the remaining water and cornflour to make a paste. Slowly bring the lemon mixture to the boil. Add the cornflour mixture and stir continuously until the sauce thickens. Remove from the heat and cool slightly. Pour over the pancakes. (See left colour plate between pages 192 and 193.)

To make the Banana Topping, add a little of the orange juice to the cornflour to make a paste. Pour the remaining orange juice and the lemon juice and apple juice concentrate into a saucepan and bring to the boil. Turn the heat down and simmer until the liquid reduces slightly. Slice the bananas and add to the sauce. Bring to the boil and cook for 1 minute. Add the cornflour and stir until the sauce boils and thickens. Pour over the pancakes and top with Whipped Ricotta Cream (see below).

To make the Fruit and Yoghurt Topping, choose any fresh seasonal fruit. Chop the fruit and scatter on the pancakes. Top with the yoghurt.

To make the Whipped Ricotta Cream, beat the ricotta cheese until smooth. Add the vanilla essence and thin to the desired consistency with the pear juice.

Orange Oat-bran Buckwheat Pancakes

MAKES 6

100 g/3½ oz/¾ cup buckwheat flour
100 g/3½ oz/¾ cup oat bran
1 teaspoon baking powder
250 ml/8 fl oz/1 cup reduced-fat
    soymilk
125 ml/4 fl oz/½ cup unsweetened
    orange juice
1 tablespoon/1 tablespoon plus
    1 teaspoon apple juice concentrate
grated rind of 1 orange
2 egg whites

Combine all the ingredients in a food processor or blender and purée until smooth. Cook a little mixture in a lightly greased non-stick pancake pan or frying pan until browned. Turn over to brown the other side. Repeat to make six pancakes.

Corn-meal and Oat-bran Pancakes

MAKES 6

150 g/5 oz/1 cup corn meal
60 g/2 oz/½ cup oat bran
2 teaspoons baking powder
1 tablespoon/1 tablespoon plus
    1 teaspoon cold-pressed grapeseed oil
2 tablespoons/2 tablespoons plus
    2 teaspoons apple juice concentrate
2 teaspoons vanilla essence
500 ml/16 fl oz/2 cups reduced-fat
    soymilk
4 egg whites

Combine the corn meal, oat bran and baking powder, and mix well. Combine the oil, apple juice concentrate and vanilla essence, and stir into the corn-meal mixture. Beat the egg whites until stiff and gently fold through. Stand for 10 minutes and then mix again. Cook a little mixture in a lightly greased non-stick pancake pan or frying pan until browned. Turn over to brown the other side. Repeat to make six pancakes. Stir the mixture well between each pancake. Serve with fresh bananas and Lemon Sauce (see page 237).

Oat Pancakes

MAKES 6

125 g/¼ lb/1 cup rolled oats
60 g/2 oz/½ cup oat bran
125 g/¼ lb/1 cup wholemeal plain flour
2 teaspoons baking powder
65 ml/2 fl oz/¼ cup apple juice
    concentrate
500 ml/16 fl oz/2 cups water or skim
    milk
1 teaspoon vanilla essence
2 egg whites

In a large bowl, combine the rolled oats and bran. In another bowl, combine the flour and baking powder and sift over the oats, returning the husks to the mixture. Combine the apple juice concentrate, water and vanilla essence, and stir through the oat and flour mixture. Beat the egg whites until stiff and gently fold through the mixture.

Cook a little mixture in a lightly greased non-stick pancake pan or frying pan until browned. Turn over to brown the other side. Repeat to make six pancakes. (See left colour plate between pages 192 and 193.)

Lemon Meringue Pie

SERVES 8

Pastry

125 g/¼ lb/1 cup wholemeal plain flour
125 g/¼ lb/1 cup rolled oats
65 ml/2 fl oz/¼ cup cold-pressed grapeseed oil
2 tablespoons/2 tablespoons plus 2 teaspoons apple juice concentrate
65 ml/2 fl oz/¼ cup lemon juice

Lemon Filling

200 ml/7 fl oz/¾ cup lemon juice
125 ml/4 fl oz/½ cup apple juice concentrate
grated rind of 1 orange
grated rind of 1 lemon
300 ml/10 fl oz/1¼ cups water
60 g/2 oz/½ cup cornflour

Meringue

4 egg whites
125 g/¼ lb/¾ cup raw almonds, finely ground
1 teaspoon vanilla essence
2 tablespoons/2 tablespoons plus 2 teaspoons apple juice concentrate

Preheat the oven to 200°C/400°F.

Combine all the Pastry ingredients in a food processor or blender and blend until the pastry binds together. Roll out to fit a fluted pie dish. Bake for 10–15 minutes. Cool.

To make the lemon filling, place the lemon juice, apple juice concentrate, orange and lemon rind and 250 ml/8 fl oz/1 cup of the water in a small saucepan and bring to the boil. Combine the remaining water with the cornflour and make into a paste. Stir into the lemon mixture and stir continuously as it boils and thickens. Cook for 2 minutes. Cool slightly. Pour into the pastry base and leave to set.

The lemon filling should be quite cold and firm before you make the meringue topping.

Preheat the oven to 200°C/400°F. To make the Meringue, beat the egg whites until stiff peaks form. Add all the other ingredients separately, mixing well after each addition. Spoon over the lemon filling. Bake for 10–15 minutes or until the top has browned.

This pie should be kept out of the refrigerator for the best flavour. Serve with non-fat frozen yoghurt or Home-made Vanilla Ice Cream (see page 199). (See colour plate opposite.)

Banana Yoghurt Pie

SERVES 6

225 g/½ lb/2 cups rolled oats
200 g/7 oz/1 cup stoned dates
1 tablespoon/1 tablespoon plus 1 teaspoon vanilla essence
2 tablespoons/2 tablespoons plus 2 teaspoons unsweetened orange juice
2 tablespoons/2 tablespoons plus 2 teaspoons carob powder
65 ml/2 fl oz/¼ cup boiling water
1 tablespoon/1 tablespoon plus 1 teaspoon gelatine
2 frozen bananas, peeled and chopped
250 ml/8 fl oz/1 cup low-fat evaporated milk, well chilled
½ teaspoon extra vanilla essence
250 ml/8 fl oz/1 cup low-fat yoghurt
1 extra banana, finely sliced
65 ml/2 fl oz/¼ cup lemon juice
1 teaspoon ground nutmeg

Combine the rolled oats, dates, vanilla essence, orange juice and carob powder in a food processor or blender and blend for 3 minutes or until the mixture begins to stick together. Do not over-blend. Press the mixture thinly around the sides and base of a 23-cm/9″ pie dish. Press down firmly, and refrigerate.

Pour the boiling water over the gelatine and stir to dissolve. Set aside to cool. Place the frozen banana in a food processor or blender and blend until smooth. Add the milk. Blend for a further 3–5 minutes or until thick and creamy and doubled in size. Add the vanilla essence and yoghurt, and mix well. Add the gelatine dissolved in the boiling water. Pour over the base of the pie dish. Refrigerate for at least 2–3 hours or until firm.

Soak the extra banana in the lemon juice, drain, and place on top of the pie. Sprinkle the nutmeg on top. (See right colour plate overleaf.)

Lemon Meringue Pie (opposite page).

Oat Pancakes (page 191) with Blueberry Topping and with Lemon Topping (page 190); Home-made Vanilla Ice Cream (page 199).

Banana Yoghurt Pie (page 192).

*W*inter Pears (opposite page).

Winter Pears

xxxxxxxxxxxxxxxxxxxxxxxxxxxxxxxxxxxxxxxxxxxxxxxxxxxxxxxxxxxxxxxxxxxxxxxxxx

SERVES 6

6 pears
500 ml/16 fl oz/2 cups unsweetened
  dark grape juice
2 teaspoons finely grated orange rind
2 teaspoons arrowroot
65 ml/2 fl oz/¼ cup water

Vanilla Custard
250 ml/8 fl oz/1 cup skim milk
1 tablespoon/1 tablespoon plus
  1 teaspoon vanilla essence
2 tablespoons/2 tablespoons plus
  2 teaspoons extra skim milk
2 tablespoons/2 tablespoons plus
  2 teaspoons cornflour

Peel the pears and leave the stems on. Pour the grape juice into a large saucepan, and stand the pears upright in it. Cover, and simmer until the pears are tender. Remove from the heat and leave, covered, for 1 hour. Put the pears into individual serving bowls. Return the remaining juice to the heat and slowly bring to the boil. Add the orange rind. Mix the arrowroot with the water to make a paste. Add to the saucepan. Turn off the heat. Stir briskly as the sauce thickens. Pour a small amount over each pear.

To make the Vanilla Custard, combine the skim milk and vanilla essence in a small saucepan. Make a paste with the extra skim milk and cornflour. Bring the skim milk and vanilla to the boil. As bubbles appear, stir in the cornflour paste. Turn the heat down and stir for at least 2 minutes. Serve with the pears. (See colour plate opposite.)

Ginger Pears

xxxxxxxxxxxxxxxxxxxxxxxxxxxxxxxxxxxxxxxxxxxxxxxxxxxxxxxxxxxxxxxxxxxxxxxxxx

SERVES 6

6 pears
350 ml/12 fl oz/1½ cups unsweetened
  apple juice
2-cm/¾″ piece fresh ginger, peeled
2 teaspoons finely grated lemon rind

Peel the pears and leave the stems on. Pour the apple juice into a large saucepan, and stand the pears upright in it. Add the ginger and lemon rind. Simmer until the pears are soft, but do not over-cook. Remove from the heat. Cover, and leave to stand until cold.

Place the pears in a serving bowl. Remove the ginger, and refrigerate. Serve chilled with a small amount of the juice.

Fruit Salad

xxxxxxxxxxxxxxxxxxxxxxxxxxxxxxxxxxxxxxxxxxxxxxxxxxxxxxxxxxxxxxxxxxxxxxxxxxxxxxxxxxxxxxxxxxx

Fruit salad can be served as a nutritious finish to a meal, for breakfast or for a snack meal. It need never become boring if you change the combinations of the fruit and soak it in a little juice. Serve plain, with home-made ice cream, custard, or non-fat or low-fat yoghurt. (See left colour plate between pages 200 and 201.)

Some Fruit-salad Combinations

- Orange segments, grapefruit segments, pineapple chunks, passionfruit pulp and orange juice.
- Strawberries, watermelon balls and sparkling apple juice.
- Cantaloup balls, honeydew melon balls, green grapes, grated fresh ginger and unsweetened pear juice.
- Banana chunks, pineapple chunks, apple chunks, purple grapes, lemon juice and unsweetened apple juice.
- Honeydew melon chunks, cantaloup chunks, pineapple chunks, purple and green grapes, blueberries and dark grape juice.
- Orange chunks, apple chunks, pear chunks, pineapple chunks, strips of dried apricot, and orange or apple juice.
- Apricot halves, peach pieces, nectarine pieces and apricot nectar.
- Pineapple chunks, banana chunks, passionfruit pulp and unsweetened pineapple juice.
- Strawberries, kiwi fruit chunks, green grapes, grated rind of orange and lemon and unsweetened orange juice.
- Banana slices, kiwi fruit slices, pineapple wedges, orange segments, water chestnut slices, glazed cherries (rinsed to remove sugar) and lemon and orange juice.
- Mango, pineapple, passionfruit pulp, strips of dried apricot (optional) and unsweetened orange juice.
- Dark plum halves, blueberries, purple grapes and dark grape juice.
- Watermelon balls, honeydew melon balls, cantaloup balls, sparkling apple juice and lemon juice.
- Mango, pineapple and orange chunks, passionfruit pulp and fresh halved dates.
- Banana chunks, passionfruit pulp and fresh halved dates.

Frozen Fruit Salad

xxxxxxxxxxxxxxxxxxxxxxxxxxxxxxxxxxxxxxxxxxxxxxxxxxxxxxxxxxxxxxxxxxxxxxxxxxxxxxxxxxxxxxxxxxx

SERVES 6–8

2 teaspoons gelatine
2 tablespoons / 2 tablespoons plus
    2 teaspoons boiling water
2 tablespoons / 2 tablespoons plus
    2 teaspoons skim milk powder
350 ml / 12 fl oz / 1½ cups low-fat
    evaporated milk, well chilled
2 tablespoons / 2 tablespoons plus
    2 teaspoons apple juice concentrate
2 bananas, finely sliced
3 passionfruit
2 apricots, stoned and finely chopped
2 peaches or nectarines, stoned and
    finely chopped
150 g / 5 oz strawberries, sliced
½ small cantaloup, peeled, seeds removed
    and finely chopped
2 teaspoons vanilla essence

Dissolve the gelatine in the boiling water. Beat together the milk powder, evaporated skim milk and apple juice concentrate. Beat in the gelatine and water. Place in chilled freezer trays and freeze until just mushy. Pour into a chilled bowl and beat until smooth and doubled in volume. Fold the fruits and vanilla essence through the mixture. Pour into a mould or basin lined with foil. Freeze overnight. Remove from the freezer, let soften slightly, and serve.

Winter Fruit Salad

SERVES 4 – 6

100 g / 3½ oz / ½ cup dates, stoned and halved

100 g / 3½ oz / ½ cup prunes, stoned and halved

100 g / 3½ oz / ½ cup dried figs, stalks removed and halved

90 g / 3 oz / ½ cup raw almonds

30 g / 1 oz / ¼ cup walnut halves

1 teaspoon ground cinnamon

250 ml / 8 fl oz / 1 cup unsweetened orange juice

2 small cantaloup for serving, halved (optional)

small bunch seedless grapes

1 orange, segmented

quantity Home-made Vanilla Ice Cream *(see p. 199)*

Combine the dried fruits, nuts and cinnamon and place in a clean jar. Pour the orange juice over them. Shake to coat the fruit with the juice. Allow to soak for at least 4 hours. Store in the refrigerator.

Remove a small amount of flesh from the halved cantaloup. Spoon the dried fruit and nut mixture, grapes and orange segments into the halved cantaloup. Serve with Home-made Vanilla Ice Cream (see page 199).

Variation

■ Substitute half the orange juice for 125 ml / 4 fl oz / ½ cup muscat for a dinner-party dessert.

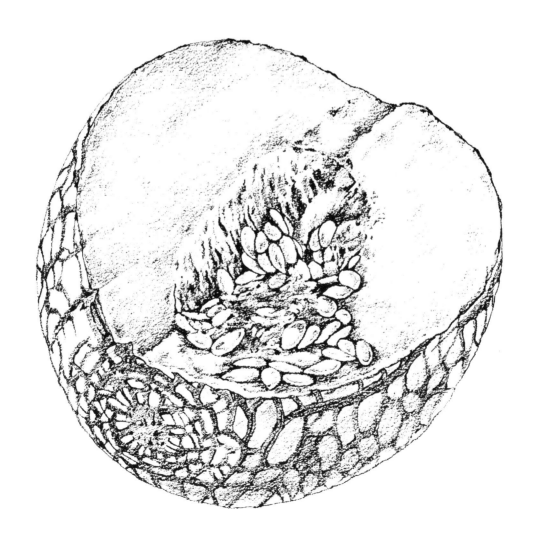

Chunky Banana Ice Cream

SERVES 8–10

350 ml/12 fl oz/1½ cups low-fat
    evaporated milk, well chilled
3 teaspoons vanilla essence
2 tablespoons/2 tablespoons plus
    2 teaspoons lemon juice
4 bananas, roughly chopped

In a large bowl, beat the milk until thick and at least doubled in size. Add the vanilla essence and lemon juice. Add the chopped banana, and beat lightly. Pour into an ice-cream maker and follow the manufacturer's freezing instructions. (See right colour plate between pages 200 and 201.)

Boysenberry Ice Cream

SERVES 8

310 g/10½ oz/2¼ cups frozen
    unsweetened boysenberries
2 tablespoons/2 tablespoons plus
    2 teaspoons apple juice concentrate
1 teaspoon vanilla essence or ½ teaspoon
    orange essence
350 ml/12 fl oz/1½ cups low-fat
    evaporated milk, well chilled, or 250 ml/
    8 fl oz/1 cup reduced-fat soymilk,
    well chilled

Crush the boysenberries in the palm of your hand. Blend in a food processor or blender until soft but still icy, like a sorbet. Add to the remaining ingredients in a large bowl. Beat until at least doubled in size. Pour into an ice-cream maker and follow the manufacturer's freezing instructions. (See left colour plate between pages 200 and 201.)

Rich Carob Ice Cream

SERVES 6

350 ml/12 fl oz/1½ cups low-fat
    evaporated milk, well chilled
30 g/1 oz/¼ cup carob powder
65 ml/2 fl oz/¼ cup apple juice
    concentrate
2 teaspoons vanilla essence

In a large bowl, beat the milk until thick and at least doubled in size. Combine the carob powder, apple juice concentrate and vanilla essence to make a thick paste. Add this mixture to the milk while still beating. Pour into an ice-cream maker and follow the manufacturer's freezing instructions.

Variation
- Add 2 tablespoons/2 tablespoons plus 2 teaspoons of finely chopped roasted almonds, toasted coconut or finely chopped raisins.

Light Carob Ice Cream

SERVES 6

350 ml/12 fl oz/1½ cups low-fat evaporated milk, well chilled, or 750 ml/1⅓ pints/3 cups non-fat or low-fat yoghurt
1 tablespoon/1 tablespoon plus 1 teaspoon carob powder
2 teaspoons vanilla essence
2 tablespoons/2 tablespoons plus 2 teaspoons apple juice concentrate

In a large bowl, beat the milk (not the yoghurt) until thick and at least doubled in size. Combine the carob powder, vanilla essence and apple juice concentrate. Add to the milk. (If using yoghurt, fold through. Do not beat or you will lose the creamy texture.) Pour into an ice-cream maker and follow the manufacturer's freezing instructions.

Kiwi Fruit Ice

SERVES 2

2 kiwi fruit
1 extra kiwi fruit, sliced
fresh pineapple slices

Peel the 2 kiwi fruit and cut into four pieces. Place in a plastic container and put into the freezer for at least 8 hours. Remove from the freezer and let stand for 15 minutes. Place in a food processor or blender and blend until thick and creamy.

Use a small melon baller to scoop the kiwi ice into small balls. Serve with slices of fresh kiwi fruit and pineapple. (See right colour plate between pages 200 and 201.)

Lemon Pear Sorbet

SERVES 8 – 10

850 g/2 lb canned unsweetened pears in natural juice
65 ml/2 fl oz/¼ cup apple juice concentrate
65 ml/2 fl oz/¼ cup lemon juice
8–10 sugar-free ice-cream cones
fresh fruit for decorating

Purée all the ingredients in a food processor or blender. Pour into an ice-cream maker and follow the manufacturer's freezing instructions. Serve in the sugar-free ice-cream cones. Decorate with a piece of fresh fruit.

Orange-flavoured Ice Cream

SERVES 6

350 ml/12 fl oz/1½ cups low-fat
   evaporated milk, well chilled
2 teaspoons vanilla essence
1 teaspoon orange essence
65 ml/2 fl oz/¼ cup apple juice
   concentrate

In a large bowl, beat the milk until thick and at least doubled in size. Add the remaining ingredients while still beating. Pour into an ice-cream maker and follow the manufacturer's freezing instructions.

Orange Tang

SERVES 1

2 oranges
1 tablespoon/1 tablespoon plus
   1 teaspoon apple juice concentrate
orange segments for garnishing

Peel the oranges and remove all the pith. Cut into quarters and place in the freezer for at least 8 hours. Remove from the freezer and let stand for 15 minutes. Place in a food processor or blender with the apple juice concentrate and blend until smooth. Spoon into a glass. Top with the orange segments. This dish is delightful served on a hot summer's day. (See right colour plate between pages 200 and 201.)

Pineapple-flavoured Ice Cream

SERVES 10 – 12

350 ml/12 fl oz/1½ cups low-fat
   evaporated milk, well chilled
2 teaspoons vanilla essence
500 ml/16 fl oz/2 cups unsweetened
   pineapple juice
125 ml/4 fl oz/½ cup apple juice
   concentrate

In a large bowl, beat the milk until thick and at least doubled in size. Add the remaining ingredients while still beating. Pour into an ice-cream maker and follow the manufacturer's freezing instructions. (See left colour plate between pages 200 and 201.)

Home-made Vanilla Ice Cream

SERVES 6

350 ml/12 fl oz/1½ cups low-fat evaporated milk, well chilled
65 ml/2 fl oz/¼ cup apple juice concentrate
2 teaspoons vanilla essence
a little grated lemon rind

In a large bowl, beat the milk until thick and at least doubled in quantity. Add the remaining ingredients while still beating. Pour into an ice-cream maker and follow the manufacturer's freezing instructions. (See colour plate opposite page 177, and left colour plate between pages 192 and 193.)

Variation
- You can add 150 g/5 oz/1 cup of the fresh fruit of your choice to the above recipe (for example, mashed banana, puréed mango, sliced strawberries, blueberries or raspberries). Reduce the amount of apple juice concentrate when using very sweet fruits.

Passionfruit Ice Cream

SERVES 6

200 ml/7 fl oz/¾ cup low-fat evaporated milk, well chilled
250 ml/8 fl oz/1 cup unsweetened fruit juice cocktail (combination of apple, orange, peach and passionfruit juices)
½ teaspoon orange essence
65 ml/2 fl oz/¼ cup apple juice concentrate
2 tablespoons/2 tablespoons plus 2 teaspoons passionfruit pulp

In a large bowl, beat the milk until thick and at least doubled in size. Add the remaining ingredients, except the passionfruit, while still beating. Pour into an ice-cream maker and follow the manufacturer's freezing instructions. When the ice cream begins to thicken, add the passionfruit pulp.

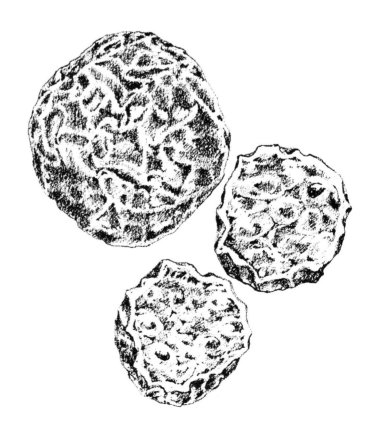

Frozen-yoghurt Ice Cream

SERVES 8

750 ml/1⅓ pints/3 cups non-fat or low-
    fat yoghurt
2 tablespoons/2 tablespoons plus
    2 teaspoons apple juice concentrate
1–2 teaspoons vanilla essence

Combine all the ingredients. Pour into an ice-cream maker and follow the manufacturer's freezing instructions. If you do not have an ice-cream maker, pour into a stainless-steel bowl and place in the freezer. As the yoghurt freezes around the edge of the bowl, stir the frozen particles into the mixture. Continue to do this until all the yoghurt is frozen.

The dish should be served more as a soft dessert than a hard ice cream. Do not beat the yoghurt as the mixture will easily separate. (See colour plate opposite.)

Strawberry Ice Cream

SERVES 8 – 10

350 ml/12 fl oz/1½ cups low-fat
    evaporated milk, well chilled
2 teaspoons vanilla essence
1 tablespoon/1 tablespoon plus
    1 teaspoon apple juice concentrate
575 g/1¼ lb strawberries, washed and
    hulled

In a large bowl, beat the milk until thick and at least doubled in size. Add the vanilla essence and apple juice concentrate. Mash half the strawberries and cut the rest in half. Add both the mashed and halved strawberries. Pour into an ice-cream maker and follow the manufacturer's freezing instructions. (See left colour plate overleaf.)

Strawberry Ice-cream Cake

SERVES 8 – 10

1 quantity Home-made Vanilla Ice
    Cream (see p. 199)
800 g/1¾ lb strawberries, washed and
    hulled
90 g/3 oz/½ cup toasted almond flakes
extra strawberries for decorating

Follow the Home-made Vanilla Ice Cream recipe, but do not freeze in the final step. Pour one-third of the ice-cream mixture into a foil-lined, round cake tin. Slice the strawberries finely and use half in a layer on top of the ice-cream mixture. Pour half the remaining ice-cream mixture on top, cover with another layer of strawberry slices, and then pour the remaining ice-cream mixture on top. Freeze.

Turn the cake out of the tin, remove the foil, and place on a serving plate. Sprinkle the toasted almond flakes on top and decorate the edge of the cake with fresh whole strawberries. (See colour plate opposite page 201.)

Frozen-yoghurt Ice Cream (opposite page) with fresh fruit.

Back (left to right): Pineapple-flavoured Ice Cream (page 198); fruit-salad combination (page 194). Front: Boysenberry Ice Cream (page 196); Strawberry Ice Cream (page 200).

Kiwi Fruit Ice (page 197); Chunky Banana Ice Cream (Page 196); Orange Tang (page 198).

Strawberry Ice-cream Cake (page 200).

CAKES, COOKIES & SLICES

Often when we think of cakes, cookies and slices we think of all those extra kilojoules we do not need. But by simply using wholemeal ingredients, low-fat ingredients, a sugar substitute, and egg whites instead of egg yolks, we can create recipes that complement a well-balanced diet rather than contribute to an unhealthy diet.

Cakes are usually best eaten within a couple of days of being made, and muffins should be devoured straight from the oven.

You'll find here lots of interesting health slices that are excellent to pack in children's lunch boxes.

Apple and Cinnamon Yoghurt Slice

MAKES 16

Base

60 g/2 oz/1 cup fresh wholemeal
  breadcrumbs
125 g/¼ lb/1 cup rolled oats
1 teaspoon ground cinnamon
1 tablespoon/1 tablespoon plus
  1 teaspoon unsweetened orange juice
1 egg white

Filling

200 g/7 oz/¾ cup low-fat cottage
  cheese
400 g/14 oz cooked apple chunks
1 teaspoon vanilla essence
1 teaspoon ground cinnamon
1 teaspoon ground nutmeg
125 ml/4 fl oz/½ cup non-fat or low-
  fat yoghurt
225 g/½ lb/1 cup sultanas
40 g/1½ oz/¼ cup wholemeal plain
  flour
2 teaspoons finely grated lemon rind
2 egg whites

Preheat the oven to 160°C/325°F.

To make the Base, blend the breadcrumbs, oats, cinnamon and orange juice in a food processor or blender until the breadcrumbs begin to stick together. Add the egg whites and blend lightly until absorbed by the breadcrumbs. Do not over-blend.

Spread the breadcrumb mixture evenly over a 20-cm × 30-cm/8″ × 12″ foil-lined slice tin. Press down firmly. Bake for 10 minutes. Remove from the oven. Turn the oven up to 180°C/350°F.

To make the Filling, press the cottage cheese through a fine sieve. Add all the other ingredients, except the egg whites, and mix well. Beat the egg whites until stiff. Gently fold through the mixture. Pour over the slice base and spread out evenly. Bake for 45 minutes. Leave to cool in the tin, and cut into slices before removing. Store in the refrigerator.

Variation

- Substitute apricot for the cooked apple, and omit the vanilla essence. Add 1 teaspoon of mixed spice.

Apple and Date Bars

MAKES 24

Pastry

280 g/10 oz/2 cups wholemeal plain
  flour
225 g/½ lb/2 cups rolled oats
125 ml/4 fl oz/½ cup cold-pressed
  grapeseed oil
65 ml/2 fl oz/¼ cup apple juice
  concentrate
125 ml/4 fl oz/½ cup unsweetened
  orange juice or equal quantities of
  unsweetened orange juice and lemon
  juice

Filling

225 g/½ lb/1⅔ cups stoned dates, finely
  chopped
2 Granny Smith apples, peeled, cored
  and sliced
250 ml/8 fl oz/1 cup unsweetened
  orange juice
1 teaspoon finely grated orange rind

Preheat the oven to 180°C/350°F.

Combine the flour and oats in a food processor or blender and blend lightly. Add the oil, apple juice concentrate and orange juice. Blend until the pastry binds together. Divide in half. Roll out the pastry to make two rectangles. One should be approximately 20 cm × 30 cm/8″ × 12″, the other slightly bigger. Place the larger piece of pastry on the base of a 20-cm × 30-cm/8″ × 12″ foil-lined slice tin.

Place all the Filling ingredients in a small saucepan. Simmer for 20 minutes or until the mixture is soft and most of the orange juice absorbed. Cool slightly.

Pour the Filling over the pastry base and spread evenly. Carefully cover with the top piece of pastry, ensuring it does not break. Press down at the edges to meet the bottom layer. Bake for 20–30 minutes. Cool in the tin before cutting into bars.

Egg-free Apple and Date Cake

SERVES 12

310 g/10½ oz/2½ cups wholemeal plain
    flour
3 teaspoons baking powder
1 teaspoon ground cinnamon
1 teaspoon mixed spice
3 Granny Smith apples
1 teaspoon finely grated lemon rind
200 g/7 oz/1 cup stoned dates, finely
    chopped
1 teaspoon vanilla essence
65 ml/2 fl oz/¼ cup cold-pressed
    grapeseed oil
125 ml/4 fl oz/½ cup non-fat yoghurt
    or non-fat buttermilk
125 ml/4 fl oz/½ cup apple juice
    concentrate

Preheat the oven to 180°C/350°F.

Sift the flour, baking powder, cinnamon and mixed spice twice into a large bowl. Peel and finely chop the apples. Add the lemon rind, chopped apple and dates. Coat well with the flour. Combine the vanilla essence, oil, yoghurt and apple juice concentrate. Add to the bowl and mix well. Spoon into a foil-lined 20-cm/8″ round cake tin. Bake for 50–60 minutes or until firm to touch and an inserted skewer comes out dry. Cool in the tin. (See left colour plate between pages 216 and 217.)

Apple and Date Munchies

MAKES 20 – 24

225 g/½ lb/2 cups rolled oats
125 g/¼ lb/1 cup wholemeal plain flour
1 teaspoon baking powder
½ teaspoon mixed spice
½ teaspoon ground nutmeg
100 g/3½ oz dates, finely chopped
30 g/1 oz dried apple, finely chopped
125 ml/4 fl oz/½ cup apple juice
    concentrate
65 ml/2 fl oz/¼ oz cold-pressed
    grapeseed oil
2 egg whites, lightly beaten

Preheat the oven to 200°C/400°F.

In a large bowl, combine the oats, flour, baking powder, mixed spice, nutmeg, chopped date and apple. In another bowl, carefully combine the apple juice concentrate, oil and beaten egg white, and then add to the oat mixture. Mix together until well combined and sticky. Place spoonfuls on a non-stick baking tray. Bake for 10–15 minutes or until golden.

Almond Apricot Biscuits

MAKES 24

225 g/½ lb/1½ cups raw almonds
20 dried apricots
1 teaspoon vanilla essence
1 teaspoon apple juice concentrate
1 teaspoon cider vinegar
2 egg whites
40 g/1½ oz/¼ cup wholemeal plain
    flour

Preheat the oven to 200°C/400°F.

Blend the almonds and apricots in a food processor or blender for 3 minutes. Add the vanilla essence, apple juice concentrate and vinegar. Beat the egg whites until stiff. Fold through the mixture. Roll into small balls, and roll them in the plain flour. Place on a lightly greased non-stick baking tray, and press down flat.

Bake for 10 minutes. The biscuits should be lightly browned around the edges. Do not over-cook. Cool on a wire rack and store in an airtight container.

Egg-free Apricot Loaf

MAKES 10 – 12

125 g/¼ lb/1 cup wheat bran
200 g/7 oz/1 cup dried apricots,
    chopped
125 g/¼ lb/¾ cup mixed peel or dried
    nectarines or dried peaches, finely
    chopped
500 ml/16 fl oz/2 cups skim milk
200 g/7 oz/1½ cups wholemeal plain
    flour
60 g/2 oz/½ cup unbleached white plain
    flour
2 teaspoons baking powder

Preheat the oven to 180°C/350°F.

Mix the oat bran, chopped apricot, mixed peel and milk together in a large bowl. Cover and let stand for at least 2 hours.

Sift the flours and baking powder. Add to the apricot mixture in small amounts and mix well. Pour the mixture into a 23-cm × 12-cm/9″ × 5″ foil-lined, non-stick loaf tin. Bake for 45–60 minutes or until firm to touch and an inserted skewer comes out dry.

Apricot Nibbles

MAKES 20

150 g/5 oz/¾ cup dried apricots
boiling water
40 g/1½ oz/¾ cup shredded coconut
1 teaspoon grated lemon rind
1 teaspoon grated orange rind
1 tablespoon/1 tablespoon plus
    1 teaspoon unsweetened orange juice
30 g/1 oz/½ cup extra shredded
    coconut, toasted

Cover the apricots with the boiling water and stand 10 minutes. Drain off the liquid. Mince the apricots in a food processor or blender and mix lightly with the coconut. Add the remaining ingredients except the toasted coconut. Knead until well combined. If the mixture is too dry add more orange juice. If the mixture is too wet add more coconut. Shape into small balls and roll in the toasted coconut. Refrigerate.

Apricot and Almond Health Chews

MAKES 24

100 g/3½ oz/½ cup dried apricots,
    chopped
65 ml/2 fl oz/¼ cup unsweetened
    orange juice
2 tablespoons/2 tablespoons plus
    2 teaspoons apple juice concentrate
40 g/1½ oz/½ cup skim milk powder
30 g/1 oz/¼ cup almonds, roughly
    chopped
1 tablespoon/1 tablespoon plus
    1 teaspoon sesame seeds, toasted
1 teaspoon grated orange rind
100 g/3½ oz/½ cup sultanas or
    currants
15 g/½ oz/¼ cup shredded coconut
30 g/1 oz/½ cup extra shredded
    coconut, toasted

Place the chopped apricot, orange juice and apple juice concentrate in a saucepan and simmer for 10 minutes. Do not drain. Remove the saucepan from the heat. Add the skim milk powder, and mix. Add the chopped almond, sesame seeds, orange rind, sultanas and coconut. Mix well and leave to cool slightly.

Roll the mixture into a log shape and roll in the toasted coconut. Roll up in foil and refrigerate. Cut into rounds as required. Wrap individual pieces in coloured cellophane to use as gifts.

Apricot and Apple Oat Slice

MAKES 24

200 g/7 oz/1 cup dried apricots
60 g/2 oz/1 cup dried apple
150 g/5 oz/1 cup raw almonds
60 g/2 oz/1 cup shredded coconut
225 g/½ lb/2 cups rolled oats
2 teaspoons finely grated orange rind
2 teaspoons finely grated lemon rind
125 ml/4 fl oz/¼ cup unsweetened
   orange juice

Chop the apricots and dried apple finely in a food processor or blender. While the machine is operating, add the almonds, coconut, oats, and orange and lemon rind. The mixture should resemble coarse breadcrumbs. Slowy add the orange juice until the mixture just starts to stick together.

Press firmly into a 20-cm × 30-cm/8″ × 12″ foil-lined slice tin. Use a round-shaped glass to roll the mixture down firmly in the tin. Refrigerate. Cut into squares or shapes and keep refrigerated.

Banana and Carob Cake

SERVES 8

225 g/½ lb/1¾ cups wholemeal plain
   flour
3 tablespoons/3 tablespoons plus
   3 teaspoons carob powder
3 teaspoons baking powder
1 teaspoon ground cinnamon
1 teaspoon mixed spice
2 bananas, mashed
125 ml/4 fl oz/½ cup apple juice
   concentrate
65 ml/2 fl oz/¼ cup cold-pressed
   grapeseed oil
65 ml/2 fl oz/¼ cup non-fat or low-fat
   yoghurt
2 teaspoons vanilla essence
4 egg whites
250 ml/8 fl oz/1 cup low-fat cream or
   Custard (see p. 182)
150 g/5 oz strawberries

Preheat the oven to 180°C/350°F.

Sift the flour, carob powder, baking powder, cinnamon and mixed spice twice into a large bowl. Combine the banana, apple juice concentrate, oil, yoghurt and vanilla essence. Add to the flour mixture and beat well. Beat the egg whites and until stiff peaks form and carefully fold into the mixture.

Spoon into a 20-cm/8″ round, foil-lined cake tin. Bake for 45–50 minutes. Remove from the oven and cover lightly until cool. Slice in half and fill with the low-fat cream or Custard and strawberries.

To fill with custard, line the tin with foil. Place the bottom half of the cake back in the tin and press the cake down. Add the cool custard. Place the cake top on and press down lightly. Refrigerate.

Variations
- Use 185 g/6 oz/1 cup of grated apple instead of the mashed banana.
- Scatter 60 g/2 oz/½ cup of chopped walnuts or pecan nuts over the mixture in the tin before baking.
- Fill with whipped low-fat cream and strawberries (see left colour plate between pages 216 and 217).

Carob Hedgehog Slice

MAKES 36

200 g/7 oz/1 cup dates
200 g/7 oz/1 cup sultanas
90 g/3 oz/½ cup raw almonds
225 g/½ lb/2 cups rolled oats
1 tablespoon/1 tablespoon plus 1
   teaspoon vanilla essence
2 tablespoons/2 tablespoons plus
   2 teaspoons carob powder

Combine all the ingredients in a food processor or blender. Blend until the mixture begins to stick together. Press into a 20-cm × 30-cm/8″ × 12″ foil-lined slice tin, and refrigerate.

Carrot Cake with Lemon Cheese

SERVES 12

310 g/10½ oz/2 cups finely grated
    carrot
200 g/7 oz/1 cup sultanas
1½ teaspoons ground cinnamon
125 ml/4 fl oz/½ cup unsweetened
    orange juice
125 ml/4 fl oz/½ cup apple juice
    concentrate
75 ml/3 fl oz/⅓ cup cold-pressed
    grapeseed oil
125 g/¼ lb/1 cup wholemeal plain flour
125 g/¼ lb/1 cup unbleached white
    plain flour
3 teaspoons baking powder
2 egg whites

Lemon Cheese Topping
250 ml/8 fl oz/1 cup cold Lemon
    Topping (see Pancake Toppings,
    p. 190)
125 g/¼ lb/½ cup low-fat ricotta cheese

Preheat the oven to 180°C/350°F.

Place the carrot, sultanas, cinnamon, orange juice and apple juice concentrate in a large saucepan and gently bring to the boil. Simmer for 5–7 minutes or until the sultanas are soft. Remove from the heat and leave to cool completely. Add the oil and mix well. Sift the flours. Combine with the baking powder and carrot mixture in two lots, mixing well. Beat the egg whites until stiff and gently fold through the mixture. Spoon into a foil-lined ring tin. Bake for 45–50 minutes.

The cake should be completely cool before adding the topping. To make the Lemon Cheese Topping, mix the ingredients until smooth and refrigerate until quite firm. Spread evenly over the top of the cake.

Christmas Cake

SERVES 24

125 g/¼ lb dried apricots
125 g/¼ lb/½ cup raisins
125 g/¼ lb/½ cup mixed dried peel
125 g/¼ lb/½ cup currants
225 g/½ lb/1½ cups stoned prunes
225 g/½ lb/1½ cups stoned dates
2 tablespoons/2 tablespoons plus
    2 teaspoons brandy, and unsweetened
    orange juice to make up 1 cup
60 g/2 oz/⅓ cup raw almonds
500 g/1 lb 2 oz/2 cups mashed pumpkin
125 ml/4 fl oz/½ cup apple juice
    concentrate
500 g/1 lb 2 oz/4 cups wholemeal plain
    flour
4 teaspoons baking powder
2 teaspoons bicarbonate of soda
1 teaspoon ground cinnamon
1 teaspoon mixed spice
½ teaspoon ground nutmeg
6 egg whites
1 tablespoon/1 tablespoon plus
    1 teaspoon vanilla essence

Preheat the oven to 160°C/325°F.

Chop the fruits and soak in the brandy and orange juice, covered, overnight. Roughly chop the almonds and add to the fruit. Add the pumpkin and apple juice concentrate, and mix well. Sift the flour, baking powder, bicarbonate of soda, cinnamon, mixed spice and nutmeg twice. Fold into the fruit mixture in three lots, and mix well. Beat the egg whites until stiff. Gently fold through the mixture. Add the vanilla essence.

Line a 23-cm/9″ round cake tin, 8 cm/3″ deep, with foil or non-stick baking paper. Cut out a long 10-cm/4″ wide strip of brown paper and secure it around the top of the tin so that 8 cm/3″ of brown paper is above the tin. Pour the cake mixture into the tin and spread evenly. Decorate with almonds if desired.

Bake the cake for 2½–3 hours. Test after 2½ hours with a fine skewer. Remove from the oven and cover with brown paper and tea towels to keep the moisture in the cake. When cool, wrap in foil or plastic wrap and store in a sealed container. (See left colour plate between pages 208 and 209.)

Currant Munchies

MAKES 20

225 g / ½ lb / 2 cups rolled oats
125 g / ¼ lb / 1 cup wholemeal plain flour
1 teaspoon baking powder
1½ teaspoons mixed spice
150 g / 5 oz / 1 cup currants
2 teaspoons finely grated lemon rind
125 ml / 4 fl oz / ½ cup apple juice
   concentrate
65 ml / 2 fl oz / ¼ cup cold-pressed
   grapeseed oil
2 egg whites, lightly beaten

Preheat the oven to 200°C / 400°F.

In a large bowl, combine the oats, flour, baking powder, mixed spice, currants and rind. In another bowl, carefully mix the apple juice concentrate, oil and beaten egg white, and then add to the oat mixture. Mix together until well combined and sticky. Place spoonfuls on a non-stick baking tray. Bake for 10–15 minutes or until golden.

Currant and Zucchini Cake

SERVES 8

310 g / 10½ oz / 2½ cups wholemeal plain
   flour
2 teaspoons baking powder
1 teaspoon bicarbonate of soda
1 teaspoon ground cinnamon
1 teaspooon mixed spice
65 ml / 2 fl oz / ¼ cup cold-pressed
   almond oil
125 ml / 4 fl oz / ½ cup low-fat yoghurt
1 tablespoon / 1 tablespoon plus
   1 teaspoon maple syrup
350 g / ¾ lb / 2 cups grated zucchini
   (juice squeezed out)
150 g / 5 oz / 1 cup currants
4 egg whites

Preheat the oven to 180°C / 350°F.

Sift the flour, baking powder, bicarbonate of soda, cinnamon and mixed spice twice. Combine the oil, yoghurt and maple syrup, and mix well. Add the zucchini and currants. Mix again. Fold the flour into the mixture. Beat the egg whites until stiff peaks form. Gently fold through mixture. Turn it into a foil-lined, deep-sided 20-cm/8″ square tin.

Bake for 1 hour. Remove from the oven and cover with foil for 10 minutes. Remove the foil and leave in the tin to cool.

Basic Oat Munchies

MAKES 20 – 24

225 g / ½ lb / 2 cups rolled oats
125 g / ¼ lb / 1 cup wholemeal plain flour
1 teaspoon baking powder
½ teaspoon mixed spice
½ teaspoon ground cinnamon
150 g / 5 oz / 1 cup mixed dried fruit
60 g / 2 oz / ¼ cup sunflower seeds
125 ml / 4 fl oz / ½ cup apple juice
   concentrate
125 ml / 4 fl oz / ½ cup cold-pressed
   grapeseed oil
2 egg whites, lightly beaten

Preheat the oven to 200°C / 400°F.

In a large bowl, combine the oats, flour, baking powder, mixed spice, cinnamon and dried fruit. In another bowl, carefully combine the apple juice concentrate, oil and beaten egg white, and then add to the oat mixture. Mix together until well combined and sticky. Place spoonfuls on a non-stick baking tray. Bake for 10–15 minutes or until golden.

Blueberry Cake

SERVES 12

280 g/10 oz/2 cups wholemeal plain flour

3 teaspoons baking powder

1 teaspoon ground cinnamon

200 g/7 oz/1½ cups blueberries (fresh or frozen, not canned)

65 ml/2 fl oz/¼ cup cold-pressed grapeseed oil

125 ml/4 fl oz/½ cup apple juice concentrate

65 ml/2 fl oz/¼ cup non-fat or low-fat buttermilk

2 teaspoons vanilla essence

2 egg whites

Preheat the oven to 190°C/375°F.

Sift the flour, baking powder and cinnamon twice into a large bowl. Add the blueberries and toss to coat well. In another bowl, combine the oil, apple juice concentrate, buttermilk and vanilla essence. Add to the flour mixture and mix well. Beat the egg whites until stiff peaks form and fold carefully through the mixture. Spoon into a 20-cm/8" round foil-lined cake tin. Bake for 35–40 minutes. (See colour plate opposite and left colour plate between pages 216 and 217.)

Energy Biscuits

MAKES 20

225 g/½ lb/2 cups untoasted muesli

125 g/¼ lb/1 cup wholemeal self-raising flour

125 g/¼ lb/1 cup unbleached white plain flour

2 tablespoons/2 tablespoons plus 2 teaspoons carob powder

10 dried apricots, chopped

10 dates, chopped

2 tablespoons/2 tablespoons plus 2 teaspoons mixed peel

2 tablespoons/2 tablespoons plus 2 teaspoons chopped mixed nuts (optional)

125 ml/4 fl oz/½ cup cold-pressed grapeseed oil

125 ml/4 fl oz/½ cup apple juice concentrate

3 egg whites

1 teaspoon vanilla essence

Preheat the oven to 180°C/350°F.

Combine the muesli, flours, carob powder, fruit, peel and nuts. Add the oil and apple juice concentrate, and mix well.

Beat the egg whites in a bowl and add the vanilla essence. Fold through the muesli mixture.

Make 20 biscuits, using your hands to flatten them onto a biscuit tray lined with non-stick baking paper. Bake for 8–10 minutes.

Variation

■ To make a decorative icing for the biscuits, melt blocks of carob. Spoon the melted carob over the biscuits and sprinkle with a mixture of pumpkin seeds and sesame seeds. (See right colour plate overleaf.)

Blueberry Cake (opposite page) with Whipped Ricotta Cream (page 190).

Christmas Cake (page 206); Cold Christmas Pudding (page 182); Baked Herb Tomatoes (page 165); Hot Chicken Terrine (page 83); Baked Peeled Potatoes (page 158).

Energy Biscuits (page 208) topped with melted carob and pumpkin and sesame seeds.

Banana Logs (page 210); Apricot Crumble Slice and Carob Peppermint Hedgehog Balls (opposite page).

Apricot Crumble Slice

MAKES 20–24

Base

125 g / ¼ lb / 1 cup wholemeal plain flour
125 g / ¼ lb / 1 cup rolled oats
65 ml / 2 fl oz / ¼ cup cold-pressed
grapeseed oil
2 tablespoons / 2 tablespoons plus
2 teaspoons apple juice concentrate

Filling

225 g / ½ lb dried apricots
250 ml / 8 fl oz / 1 cup water
1 teaspoon finely grated orange rind

Crumble Topping

2 egg whites
125 g / ¼ lb / ¾ cup raw almonds, finely
ground
1 teaspoon vanilla essence
2 tablespoons / 2 tablespoons plus
2 teaspoons apple juice concentrate
2 tablespoons / 2 tablespoons plus
2 teaspoons shredded coconut

Combine all the Base ingredients in a food processor or blender and blend until they bind together. Firmly press into a 20-cm × 30-cm/8″ × 12″ foil-lined slice tin. Set aside.

To make the Filling, place the apricots, water and orange rind in a saucepan. Simmer for 10–15 minutes or until the apricots are soft. Purée and cool slightly. Pour over the slice base.

While the apricots are cooking preheat the oven to 180°C/ 350°F.

To make the Crumble Topping, beat the egg whites until stiff peaks form. Fold in all the other ingredients in the order they are listed. Pour over the Filling. Bake for 20–25 minutes or until the top is firm and lightly brown. Cut into squares or shapes and keep refrigerated. (See colour plate opposite.)

Carob Peppermint Hedgehog Balls

MAKES 24

200 g / 7 oz / 1 cup dates
200 g / 7 oz / 1 cup raisins
150 g / 5 oz / 1 cup raw almonds
225 g / ½ lb / 2 cups rolled oats
60 g / 2 oz / 1 cup shredded coconut
2 tablespoons / 2 tablespoons plus
2 teaspoons carob powder
2 teaspoons vanilla essence
½ teaspoon peppermint essence
2 tablespoons / 2 tablespoons plus
2 teaspoons apple juice concentrate
1 tablespoon / 1 tablespoon plus
1 teaspoon extra apple juice
concentrate or unsweetened orange
juice (if necessary)

Place the dates and raisins in a food processor or blender and blend to small pieces. Add the almonds, oats, coconut and carob powder. Blend until the mixture resembles bread-crumbs. Add the essences and apple juice concentrate. The mixture should now begin to stick together. Stop the machine and check if the texture is correct by taking a small amount in the palm of your hand and rolling up firmly into a ball. If the mixture does not bind, add the extra apple juice concentrate. The mixture should not be too sticky. Roll into small balls and refrigerate until firm. Keep in the freezer and use as required. (See colour plate opposite.)

Variation

■ Omit the peppermint essence and press the mixture into a 20-cm × 30-cm/8″ × 12″ slice tin. Roll down firmly, using a round glass. Refrigerate and cut into slices when firm.

Banana Logs

MAKES 12

200 g/7 oz dried banana
100 g/3½ oz dried apple
150 g/5 oz/1 cup raw almonds
125 g/¼ lb/1 cup rolled oats
30 g/1 oz/½ cup shredded coconut
3 tablespoons/3 tablespoons plus
   3 teaspoons apple juice concentrate
squeeze of lemon or unsweetened orange
   juice (if necessary)
extra shredded coconut

Chop the banana and apple roughly in a food processor or blender. Add the almonds, oats and coconut. Blend until the mixture resembles large breadcrumbs. Add the apple juice concentrate, and blend lightly. If the mixture is too dry add the lemon juice. The mixture will come together in your hands. Roll into log shapes that are 6 cm/2½″ long. Roll in the coconut. Store in the freezer for a chewy texture. (See colour plate opposite page 209.)

Moist Mandarin and Banana Cake

SERVES 8

3 very ripe bananas or 1 banana and
   2 apples, grated (juice squeezed out)
200 g/7 oz/1 cup stoned dates
peel from ½ mandarin, pith removed
125 g/¼ lb/½ cup low-fat cottage
   cheese
4 egg whites
1 teaspoon vanilla essence
2 tablespoons/2 tablespoons plus
   2 teaspoons chopped walnuts
   (optional)
200 g/7 oz/1½ cups wholemeal self-
   raising flour
1 teaspoon bicarbonate of soda

Preheat the oven to 180°C/350°F.
   Mash the bananas. Blend the dates and mandarin peel in a food processor or blender. Add the cottage cheese and blend until quite smooth. Beat in 1 egg white at a time. Add the banana, vanilla essence and chopped walnuts. Sift the flour and bicarbonate of soda and fold through gently. Bake in a 20-cm/8″ ring tin or a deep 20-cm/8″ fluted cake tin for 35–40 minutes.

Variations
- Any fruits can be substituted for the mandarin and banana. The quantity should be 185 g/6 oz/¾ cup. You can use orange or lemon peel instead of mandarin peel.
- To make apricot tea cakes, substitute 185 g/6 oz/¾ cup of apricot pulp for the bananas, and omit the mandarin peel. Spoon the mixture into paper patty cups. Bake at 180°C/350°F for 15–20 minutes.

Sesame Fruit Loaf

SERVES 8

125 g/¼ lb/1 cup All Bran
250 ml/8 fl oz/1 cup skim milk
125 g/¼ lb/1 cup wheatgerm
1 teaspoon bicarbonate of soda
100 g/3½ oz/½ cup sultanas
100 g/3½ oz/½ cup currants
100 g/3½ oz/½ cup raisins
60 g/2 oz/½ cup chopped walnuts
1 tablespoon/1 tablespoon plus
   1 teaspoon honey or golden syrup
toasted sesame seeds

Preheat the oven to 200°C/400°F.
   Soak the All Bran in the milk for 5 minutes. Add all the other ingredients, except the sesame seeds, and mix thoroughly. Spoon into a foil-lined loaf tin. Sprinkle with toasted sesame seeds. Bake for 35–40 minutes.

Note
If All Bran is unavailable use any breakfast cereal comprised of bran flakes.

BREADS, CEREALS, MUFFINS & SCONES

For the health-conscious person, gone are the days of fried eggs, bacon and sausages or lashings of butter on white bread for breakfast. Breakfast is now recognised as one of the most important meals of the day and the opportunity to start the day right with some essential fibre as well as nutrients.

The breakfast cereal, bread, muffin and scone recipes here contain both water-soluble fibre and non-water-soluble fibre, both essential in a healthy eating plan. They are also high in complex carbohydrates, which are the source of longer-lasting energy, and lower in kilojoules than simple carbohydrates such as white flour and sugar.

Basic Breadmaking Instructions

The bread recipes that follow use this basic technique.

Place the flour, oat bran, yeast and calcium ascorbate in a large mixing bowl. Add the oil, apple juice concentrate and water. Use a knife to scrape the flour away from the sides and turn it back into the centre. Mix to a dough. (If adding fruit, nuts, vegetables, cheese and so on, do so now.)

Knead the dough on a floured bench for approximately 10 minutes, or in an electric mixer with a dough hook. If kneading by hand, take the edges of the dough and pull them into the centre with your fingers. Push the dough out over the bench using the heels of both hands. Give the dough a small turn each time you do this. The dough has been sufficiently kneaded when it springs back after a finger is pushed into it.

Place the dough in a warm, draught-free place (in a preheated oven that has been turned off, or near a heater, or in a car that is parked in the sun) for about 30 minutes or until it has doubled in size.

Knock the dough down again. Place the dough in a prepared bread tin and set aside to allow it to reach the top of the tin.

If desired, brush the top of the risen dough with water, skim milk or diluted soymilk and sprinkle with poppyseeds, sesame seeds, cracked wheat, caraway seeds or spices.

Bake the dough in a hot oven (230°C/450°F) for 30 minutes or until the bread is crisp on the outside and sounds hollow when tapped.

Basic Oat-bran Bread

MAKES 1 LOAF

225 g/½ lb/2 cups unbleached white
   plain flour
185 g/6 oz/1½ cups oat bran
1 tablespoon/1 tablespoon plus
   1 teaspoon yeast
2 teaspoons calcium ascorbate
1 tablespoon/1 tablespoon plus
   1 teaspoon cold-pressed grapeseed oil
1 tablespoon/1 tablespoon plus
   1 teaspoon apple juice concentrate
350 ml/12 fl oz/1½ cups very warm
   water or skim milk

To make the loaf, follow the Basic Breadmaking Instructions (see above).

Ensure the loaf is completely cold before slicing. If you use an electric knife you can slice finely and make excellent wholesome sandwiches, or slice it thickly for crunchy toast.

You can store half the dough in an airtight plastic bag in the refrigerator and use it the following day. Keeping it in the refrigerator stops the yeast from working. Once the dough comes back to room temperature, the yeast will begin to work.

The Basic Oat-bran Bread dough is also used to make bread rolls (see right colour plate between pages 216 and 217), two pizza bases, or one base and a small loaf of bread.

Garlic Oat-bran Bread

SERVES 3–4

½ quantity Basic Oat-bran Bread
   dough (see this page)
4 cloves garlic, crushed
a little skim milk
a little dried oregano
a little dried basil
a little grated geska herb cheese

Preheat the oven to 200°C/400°F.

Roll out the Basic Oat-bran Bread dough to the size of a pizza tray, cover with a tea towel and stand in a warm place for no more than 10 minutes.

Top the base with garlic, brushing with skim milk to spread the garlic evenly. Sprinkle with oregano, basil and cheese. Bake for 10–15 minutes.

Apple and Lemon Oat-bran Bread

MAKES 1 LOAF

225 g / ½ lb / 2 cups unbleached white
  plain flour
185 g / 6 oz / 1½ cups oat bran
1 tablespoon / 1 tablespoon plus
  1 teaspoon yeast
2 teaspoons calcium ascorbate
100 g / 3½ oz / ½ cup grated apple,
  firmly packed (juice squeezed out)
1 tablespoon / 1 tablespoon plus
  1 teaspoon finely grated lemon rind
1 teaspoon mixed spice
1 tablespoon / 1 tablespoon plus
  1 teaspoon cold-pressed grapeseed oil
1 tablespoon / 1 tablespoon plus
  1 teaspoon apple juice concentrate
350 ml / 12 fl oz / 1½ cups very warm
  water

To make the loaf, follow the Basic Breadmaking Instructions (see page 212). This is a moist bread with a light lemony flavour. (See right colour plate between pages 216 and 217.)

Banana and Walnut Oat-bran Bread

MAKES 1 LOAF

225 g / ½ lb / 2 cups unbleached white
  plain flour
185 g / 6 oz / 1½ cups oat bran
1 tablespoon / 1 tablespoon plus
  1 teaspoon yeast
2 teaspoons calcium ascorbate
125 g / ¼ lb / ½ cup mashed banana
30 g / 1 oz / ¼ cup walnuts, chopped
1 tablespoon / 1 tablespoon plus
  1 teaspoon cold-pressed grapeseed oil
1 tablespoon / 1 tablespoon plus
  1 teaspoon apple juice concentrate
350 ml / 12 fl oz / 1½ cups very warm
  water

To make the loaf, follow the Basic Breadmaking Instructions (see page 212).

This is our favourite loaf. It smells absolutely wonderful as you take it from the oven and you will be tempted to cut it immediately, but hot bread does not slice very well, so it is best to let it stand for a good hour before slicing. It makes delicious lettuce and banana sandwiches or banana and alfalfa sprout sandwiches, or just top it with low-fat cottage cheese.

Cheese and Pecan Oat-bran Bread

MAKES 1 LOAF

225 g/½ lb/2 cups wholemeal plain
  flour
185 g/6 oz/1½ cups oat bran
1 tablespoon/1 tablespoon plus
  1 teaspoon yeast
2 teaspoons calcium ascorbate
60 g/2 oz/½ cup grated low-fat grating
  cheese, firmly packed
75 g/2½ oz/½ cup finely chopped celery
30 g/1 oz/¼ cup pecan nuts, finely
  chopped
1 tablespoon/1 tablespoon plus
  1 teaspoon cold-pressed grapeseed oil
1 tablespoon/1 tablespoon plus
  1 teaspoon apple juice concentrate
350 ml/12 fl oz/1½ cups very warm
  water

To make the loaf, follow the Basic Breadmaking Instructions (see page 212).

This is an excellent bread for pâté. It keeps its moisture, and its flavours develop with time.

Fruit Oat-bran Bread

MAKES 1 LOAF

225 g/½ lb/2 cups wholemeal plain
  flour
185 g/6 oz/1½ cups oat bran
1 tablespoon/1 tablespoon plus
  1 teaspoon yeast
2 teaspoons calcium ascorbate
1 teaspoon ground cinnamon
1 teaspoon mixed spice
1 teaspoon ground nutmeg
225 g/½ lb/1½ cups chopped mixed
  dried fruits (e.g. peaches, nectarines,
  pears, dates, raisins, sultanas, mixed
  peel)
1 tablespoon/1 tablespoon plus
  1 teaspoon cold-pressed grapeseed oil
2 tablespoons/2 tablespoons plus
  2 teaspoons apple juice concentrate
350 ml/12 fl oz/1½ cups very warm
  water
a little skim milk or water
1 tablespoon/1 tablespoon plus
  1 teaspoon poppyseeds

To make the loaf, follow the Basic Breadmaking Instructions (see page 212).

I like to cook this bread without a tin, in a 'rustic' shape, just on an oven tray. Brush the top of the dough with skim milk or water and sprinkle with the poppyseeds.

Onion and Sesame Oat-bran Bread

MAKES 1 LOAF

1 onion, chopped
2 cloves garlic, crushed (optional)
1 tablespoon/1 tablespoon plus
    1 teaspoon sesame seeds
225 g/½ lb/2 cups unbleached white
    flour
185 g/6 oz/1½ cups oat bran
1 tablespoon/1 tablespoon plus
    1 teaspoon yeast
2 teaspoons calcium ascorbate
1 tablespoon/1 tablespoon plus
    1 teaspoon cold-pressed grapeseed oil
1 tablespoon/1 tablespoon plus
    1 teaspoon apple juice concentrate
250 ml/8 fl oz/1 cup very warm water
1 tablespoon extra/1 tablespoon plus
    1 teaspoon extra sesame seeds or
    poppyseeds

Place the onion, garlic and sesame seeds in a small saucepan. Cover, and cook on a low heat until the garlic and onion are very soft. Then follow the Basic Breadmaking Instructions (see page 212), adding the slightly cooked onion mixture after the warm water.

Brush the top of the loaf with water and sprinkle with sesame seeds or poppyseeds.

Potato and Herb Oat-bran Bread

MAKES 1 LOAF

225 g/½ lb/2 cups unbleached white
    plain flour
185 g/6 oz/1½ cups oat bran
1 tablespoon/1 tablespoon plus
    1 teaspoon yeast
2 teaspoons calcium ascorbate
100 g/3½ oz/½ cup grated potato (juice
    squeezed out), firmly packed
2 teaspoons dried dill
2 tablespoons/2 tablespoons plus
    2 teaspoons sunflower seeds
1 tablespoon/1 tablespoon plus
    1 teaspoon cold-pressed grapeseed oil
1 tablespoon/1 tablespoon plus
    1 teaspoon apple juice concentrate
250 ml/8 fl oz/1 cup very warm water
2 teaspoons caraway seeds

To make the loaf, follow the Basic Breadmaking Instructions (see page 212).

Brush the top of the dough with water and sprinkle with the caraway seeds.

Raisin Oat-bran Bread

MAKES 1 LOAF

*225 g / ½ lb / 2 cups unbleached white
    plain flour*
185 g / 6 oz / 1½ cups oat bran
*1 tablespoon / 1 tablespoon plus
    1 teaspoon yeast*
2 teaspoons calcium ascorbate
2 teaspoons mixed spice
½ teaspoon ground cinnamon
½ teaspoon ground nutmeg
*1 tablespoon / 1 tablespoon plus
    1 teaspoon finely grated orange rind*
200 g / 7 oz / 1½ cups raisins
*2 tablespoons / 2 tablespoons plus
    2 teaspoons apple juice concentrate*
*1 tablespoon / 1 tablespoon plus
    1 teaspoon cold-pressed grapeseed oil*
*350 ml / 12 fl oz / 1½ cups very warm
    water*

To make the loaf, follow the Basic Breadmaking Instructions (see page 212).

This loaf develops in flavour as it keeps – that is, if you can keep it! It also makes great toast.

Zucchini Oat-bran Pancakes

MAKES 8

125 g / ¼ lb / 1 cup rolled oats
60 g / 2 oz / ½ cup oat bran
*125 g / ¼ lb / 1 cup unbleached white
    plain flour*
2 teaspoons baking powder
*350 g / ¾ lb / 2 cups grated zucchini
    (juice squeezed out), firmly packed*
*30 g / 1 oz / ¼ cup grated low-fat grating
    cheese, firmly packed*
*250 ml / 8 fl oz / 1 cup low-fat evaporated
    milk*
250 ml / 8 fl oz / 1 cup water
2 egg whites
black pepper to taste

Combine the oats and oat bran in a large bowl. Sift the flour and baking powder into the oats and combine. Add the zucchini and cheese, and mix well.

Combine the milk and water and stir into the mixture, and mix thoroughly.

Beat the egg whites until stiff and gently fold through the mixture. Cook a little mixture on a lightly greased non-stick pancake pan until browned. Turn over to brown the other side. Repeat to make eight pancakes.

Serving Suggestions
- Top with avocado, alfalfa sprouts and Soymilk Mayonnaise (see page 139) and roll up.
- Top with lettuce, tomato, cucumber slices, tuna and horseradish mayonnaise (grate fresh horseradish into Soymilk Mayonnaise, see page 139).
- Make up a basic White Sauce (see page 239) and add chopped cooked chicken, left-over fish, canned salmon or cooked vegetables, and use as a filling.
- Top with Mushroom Sauce (see page 237) and dry-fried tomato rings (see colour plate opposite).

*Zucchini Oat-bran Pancakes (opposite page) topped with tomato and
Mushroom Sauce (page 237).*

Top (left to right): Blueberry Cake (page 208); Banana and Carob Cake (page 205). Bottom: Egg-free Apple and Date Cake (page 203); Banana and Carob Muffins (page 218).

Apple and Lemon Oat-bran Bread (page 213); Apricot Jam Spread (page 232); Plum Jam Spread (page 233); Apple Jam Spread (page 232); Basic Oat-bran Bread rolls (page 212).

Blueberry Oat Muffins (opposite page).

Apple and Sultana Muffins

MAKES 12 MONSTER MUFFINS

225 g /½ lb /2 cups oat bran
225 g /½ lb /2 cups wholemeal plain
  flour
6 teaspoons baking powder
2 teaspoons ground cinnamon
1 teaspoon mixed spice
6 Granny Smith apples
boiling water
200 g /7 oz /1 cup sultanas
1 teaspoon grated lemon rind
125 ml /4 fl oz /½ cup apple juice
  concentrate
125 ml /4 fl oz /½ cup cold-pressed
  grapeseed oil
200 ml /7 fl oz /¾ cup unsweetened
  orange juice
65 ml /2 fl oz /¼ cup lemon juice
3 egg whites
a little extra oat bran

Preheat the oven to 180°C /350°F.

Place the oat bran in a large bowl. Combine the wholemeal flour, baking powder and spices, and sift into the oat bran.

Peel, core and chop the apples. Cover with the boiling water. Stand for 5 minutes, and then drain. Add the apples, sultanas and lemon rind to the flour mixture. Mix well to coat with flour.

Combine the apple juice concentrate, oil and orange and lemon juice, and add to the flour mixture.

Beat the egg whites just lightly and gently fold through the mixture. Spoon into a lightly greased muffin tray that has been coated with a little flour or oat bran. Bake for 25–30 minutes.

Remove the muffins from the tray immediately and place on a wire rack to cool. Cover with a tea towel.

Blueberry Oat Muffins

MAKES 12 MONSTER MUFFINS

225 g /½ lb /2 cups oat bran
225 g /½ lb /2 cups unbleached white
  plain flour
6 teaspoons baking powder
1 teaspoon ground cinnamon
1 teaspoon mixed spice
½ teaspoon ground ginger
400 g /14 oz /3 cups blueberries (fresh
  or frozen, not canned)
125 ml /4 fl oz /½ cup cold-pressed
  grapeseed oil
125 ml /4 fl oz /½ cup non-fat or low-
  fat buttermilk
2 teaspoons vanilla essence
3 egg whites

Preheat the oven to 180°C /350°F.

Place the oat bran in a large bowl. Sift the flour, baking powder, cinnamon, mixed spice and ginger into the oat bran, and mix through. Add the blueberries and coat well with the flour.

Combine the oil, apple juice concentrate, buttermilk and vanilla essence, and fold into the flour mixture. Try not to squash the blueberries.

Beat the egg whites until stiff and gently fold through the mixture. Spoon into a lightly greased and floured muffin tray. Bake for 25–30 minutes.

Remove the muffins from the tray immediately and place on a wire rack to cool. Cover with a tea towel. (See colour plate opposite.)

Banana and Carob Muffins

MAKES 12

225 g/½ lb/2 cups wholemeal plain
    flour
3 tablespoons/3 tablespoons plus
    3 teaspoons carob powder
3 teaspoons baking powder
1 teaspoon ground cinnamon
1 teaspoon mixed spice
225 g/½ lb/1 cup mashed banana
125 ml/4 fl oz/½ cup apple juice
    concentrate
65 ml/2 fl oz/¼ cup cold-pressed
    grapeseed oil
65 ml/2 fl oz/¼ cup non-fat or low-fat
    yoghurt
2 teaspoons vanilla essence
3 egg whites

Topping
½ teaspoon ground cinnamon
2 tablespoons/2 tablespoons plus
    2 teaspoons rolled oats
apple juice concentrate

Preheat the oven to 180°C/350°F.

Sift the flour, carob powder, baking powder, cinnamon and mixed spice twice into a large bowl. Combine the banana, apple juice concentrate, oil, yoghurt and vanilla essence. Add to the bowl and beat well. Beat the egg whites until stiff and gently fold through the mixture. Spoon into a lightly greased and floured muffin tray.

To make the Topping, add the cinnamon to the rolled oats. Sprinkle over the top of each muffin and add just a drop of the apple juice concentrate. Bake for 20–25 minutes.

Remove the muffins from the tray immediately and place on a wire rack to cool. Cover with a tea towel. To serve, cut the tops off and fill with low-fat cream and sliced bananas. (See left colour plate between pages 216 and 217.)

Banana and Cinnamon Muffins

MAKES 12

125 g/¼ lb/1 cup wholemeal plain flour
125 g/¼ lb/1 cup unbleached white
    plain flour
2 teaspoons baking powder
1 teaspoon ground cinnamon
½ teaspoon ground nutmeg
225 g/½ lb/1 cup banana, freshly
    chopped
125 ml/4 fl oz/½ cup apple juice
    concentrate
2 teaspoons vanilla essence
65 ml/2 fl oz/¼ cup cold-pressed
    grapeseed oil
65 ml/2 fl oz/¼ cup non-fat or low-fat
    buttermilk
2 egg whites
2 tablespoons/2 tablespoons plus
    2 teaspoons rolled oats
extra ground cinnamon

Preheat the oven to 180°C/350°F.

Sift the flours, baking powder, cinnamon and nutmeg twice into a large bowl. Add the banana and toss in the flour to coat well. Combine the apple juice concentrate, vanilla essence, oil and buttermilk. Add to the flour mixture and mix well. Beat the egg whites until stiff and gently fold through the mixture. Spoon into a lightly greased and floured muffin tray. Sprinkle with the rolled oats and extra cinnamon. Bake for 20–25 minutes.

Remove the muffins from the tray immediately and place on a wire rack to cool. Cover with a tea towel.

Banana and Date Muffins

MAKES 12 MONSTER MUFFINS

310 g / 10½ oz / 2½ cups oat bran
200 g / 7 oz / 1½ cups wholemeal plain flour
6 teaspoons baking powder
2 teaspoons mixed spice
1 teaspoon ground cinnamon
500 g / 1 lb 2 oz / 2 cups finely chopped banana
100 g / 3½ oz / ½ cup finely chopped dates
125 ml / 4 fl oz / ½ cup apple juice concentrate
125 ml / 4 fl oz / ½ cup cold-pressed grapeseed oil
250 ml / 8 fl oz / 1 cup low-fat evaporated skim milk
3 egg whites
a little extra oat bran

Preheat the oven to 180°C/350°F.

Place the oat bran in a large bowl. Sift the flour, baking powder and spices into the oat bran. Mix through with your hands. Add the banana and dates and toss well to break up and coat with the flour mixture.

Combine the apple juice concentrate, oil and milk, and mix into the flour mixture.

Beat the egg whites until stiff and gently fold through the mixture. Spoon into a lightly greased muffin tray that has been coated with a little oat bran. Cook for 25–30 minutes.

Remove the muffins from the tray immediately and place on a wire rack to cool. Cover with a tea towel.

Broccoli and Cauliflower Muffins

MAKES 12 MONSTER MUFFINS

200 g / 7 oz broccoli florets
200 g / 7 oz cauliflower florets
225 g / ½ lb / 2 cups oat bran
1 teaspoon grated geska herb cheese
125 g / ¼ lb / 1 cup wholemeal plain flour
125 g / ¼ lb / 1 cup unbleached white plain flour
6 teaspoons baking powder
1 teaspoon ground nutmeg
300 ml / 10 fl oz / 1¼ cups low-fat evaporated skim milk
125 ml / 4 fl oz / ½ cup cold-pressed grapeseed oil
65 ml / 2 fl oz / ¼ cup apple juice concentrate
4 egg whites
a little extra oat bran

Preheat the oven to 180°C/350°F.

Steam the broccoli and cauliflower until just tender and plunge into cold water. Drain well. Place the oat bran and cheese in a large bowl. Sift the flours, baking powder and nutmeg into the oat bran and cheese. Add the broccoli and cauliflower and toss until well coated.

Combine the milk, oil and apple juice concentrate and stir into the mixture. Be careful not to break up the cauliflower and broccoli pieces.

Beat the egg whites until stiff and gently fold through the mixture. Spoon into a lightly greased muffin tray that has been coated with a little oat bran. Bake for 25–30 minutes.

Remove the muffins from the tray immediately and place on a wire rack to cool. Cover with a tea towel. (See colour plate opposite page 17.)

Carrot and Coconut Muffins

MAKES 12 MONSTER MUFFINS

225 g/½ lb/2 cups oat bran
225 g/½ lb/2 cups wholemeal plain flour
6 teaspoons baking powder
400 g/14 oz carrots
200 g/7 oz/1⅓ cups raisins
125 g/¼ lb/½ cup shredded coconut
250 ml/8 fl oz/1 cup skim milk
2 teaspoons vanilla essence
125 ml/4 fl oz/½ cup apple juice concentrate
125 ml/4 fl oz/½ cup cold-pressed grapeseed oil
3 egg whites
a little extra oat bran

Preheat the oven to 180°C/350°F.

Place the oat bran in a bowl. Sift the flour and baking powder into the oat bran, and mix through.

Juice the carrots in a juicer. In a large bowl, combine the carrot pulp, carrot juice and raisins.

Blend the coconut with the milk in a food processor or blender. Add to the carrot mixture with the vanilla essence, apple juice concentrate and oil. Add the flour mixture in three lots, stirring well each time.

Beat the egg whites until stiff and gently fold through the mixture. Spoon into a lightly greased muffin tray that has been coated with a little oat bran. Bake for 25–30 minutes.

Remove the muffins from the tray immediately and place on a wire rack to cool. Cover with a tea towel.

Coconut is high in saturated fat, so these muffins should not be eaten excessively.

Carrot and Ginger Muffins

MAKES 12 MONSTER MUFFINS

225 g/½ lb/2 cups oat bran
125 g/¼ lb/1 cup rolled oats
125 g/¼ lb/1 cup unbleached white plain flour
6 teaspoons baking powder
400 g/14 oz carrots
125 g/¼ lb/¾ cup glacé ginger, chopped
100 g/3½ oz/½ cup dried apricots, chopped
125 ml/4 fl oz/½ cup apple juice concentrate
125 ml/4 fl oz/½ cup cold-pressed grapeseed oil
2 teaspoons grated lemon rind
4 egg whites
a little extra oat bran

Preheat the oven to 180°C/350°F.

Combine the oat bran and rolled oats in a bowl. Sift the flour and baking powder into the oats, and mix through.

Juice the carrots in a juicer. In a large bowl, combine the carrot pulp and juice with the remaining ingredients, except the egg whites. Add the flour mixture in three lots, stirring well each time.

Beat the egg whites until stiff and gently fold through the mixture. Spoon into a lightly greased muffin tray that has been coated with a little oat bran. Bake for 25–30 minutes.

Remove the muffins from the tray immediately and place on a wire rack to cool. Cover with a tea towel.

Carrot and Mixed-peel Muffins

MAKES 12 MONSTER MUFFINS

225 g/½ lb/2 cups oat bran
225 g/½ lb/2 cups unbleached white flour
6 teaspoons baking powder
1 teaspoon ground cinnamon

Preheat the oven to 180°C/350°F.

Place the oat bran in a bowl. Sift the flour, baking powder and spices into the oat bran, and mix through.

Juice the carrots in a juicer. In a large bowl, combine the carrot pulp and juice, mixed peel, apple juice concentrate, oil, vanilla essence and orange rind, and mix thoroughly. Add the flour in three lots, stirring well each time.

1 teaspoon mixed spice
400 g/14 oz carrots
200 g/7 oz/1¼ cups dried mixed peel
125 ml/4 fl oz/½ cup apple juice
    concentrate
125 ml/4 fl oz/½ cup cold-pressed
    grapeseed oil
2 teaspoons vanilla essence
2 teaspoons grated orange rind
4 egg whites
a little extra oat bran

Beat the egg whites until stiff and gently fold through the mixture. Spoon into a lightly greased muffin tray that has been coated with a little oat bran. Bake for 25–30 minutes.

Remove the muffins from the tray immediately and place on a wire rack to cool. Cover with a tea towel.

Cauliflower Cheese Oat-bran Muffins

MAKES 12 MONSTER MUFFINS

225 g/½ lb/2 cups oat bran
225 g/½ lb/2 cups unbleached white
    plain flour
6 teaspoons baking powder
1 teaspoon ground nutmeg
100 g/3½ oz/1 cup grated low-fat
    grating cheese
500 g/1 lb 2 oz very small cauliflower
    florets
125 ml/4 fl oz/½ cup cold-pressed
    grapeseed oil
350 ml/12 fl oz/1½ cups skim milk
3 egg whites

Preheat the oven to 180°C/350°F.

Place the oat bran in a large bowl. Sift the flour, baking powder and nutmeg into the oat bran. Distribute the grated cheese through the flour mixture with your hands. Steam the cauliflower until just tender. Plunge into cold water to cool. Drain well. Add the cauliflower florets to the mixture and coat well with flour.

Combine the oil and milk and stir through the mixture. Be careful not to break up the cauliflower pieces.

Beat the egg whites until stiff and gently fold through the mixture. Spoon into a lightly greased and floured muffin tray. Bake for 25–30 minutes.

Remove the muffins from the tray immediately and place on a wire rack to cool. Cover with a tea towel.

Corn-meal and Currant Bran Muffins

MAKES 12 MONSTER MUFFINS

310 g/10½ oz/2 cups corn meal
225 g/½ lb/2 cups oat bran
6 teaspoons baking powder
150 g/5 oz/1 cup currants
250 ml/8 fl oz/1 cup non-fat or low-fat
    yoghurt
250 ml/8 fl oz/1 cup skim milk
125 ml/4 fl oz/½ cup apple juice
    concentrate
125 ml/4 fl oz/½ cup cold-pressed
    grapeseed oil
2 teaspoons vanilla essence
3 egg whites
a little extra oat bran

Preheat the oven to 180°C/350°F.

Combine the corn meal, oat bran, baking powder and currants in a large bowl, and mix well.

In another bowl combine all the remaining ingredients, except the egg whites, and add to the corn-meal mixture.

Beat the egg whites only lightly and fold through the mixture. Spoon into a lightly greased muffin tray that has been coated with a little oat bran. Bake for 20–25 minutes.

Remove the muffins from the tray immediately and place on a wire rack to cool. Cover with a tea towel.

Spicy Pear and Almond Muffins

MAKES 12 MONSTER MUFFINS

2½–3 teaspoons Spice Mixture (see below)
125 g/¼ lb/1 cup rolled oats
225 g/½ lb/2 cups oat bran
125 g/¼ lb/1 cup unbleached white plain flour
6 teaspoons baking powder
500 g/1 lb 2 oz cooked pears in cooking liquid or canned unsweetened pears in natural juice
2 teaspoons grated lemon rind
125 ml/4 fl oz/½ cup apple juice concentrate
125 ml/4 fl oz/½ cup cold-pressed grapeseed oil
2 teaspoons vanilla essence
3 egg whites
a little extra oat bran
6 teaspoons ground almonds

Spice Mixture
equal quantities of ground cinnamon, cloves, peppercorns, ginger and cardamom

Preheat the oven to 180°C/350°F.

To make the Spice Mixture, combine equal portions of all the ground spices and mix. This mixture keeps well in an airtight container.

In a large bowl, combine the rolled oats and oat bran. Sift the flour, baking powder and Spice Mixture into the oats.

Drain the pears and reserve the liquid. Chop the pears and combine with the lemon rind, apple juice concentrate, 250 ml/8 fl oz/1 cup of reserved pear liquid, and oil and vanilla essence. Add to the flour mixture and combine well.

Beat the egg whites until stiff and gently fold through the mixture. Spoon into a lightly greased muffin tray that has been coated with a little oat bran. Sprinkle ½ teaspoon of the ground almonds on top of each muffin. Bake for 25–30 minutes.

Remove the muffins from the tray immediately and place on a wire rack to cool. Cover with a tea towel.

Pear and Cinnamon Muffins

MAKES 12 MONSTER MUFFINS

125 g/¼ lb/1 cup rolled oats
225 g/½ lb/2 cups oat bran
125 g/¼ lb/1 cup unbleached white plain flour
6 teaspoons baking powder
3 teaspoons ground cinnamon
65 ml/2 fl oz/¼ cup lemon juice
185 ml/6 fl oz/¾ cup unsweetened orange juice
125 ml/4 fl oz/½ cup apple juice concentrate
125 ml/4 fl oz/½ cup cold-pressed grapeseed oil
2 teaspoons vanilla essence
400 g/14 oz Packham pears, cored and chopped
3 egg whites
a little extra oat bran

Preheat the oven to 180°C/350°F.

Combine the rolled oats and oat bran. Sift the flour, baking powder and cinnamon into the oats, and combine.

In a large bowl, combine the remaining ingredients, except the egg whites. Slowly fold the flour mixture through the fruit juice mixture, stirring well until everything is combined.

Beat the egg whites until stiff and gently fold through the mixture. Spoon into a lightly greased muffin tray that has been coated with a little oat bran. Bake for 25–30 minutes.

Remove the muffins from the tray immediately and place on a wire rack to cool. Cover with a tea towel.

Pineapple and Date Muffins

MAKES 12 MONSTER MUFFINS

225 g/½ lb/2 cups oat bran
225 g/½ lb/2 cups soy flour or
  unbleached white plain flour
6 teaspoons baking powder
2 teaspoons ground cinnamon
400 g/14 oz canned unsweetened
  pineapple pieces in natural juice
225 g/½ lb/1 cup chopped dates
125 ml/4 fl oz/½ cup cold-pressed
  grapeseed oil
125 ml/4 fl oz/½ cup apple juice
  concentrate
2 teaspoons vanilla essence
3 egg whites

Preheat the oven to 180°C/350°F.

Place the oat bran in a bowl. Sift the flour, baking powder and cinnamon into the oat bran, and mix through.

Drain the pineapple and reserve the juice. Chop the pineapple pieces and, in a large bowl, combine them with the dates, 250 ml/8 fl oz/1 cup of the reserved pineapple juice, and oil, apple juice concentrate and vanilla essence. Fold the flour mixture through the fruit mixture in three lots.

Beat the egg whites until stiff and fold through the mixture. Spoon into a lightly greased and floured muffin tray. Bake for 25–30 minutes.

Remove the muffins from the tray immediately and place on a wire rack to cool. Cover with a tea towel.

Pumpkin and Poppyseed Muffins

MAKES 12 MONSTER MUFFINS

500 g/1 lb 2 oz pumpkin, peeled
225 g/½ lb/2 cups oat bran
100 g/3½ oz/½ cup poppyseeds
225 g/½ lb/2 cups soy flour or
  unbleached white plain flour
6 teaspoons baking powder
½ teaspoon ground nutmeg
1 tablespoon/1 tablespoon plus
  1 teaspoon grated lemon or orange
  rind
250 ml/8 fl oz/1 cup low-fat evaporated
  milk or reduced-fat soymilk
125 ml/4 fl oz/½ cup cold-pressed
  grapeseed oil
1 teaspoon vanilla essence
125 ml/4 fl oz/½ cup apple juice
  concentrate
3 egg whites

Preheat the oven to 180°C/350°F.

Place the pumpkin in a steamer and cook. Drain well before mashing thoroughly.

Place the oat bran and poppyseeds in a large bowl. Sift the soy flour, baking powder and nutmeg into the oat bran and poppyseeds. Mix through and add the lemon rind.

Add the pumpkin, skim milk, oil, vanilla essence and apple juice concentrate to the flour mixture, and mix thoroughly.

Beat the egg whites until stiff and gently fold through the mixture. Spoon into a lightly greased and floured muffin tray. Bake for 25–30 minutes.

Remove the muffins from the tray immediately and place on a wire rack to cool. Cover with a tea towel.

Pineapple and Blueberry Muffins

MAKES 12 MONSTER MUFFINS

225 g / ½ lb / 2 cups oat bran
225 g / ½ lb / 2 cups unbleached white
   plain flour
6 teaspoons baking powder
1 teaspoon ground cinnamon
1 teaspoon mixed spice
1 teaspoon ground ginger
400 g / 14 oz / 3 cups canned unsweetened
   pineapple pieces in natural juice
200 g / 7 oz blueberries (fresh or frozen,
   not canned)
65 ml / 2 fl oz / ¼ cup water
125 ml / 4 fl oz / ½ cup apple juice
   concentrate
125 ml / 4 fl oz / ½ cup cold-pressed
   grapeseed oil
2 teaspoons vanilla essence
3 egg whites

Preheat the oven to 180°C / 350°F.

Place the oat bran in a large bowl. Sift the flour, baking powder and spices into the oat bran, and mix through.

Drain the pineapple and reserve the juice. Chop up the pineapple pieces and add them, with the blueberries, to the bowl. Mix thoroughly so the fruit is coated well with the flour mixture.

Combine 200 ml / 7 fl oz / ¾ cup of the reserved pineapple juice with the water, apple juice concentrate, oil and vanilla essence. Add to the mixture and fold through.

Beat the egg whites until stiff and gently fold through the mixture. Spoon into a lightly greased and floured muffin tray. Bake for 25–30 minutes.

Remove the muffins from the tray immediately and place on a wire rack to cool. Cover with a tea towel. (See colour plate opposite.)

Pumpkin and Prune Muffins

MAKES 12 MONSTER MUFFINS

500 g / 1 lb 2 oz pumpkin, peeled
225 g / ½ lb / 2 cups oat bran
100 g / 3½ oz / ¾ cup rolled oats
150 g / 5 oz / 1¼ cups unbleached white
   plain flour
1 teaspoon ground cinnamon
1 teaspoon mixed spice
½ teaspoon ground nutmeg
6 teaspoons baking powder
200 g / 7 oz / 1 cup moist prunes, chopped
1 tablespoon / 1 tablespoon plus
   1 teaspoon grated lemon rind
250 ml / 8 fl oz / 1 cup unsweetened
   orange juice
125 ml / 4 fl oz / ½ cup apple juice
   concentrate
125 ml / 4 fl oz / ½ cup cold-pressed
   grapeseed oil
1 teaspoon vanilla essence
3 egg whites
a little extra oat bran

Preheat the oven to 180°C / 350°F.

Place the pumpkin in a steamer and cook until tender. Drain well before mashing thoroughly.

Place the oat bran and oats in a large bowl. Sift the flour, spices and baking powder into the oats, and mix through with your hands.

In another bowl, combine the pumpkin, prunes, lemon rind, orange juice, apple juice concentrate, oil and vanilla essence. Add to the flour mixture and mix well.

Beat the egg whites until stiff and gently fold through the mixture. Spoon into a lightly greased muffin tray that has been coated with a little oat bran. Bake for 25–30 minutes.

Remove the muffins from the tray immediately and place on a wire rack to cool. Cover with a tea towel.

Breakfast in a Glass (page 250); Pineapple and Blueberry Muffin (opposite page).

Oat-bran and Oatmeal Porridge (opposite page); Caro Cappucino (page 295).

Traditional Oat Porridge

SERVES 1

60 g / 2 oz / ½ cup rolled oats
250 ml / 8 fl oz / 1 cup water

In a saucepan, slowly bring the oats and water to the boil, stirring continuously. Turn the heat down, cover, and cook until the porridge reaches the desired consistency.

Oat-bran Porridge

SERVES 1

40 g / 1½ oz / ⅓ cup oat bran
250 ml / 8 fl oz / 1 cup water

In a saucepan, slowly bring the oat bran and water to the boil, stirring continuously. Turn the heat down, cover, and cook until the porridge reaches the desired consistency. It contains more bran than traditional porridge.

Oat-bran and Oatmeal Porridge

SERVES 1

30 g / 1 oz / ¼ cup rolled oats
2 tablespoons / 2 tablespoons plus
  2 teaspoons oat bran
250 ml / 8 fl oz / 1 cup water

In a saucepan, slowly bring all the ingredients to the boil, stirring continuously. Turn the heat down, cover, and cook until the porridge reaches the desired consistency. (See colour plate opposite.)

Rhubarb and Cinnamon Muffins

MAKES 12 MONSTER MUFFINS

125 g / ¼ lb / 1 cup rolled oats
225 g / ½ lb / 2 cups oat bran
125 g / ¼ lb / 1 cup unbleached white
  plain flour
6 teaspoons baking powder
1 teaspoon bicarbonate of soda
2 teaspoons ground cinnamon
400 g / 14 oz rhubarb, chopped
125 ml / 4 fl oz / ½ cup cold-pressed
  grapeseed oil
125 ml / 4 fl oz / ½ cup apple juice
  concentrate
250 ml / 8 fl oz / 1 cup low-fat evaporated
  skim milk
2 teaspoons vanilla essence
4 egg whites
a little extra oat bran

Preheat the oven to 180°C / 350°.

In a large bowl, combine the oats and oat bran. Sift the flour, baking powder, bicarbonate of soda and cinnamon into the oats, and mix through. Add the rhubarb and coat well with the flour.

Combine the oil, apple juice concentrate, skim milk and vanilla essence, and add to the flour mixture.

Beat the egg whites until stiff and gently fold through the mixture. Spoon into a lightly greased muffin tray that has been coated with a little oat bran. Bake for 25–30 minutes.

Remove the muffins from the tray immediately and place on a wire rack to cool. Cover with a tea towel.

Rhubarb and Pineapple Muffins

MAKES 12 MONSTER MUFFINS

225 g/½ lb/2 cups oat bran
225 g/½ lb/2 cups unbleached white
　plain flour
6 teaspoons baking powder
2 teaspoons ground cinnamon
60 g/2 oz/½ cup chopped walnuts
225 g/½ lb rhubarb, chopped
400 g/14 oz canned unsweetened
　pineapple pieces in natural juice
200 ml/7 fl oz/¾ cup apple juice
　concentrate
125 ml/4 fl oz/½ cup cold-pressed
　grapeseed oil
2 teaspoons vanilla essence
3 egg whites

Preheat the oven to 180°C/350°F.

Place the oat bran in a large bowl. Sift the flour, baking powder and cinnamon into the oat bran, and mix through. Add the chopped walnuts and rhubarb, and toss to coat with flour.

Drain the pineapple and reserve the juice, chop the pineapple pieces and add to the bowl.

Combine 200 ml/7 fl oz/¾ cup of the pineapple juice with the apple juice concentrate, oil and vanilla essence, and add to the flour mixture.

Beat the egg whites until stiff and fold gently through the mixture. Spoon into a lightly greased and floured muffin tray. Bake for 25–30 minutes.

Remove the muffins from the tray immediately and place on a wire rack to cool. Cover with a tea towel.

Spinach and Cheese Muffins

MAKES 12

125 g/¼ lb/1 cup wholemeal plain flour
125 g/¼ lb/1 cup unbleached white
　plain flour
2 teaspoons baking powder
1 teaspoon ground nutmeg
100 g/3½ oz/1 cup spinach, finely
　chopped
60 g/2 oz/½ cup grated low-fat grating
　cheese
125 ml/4 fl oz/½ cup low-fat
　evaporated milk
125 ml/4 fl oz/½ cup non-fat or low-
　fat yoghurt
2 tablespoons/2 tablespoons plus
　2 teaspoons apple juice concentrate
2 egg whites

Preheat the oven to 180°C/350°F.

Sift the flours, baking powder and nutmeg twice into a large bowl. Add the spinach and cheese and toss to coat lightly. Combine the milk, yoghurt and apple juice concentrate. Add to the mixture, and mix well. Beat the egg whites until stiff and gently fold through the mixture.

Spoon into a lightly greased and floured muffin tray. Bake for 25 minutes.

Remove the muffins from the tray immediately and place on a wire rack to cool. Cover with a tea towel.

Puffed Millet with Apple

SERVES 1

125 g/¼ lb/¾ cup puffed millet
125 ml/4 fl oz/½ cup cooked apple
dash of ground cinnamon
125 ml/4 fl oz/½ cup skim milk

Place the millet in a breakfast bowl. Top with the apple and cinnamon, and add the milk.

Creamy Millet

SERVES 2

225 g/½ lb/1 cup millet
750 ml/1⅓ pints/3 cups boiling water
1 apple, peeled and grated
pinch of ground cinnamon

In a saucepan, add the millet to the boiling water and stir briskly. Add the apple and cinnamon. Turn the heat down low and cover the saucepan. Stir occasionally so the millet does not stick to the saucepan. Millet is cooked when it becomes creamy and loses its gritty texture.

Home-made Muesli

MAKES 12 CUPS

125 g/¼ lb/1 cup wheatgerm
200 g/7 oz/1 cup buckwheat
400 g/14 oz/2 cups All Bran
500 g/1 lb 2 oz/4 cups rolled oats
125 g/¼ lb/½ cup sunflower seeds
150 g/5 oz/1 cup raw almonds
100 g/3½ oz/½ cup chopped dates
100 g/3½ oz/½ cup dried pineapple
100 g/3½ oz/½ cup dried papaw
100 g/3½ oz/½ cup chopped dried
  apricots

Combine all the ingredients and keep in an airtight container. Serve with skim milk.

Rice and Apple

SERVES 1

90 g/3 oz/½ cup uncooked brown rice
1 Granny Smith apple or pear or apricot
  or peach
125 ml/4 fl oz/½ cup unsweetened
  orange juice
350 ml/12 fl oz/1½ cups water

Combine all the ingredients in a saucepan. Cover, and simmer for 40 minutes or until all the liquid is absorbed and the rice cooked.

The rice can be cooked the night before if required and reheated in the microwave oven the next morning, or it can be eaten cold. It can also be served with a little skim milk.

Shredded Wheats with Strawberries

SERVES 1

4 Shredded Wheats
150 g/5 oz/1 cup strawberries, washed
    and hulled
3 tablespoons/3 tablespoons plus
    3 teaspoons Whipped Ricotta Cream
    (see Pancake Toppings, p. 190)

Place the Shredded Wheats in a breakfast bowl. Top with the strawberries and Whipped Ricotta Cream. The three very different textures of the ingredients create an interesting as well as tasty combination.

Note
If Shredded Wheats are unavailable, use any cereal biscuit that is low in sugar and salt.

Plain Pikelets

MAKES 15

125 g/¼ lb/1 cup wholemeal plain flour
2 teaspoons baking powder
125 ml/4 fl oz/½ cup skim milk
1 teaspoon vanilla essence
2 egg whites

Sift the flour and baking powder into a large bowl. Add the milk and vanilla essence and beat until the mixture is smooth. Add the egg whites and beat until they are absorbed and the mixture is smooth.

Place dessertspoonfuls of the mixture on a hot, lightly greased, non-stick frying pan. As bubbles appear on top of the mixture, quickly turn over. Cook until both sides are brown.

Serve with the topping of your choice, for example, sliced tomato, low-fat cottage cheese and herbs, sugar-free jam spread, or mashed banana.

Cheese and Spice Pikelets

MAKES 15

125 g/¼ lb/1 cup wholemeal plain flour
2 teaspoons baking powder
½ teaspoon curry powder
175 ml/6 fl oz/⅔ cup skim milk
30 g/1 oz/¼ cup grated low-fat grating
    cheese

Sift the flour, baking powder and curry powder into a large bowl. Add the milk and beat until the mixture is smooth. Add the cheese and beat again until the mixture is smooth.

Place spoonfuls of the mixture on a hot, lightly greased, non-stick frying pan. As bubbles appear on top of the mixture, quickly turn over. Cook until both sides are brown.

Serve with the topping of your choice, for example, sliced tomato and alfalfa sprouts, or low-fat ricotta cheese with finely sliced celery.

Date and Cinnamon Pikelets

MAKES 15

125 g/¼ lb/1 cup wholemeal plain flour
2 teaspoons baking powder
1 teaspoon ground cinnamon
10 dates, finely chopped
125 ml/4 fl oz/½ cup skim milk
1 teaspoon vanilla essence
2 egg whites

Sift the flour and baking powder into large bowl. Mix the cinnamon and chopped dates through the flour. Add the milk and vanilla essence and beat until the mixture is smooth. Add the egg whites and beat again until the mixture is smooth.

Place spoonfuls of the mixture on a hot, lightly greased, non-stick frying pan. As bubbles appear on top of the mixture, quickly turn over. Cook until both sides are brown. Serve plain or with the topping of your choice.

Wholemeal Scones

SERVES 24

500 g/1 lb 2 oz/4 cups unbleached white plain flour

280 g/10 oz/2 cups wholemeal plain flour

3 tablespoons/3 tablespoons plus 3 teaspoons baking powder

1 teaspoon bicarbonate of soda

65 ml/2 fl oz/¼ cup lemon juice

250 ml/8 fl oz/1 cup non-fat or low-fat yoghurt

500 ml/16 fl oz/2 cups low-fat evaporated milk

a little water

Preheat the oven to 200°C/400°F.

Sift the flours, baking powder and bicarbonate of soda into a large bowl. Combine the lemon juice and yoghurt. Use a knife to mix it through the flour. Add the skim milk and use the knife to continue mixing. Put the dough onto a well-floured bench. Press down with the palm of your hand. Lightly flour over the top so it does not stick to your hands. Press down to a 2.5-cm/1″ thickness. Using a scone cutter, cut into the desired shapes. Place close together on a lightly greased non-stick baking tray. Brush the top of the scones lightly with water (just enough to remove the flour). Bake for 10–15 minutes.

Banana and Date Wholemeal Scones

MAKES 10

280 g/10 oz/2 cups wholemeal plain flour

3 teaspoons baking powder

¼ teaspoon ground cinnamon

¼ teaspoon mixed spice

225 g/½ lb/1 cup very finely chopped dates

1 teaspoon finely grated lemon rind

1 small banana, mashed

200 ml/7 fl oz/¾ cup skim milk

1 teaspoon lemon juice

Preheat the oven to 200°C/400°F.

Sift the flour, baking powder, cinnamon and mixed spice twice into a large bowl. Add the dates and lemon rind, and mix through. Combine the banana, milk and lemon juice, and add to the flour mixture. Mix together and knead lightly. Using a scone cutter, cut into the desired shapes. Place on a non-stick baking tray. Bake for 10–15 minutes. Serve while still warm.

Herb Scones

MAKES 10

225 g/½ lb/2 cups unbleached white
    plain flour
3 teaspoons baking powder
1 tablespoon/1 tablespoon plus
    1 teaspoon finely chopped fresh chives
1 tablespoon/1 tablespoon plus
    1 teaspoon finely chopped fresh
    parsley
1 tablespoon/1 tablespoon plus
    1 teaspoon finely chopped fresh
    rosemary or basil
2 tablespoons/2 tablespoons plus
    2 teaspoons non-fat or low-fat
    yoghurt
1 tablespoon/1 tablespoon plus
    1 teaspoon lemon juice
250 ml/8 fl oz/1 cup skim milk or
    reduced-fat soymilk

Preheat the oven to 200°C/400°F.

Sift the flour and baking powder into a large bowl. Add the herbs, and coat with the flour. Add the yoghurt and lemon juice and mix through until the flour resembles fine breadcrumbs. Add the milk and, using a knife, mix through. Place the dough on a lightly floured bench and knead lightly. Using a scone cutter, cut into the desired shapes. Place on a non-stick baking tray. Bake for 10–15 minutes.

Pumpkin Wholemeal Scones

MAKES 10

125 g/¼ lb/1 cup wholemeal plain flour
125 g/¼ lb/1 cup unbleached white
    plain flour
1 tablespoon/1 tablespoon plus
    1 teaspoon baking powder
1 teaspoon ground nutmeg
75 g/2½ oz/¼ cup grated pumpkin,
    lightly packed
2 tablespoons/2 tablespoons plus
    2 teaspoons non-fat or low-fat
    yoghurt
1 tablespoon/1 tablespoon plus
    1 teaspoon lemon juice
2 teaspoons apple juice concentrate
250 ml/8 fl oz/1 cup skim milk

Preheat the oven to 200°C/400°F.

Sift the flours, baking powder and nutmeg twice into a large bowl. Add the pumpkin and toss in the flour to coat well. Add the yoghurt, lemon juice and apple juice concentrate. Use a knife to mix together. Slowly add the milk, still using the knife to bind the ingredients. The mixture will be slightly sticky.

Scrape the dough from the bowl and put onto a lightly floured board. Knead gently (too much kneading will make the scones heavy). Using a scone cutter, cut into the desired shapes. Place on a non-stick baking tray. Bake for 10–15 minutes.

JAM & SAVOURY SPREADS, CHUTNEYS, SAUCES & PRESERVES

Commercially prepared condiments such as jams, chutneys, preserves and sauces are usually very high in sugar, fat, salt and, very often, artificial flavouring and preservative. It is cheaper and healthier to make your own at home, especially if you have an orchard, vegetable garden or herb garden. It is also very satisfying. You can enjoy your shelves, laden with the fruits of your harvest, as well as all those delicious things you can make with your home-made condiments.

Apple Jam Spread

MAKES 2 × 250-ML/8-FL-OZ JARS

225 g/½ lb/3⅓ cups dried apples
750 ml/1⅓ pints/3 cups unsweetened
  pineapple juice
2 tablespoons/2 tablespoons plus 2
  teaspoons lemon juice
2 teaspoons grated lemon rind
2 teaspoons ground cinnamon

Combine all the ingredients in a large saucepan and simmer over a gentle heat until the apples are soft. Purée the mixture in a food processor or blender. Pour into hot sterilised jars and seal when cool. Refrigerate. (See right colour plate between pages 216 and 217.)

Apricot Jam Spread

MAKES 3 × 250-ML/8-FL-OZ JARS

250 ml/8 fl oz/1 cup unsweetened apple
  and pear juice
250 ml/8 fl oz/1 cup unsweetened
  orange juice
125 ml/4 fl oz/½ cup apple juice
  concentrate
2 teaspoons agar powder
1 tablespoon/1 tablespoon plus 1
  teaspoon lemon juice
400 g/14 oz apricots, stoned and
  roughly chopped

Place all the ingredients, except the chopped apricots, in a saucepan and slowly bring to the boil. Simmer for 5 minutes. Add the apricots and simmer for a further 15–20 minutes. Pour the mixture into hot sterilised jars and seal when cool. Refrigerate. (See right colour plate between pages 216 and 217.)

Blueberry Jam Spread

MAKES 3 × 250-ML/8-FL-OZ JARS

350 ml/12 fl oz/1½ cups unsweetened
  pear juice
75 ml/3 fl oz/⅓ cup apple juice
  concentrate
1 tablespoon/1 tablespoon plus 1
  teaspoon lemon juice
2 teaspoons agar powder
425 g/15 oz/3 cups blueberries (fresh or
  frozen, not canned)

Combine the pear juice, apple juice concentrate, lemon juice and agar powder in a saucepan. Slowly bring to the boil and stir to dissolve the powder. Boil for 5 minutes. Add the blueberries and boil for another 10 minutes. Pour the mixture into hot sterilised jars and seal when cool. Refrigerate.

When blueberries are in season, Blueberry Jam Spread will undoubtedly become one of your favourites.

Cherry Jam Spread

✕✕

MAKES 3 × 250-ML/8-FL-OZ JARS

250 ml/8 fl oz/1 cup unsweetened
orange juice
250 ml/8 fl oz/1 cup apple juice
concentrate
1 tablespoon/1 tablespoon plus 1
teaspoon lemon juice
¼ teaspoon grated lemon rind
2 teaspoons agar powder
500 g/1 lb 2 oz/3 cups stoned cherries

Place all the ingredients, except the cherries, in a saucepan. Slowly bring to the boil. Simmer for 15 minutes, stirring occasionally. Add the cherries and slowly bring to the boil again. Simmer for 5 minutes. Pour the mixture into hot sterilised jars and seal when cool. Refrigerate.

Fruit Jam Spread

✕✕

MAKES 2 × 250-ML/8-FL-OZ JARS

125 g/¼ lb/½ cup dried apricots
90 g/3 oz/1⅓ cups dried apples
60 g/2 oz/¼ cup raisins
875 ml/1½ pints/3½ cups unsweetened
orange juice

Combine all the ingredients in a large saucepan and simmer over a gentle heat until the fruit is soft. Purée the mixture in a food processor or blender. Pour into hot sterilised jars and seal when cool. Refrigerate.

Clear Marmalade

✕✕

MAKES 1¼ × 250-ML/8-FL-OZ JARS

350 ml/12 fl oz/1½ cups unsweetened
apple and pear juice
2 teaspoons apple juice concentrate
1 teaspoon finely grated lemon rind
1 teaspoon agar powder

Place all the ingredients in a saucepan. Slowly bring to the boil and stir to dissolve the agar powder. As the mixture comes to the boil, turn the heat down. Simmer for 5 minutes. Pour the mixture into hot sterilised jars. As it begins to set, stir with a spoon to keep the lemon rind evenly distributed through the marmalade. Seal when cool. Refrigerate.

Plum Jam Spread

✕✕

MAKES 3 × 250-ML/8-FL-OZ JARS

1 kg/2¼ lb plums
1 litre/1¾ pints/4 cups unsweetened
orange juice
finely grated rind of 1 orange

Place all the ingredients in a saucepan and slowly bring to the boil. Simmer over a gentle heat until the liquid has reduced and the plums are quite mushy. Remove the stones and mash the pulp with a potato masher. Pour into hot sterilised jars and seal when cool. Refrigerate. (See right colour plate between pages 216 and 217.)

Raspberry Jam Spread

MAKES 3½ × 250-ML/8-FL-OZ JARS

300 ml/10 fl oz/1¼ cups unsweetened apple and pear juice
2 teaspoons agar powder
65 ml/2 fl oz/¼ cup apple juice concentrate
425 g/15 oz/3 cups raspberries (fresh or frozen, not canned)

Place the apple and pear juice, agar powder and apple juice concentrate in a saucepan. Slowly bring to the boil. Simmer for 5 minutes. Add the raspberries, and slowly bring to the boil again. Simmer for 5 minutes. Pour the mixture into hot sterilised jars and seal when cool. Refrigerate.

Strawberry Jam Spread

MAKES 6 × 250-ML/8-FL-OZ JARS

500 ml/16 fl oz/2 cups unsweetened apple and pear juice or unsweetened orange juice
1 tablespoon/1 tablespoon plus 1 teaspoon agar powder
200 ml/7 fl oz/¾ cup apple juice concentrate
1 kg/2¼ lb strawberries, washed and hulled

Place all the ingredients, except the strawberries, in a saucepan and slowly bring to the boil. Simmer for 5 minutes. Add the strawberries and bring to the boil. Simmer for 20–25 minutes. Remove from the heat. Pour into hot sterilised jars and seal when cool. Refrigerate.

Chicken Spread

MAKES 2 × 250-ML/8-FL-OZ JARS

225 g/½ lb/1 cup cooked minced chicken (all fat and skin removed before cooking)
1 tablespoon/1 tablespoon plus 1 teaspoon grated mild onion
1 tablespoon/1 tablespoon plus 1 teaspoon finely chopped fresh parsley
150 g/5 oz/1 cup chopped blanched almonds
3 tablespoons/3 tablespoons plus 3 teaspoons mayonnaise
pinch of dried thyme
1 teaspoon lemon juice

Blend all the ingredients in a food processor or blender until smooth. Pour into a small airtight container and refrigerate. Serve with wholemeal toast fingers or fresh wholemeal bread.

Savoury Spread

xxxxxxxxxxxxxxxxxxxxxxxxxxxxxxxxxxxxxxxxxxxxxxxxxxxxxxxxxxxxxxxxxxxxxxxxxxxxxxxxxxxxxxx

MAKES 1½ × 250-ML/8-FL-OZ JARS

225 g/½ lb ripe tomatoes, skinned,
*   seeded and chopped*
1 tablespoon/1 tablespoon plus 1
*   teaspoon grated onion*
1 tablespoon/1 tablespoon plus 1
*   teaspoon grated low-fat grating cheese*
1 tablespoon/1 tablespoon plus 1
*   teaspoon non-fat or low-fat yoghurt*
1 teaspoon mixed dried herbs
black pepper to taste
⅛ teaspoon cayenne pepper
fresh wholemeal breadcrumbs (use more
*   or less according to desired*
*   consistency)*

Place all the ingredients, except the breadcrumbs, in a saucepan. Slowly bring to the boil and boil for 1 minute. Remove from the heat. Add the wholemeal breadcrumbs and mix to make a paste. Store in an airtight container in the refrigerator. Serve with wholemeal toast fingers or fresh wholemeal bread.

Steak Paste

xxxxxxxxxxxxxxxxxxxxxxxxxxxxxxxxxxxxxxxxxxxxxxxxxxxxxxxxxxxxxxxxxxxxxxxxxxxxxxxxxxxxxxx

MAKES 1 × 250-ML/8-FL-OZ JAR

500 g/1 lb 2 oz topside steak
1 bay leaf
1 tablespoon/1 tablespoon plus 1
*   teaspoon water*
½ teaspoon black pepper
½ teaspoon ground mace
½ teaspon ground nutmeg
¼ teaspoon cayenne pepper
squeeze of lemon juice

Cut the steak into small pieces and remove all the fat and sinew. Put all the ingredients, except the lemon juice, into a heatproof dish. Cover, and steam gently for 3 hours. When cool, finely mince in a food processor or blender. Mix with the lemon juice. Store in an airtight container in the refrigerator. Serve with wholemeal toast fingers or fresh wholemeal bread.

Date and Apple Chutney

xxxxxxxxxxxxxxxxxxxxxxxxxxxxxxxxxxxxxxxxxxxxxxxxxxxxxxxxxxxxxxxxxxxxxxxxxxxxxxxxxxxxxxx

MAKES 4 × 250-ML/8-FL-OZ JARS

4 cooking apples, peeled, cored and
*   grated*
500 g/1 lb 2 oz/3⅓ cups chopped dates
2 onions, finely chopped
225 g/½ lb/1 cup raisins or sultanas or
*   stoned apricots*
1 teaspoon chilli powder
500 ml/16 fl oz/2 cups unsweetened
*   orange juice*
6 cloves
¼ teaspoon ground allspice
350 ml/12 fl oz/1½ cups white wine
*   vinegar or cider vinegar*

Place all the ingredients in a large saucepan and slowly bring to the boil over a low heat. Simmer, stirring occasionally, for 1 hour or until the mixture has a thick, soft consistency. Pour into hot sterilised jars and seal when cool. Refrigerate. The flavour will improve if left for at least 1 week before using.

   This is an excellent savoury spread for sandwiches, a dip to serve with vegetable and fruit platters, and a chutney with chicken, fish and vegetables.

Mango Chutney

MAKES 2 × 250-ML/8-FL-OZ JARS

1 onion, chopped
1 teaspoon finely chopped fresh ginger
65 ml/2 fl oz/¼ cup water or Chicken
  Stock (see p. 14)
flesh of 2 mangoes
2 Granny Smith apples, peeled and
  grated (juice squeezed out)
250 ml/8 fl oz/1 cup unsweetened
  orange juice
75 ml/3 fl oz/⅓ cup brown rice vinegar
½ teaspoon chilli powder
½ teaspoon ground cummin
1 tablespoon/1 tablespoon plus 1
  teaspoon orange rind
125 ml/4 fl oz/½ cup apple juice
  concentrate

In a saucepan, simmer the onion and ginger in the water for 5 minutes. Add the remaining ingredients. Cover, and bring to the boil. Remove the lid, and cook for 1 hour. Stir frequently to prevent the mixture from sticking to the base of the saucepan. Pour into hot sterilised jars and seal when cool. Refrigerate.

Variation
■ When mangoes are out of season you can substitute canned unsweetened peaches. Drain before using.

Apple Sauce

MAKES 500 ML/16 FL OZ/2 CUPS

6 cooking apples, peeled, cored and sliced
½ lemon
250 ml/8 fl oz/1 cup water
1 tablespoon/1 tablespoon plus 1
  teaspoon cornflour
1 tablespoon/1 tablespoon plus 1
  teaspoon extra water

Place the apple, lemon and water in a saucepan. Cover, and cook until the apple is soft. Remove the lemon. Mix the cornflour with 1 tablespoon/1 tablespoon plus 1 teaspoon of water to make a paste. Stir through the apple and continue cooking and stirring until the sauce thickens. Serve hot or cold.

Store the sauce in an airtight container in the refrigerator or freezer (it freezes well).

Blueberry Sauce

MAKES 625 ML/1 PINT/2½ CUPS

500 ml/16 fl oz/2 cups unsweetened
  pear juice or water
30 g/1 oz/¼ cup cornflour
75 ml/3 fl oz/⅓ cup apple juice
  concentrate
450 g/1 lb/3 cups blueberries (fresh or
  frozen, not canned)
1 tablespoon/1 tablespoon plus 1
  teaspoon lemon juice

This sauce is a delicious accompaniment to pancakes.

Mix 65 ml/2 fl oz/¼ cup of the pear juice with the cornflour to make a paste. Combine all the remaining ingredients in a small saucepan and slowly bring to the boil. Add the cornflour paste and stir continuously until the sauce thickens.

Remove from the heat and cool slightly. Pour over pancakes and serve.

Any left-over sauce will keep in the refrigerator for about 1 week. Reheat and add a little water for a pouring consistency.

Lemon Sauce

MAKES 625 ML/1 PINT/2½ CUPS

200 ml/7 fl oz/¾ cup freshly squeezed
    lemon juice
125 ml/4 fl oz/½ cup apple juice
    concentrate
½ teaspoon orange essence
2 teaspoons finely grated orange rind
350 ml/12 fl oz/1½ cups water
30 g/1 oz/¼ cup cornflour

This sauce is a delicious accompaniment to pancakes.

Combine the lemon juice, apple juice concentrate, orange essence, rind and 250 ml/8 fl oz/1 cup of the water in a small saucepan. Slowly bring to the boil. Mix the remaining water and cornflour to make a paste. Add to the lemon mixture in the saucepan and stir continuously until the sauce thickens.

Remove from the heat and cool slightly. Pour over pancakes and serve.

Any left-over sauce will keep in the refrigerator for about 1 week. Reheat and add a little water for a pouring consistency.

Mushroom Sauce

MAKES 300 ML/10 FL OZ/1¼ CUPS

200 g/7 oz sliced mushrooms
1 teaspoon light olive oil
¼ teaspoon dried dill
¼ teaspoon dried thyme
200 ml/7 fl oz/¾ cup skim milk
1 tablespoon/1 tablespoon plus 1
    teaspoon cornflour
1 tablespoon/1 tablespoon plus 1
    teaspoon finely chopped fresh parsley

In a saucepan, cook the mushrooms in the oil with the dill and thyme until the mushrooms have softened and changed colour. Mix a little of the milk with the cornflour to make a paste and add to the remaining milk. Combine thoroughly and add to the mushroom mixture. Keep stirring until the sauce thickens. Just before serving add the parsley. (See colour plate opposite page 216.)

Orange Sauce

MAKES 625 ML/1 PINT/2½ CUPS

200 ml/7 fl oz/¾ cup freshly squeezed
    orange juice
125 ml/4 fl oz/½ cup apple juice
    concentrate
½ teaspoon orange essence
2 teaspoons grated orange rind
350 ml/12 fl oz/1½ cups water
30 g/1 oz/¼ cup cornflour

This sauce is a delicious accompaniment to pancakes.

Combine the orange juice, apple juice concentrate, orange essence, rind, and 250 ml/8 fl oz/1 cup of the water in a small saucepan. Slowly bring to the boil. Mix the remaining water and cornflour to make a paste. Add to the orange mixture in the saucepan and stir continuously until the sauce thickens. Remove from the heat and cool slightly. Pour over pancakes and serve.

Orange Curry Sauce

MAKES 250 ML/8 FL OZ/1 CUP

2 teaspoons arrowroot
1–2 teaspoons curry powder
250 ml/8 fl oz/1 cup unsweetened
    orange juice

Mix the arrowroot and curry powder with a small amount of the orange juice to make a paste. Stir this through the remaining orange juice. Place in a small saucepan. Slowly bring to the boil until the sauce thickens. Cool and refrigerate.

Use Orange Curry Sauce as required. It is excellent poured over chicken, turkey, cantaloup, cucumber and pineapple.

Raspberry Sauce

MAKES 625 ML/1 PINT/2½ CUPS

500 ml/16 fl oz/2 cups unsweetened
  pear juice or water
30 g/1 oz/¼ cup cornflour
75 ml/3 fl oz/⅓ cup apple juice
  concentrate
450 g/1 lb/3 cups raspberries (fresh or
  frozen, not canned)
1 tablespoon/1 tablespoon plus 1
  teaspoon lemon juice

This sauce is a delicious accompaniment to pancakes.

Mix 65 ml/2 fl oz/¼ cup of the pear juice with the cornflour to make a paste. Combine all the remaining ingredients in a small saucepan and slowly bring to the boil. Add the cornflour paste and stir continuously until the sauce thickens.

Remove from the heat and cool slightly. Pour over pancakes and serve.

Any left-over sauce will keep in the refrigerator for about 1 week. Reheat and add a little water for a pouring consistency.

Sweet-and-sour Sauce

MAKES 500 ML/16 FL OZ/2 CUPS

250 ml/8 fl oz/1 cup vegetable juice
125 ml/4 fl oz/½ cup unsweetened
  pineapple juice
125 g/¼ lb/½ cup unsweetened
  pineapple pieces
2 tablespoons/2 tablespoons plus 2
  teaspoons wine vinegar
black pepper to taste
1 teaspoon cornflour
2 tablespoons/2 tablespoons plus 2
  teaspoons salt-free tomato paste
½ small red capsicum, finely chopped
½ small green capsicum, finely chopped
a little freshly chopped parsley or chives
  for garnishing

In a saucepan, combine all the ingredients and bring to the boil, stirring frequently. Boil gently until the sauce thickens. Garnish with the parsley.

Spicy Tomato Sauce

MAKES 3 LITRES/5 PINTS/12 CUPS

3 kg/6½ lb ripe tomatoes, skinned and
  seeded
2 large onions, finely chopped
3 large Granny Smith apples, peeled and
  chopped
2 large carrots, grated
250 ml/8 fl oz/1 cup vinegar
250 ml/8 fl oz/1 cup water
½ teaspoon ground mace
⅛ teaspoon ground cloves
¼ teaspoon cayenne pepper

Combine all the ingredients in a large saucepan and bring to the boil. Simmer, uncovered, for 1–1½ hours or until the sauce is thick, stirring occasionally. Remove from the heat. Purée in a food processor or blender. Pour into sterilised bottles and seal when cool. Refrigerate. (See left colour plate between pages 72 and 73.)

Fresh Tomato Sauce

MAKES 625 ML/1 PINT/2½ CUPS

1 kg/2¼ lb ripe tomatoes, skinned, seeded and chopped
1 bay leaf
6 peppercorns
6 cloves
65 ml/2 fl oz/¼ cup water
black pepper to taste

Place the tomato, bay leaf, peppercorns, cloves and water in a saucepan and bring to the boil over a high heat. Reduce the heat and simmer, covered, until the tomato is very soft. Purée by pushing through a sieve and discard the bay leaf, peppercorns and cloves. Season with black pepper. Cool and refrigerate until required. Can also be used in soups, sauces and casseroles.

Sweet Tomato Sauce

MAKES 500 ML/16 FL OZ/2 CUPS

1 small onion, chopped
1 teaspoon crushed garlic
1 teaspoon light olive oil or *a little water*
150 g/5 oz/1 cup grated carrot or *pumpkin*
125 ml/4 fl oz/½ cup dry red wine
425 g/15 oz canned whole tomatoes in natural juice, salt-free
2 tablespoons/2 tablespoons plus 2 teaspoons salt-free tomato paste
2 teaspoons finely chopped fresh parsley

In a saucepan, cook the onion and garlic in the oil until the onion is soft. Add the carrot and cook until soft. Add the wine.

Chop the tomatoes and add to the pan with their juice. Stir in the tomato paste. Simmer for 20 minutes, stirring frequently. Just before serving add the parsley.

White Sauce

MAKES 250 ML/8 FL OZ/1 CUP

250 ml/8 fl oz/1 cup skim milk or *reduced-fat soymilk*
2 tablespoons/2 tablespoons plus 2 teaspoons cornflour
black pepper to taste

Pour all but 2 tablespoons/2 tablespoons plus 2 teaspoons of the milk into a saucepan and bring to the boil. Mix the cornflour with the remaining milk until smooth. Just as bubbles appear prior to boiling, add the cornflour paste and beat well. Season with black pepper.

Variations
Add to the basic White Sauce one of the following:

- 2 tablespoons/2 tablespoons plus 2 teaspoons of grated low-fat grating cheese
- 2 tablespoons/2 tablespoons plus 2 teaspoons of freshly chopped chives
- 1 tablespoon/1 tablespoon plus 1 teaspoon of freshly chopped parsley
- 2 teaspoons of Dijon mustard
- 2 teaspoons of freshly chopped dill
- 2 teaspoons of freshly chopped mint
- squeeze of lemon juice.

FRUIT & VEGETABLE PRESERVES

Recently I discovered the art of preserving my own fruit and vegetables in bottles without the need to add any sugar, salt, preservative or colour. Preserving is effortless, the results are great, and it enables us to enjoy the natural goodness and flavour of fruit and vegetables long after their season has ended. The compliments I receive about 'my shelves of many colours' are reward enough, but the real bonus is that we can enjoy top-quality fruit and vegetables all year round.

If you do not have a preserving unit, I would encourage you to save your extra cents and invest in one. The latest model is inexpensive. It is simply filled with water and switched on for the required amount of time – usually about 1 hour. The bottles are then removed from the unit, cooled, and stored to be enjoyed as you require them.

In any recipes calling for cooked fruit, use bottled fruit. Drain the vegetables and use in salads or other suitable recipes. All the recipes given use No. 27 Fowlers Vacola bottles.

Apples

apples
2 tablespoons/2 tablespoons plus 2
teaspoons lemon juice or 65 ml/2 fl
oz/¼ cup unsweetened orange juice or
unsweetened pear juice
a little water
1 stick cinnamon (optional)

Cut the apples in quarters and, working quickly to avoid discoloration, pack into the bottles. Add the lemon juice and top up with water.

For an interesting flavour, put the stick of cinnamon down the side of the bottle before sealing. Process using the usual method. Serve with porridge, muesli or non-fat or low-fat yoghurt.

Variations
- To make preserved apples for desserts, spreads, cakes and muffins add 1–2 tablespoons/1–2 tablespoons plus 1–2 teaspoons lemon juice and a few cloves to the apples and top up with water. Process using the usual method.
- Rhubarb and apple make good preserving partners. Roughly chop equal quantities of the fruits and fill the bottles. Add 125 ml/4 fl oz/½ cup unsweetened grape juice and 125 ml/4 fl oz/½ cup water or unsweetened orange juice to each bottle. Process using the usual method.

Apricots

apricots
65 ml–125 ml/2 fl oz–4 fl oz/¼ cup–
½ cup unsweetened orange juice and a
little water or 1 litre/1¾ pints/
4 cups water
dash of brandy (optional)

I like to preserve apricots whole, even though it is a little more difficult to pack them into the bottles, because the stone imparts an almond flavour to the preserve after the bottles have been on the shelf for a while.

Wash and stone the apricots. Pack them into the bottles very tightly. Add the orange juice and top up with water; or cook some of the apricots, unstoned, in 1 litre/1¾ pints/ 4 cups of water until quite soft, remove the stones and push through a sieve. Pour this liquid over the apricots in the bottles. For special occasions add a dash of brandy. Process using the usual method. Serve in dessert goblets. (See left colour plate between pages 248 and 249.)

Bananas

〰〰〰〰〰〰〰〰〰〰〰〰〰〰〰〰〰〰〰〰〰〰〰〰〰〰〰〰〰〰〰〰

bananas
2 tablespoons/2 tablespoons plus 2
* teaspoons lemon juice*
water

This is an original and tasty way to eat bananas.

Peel and slice the bananas and pack tightly into the bottles. Add the lemon juice and top with water (unsweetened orange, pineapple or grape juice can also be used). Process using the usual method. Serve with porridge, muesli or non-fat or low-fat yoghurt.

Variation

- To preserve bananas for use as a dessert, pack banana slices, chopped dried apricots and the pulp of 3 large passionfruit into a bottle. Add 2 tablespoons/2 tablespoons plus 2 teaspoons lemon juice and top up with unsweetened orange juice or water. Process using the usual method. Serve topped with non-fat or low-fat yoghurt, or a light warm custard.

Beetroot

〰〰〰〰〰〰〰〰〰〰〰〰〰〰〰〰〰〰〰〰〰〰〰〰〰〰〰〰〰〰〰〰

beetroot
water and cider vinegar or *unsweetened*
* orange juice and cider vinegar*

Wash the beetroot thoroughly, being careful not to break the skin. Place in a saucepan with enough water to cover the beetroot. Bring to the boil and simmer for 1–2 hours or until the beetroot skin comes away easily. Remove from the heat. Run under cold water to remove the skin. Cut as desired or leave whole (if small). Pack tightly into the bottles. Top up with water and cider vinegar. Process using the usual method. Use in salads and sandwiches.

Variation

- Wash the beetroot thoroughly. Peel and cut into small chips. Pack into the bottles tightly. Top up with cider vinegar (you can dilute the vinegar with water, if you desire). Process using the usual method. Use in salads or on a vegetable platter.

Citrus Fruits

〰〰〰〰〰〰〰〰〰〰〰〰〰〰〰〰〰〰〰〰〰〰〰〰〰〰〰〰〰〰〰〰

grapefruit
mandarins
oranges
water

Peel the citrus fruit and cut away the pith. Cut into segments, removing the membrane and pips. Mandarins need not have the membrane removed but should have the pips removed to avoid a bitter taste. Pack tightly into bottles and top up with water (unsweetened orange or pineapple juice can also be used – dilute with water if desired). Process using the usual method. Serve as the base for a fruit salad or chilled as a first course on a hot summer's night.

Mixed Fruit

any combination of the following:
pineapple, peaches, apricots, pears,
mandarins, oranges, grapefruit, stoned
cherries, green and purple grapes,
passionfruit, kiwi fruit, nectarines,
plums
unsweetened apple juice
2 teaspoons brandy (optional)

Wash all the fruit and cut into even-sized pieces or leave whole. Pack tightly into the bottles and top up with unsweetened apple juice (unsweetened orange or pineapple juice can also be used). For a special occasion add the brandy. Process using the usual method. Serve chilled as a fruit salad.

Peaches

clingstone peaches, peeled
a few almonds (optional)
several thin strips orange peel or *2*
teaspoons finely grated lemon rind
(optional)
a little water or *water and unsweetened*
orange juice
1 cinnamon stick (optional)

Leave the peaches whole, or halve them, or halve and cut each half into four slices. Pack tightly into the bottles.

I like to add a few raw almonds and some thin strips of orange peel (pith removed) or 2 teaspoons of finely grated lemon rind to each bottle before topping up with water or water and unsweetened orange juice. You might also like to add a cinnamon stick to each bottle. Process using the usual method. Serve plain or with cheesecake. (See left colour plate between pages 248 and 249.)

Pears

pears, peeled and cored
a little water
a few fresh mint leaves

Pears can be preserved whole, halved or quartered. The stalks can be left on if you are preserving the pears whole. Pack tightly into the bottles. Top up with water and add a few mint leaves (you can also top up with water and unsweetened grape juice). The mint pear preserve can be served as a first course. (See left colour plate between pages 248 and 249.)

Variation
- To preserve pears for a dessert, cook some extra pears in unsweetened orange juice until soft. Strain and use this liquid to top up the bottles. Add the pulp of 6 passionfruit to each bottle and top up with water. Process using the usual method.

Pineapple

2 pineapples
water

Remove the top and bottom of 1 pineapple. Cut into slices and then peel and core. Leave in chunky circles, or cut into small chunks, or just roughly chop the flesh. Peel the other pineapple and remove the ends. Juice. Add an equal quantity of water to the quantity of pineapple juice. Pack the pineapple firmly into the bottles and top up with the diluted pineapple juice. Process using the usual method. Use in fruit salads, vegetable salads, with steamed chicken or in sweet-and-sour dishes. It is best eaten just as it is.

Strawberries

strawberries, washed and hulled
water
unsweetened orange juice

If you are lucky enough to have your own strawberry patch, it is worthwhile preserving this fruit to use when not in season for sauces and spreads. During the processing, strawberries tend to shrink and lose some of their bright colour, which detracts from their appearance and suitability for many other dishes.

Place the strawberries in a saucepan. Cover with water and unsweetened orange juice. Slowly bring to the boil. Remove from the heat, cover, and let stand for 4 hours. Strain and reserve the liquid. Place the strawberries in the bottles.

Return the liquid to the saucepan and bring to the boil. Boil until reduced by half. Leave to cool slightly. Pour into the bottles. Process using the usual method.

Serving Suggestions
- Fold through an equal quantity of apple purée, chill, and serve for a summer breakfast treat.
- Thicken with arrowroot to make a sauce and use as a pancake or cheesecake topping.
- Add fruit pectin to make a strawberry jam spread.

Tomatoes

tomatoes
1 tablespoon / 1 tablespoon plus 1 teaspoon lemon juice

Tomatoes are a versatile fruit and, although available nearly all year round, they are at their best at the beginning of the year. They can be preserved peeled or unpeeled, whole, halved or roughly chopped. Pack them firmly into bottles so there is no need to add any liquid except the lemon juice. Process using the usual method. (See left colour plate between pages 248 and 249.)

Serving Suggestions
- Purée to make a quick tomato juice.
- Use as a base for a tomato soup.
- Add to casseroles and sauces.

Tomatoes and Leeks

tomatoes
leeks
1 tablespoon / 1 tablespoon plus 1 teaspoon lemon juice
2 tablespoons / 2 tablespoons plus 2 teaspoons cider vinegar
a little water

Peel the tomatoes and roughly chop. Use only the white part of the leeks and wash thoroughly. Slice the leeks very finely. Combine equal quantities of tomato and leek and mix well before packing tightly into the bottles. Top up with the lemon juice, cider vinegar and water. Process using the usual method.

Serving Suggestions
- Add to casseroles and soups.
- Thicken with cornflour and use on a pizza base or in sandwiches and salads.

Tomatoes and Zucchini

tomatoes
zucchini
1 tablespoon/1 tablespoon plus 1
   teaspoon lemon juice
2 tablespoons/2 tablespoons plus 2
   teaspoons cider vinegar
a little water

Peel the tomatoes and roughly chop. Remove the ends of the zucchini. Wash and finely slice. Pack equal amounts of the tomato and zucchini tightly into the bottles. Top up with the lemon juice, cider vinegar and water. Process using the usual method.

Serving Suggestions
- Add to casseroles.
- Thicken with cornflour to make a sauce.
- Thicken with cornflour, top with breadcrumbs and finely grated low-fat grating cheese, bake, and serve as an accompaniment to a main meal.

Mixed Vegetables

any combination of the following:
   carrots, radishes, turnips, cucumber,
   red and green capsicums, celery,
   butternut pumpkin, green beans, snow
   peas, zucchini
cider vinegar
water

Wash all vegetables and peel if necessary. Cut into strips or 3-cm/1″ cubes, or slice diagonally. Pack into bottles tightly. Fill two-thirds with the cider vinegar and top up with water. Process using the usual method. Serve on a vegetable platter for special occasions and use in salads. (See left colour plate between pages 248 and 249.)

JUICES, DRINKS & PUNCHES

Fresh juices have been used therapeutically for centuries, and they are still used extensively in many European health clinics for fasting, cleansing, cancer-healing processes and for their rejuvenating effect. They are rich in enzymes, vitamins, minerals, trace elements and natural sugars. They require little energy from the body for their absorption, assimilation and elimination.

A special juicer is required to extract the juice from fruits and vegetables. It extracts the juice from the pulp, which is high in fibre and nutrients. Experiment with recipes using the pulp.

It is important that juices are drunk immediately after juicing, otherwise the oxidation process will not only turn the juices brown in colour, but will also destroy their goodness. Some people believe that it is better not to combine fruit juices with vegetable juices, as they think it impairs the digestion and assimilation of nutrients.

You will find lots of ideas for healthy, non-alcoholic, non-sugary drinks in these recipes.

Do not forget the importance of water in your diet. You need between six to eight glasses of water each day for normal bodily functions. Drinks like alcohol, coffee and tea actually dehydrate the body. Keep these drinks to an absolute minimum and look for caffeine- and alcohol-free alternatives.

Sparkling Apple Juice

SERVES 1

400 g/14 oz apples, cored and chopped

Apple juice is rich in vitamin C, the B group vitamins, potassium and folic acid. It is considered to be an excellent body cleanser and blood purifier. There is absolutely no comparison between bottled and fresh apple juice! Apple juice also combines well with other juices.

Place the apple in a juicer and juice. (See colour plate opposite page 249.)

Apple, Celery and Ginger Juice

SERVES 1

310 g/10½ oz apples, cored and chopped
60 g/2 oz celery
1 teaspoon chopped fresh ginger

Place the apple, celery and ginger in a juicer and juice.

Apple and Cucumber Juice

SERVES 1

310 g/10½ oz apples, cored and chopped
100 g/3½ oz cucumber, peeled and chopped

Place the apple and cucumber in a juicer and juice.

Apple and Grape Juice

SERVES 1

200 g/7 oz apples, cored and chopped
150 g/5 oz grapes

Place the apple and grapes in a juicer and juice.

Apple and Lemon Juice

SERVES 1

310 g/10½ oz apples, cored and chopped
65 ml/2 fl oz/¼ cup freshly squeezed lemon juice

Place the apple in a juicer and juice. Mix the apple juice and lemon juice together.

Apricot Juice

SERVES 1

400 g/14 oz apricots, stoned and chopped

Apricot juice contains potassium, iron, vitamins A and B6, folic acid and other essential vitamins. It is a cleansing juice and highly prized for its nutrients.

The people of the Hunza Valley in Kashmir, who live long healthy lives, eat a lot of apricots.

Apricot juice is a meal all on its own. It is a delicious thick purée, full of goodness. You may prefer to thin it down with water, fresh orange juice, mango juice, grape juice or apple juice. It combines well with all of these, and passionfruit pulp gives it a delicious bite.

Place the apricot in a juicer and juice.

Beetroot Juice

SERVES 1

310 g/10½ oz beetroot, peeled and chopped

If you have your own vegetable patch, beetroot is one vegetable of which you should have plenty. It makes an excellent juice that combines well with other juices.

This is a strong-flavoured juice, so you might like to dilute it with celery juice, cucumber juice or carrot juice.

Place the beetroot in a juicer and juice.

Carrot Juice

SERVES 1

350 g/¾ lb carrots, chopped

This is a popular juice, rich in carotene, which the body turns into vitamin A. It also contains vitamins C, D, E, and K.

Place the carrot in a juicer and juice.

Carrot and Celery Juice

SERVES 1

310 g/10½ oz carrots, chopped
60 g/2 oz celery, chopped

Place the carrot and celery in a juicer and juice.

Carrot, Celery and Ginger Juice

SERVES 1

310 g/10½ oz carrots, chopped
60 g/2 oz celery, chopped
1 teaspoon chopped fresh ginger

This makes an excellent breakfast juice to start the day.

Place the carrot, celery and ginger in a juicer and juice.

Citus Combination Juice

SERVES 2

1 grapefruit, peeled
1 orange, peeled and chopped
1 lemon, peeled and chopped
200 g/7 oz pineapple flesh, chopped

Citrus juices include orange, grapefruit, lemon and lime and are all excellent sources of vitamin C and potassium.
Place all the fruit in a juicer and juice.

Grape Juice

SERVES 1

350 g/¾ lb green or purple grapes

Grape juice is one of the most delicious juices of all. It has been used for centuries as a 'spring-cleaning' juice, and is still used today for cancer patients in some detoxifying programmes. It has a high concentration of fruit sugar, which promotes the burning of stored fat and the release of toxic substances. It is also high in iron.

Grape juice combines well with nearly all other fruit juices, so enjoy making up your own combinations.

Place the grapes in a juicer and juice.

Grapefruit and Orange Juice

SERVES 1

1 grapefruit, peeled and chopped
2 oranges, peeled and chopped

Place the grapefruit and orange in a juicer and juice. (See colour plate opposite.)

Green Juice

any combination of the following: lettuce, spinach, a little cabbage, parsley, kale, wild carrot tops, radish tops, cress, wheat grass, alfalfa sprouts, comfrey, cucumber, celery and especially celery leaves

Green juice is a combination of any green vegetables that will pass through your juicer. Its benefits are thought to be many because it supplies chlorophyll and many vitamins and minerals, trace elements, enzymes and other components of nature's 'natural medicines'. This juice can also be added to others like carrot juice, celery juice or beetroot juice.

Chop your selection of green vegetables and place in a juicer and juice.

Lemon Zinger Juice

SERVES 1

125 ml/4 fl oz/½ cup freshly squeezed lemon juice
200 ml/7 fl oz/¾ cup mineral water

Mix together the lemon juice and mineral water.

Grapefruit and Orange Juice (opposite page); Tomato Spicer (page 254);
Orange Juice (page 249).

Preserves. Back (left to right): Tomatoes (page 243); Apricots (page 240); Pears (page 242). Front: Peaches (page 242); Mixed Vegetables (page 244); Peaches; blueberries.

Back (left to right): Summer Party Punch (page 254); Fruit Punch (page 253).
Front: Pineapple Milkshake and Apple Milk Drink (page 251).

Back (left to right): mineral water with fruits; Apricot Thickshake (opposite page). Middle: Sparkling Apple Juice (page 246); Blueberry Thickshake and Carob Thickshake (page 250). Front: Peppermint Refresher (page 254); Pink Fizz (page 253).

Orange Juice

〜〜〜〜〜〜〜〜〜〜〜〜〜〜〜〜〜〜〜〜〜〜〜〜〜〜〜〜〜〜〜〜〜〜〜〜〜〜

SERVES 1

3 oranges, peeled and chopped

Oranges are high in vitamin C, calcium and phosphorus.
Place the orange in a juicer and juice. (See colour plate opposite page 248.)

Pineapple Juice

〜〜〜〜〜〜〜〜〜〜〜〜〜〜〜〜〜〜〜〜〜〜〜〜〜〜〜〜〜〜〜〜〜〜〜〜〜〜

SERVES 1

400 g/14 oz pineapple flesh, chopped

Pineapple juice combines well with orange, mango, papaw and passionfruit. Pineapple sage and fresh mint can also enhance the flavour. Place the pineapple in a juicer and juice.

Tomato Juice

〜〜〜〜〜〜〜〜〜〜〜〜〜〜〜〜〜〜〜〜〜〜〜〜〜〜〜〜〜〜〜〜〜〜〜〜〜〜

SERVES 1

350 g/¾ lb ripe tomatoes, chopped

Tomato juice combines well with carrot juice and cucumber juice. You can also add crushed garlic or crushed fresh ginger, for a change of flavour. Tomato juice is a good source of vitamins A and C. Place the tomato in a juicer and juice.

Watermelon Juice

〜〜〜〜〜〜〜〜〜〜〜〜〜〜〜〜〜〜〜〜〜〜〜〜〜〜〜〜〜〜〜〜〜〜〜〜〜〜

SERVES 1

350 g/¾ lb watermelon flesh

Watermelon juice is a wonderful natural diuretic.
Seed and chop the watermelon, place in a juicer and juice.

Apricot Thickshake

〜〜〜〜〜〜〜〜〜〜〜〜〜〜〜〜〜〜〜〜〜〜〜〜〜〜〜〜〜〜〜〜〜〜〜〜〜〜

SERVES 2

*250 ml/8 fl oz/1 cup skim milk or
reduced-fat soymilk or goat's milk,
well chilled*
*150 g/5 oz/½ cup fresh apricots, stoned
and finely chopped*
2 ice blocks
1 teaspoon apple juice concentrate
¼ teaspoon ground cinnamon (optional)
*2 tablespoons/2 tablespoons plus
2 teaspoons low-fat ricotta cheese
(optional)*

Blend all the ingredients in a food processor or blender until thick and creamy. Add the ricotta cheese and blend for a richer, creamier thickshake. (See colour plate opposite.)

Variation
- Canned apricots in natural juice can be used if fresh apricots are not available. Drain and chill apricots before use.

Apricot and Almond Thickshake

SERVES 1

125 ml/4 fl oz/½ cup reduced-fat
  soymilk, well chilled
125 ml/4 fl oz/½ cup unsweetened
  apple juice, well chilled
4 dried apricots, soaked and drained
5 raw almonds

Blend all the ingredients in a food processor or blender until thick and frothy.

Blueberry Thickshake

SERVES 2

250 ml/8 fl oz/1 cup skim milk, well
  chilled
65 ml/2 fl oz/¼ cup low-fat yoghurt,
  well chilled
250 ml/8 fl oz/1 cup blueberries (fresh
  or frozen, not canned)
1 teaspoon apple juice concentrate

Combine all ingredients in a food blender or processor and blend until thick and frothy. (See colour plate opposite page 249.)

Carob Thickshake

SERVES 2

250 ml/8 fl oz/1 cup skim milk, well
  chilled
2 tablespoons/2 tablespoons plus
  2 teaspoons skim milk powder
1 tablespoon/1 tablespoon plus
  1 teaspoon carob powder
1 teaspoon vanilla essence
½ banana, chopped (optional)
ice blocks
ground nutmeg for garnishing

Blend all the ingredients, except the nutmeg and the ice blocks, in a food processor or blender until smooth and frothy. Pour into two tall glasses containing ice blocks. Garnish with the nutmeg. (See colour plate opposite page 249.)

Breakfast in a Glass

SERVES 1

250 ml/8 fl oz/1 cup skim milk or
  reduced-fat soymilk, well chilled
1–2 teaspoons vanilla essence
2–4 dates, stoned
1 banana or apple, peeled and cored
2 teaspoons oat bran

Blend all the ingredients in a food processor or blender until smooth and thick. Drink immediately. (See colour plate opposite page 224.)

Apple Milk Drink

SERVES 2

250 ml/8 fl oz/1 cup unsweetened apple juice, well chilled
250 ml/8 fl oz/1 cup skim milk, well chilled
dash of ground cinnamon

Blend the apple juice and skim milk in a food processor or blender until thick and frothy. Sprinkle the cinnamon on top. (See right colour plate between pages 248 and 249.)

Banana Milk Drink

SERVES 1

250 ml/8 fl oz/1 cup skim milk, well chilled
1 banana, mashed
2 teaspoons skim milk powder
1 teaspoon brewer's yeast
dash of ground nutmeg

Blend the skim milk, banana, skim milk powder and brewer's yeast in a food processor or blender until thick and frothy. Sprinkle the nutmeg on top.

Pineapple Milkshake

SERVES 2

250 ml/8 fl oz/1 cup skim milk, well chilled
200 ml/7 fl oz/¾ cup unsweetened pineapple juice, well chilled
2 teaspoons skim milk powder or *1 tablespoon/1 tablespoon plus 1 teaspoon ice cream*
fresh mint leaves for garnishing

Blend all the ingredients, except the mint, in a food processor or blender until thick and frothy. Garnish with mint leaves. (See right colour plate between pages 248 and 249.)

Banana Fruit Smoothie

SERVES 1

1 small ripe banana, roughly chopped
250 ml/8 fl oz/1 cup skim milk, well chilled
½ teaspoon vanilla essence
4 ice blocks
dash of ground nutmeg (optional)

Blend all the ingredients in a food processor or blender until smooth and frothy.

Variation
■ Substitute non-fat or low-fat yoghurt for the skim milk, or use a frozen banana, for a creamier consistency.

Berry Fruit Smoothie

SERVES 2

250 ml/8 fl oz/1 cup skim milk, well
   chilled
65 ml/2 fl oz/¼ cup non-fat or low-fat
   yoghurt, well chilled
150 g/5 oz/1 cup fresh berries, well
   chilled
1 teaspoon apple juice concentrate

Blend all the ingredients in a food processor or blender until thick and frothy.

Honey and Almond Smoothie

SERVES 1

200 ml/7 fl oz/¾ cup reduced-fat
   soymilk, well chilled
5 raw almonds
1 teaspoon honey
2 teaspoons wheatgerm

Blend all the ingredients in a food processor or blender until thick and frothy.

Strawberry Smoothie

SERVES 2

150 g/5 oz/1 cup strawberries, washed
   and hulled
2 tablespoons/2 tablespoons plus
   2 teaspoons unsweetened orange juice
1 tablespoon/1 tablespoon plus
   1 teaspoon apple juice concentrate
500 ml/16 fl oz/2 cups skim milk, well
   chilled
125 ml/4 fl oz/½ cup non-fat or low-
   fat yoghurt, well chilled

In a small saucepan, simmer the strawberries in the orange juice and apple juice concentrate until the strawberries are soft. Chill. Purée all the ingredients in a food processor or blender, and serve.

Variation
■ Substitute 2 tablespoons/2 tablespoons plus 2 teaspoons of skim milk powder for the yoghurt.

Barley Water

SERVES 10

3 tablespoons/3 tablespoons plus
   3 teaspoons pearl barley
250 ml/8 fl oz/1 cup water
2.25 litres/4 pints/9 cups extra water
250 ml/8 fl oz/1 cup orange juice
1 tablespoon/1 tablespoon plus
   1 teaspoon grated orange rind
250 ml/8 fl oz/1 cup lemon juice
1 tablespoon/1 tablespoon plus
   1 teaspoon grated lemon rind
1 tablespoon/1 tablespoon plus
   1 teaspoon honey

Cover the pearl barley with water. Bring to the boil, strain and discard the water. Cover the barley with the extra water, bring to the boil, and simmer for 15 minutes.

In a large jug, combine the honey and juice and rind of the oranges and lemons. Add the barley water through a sieve. Discard the barley, and leave to cool. Remove the rind and refrigerate.

This is an excellent thirst quencher or a pick-me-up if you are not feeling well.

Pink Fizz

SERVES 1

350 g/¾ lb watermelon flesh, seeded and
   chopped
250 ml/8 fl oz/1 cup soda water, well
   chilled

Push the watermelon flesh through a fine sieve, and add the soda water. Serve with pink straws and a little pink parasol. (See colour plate opposite page 249.)

Fruit Punch

SERVES 10

500 ml/16 fl oz/2 cups unsweetened
   orange juice
500 ml/16 fl oz/2 cups unsweetened
   apple juice
500 ml/16 fl oz/2 cups unsweetened
   pineapple juice
125 ml/4 fl oz/½ cup passionfruit pulp
ice blocks
1 litre/1¾ pints/4 cups mineral water or
   soda water

Combine the orange juice, apple juice and pineapple juice. Stir through the passionfruit pulp. Add ice blocks and dilute with the mineral water. (See right colour plate between pages 248 and 249.)

Summer Party Punch

SERVES 10 – 14

*1 litre/1¾ pints/4 cups unsweetened
   orange juice*
*500 ml/16 fl oz/2 cups unsweetened
   pineapple juice*
*500 g/1 lb 2 oz strawberries, washed,
   hulled and puréed*
1.5 litres/2½ pints/6 cups soda water
ice blocks

Combine the orange juice, pineapple juice and strawberry purée, and chill well. Add the soda water and ice blocks just prior to serving.

Thread the fruit onto the cocktail sticks and place one in each glass of punch. (See right colour plate between pages 248 and 249.)

Variation

■ For a festive occasion, thread cubes of peeled apple, chunks of pineapple and washed and hulled strawberries onto cocktail sticks and place one in each glass.

Peppermint Refresher

SERVES 1

*125 ml/4 fl oz/½ cup peppermint tea,
   well chilled*
*125 ml/4 fl oz/½ cup soda water, well
   chilled*
ice blocks
fresh peppermint leaves or *mint leaves for
   garnishing*

Mix the tea with the soda water, add the ice blocks, and garnish with peppermint leaves. (See colour plate opposite page 249.)

Tomato Spicer

SERVES 3

*500 ml/16 fl oz/2 cups salt-free tomato
   juice*
250 ml/8 fl oz/1 cup non-fat or *low-fat
   yoghurt*
a little crushed garlic
1 teaspoon finely grated lemon rind
2 teaspoons finely chopped red capsicum
*strips red and green capsicum for
   garnishing*

Blend all the ingredients, except the red and green capsicum strips, in a food processor or blender until smooth. Chill well. Serve in long thin glasses and garnish with the capsicum strips. (See right colour plate between pages 40 and 41, and opposite page 248.)

RECIPES FOR THE MICROWAVE

The microwave oven is now a popular addition to many kitchens. Its benefits are not only that it offers fast and convenient cooking but that cooking with a microwave oven is much healthier than using many traditional methods. With a microwave oven most foods can be cooked in less than half their conventional cooking time and the cooking process does not require the addition of fat, butter or oil. Even cooking liquid is kept to a minimum. Vegetables, chicken, fish and fruit, for example, cook to perfection with little preparation other than the addition of herbs or spices. The shorter cooking time ensures that the nutrients and the subtle, natural flavours of these foods are retained.

Cakes and muffins cook in just minutes in a microwave oven, while the preparation of porridge, custards and sauces is much easier and cleaner than when using the stove-top.

Once you are familiar with the workings of your microwave oven and understand its cooking times you will find that microwave cooking is foolproof and your recipes will turn out perfectly every time.

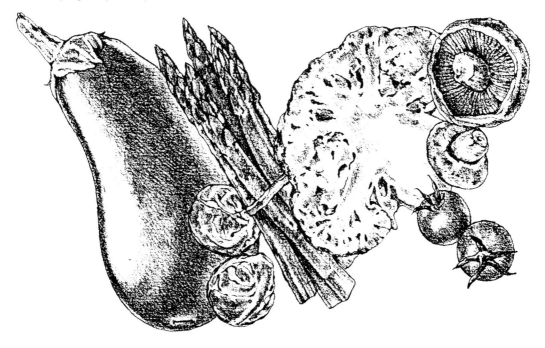

HOW DOES A MICROWAVE WORK?

Basics
- In a conventional oven, food is brought to the temperature of the oven cavity, then the cooking process begins. In a microwave oven, the cooking process occurs by direct penetration of the food by microwaves (also known as microwave energy). Cooking actually occurs with the vibration of the moisture molecules in the food.
- The microwave energy is absorbed by the food and the oven cavity itself remains cool.
- Microwave energy passes through glass, ceramics, plastic and paper. It will not pass through metal, however, so foil and metal containers, spoons and utensils are not suitable for use in a microwave oven.
- Microwaves penetrate foods to a depth of 2–4 cm on all surfaces: top, bottom and sides.
- The interior of foods greater than 5 cm in diameter heats by conduction, as it would in a conventional oven.

Advantages
- The most obvious advantage is the reduction in cooking time.
- There will be a saving on energy because of the reduced cooking time.
- The oven itself remains cool, so you will not burn yourself, and you can cook in the summer without heating the kitchen.
- It is an easy appliance to clean. Merely wipe over surfaces after use. Spilt food will not adhere to the surface because the oven cavity and doors do not get hot.
- Food can be cooked and presented in one dish, saving washing up.
- Faster cooking ensures that the flavour and natural nutrients are retained.
- Reheating foods only takes minutes, so you do not destroy vital nutrients and dry foods out, both of which can easily occur in a conventional oven.
- Cooking sauces, custards and porridge, and heating milk, in the microwave oven is easier and cleaner, avoiding dirty, sticky saucepans needing to be soaked at the end of the cooking time.

Converting Recipes
- Most recipes can be adapted to microwave cooking.
- Some recipes only need a shorter cooking time. Other recipes need to have the liquid content reduced as there is little evaporation in a microwave oven.
- Generally, use two-thirds of the liquid normally used and add more as it is needed.
- It may be necessary to reduce the quantities of herbs and spices because of the shorter cooking times. You may like to add dried or fresh herbs and spices at the end of the cooking time.
- It may be necessary to slice vegetables, fruits or meats in a special manner for quicker cooking.
- Low-fat cheese, which is substituted for other cheese in this book, should be added near the end of the cooking time, otherwise it will completely dry out.

Reheating Foods
- Foods reheated in the microwave often taste fresh rather than reheated.
- Valuable nutrient content is not lost in moisture evaporation, which occurs in a conventional oven.
- Foods that can be stirred can be reheated on HIGH.
- Foods that contain sensitive ingredients such as cheese, milk and egg whites, and cannot be stirred, should be reheated on MEDIUM over a long period of time.

Cooking Times
If your recipes are taking longer to cook than the times indicated in this book, or if food is over-cooked, you can avoid ruined meals by checking the following.
- Is your microwave the same voltage as the model in which the recipes in this book have been tested? If not you need to add or subtract time according to your oven. Follow the chart on page 258.
- Did you select the power setting and time indicated in the recipe?

Some Quick Tips

	Amount	**Cooking**	**Guidelines**
Toasted Wholemeal Breadcrumbs	15 g/½ oz/¼ cup	2 minutes on HIGH	Spread the breadcrumbs evenly over a sheet of non-stick baking paper. Stir once or twice during cooking. Cool. Store in an airtight container.
	60 g/2 oz/1 cup	4½ minutes on HIGH	
	125 g/¼ lb/2 cups	6 minutes on HIGH	
Toasted Sesame Seeds	2 tablespoons/2 tablespoons plus 2 teaspoons	40 seconds – 1 minute on HIGH	Spread the sesame seeds evenly over a sheet of non-stick baking paper. Stir once or twice during cooking. Store in an airtight container.
	3 tablespoons/¼ cup	1–3 minutes on HIGH	
	30 g/1 oz/½ cup	2–4 minutes on HIGH	
Toasted Rolled Oats	2 tablespoons/2 tablespoons plus 2 teaspoons	1–2 minutes on HIGH	Cover the oats while cooking and stand for 10 minutes after cooking.
	60 g/2 oz/½ cup	2–4 minutes on HIGH	
Dried Grated Rind	grated lemon or orange rind	1–2 minutes on HIGH	Place on a sheet of non-stick baking paper. Microwave until rind is dry. Stir once during cooking.
Dried Herbs	fresh herbs	4–6 minutes on HIGH	Remove leaves from stems and place in a single layer on absorbent paper towel. Microwave, checking after 4 minutes, until the herbs are dry and brittle. Allow to cool on the paper towel. Crush leaves and store in an airtight container.
Gelatine	125 ml/4 fl oz/½ cup water and 1 tablespoon/ 1 tablespoon plus 1 teaspoon gelatine	Microwave the water for 2 minutes on HIGH. Add the gelatine and mix well. Microwave for 1 minute on HIGH.	Cool before using.
Agar Powder	350 ml/12 fl oz/1½ cups water and 1 tablespoon/ 1 tablespoon plus 1 teaspoon agar powder	Microwave the water for 2 minutes on HIGH. Add the agar powder and mix well. Microwave for 1–2 minutes on HIGH.	Cool before using.

- Is the food at room temperature when cooking commences? If not, cooking times will be different, depending on whether the food has come straight from the refrigerator or been preheated.
- Always pay particular attention to the way in which ingredients are cut up or sliced and positioned in the cooking dish.
- Try to use dishes that are a similar size to those recommended in the recipes.

Use the times given in this book as a guide only, remembering to check your microwave oven handbook or manual for any specific features offered by your own microwave oven.

The recipes in this book have been tested in a 600–650 watt oven. If you need to adapt cooking times for an oven with a different wattage, use the following chart as a guide.

Adapting Cooking Times		
600–650 watt	550–600 watt	400–500 watt
15 sec	17 sec	20 sec
30 sec	35 sec	41 sec
1 min	1 min 9 sec	1 min 21 sec
2 min	2 min 22 sec	2 min 42 sec
3 min	3 min 27 sec	4 min 3 sec
4 min	4 min 36 sec	5 min 24 sec
5 min	5 min 45 sec	6 min 45 sec
10 min	11 min 30 sec	13 min 30 sec
15 min	17 min 15 sec	20 min 15 sec
20 min	23 min	27 min
25 min	28 min 45 sec	33 min 45 sec
30 min	34 min 30 sec	40 min 30 sec

Most microwave ovens have a turntable. If your oven does not, you may need to rotate your dishes during the cooking process. Check your oven manual to see how often this is necessary.

Some Microwave Facts

- The beauty of a microwave oven is that it will only do what you ask it to do. If a dish requires 6 minutes' cooking and you are called to the door or telephone, the microwave will not go on cooking – it switches off automatically at the set time.
- You need to become confident about cooking times. The only way to do this is to open the oven door and test the food as it cooks. This method is not successful in a conventional oven, because as you open and close the door the oven cavity loses temperature and so does

the food you are cooking. This does not occur in a microwave oven because the oven cavity remains cool. The microwave heat is so intense in the food itself that taking the food from the oven to check if it is cooked will not affect it greatly. When you return the food to the microwave there is not a slow build-up of heat as in a conventional oven – the heat is intense immediately on operation.

- Most foods taste exactly the same cooked in a microwave oven as in a conventional oven, but some foods, such as cakes and muffins, will look different because there is no browning process in the basic microwave oven. Personally, I would prefer cakes, muffins, and so on, cooked in a conventional oven for their appearance and light texture. However, the benefit of cooking these foods in a microwave oven is that they cook in far less time than in a conventional oven; for example, a cake takes approximately 8–12 minutes, muffins approximately 1½–3 minutes. When visitors arrive unexpectedly, or children arrive home ravenous on a cold day, these foods can be prepared quickly, with little fuss.
- Vegetables are especially good cooked in a microwave oven. They take only a short time, in a minimal quantity of water, stock, soy sauce, or dry white wine. They retain their bright colours and crispy, crunchy texture, and taste fresh and sweet. This is also the case for fruits. Fruit and vegetables contain a lot of moisture and natural sweetness and need little added in the cooking process.
- Cheese will not brown in a microwave oven, so sprinkle it with paprika or finely chopped fresh herbs for a better visual effect.
- It is best to start with the shortest time recommended in the recipe and cook further if necessary.
- The energy generated within the food by the cooking is so intense that some cooking will continue to occur after the food has been taken from the oven. Some foods can take a short standing time after cooking, whereas large, dense items, like a chicken or turkey, will take a longer standing time.
- Positioning food in a microwave oven is very important. The food on the outside of the dish cooks quicker than that on the inside; unevenly shaped foods like chicken drumsticks and broccoli florets should be positioned with the thickest part to the outside of the dish.
- When reheating food, make sure that any

bulky pieces of food are placed on the outer part of the plate to ensure even reheating.

- Food used in the recipes in this book should be at room temperature. Foods taken straight from the refrigerator may take longer to cook.
- Many recipes call for the food to be covered during cooking. You can cover containers with their own lids or use microwave-safe plastic wrap. Covering foods will enable them to heat more quickly, with less cooking liquid required. Steam is trapped inside the container and will make food more moist.
- It may be necessary with some ovens to shield the corners or edges of some foods so that the whole food cooks evenly and the corners and edges do not over-cook. To shield parts of the food, cover with small pieces of foil. Check your oven manual to see if this is necessary.
- Be sure that the utensils and cooking ware you use are microwave safe. Check your oven manual to find lists of suitable equipment. I like using glass jugs, bowls and containers in the microwave oven because I can see the food through the oven door.
- If you adapt any of these recipes by adding extra ingredients or omitting others, then you must adjust the cooking times accordingly.
- Because browning does not occur naturally in the microwave oven, you may like to place food under a grill for a short time only.

SOUPS

*M*any low-fat soups, flavoured with different herbs and spices instead of salt, can be cooked quickly in your microwave oven. The larger the quantity of soup, the longer it will take to cook because of the density of the liquid.

Cooking soups in the microwave oven is much cleaner than the conventional method with that large, heavily stained saucepan to wash at the end of the cooking process. You can reheat soups in individual serving bowls or in soup mugs for a quick lunch snack or a first course to a main meal.

Creamy Corn Soup

SERVES 4 – 6

3 large potatoes, peeled and chopped
1 onion, finely chopped
60 g/2 oz/1 cup finely chopped celery leaves
1.25 litres/2¼ pints/5 cups Vegetable Stock or Chicken Stock (*see p. 14*)
2 cups corn kernels
black pepper to taste
250–500 ml/8–16 fl oz/1–2 cups skim milk

Place the potato, onion and chopped celery leaves in a large casserole dish. Add 2 tablespoons of the stock. Cover, and microwave for 4–6 minutes on HIGH. Add the remaining stock and corn. Cover, and microwave for 4–6 minutes on HIGH. Purée the soup in a food processor or blender. Season with black pepper and thin down using the skim milk. Microwave for 1 minute on HIGH. Serve.

Cauliflower Soup

SERVES 8

8 garlic cloves, crushed
1 leek, thoroughly washed and finely
    sliced
3 potatoes, peeled
65 ml/2 fl oz/¼ cup water
1 litre/1¾ pints/4 cups extra water or
    Vegetable Stock (see p. 14)
1 cauliflower, cut into florets
2–3 tablespoons finely chopped fresh
    parsley
pinch of ground nutmeg
black pepper to taste
250ml/8 fl oz/1 cup skim milk

Place the garlic, leek, potatoes and 65 ml/2 fl oz/¼ cup of water in a 4-litre/7-pint/16-cup casserole dish. Cover, and microwave for 2½ minutes on HIGH. Stir well. Microwave for 2½ minutes more on HIGH.

Place the extra water in a 1-litre/1¾-pint/4-cup glass jug. Microwave for 3–4 minutes on HIGH. Pour into the casserole dish and add the cauliflower, parsley and nutmeg. Microwave for 15–20 minutes.

Purée the soup in a food processor or blender. Season with black pepper and thin down using the skim milk. Stir through and serve.

Pumpkin Soup with Basil

SERVES 4–6

500 g/1 lb 2 oz pumpkin, peeled
225 g/½ lb carrots
1.5 litres/2½ pints/6 cups Chicken
    Stock (see p. 14)
2 onions, finely chopped
225 g/½ lb ripe tomatoes or canned
    whole tomatoes in natural juice, salt-
    free
black pepper to taste
2 tablespoons/2 tablespoons plus
    2 teaspoons freshly chopped basil or
    1 teaspoon dried basil
fresh basil leaves for garnishing

Slice the pumpkin and carrots finely – a food processor will make this a speedy job. Place the stock in a 2-litre/3½-pint/8-cup glass jug. Microwave for 3–4 minutes on HIGH. Place the onion and vegetables in a 4-litre/7-pint/16-cup casserole dish. Add the stock. Cover, and microwave for 15 minutes on HIGH. Skin and seed the tomatoes. Chop roughly. Add the tomato, pepper and basil, and stir through. Microwave for 3–4 minutes on HIGH.

Serve garnished with fresh basil.

Tomato Soup

SERVES 4–6

1 onion, chopped
2 sticks celery with leaves, finely sliced
1 tablespoon/1 tablespoon plus
    1 teaspoon finely chopped fresh ginger
2 tablespoons/2 tablespoons plus
    2 teaspoons water
½ teaspoon dried oregano
½ teaspoon dried basil
850 g/2 lb canned whole tomatoes in
    natural juice, salt-free
2 tablespoons/2 tablespoons plus
    2 teaspoons salt-free tomato paste

Combine the onion, celery and ginger in a 2-litre/3½-pint/8-cup casserole dish. Add the water. Cover, and microwave for 4 minutes on HIGH. Purée the remaining ingredients in a food processor or blender and add to the dish. Stir well. Microwave for 5 minutes on HIGH.

Serve hot – or cool, refrigerate and serve chilled.

Variations
- Add 150 g/5 oz/1 cup of finely grated carrot prior to serving.
- Add 150 g/5 oz/1 cup of finely sliced celery prior to serving.
- Add 150 g/5 oz/1 cup of finely chopped capsicum prior to serving.
- Add a handful of finely chopped fresh chives prior to serving.
- Serve with non-fat or low-fat yoghurt and a sprinkling of your favourite herbs.
- Serve with vegetable sticks to munch on, for example, carrot, celery, cucumber and zucchini.

Zucchini Soup

SERVES 6

1 onion, chopped
2 tablespoons/2 tablespoons plus
    2 teaspoons water
500 g/1 lb 2 oz zucchini, cut into
    diagonal thin rounds
1 potato, peeled and chopped
1 carrot, grated
1.25 litres/2¼ pints/5 cups Chicken
    Stock (see p. 14)
2 tablespoons/2 tablespoons plus
    2 teaspoons finely chopped fresh chives
1 tablespoon/1 tablespoon plus
    1 teaspoon finely chopped fresh mint
black pepper to taste or dash of cayenne
    pepper

Place the onion in a 4-litre/7-pint/16-cup casserole dish with the water. Cover, and microwave for 3 minutes on HIGH. Add the zucchini, potato and carrot.

Place the stock in a 2-litre/3½-pint/8-cup jug and microwave for 6 minutes on HIGH. Pour into the casserole dish. Cover, and microwave for 20–25 minutes on HIGH or until the potato is cooked through.

Purée the soup in a food processor or a blender. Add the chives, mint and pepper to taste.

VEGETARIAN DISHES

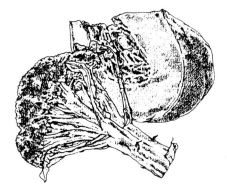

*V*egetables are full of nutrients and essential fibre. Combined with grains, cereals, pasta and tasty sauces they make for delicious main meals. With a microwave oven you can cook these dishes with little fuss and without the need to use cooking oils or salt.

Adzuki Beans

MAKES 400 G/14 OZ/2¼ CUPS

185 g/6 oz/1 cup adzuki beans
cold water
500 ml/16 fl oz/2 cups extra hot water

Soak the beans in cold water overnight. Drain. Place the beans in a small casserole dish. Add the hot water. Cover, and microwave for 40 minutes on HIGH. Let the beans stand for 10 minutes. Drain.

To store the beans in the refrigerator they should be very well drained. Store in an airtight container for no more than 5 days.

Serving Suggestions
- Add fresh herbs and a flavoured herb vinegar to make a bean salad.
- Add to your favourite vegetable casserole or soup.

Cauliflower Cheese Bake

SERVES 4

310 g/10½ oz carrots
500 g/1 lb 2 oz cauliflower florets
2 tablespoons/2 tablespoons plus
    2 teaspoons water
500 ml/16 fl oz/2 cups reduced-fat
    soymilk or skim milk
2 bay leaves
black pepper to taste
30 g/1 oz/¼ cup cornflour
2 tablespoons/2 tablespoons plus
    2 teaspoons finely chopped fresh
    parsley
100 g/3½ oz/1 cup grated low-fat
    grating cheese
a little paprika (optional)

Slice the carrots on an angle into thin rounds. Place around the outer part of a round, glass baking dish. Leave the cauliflower florets in large pieces. Place them in the centre of the carrot. Add the water. Cover with plastic wrap. Microwave for 9 minutes on HIGH or until the vegetables are tender. Drain off the liquid. Arrange the carrot and cauliflower florets as before, but this time with the cauliflower heads facing out and clumped to make a whole cauliflower head.

Place the soymilk, bay leaves, black pepper and cornflour in a 1-litre/1¾-pint/4-cup glass jug. Mix the ingredients thoroughly. Microwave for 2 minutes on HIGH. Stir well. Microwave for 1½ minutes more on HIGH. Remove the bay leaves and fold parsley through the mixture. Pour over the cauliflower. Sprinkle the cheese and paprika on top. Microwave for 2 minutes on HIGH. Serve.

Red Kidney Beans

MAKES 400 G/14 OZ/2¼ CUPS

185 g/6 oz/1 cup kidney beans
cold water
500 ml/16 fl oz/2 cups extra hot water

Soak the beans in the cold water overnight. Drain. Place the beans in a small casserole dish. Add the hot water. Cover, and microwave for 20 minutes on HIGH. Let the beans stand for 10 minutes. Drain.

To store the beans in the refrigerator they should be well drained. Store in an airtight container for no more than 5 days.

Serving Suggestions
- Add fresh herbs and a flavoured herb vinegar to make a bean salad.
- Add to your favourite vegetable casserole or soup.

Spinach Lasagne Slice

SERVES 6–8

9–12 spinach lasagne noodles
a little paprika

Vegetable Sauce
2 small onions, chopped
2 cloves garlic, crushed
2 tablespoons/2 tablespoons plus
* 2 teaspoons water*
1 stick celery, finely sliced
150 g/5 oz/1 cup finely sliced green
* beans*
150 g/5 oz/1 cup finely sliced zucchini
150 g/5 oz/1 cup grated carrot
150 g/5 oz/1 cup capsicum, cut into
* thin strips*
60 g/2 oz/½ cup finely sliced
* mushrooms*
310 g/10½ oz spinach, chopped
1 teaspoon dried oregano
1 teaspoon dried basil
1 teaspoon dried rosemary
850 g/2 lb canned salt-free tomatoes,
* drained*
100 g/3½ oz/⅓ cup salt-free tomato
* paste*

White Sauce with Cheese
30 g/1 oz/¼ cup cornflour
500 ml/16 fl oz/2 cups reduced-fat
* soymilk*
2 bay leaves
100 g/3½ oz/1 cup grated low-fat
* grating cheese*

To make the Vegetable Sauce, place the onion, garlic and water in a 4-litre/7-pint/16-cup casserole dish. Microwave for 2 minutes on HIGH. Add all the remaining ingredients. Mix well. Microwave for 10 minutes on HIGH. Stir well. Microwave for 10–15 minutes more on HIGH.

To make the White Sauce with Cheese, mix the cornflour with a little of the milk to make a paste. Add the remaining milk, bay leaves and cheese. Microwave for 2 minutes on HIGH. Stir well. Microwave for 1½–2 minutes more on HIGH. Remove the bay leaves.

To assemble the dish, place some Vegetable Sauce on the base of a large deep-sided oblong dish. Top with some of the lasagne noodles and white sauce. Continue the layers ending with a layer of white sauce. (Be careful to completely cover all the noodles with the last layer of white sauce.) Sprinkle with paprika. Cover with plastic wrap. Microwave for 15–18 minutes on HIGH on an elevated rack.

The lasagne will hold its shape better if it is left to go completely cold and then refrigerated. Cut into portions and reheat. To reheat, microwave for 2–3 minutes on HIGH. Serve with a tossed salad. (See left colour plate between pages 264 and 265.)

Carrot Terrine

xxxxxxxxxxxxxxxxxxxxxxxxxxxxxxxxxxxxxxxxxxxxxxxxxxxxxxxxxxxxxx

SERVES 8 – 10

500 g/1 lb 2 oz carrots, finely sliced
225 g/½ lb potatoes, peeled and finely sliced
2 bay leaves
125 ml/4 fl oz/½ cup salt-free tomato juice
65 ml/2 fl oz/¼ cup Chicken Stock (see p. 14) or water
1 large onion, finely chopped
60 g/2 oz/½ cup wholemeal plain flour
½ teaspoon dried sage
2 teaspoons dried basil
1 teaspoon dried oregano
1 teaspoon ground nutmeg
4 egg whites
a little whipped low-fat ricotta cheese for garnishing
a little skim milk (optional)
sprigs fresh parsley for garnishing
black pepper to taste

Place the carrot, potato, bay leaves, tomato juice, stock and onion in a 4-litre/7-pint/16-cup casserole dish. Cover, and microwave for 20 minutes on HIGH or until the vegetables are soft. Remove the bay leaves and purée the mixture in a food processor or blender until smooth. Add the flour, herbs and nutmeg, and mix well.

Beat the egg white until light and fluffy. Fold through the mixture. Place a piece of greaseproof paper or non-stick baking paper on the base of a 25-cm × 10-cm/10″ × 4″ loaf dish. Pour the mixture into the loaf dish. Elevate, uncovered, on a cake stand in the oven. Microwave for 5 minutes on HIGH and 10 minutes more on MEDIUM–LOW or DEFROST. Leave to cool before turning out.

Garnish the terrine with whipped low-fat ricotta cheese, or skim milk for a thinner consistency, and sprigs of fresh parsley. Season with black pepper. Serve with wholemeal crackers or toasted pita bread triangles. (See colour plate opposite.)

Mushroom Terrine

xxxxxxxxxxxxxxxxxxxxxxxxxxxxxxxxxxxxxxxxxxxxxxxxxxxxxxxxxxxxxx

SERVES 8 – 10

2 onions, finely chopped
1 tablespoon/1 tablespoon plus 1 teaspoon Chicken Stock (see p. 14) or water
500 g/1 lb 2 oz mushrooms, finely chopped
1½ teaspoons dry mustard
1 teaspoon dried dill
⅛–¼ teaspoon cayenne pepper
black pepper to taste
30 g/1 oz/¼ cup oat bran
750 g/1½ lb low-fat ricotta cheese or low-fat cottage cheese
handful of finely chopped fresh parsley
a little paprika

Place the onion in a large casserole dish with the stock. Cover, and microwave for 4 minutes on HIGH. Add the mushrooms. Cover, and microwave for 4 minutes on HIGH. Remove the lid, and microwave for 4 minutes more on HIGH. Drain off the juice. Add the mustard, dill, cayenne pepper, black pepper and oat bran, and fold through. Break up the ricotta cheese, stir, and mix through. Blend all the ingredients, except the parsley and paprika, in a food processor or blender until smooth.

Line the base of a 25-cm × 10-cm/10″ × 4″ glass terrine dish with non-stick baking paper. Spoon the mixture in and smooth down. Elevate in the oven on a cake stand. Microwave for 6 minutes on HIGH. Microwave for 6 minutes more on MEDIUM–HIGH. Cool in the dish for 10–15 minutes. Turn out onto a flat plate. Sprinkle the parsley and paprika over the top.

Serve with wholemeal crackers or vegetable crudités. (See colour plate opposite.)

Mushroom Terrine and Carrot Terrine
(opposite page).

Top: Spinach Lasagne Slice (page 263).
Super-quick Salmon Lasagne (page 268).

Vegetable and Eggplant Curry (page 266).

Mushroom Pizza and Hawaiian Pizza
(opposite page).

Hawaiian Pizza

MAKES 1

1 quantity Pizza Tomato Sauce
  (see p. 293)
1 large wholemeal pita bread
*100 g / 3½ oz / ¾ cup green capsicum, cut
  into thin strips*
*100 g / 3½ oz / ¾ cup red capsicum, cut
  into thin strips*
*200 g / 7 oz / 1½ cups canned
  unsweetened crushed pineapple, well
  drained*
*60 g / 2 oz / ½ cup grated low-fat grating
  cheese*

Spread the Pizza Tomato Sauce over the pita bread evenly. Top with the capsicum, pineapple and cheese. Microwave for 4–5 minutes on HIGH. (See colour plate opposite.)

Mushroom Pizza

MAKES 1

1 quantity Pizza Tomato Sauce
  (see p. 293)
1 large wholemeal pita bread
*225 g / ½ lb / 2 cups mushrooms, finely
  sliced*
*100 g / 3½ oz / 1 cup grated low-fat
  grating cheese*

Spread the Pizza Tomato Sauce over the pita bread evenly. Top with the mushrooms and cheese. Microwave for 4 minutes on HIGH. (See colour plate opposite.)

Stir-fry Vegetable Combination

SERVES 4–6

*1 kg / 2¼ lb any combination of the
  following: carrots, zucchini, beans,
  cauliflower, broccoli, mushrooms, red
  capsicum, celery, bean shoots*
2 cloves garlic, crushed
1 teaspoon finely chopped fresh ginger
*2 tablespoons / 2 tablespoons plus
  2 teaspoons low-salt soy sauce*

Cut the carrot and zucchini into julienne strips. Cut the beans into thin diagonal strips. Break the cauliflower and broccoli into small florets. Slice the mushrooms finely. Cut the capsicum into thin strips. Slice the celery into thin diagonal strips.

Place the carrot and bean strips, garlic, ginger and about a tablespoon of the soy sauce in a 4-litre / 7-pint / 16-cup casserole dish. Cover, and microwave for 4 minutes on HIGH. Add all the remaining vegetables, except the bean shoots, and the remaining soy sauce. Cover, and microwave for 7 minutes on HIGH. Add the bean shoots and stir. Microwave for 2–3 minutes on HIGH.

Serve immediately. The stir-fry is excellent with fish or chicken. If refrigerating do not cover.

Vegetarian Chili con Carne

SERVES 6–8

225 g/½ lb/1¼ cups kidney beans
cold water
boiling water
1 onion, finely chopped
2 cloves garlic, crushed
225 g/½ lb/1¼ cups carrots, finely
    chopped
225 g/½ lb green beans, finely chopped
1 small red capsicum, finely chopped
1 small green capsicum, finely chopped
65 ml/2 fl oz/¼ cup Chicken Stock
    (see p. 14) or water
½ teaspoon chilli powder
½ teaspoon ground cummin
425 g/15 oz canned whole tomatoes in
    natural juice, salt-free
75 g/2½ oz/¼ cup salt-free tomato
    paste
finely chopped fresh parsley for
    garnishing

Soak the beans in cold water overnight. Drain. Cover with boiling water. Microwave for 20 minutes on HIGH. Let the beans stand for 10 minutes. Drain.

Place the onion, garlic, carrot, chopped beans and capsicum in a large casserole dish. Add the Chicken Stock. Cover. Microwave for 10 minutes on HIGH. Add all the remaining ingredients, except the parsley. Microwave for 15–20 minutes on HIGH. Stir once during cooking. Add the beans. Microwave for 5 minutes on HIGH or until the beans are heated through. Sprinkle with the parsley. (See colour plate opposite page 161.)

Serving Suggestions
- Fill a baked potato with Vegetarian Chili con Carne.
- Fill a pita bread with shredded lettuce and Vegetarian Chili con Carne.

Vegetable and Eggplant Curry

SERVES 6–8

1 teaspoon garlic, crushed
1 large onion, chopped
1 large eggplant, cubed
310 g/10½ oz carrots, cut into rounds
    and in half again
1 large green capsicum, roughly chopped
100 g/3½ oz beans, finely sliced
125 g/¼ lb/1 cup frozen peas
400 g/14 oz potatoes, peeled and cubed
100 g/3½ oz/½ cup raisins or sultanas
425 g/15 oz canned whole tomatoes in
    natural juice, salt-free
2 tablespoons/2 tablespoons plus
    2 teaspoons salt-free tomato paste
1 tablespoon/1 tablespoon plus
    1 teaspoon low-salt soy sauce
1 tablespoon/1 tablespoon plus
    1 teaspoon curry powder
1 teaspoon ground cummin
1 teaspoon ground ginger
6–8 par-baked eggplant shells (optional)

Combine all the ingredients in a 4-litre/7-pint/16-cup casserole dish. Cover. Microwave for 5 minutes on HIGH. Stir. Microwave for 15 minutes on MEDIUM. Stir. Microwave for 15–20 minutes more on MEDIUM.

Serve in eggplant shells, if desired, or with fruit accompaniments. (See right colour plate between pages 264 and 265.)

Serving Suggestions
- Yoghurt, chilled banana slices and pineapple wedges make delicious accompaniments to Vegetable and Eggplant Curry.

FISH & SEAFOOD

𝓕ish cooks very quickly in the microwave oven. It retains its flavour and moistness, and therefore it needs little added liquid. Cooking times may vary according to the density of the fish. To arrange fish fillets in a baking dish, always place the thickest parts on the outer area of the dish. If long fillets are thin at one end, overlap the ends in the centre of the dish. Check if the fish is cooked after the minimum suggested cooking time. Fish is easily over-cooked and can become very tough or completely break up. As it stands it will complete cooking.

Prawns in Chilli Sauce

SERVES 4–5

500 g/1 lb 2 oz green king prawns
1 clove garlic, crushed
125 ml/4 fl oz/½ cup Chicken Stock
  (see p. 14) or dry white wine
2 tablespoons/2 tablespoons plus
  2 teaspoons lemon juice
1 tablespoon/1 tablespoon plus
  1 teaspoon low-salt soy sauce
2 tablespoons/2 tablespoons plus
  2 teaspoons finely chopped fresh
  parsley

Sauce
2 teaspoons finely chopped fresh ginger
3 cloves garlic, crushed
75 g/2½ oz/¼ cup salt-free tomato
  paste
65 ml/2 fl oz/¼ cup salt-free tomato
  juice
2 tablespoons/2 tablespoons plus
  2 teaspoons apple juice concentrate
1 tablespoon/1 tablespoon plus
  1 teaspoon low-salt soy sauce
1 tablespoon/1 tablespoon plus
  1 teaspoon dry sherry
2 tablespoons/2 tablespoons plus
  2 teaspoons water
2 teaspoons finely chopped chilli or
  2 teaspoons chopped red capsicum
⅛–¼ teaspoon chilli powder

Shell and devein the prawns. Combine all the ingredients, except the prawns and the Sauce ingredients, in a shallow glass casserole dish. Microwave for 1–2 minutes on HIGH or until the liquid is quite hot. Add the prawns and toss through the cooking liquid. Microwave for 3½–5½ minutes on HIGH or until the prawns have changed colour and are tender. Thick prawns will take longer to cook than thin ones. Check at 2½–3 minutes and toss through the cooking liquid again, turning each prawn over. The prawns will be very tough if over-cooked.

To make the sauce, combine all the ingredients in a glass jug. Microwave for 1½–2 minutes on HIGH. Pour over the prawns and serve. (See left colour plate between pages 280 and 281.)

Super-quick Salmon Lasagne

SERVES 6

*425 g/15 oz canned pink salmon,
    drained*
150 g/5 oz/1 cup chopped celery
*150 g/5 oz/1 cup finely sliced spring
    onion*
150 g/5 oz/1 cup chopped zucchini
150 g/5 oz/1 cup chopped red capsicum
*2 tablespoons/2 tablespoons plus
    2 teaspoons finely chopped fresh
    parsley*
¼ teaspoon dried thyme
black pepper to taste
10 spinach lasagne noodles
*100 g/3½ oz/1 cup grated low-fat
    grating cheese*

Sauce
*500 ml/16 fl oz/2 cups reduced-fat
    soymilk or skim milk*
30 g/1 oz/¼ cup cornflour
3 bay leaves
black pepper to taste

Mix the salmon, celery, spring onion, zucchini, capsicum, parsley, thyme and black pepper together and set aside.

To make the Sauce, mix a little milk with the cornflour to make a paste. Add the remaining milk, bay leaves and black pepper, and stir well. Microwave for 3 minutes on HIGH. Stir well. Microwave for 3 minutes more on HIGH. Stir well. Microwave for 1 minute further on HIGH for a smooth and thick consistency. Remove the bay leaves.

Place three lasagne noodles on the base of a deep-sided 20-cm × 30-cm/8″ × 12″ (or larger) baking dish. Top with one-third of the salmon mixture and spoon a generous cup of sauce over the top. Repeat the layers, finishing with a layer of sauce. Cover with plastic wrap. Microwave for 10 minutes on HIGH and then 5 minutes on MEDIUM. Sprinkle the cheese on top. Microwave for 3 minutes more on HIGH. Serve.

To reheat one serve of the dish, microwave for 1½ minutes on HIGH. (See left colour plate between pages 264 and 265.)

Curried Scallops

SERVES 6–8

500 g/1 lb 2 oz scallops
1 tablespoon water

Sauce
*2 Granny Smith apples, peeled and finely
    sliced*
65 ml/2 fl oz/¼ cup water
1 clove garlic
1 onion, finely chopped
75 g/2½ oz/½ cup finely chopped celery
*625 ml/1 pint/2½ cups Chicken Stock
    (see p. 14)*
30 g/1 oz/¼ cup cornflour
1½ tablespoons curry powder
*75 g/2½ oz/¼ cup salt-free tomato
    paste*
*1 tablespoon/1 tablespoon plus
    1 teaspoon lemon juice*
*2 tablespoons/2 tablespoons plus
    2 teaspoons finely chopped fresh
    parsley*

To make the Sauce, place the apple in a small casserole dish with the water. Cover, and microwave for 6 minutes on HIGH. Mash slightly. Microwave for 3 minutes more on HIGH. Purée in a food processor or blender. Set aside.

Place the garlic, onion, celery and about a tablespoon of the stock in a large glass jug. Microwave for 3 minutes on HIGH. Set aside.

Combine the cornflour and curry powder. Mix a little of the remaining stock with the combined cornflour and curry powder to make a paste. Add the tomato paste, lemon juice and the rest of the stock. Microwave for 2½ minutes on HIGH. Stir. Microwave for 2½–3 minutes more on HIGH or until thick.

Fold the apple, onion and celery through the mixture. Microwave for 2–3 minutes more on HIGH.

Wash and devein the scallops. Place them in a shallow microwave dish. Add the water. Cover, and microwave for 2–5 minutes on MEDIUM, depending on the size of the scallops. They are cooked when they just turn snow white. Stand, covered, for 1–2 minutes.

Add the parsley and the scallops to the sauce, and serve on a bed of rice.

Whole Stuffed Baby Trout

SERVES 2

juice of ½ lemon
2 × 200-g/7-oz trout
1 small onion, finely chopped
1 stick celery, finely chopped
75 g/2½ oz/½ cup grated carrot
1 teaspoon finely chopped fresh ginger
½ teaspoon crushed garlic
½ teaspoon ground coriander
2 tablespoons/2 tablespoons plus 2
  teaspoons Chicken Stock (see p. 14)
60 g/2 oz/1 cup fresh wholemeal
  breadcrumbs
1 tablespoon/1 tablespoon plus
  1 teaspoon finely chopped fresh chives
1 tablespoon/1 tablespoon plus
  1 teaspoon finely chopped fresh
  parsley
black pepper to taste

Sauce
65 ml/2 fl oz/¼ cup white wine vinegar
200 ml/7 fl oz/¾ cup unsweetened
  orange juice
1½ teaspoons cornflour

Rub the lemon juice on the inside and outside of the fish. Combine the onion, celery, carrot, ginger, garlic, coriander and stock in a small casserole dish. Cover, and microwave for 5 minutes on HIGH. Add the remaining ingredients. Divide the mixture evenly between the two fish. Fill the fish cavity, and place the fish in an oblong glass dish. Microwave for 4–6½ minutes on HIGH. Turn the fish over. Microwave for 4–6½ minutes more on HIGH.

To make the Sauce, combine all the ingredients in a glass jug and mix well. Microwave for 2 minutes on HIGH. Stir. Microwave for 1–2 minutes more on HIGH. Pour over the fish and serve immediately. Serve with a tossed salad. (See left colour plate between pages 280 and 281.)

Fish with Celery

SERVES 2

3 large sticks celery
1 large tomato, thickly sliced
225 g/½ lb fish fillets (preferably blue
  grenadier)
2 spring onions, finely sliced
finely chopped fresh basil
black pepper to taste

Prepare the fish on a serving plate. Place half the celery on the plate. Top with half the tomato slices. Place the fillets on top. Repeat the layers of celery and tomato. Top with the spring onion and sprinkle with basil. Season with black pepper. Microwave for 6 minutes on HIGH or until the fish is cooked. Drain off any liquid.

Serve with a salad or steamed vegetables and a baked potato. (See left colour plate between pages 280 and 281.)

CHICKEN

*C*hicken is a favourite food cooked microwave style. It is a low-fat meat once you have removed the skin and fat. You can achieve a browning effect on chicken meat by basting with combined low-salt soy sauce and salt-free tomato paste. Do this during the cooking procedure and sprinkle with paprika or your favourite finely chopped fresh herbs. Chicken is juicy and tender cooked in the microwave oven and can be complemented by the addition of vegetables, fruit and sauces.

Whole Steamed Chicken

SERVES 6

1 × 1.5-kg / 3½-lb chicken
½ lemon
3 sprigs of parsley
1 stick celery, finely sliced
½ carrot, cut into strips
65 ml / 2 fl oz / ¼ cup unsweetened
    orange juice or water
black pepper to taste (optional)

Remove all the skin and fat from the chicken. Put the lemon half in the chicken cavity, and place the chicken in a 4-litre/ 7-pint/16-cup casserole dish. Place the parsley, celery and carrot around the chicken. Pour the orange juice over the top and season with pepper. Cover the chicken. Microwave for 15 minutes on HIGH. Turn the chicken for more even cooking and baste with the juice. Microwave for 15 minutes more on HIGH.

    Serve the chicken hot with a sauce of your choice, or serve cold in salads and sandwiches or for picnics.

Chicken in a Bag

SERVES 6

75 g / 2½ oz / ¼ cup salt-free tomato
    paste
1 tablespoon / 1 tablespoon plus 1
    teaspoon low-salt soy sauce
1 teaspoon dried basil
1 teaspoon dried oregano
black pepper to taste
1 × 1.5-kg / 3½-lb chicken (all skin and
    fat removed)
425 g / 15 oz canned salt-free tomatoes,
    drained
1 red capsicum, cut into strips
1 green capsicum, cut into strips
1 onion, sliced into half rings

Combine the tomato paste, soy sauce, basil, oregano and pepper to make a paste. Use a pastry brush to wipe the paste over the chicken. Coat well. Carefully put the chicken into an oven bag. Add the remaining ingredients to the oven bag and seal. Insert two or three holes in the top of the bag. Place on a microwave dish. Microwave for 20–22 minutes on HIGH.

    Serve hot or cold with vegetables or salad.

Stuffed Chicken in Mustard Sauce

SERVES 4–6

4–6 chicken breasts (all skin and fat
    removed)
60 g/2 oz/½ cup spinach, well packed
200 g/7 oz/¾ cup low-fat ricotta cheese
¼ teaspoon ground nutmeg

Marinade
125 ml/4 fl oz/½ cup unsweetened
    orange juice
125 ml/4 fl oz/½ cup dry sherry
2 tablespoons/2 tablespoons plus
    2 teaspoons apple juice concentrate
2 teaspoons wholegrain mustard
1 tablespoon/1 tablespoon plus
    1 teaspoon cornflour

Using a very sharp knife, cut a pocket in each chicken breast without cutting completely through. Wash the spinach and place in a small casserole dish. Microwave for 2 minutes on HIGH. Drain very well and chop up finely. Combine the spinach, ricotta cheese and nutmeg, and mix well. Spoon this mixture equally into the pockets. Mix all the Marinade ingredients together, except the cornflour, and pour over the chicken. Marinate for at least 3 hours. Drain off the marinade and remove the mustard seeds, and reserve both.

Place the chicken breasts evenly around the base of a glass casserole dish. Spoon the mustard seeds on top. Cover, and microwave for 6–6½ minutes on HIGH. Turn over carefully. Microwave for 6–6½ minutes more on HIGH.

Combine all the reserved marinade liquid with any remaining liquid from the cooked chicken. Mix the cornflour with a little of the liquid to make a paste. Stir this into the remaining liquid. Microwave for 1½–2 minutes on HIGH. Stir. Microwave for 1 minute more on HIGH. Pour the sauce over the chicken and top with the remaining mustard seeds.

Serve hot or cold with steamed vegetables or a tossed salad. (See colour plate opposite page 272.)

Chicken, Pineapple and Chestnut Curry

SERVES 4–6

400 g/14 oz chicken breasts (all fat and
    skin removed), cut into bite-sized
    pieces
1 large onion, chopped
2 cloves garlic
1 tablespoon/1 tablespoon plus
    1 teaspoon curry powder
3 tablespoons/3 tablespoons plus
    3 teaspoons Chicken Stock (see p. 14)
2 bay leaves
225 g/½ lb fresh pineapple, sliced into
    thin wedges
200 g/7 oz/1 cup canned water
    chestnuts, drained
60 g/2 oz/½ cup frozen peas
125 ml/4 fl oz/½ cup reduced-fat
    soymilk
1–2 tablespoons cornflour

Combine the chicken, onion, garlic, curry powder and stock in a casserole dish. Cover, and microwave for 3 minutes on HIGH. Stir. Microwave for 2 minutes more on HIGH. Add the remaining ingredients, except the soymilk and cornflour. Cover, and microwave for 10 minutes on MEDIUM. Mix the soymilk and cornflour until smooth, and stir through the mixture. Microwave for 5 minutes on MEDIUM.

Serve with brown rice and a cooked orange vegetable such as carrot or pumpkin.

Chicken and Ginger Balls

MAKES 20

2 *Granny Smith apples*
400 *g/14 oz minced chicken (all skin and fat removed)*
60 *g/2 oz/1 cup fresh wholemeal breadcrumbs*
1 *teaspoon finely chopped fresh ginger*
½ *teaspoon grated lemon rind*
1 *onion, finely chopped*

Grate the apples and squeeze out the juice. Combine all the ingredients using your hands. Shape the mixture into small balls. Place in a shallow, rectangular glass dish. Microwave for 4 minutes on HIGH. Turn over and rotate the centre ones to the outside. Microwave for 4 minutes more on HIGH.

Serve the balls hot or cold. They are delicious served hot with mango chutney or threaded on wooden skewers with some chunks of raw vegetables. (See colour plate opposite.)

Chicken Tandoori Kebabs

MAKES 16

400 *g/14 oz chicken breasts (all skin and fat removed)*
juice of 1 lemon
16 *wooden skewers*
100 *g/3½ oz small mushrooms, cut into pieces*
2 *large green capsicums, cut into pieces*

Marinade
250 *ml/8 fl oz/1 cup non-fat or low-fat yoghurt*
1 *small onion, finely chopped*
2 *teaspoons garam masala*
½ *teaspoon ground cummin*
¼ *teaspoon chilli powder*
¼ *teaspoon ground coriander*

Cut the chicken breasts into 2-cm/¾″ cubes. Squeeze the lemon juice over the top and stand for 30 minutes.

Combine the Marinade ingredients. Add to the chicken and lemon. Marinate for at least 12 hours.

Thread three pieces of chicken and some of the mushroom and capsicum pieces onto each wooden skewer, alternating between items. Cook eight kebabs at a time in an oblong glass casserole dish. Place four in one direction and four in the opposite direction. Microwave for 3–4 minutes on HIGH. Drain off juices and turn over. Microwave for 3–4 minutes more on HIGH. Repeat with the remaining eight kebabs.

Serve on a bed of brown rice with mango chutney. (See colour plate opposite.)

Chicken Tandoori Kebabs and Chicken and Ginger Balls (opposite page); Mango Chutney (page 292); Stuffed Chicken in Mustard Sauce (page 271).

Beef Burger Meatloaf (page 275); Zucchini Meatloaf and Spicy Lamb Balls (opposite page) with Pizza Tomato Sauce (page 293); French Beans (page 282).

MEAT

To keep your diet low in fat, you should have no more than 100 g/3½ oz of meat daily. Always buy the best quality meat available and remove all fat and sinew before cooking. Your meat will have a different colour from meat cooked in the conventional manner, but red meat correctly cooked in the microwave keeps its natural moistness.

Spicy Lamb Balls

MAKES 24

400 g/14 oz lean minced lamb
60 g/2 oz/1 cup fresh wholemeal
   breadcrumbs
200 g/7 oz/1¼ cups finely grated
   potato, juice squeezed out
1 onion, finely chopped
¼ teaspoon chilli powder
¼ teaspoon ground coriander
¼ teaspoon ground cummin
¼ teaspoon garam masala

Combine all the ingredients, using your hands. Shape into 24 small balls. Place in a shallow glass rectangular dish. Microwave for 5 minutes on MEDIUM-HIGH. Turn over and rotate the centre ones to the outside. Microwave for 5 minutes more on MEDIUM-HIGH. Cover and stand for 2–3 minutes.

Serve the balls hot with Sweet Tomato Sauce (see page 239) or dip into a bowl of chilled non-fat or low-fat yoghurt mixed with grated cucumber. (See colour plate opposite.)

Zucchini Meatloaf

SERVES 8

400 g/14 oz coarsely grated zucchini,
   juice squeezed out
500 g/1 lb 2 oz lean minced beef
1 onion, finely chopped
1 small red capsicum, finely chopped
125 g/¼ lb/2 cups fresh wholemeal
   breadcrumbs
1 egg white
1 tablespoon/1 tablespoon plus
   1 teaspoon finely chopped fresh
   parsley
1 tablespoon/1 tablespoon plus
   1 teaspoon finely chopped fresh basil
black pepper to taste
1 teaspoon low-salt soy sauce
75 g/2½ oz/¼ cup salt-free tomato
   paste
30 g/1 oz/¼ cup grated low-fat grating
   cheese

Combine all the ingredients, except the tomato paste and cheese, and mix with your hands. Press the mixture into a 23-cm/9″ cake ring 8 cm/3″ deep. Microwave for 15 minutes on HIGH. Turn out onto a serving platter. Spread the tomato paste evenly over the top of the loaf and cover with the cheese. Microwave for 3 minutes on HIGH.

Serve hot or cold with a selection of salads, as a lunch dish or for a picnic. (See colour plate opposite.)

Variations
- Fresh tarragon can be substituted for the parsley.
- If fresh herbs are not available use ½–1 teaspoon dried herbs.

Beef Burgers

xxxxxxxxxxxxxxxxxxxxxxxxxxxxxxxxxxxxxxxxxxxxxxxxxxxxxxxxxxxxxxxxxxxxxxxxxxxxxxxxxxxxxxxxxxxxxxxxxxxxx

SERVES 10

500 g/1 lb 2 oz lean minced beef
200 g/7 oz/1¼ cups carrots, grated
200 g/7 oz/1¼ cups zucchini, grated
   (juice squeezed out)
200 g/7 oz/1¼ cups Granny Smith
   apples, grated
400 g/14 oz/1½ cups grated, peeled
   potato
60 g/2 oz/1 cup fresh wholemeal
   breadcrumbs
2 tablespoons/2 tablespoons plus
   2 teaspoons wholemeal plain flour
handful of finely chopped fresh parsley
½ teaspoon ground nutmeg
½–1 teaspoon dried mixed herbs

Combine all the ingredients and mix with your hands. Shape into 10 equal-sized burgers. Cook four at a time on a roasting rack or use your microwave cake stand. Microwave for 7–8 minutes on HIGH.

Serve on a wholemeal bun or between two wholemeal pita breads with salad ingredients of your choice, such as shredded lettuce, alfalfa sprouts, sliced tomato, sliced cucumber, onion rings, grated carrot and red and green capsicum rings. Flavour with a suitable chutney or tomato sauce.

Beef Burger Pizzas

xxxxxxxxxxxxxxxxxxxxxxxxxxxxxxxxxxxxxxxxxxxxxxxxxxxxxxxxxxxxxxxxxxxxxxxxxxxxxxxxxxxxxxxxxxxxxxxxxxxxx

MAKES 6

Base
500 g/1 lb 2 oz lean minced beef
185 g/6 oz/3 cups fresh wholemeal
   breadcrumbs
1 clove garlic, crushed
1 onion, grated
150 g/5 oz/1 cup cooked brown rice
2 teaspoons low-salt soy sauce
black pepper to taste
½ teaspoon dried oregano or curry
   powder or paprika

Topping
100 g/3½ oz/⅓ cup salt-free tomato
   paste
125 g/¼ lb/1 cup mushrooms, finely
   chopped
1 small green capsicum, finely sliced
6 spring onions, finely sliced
125 g/¼ lb/1¼ cups grated low-fat
   grating cheese
18 cherry tomatoes

Combine all the Base ingredients and mix well using your hands. Divide into six portions. Press each portion onto a flat bread-and-butter plate. Spread 1 tablespoon of the tomato paste on each base. Top with equal portions of mushrooms, capsicum, spring onion and cheese. Cut the cherry tomatoes in half. Place 6 halves on top of each pizza. Cook three pizzas at a time. Microwave for 6 minutes on HIGH or until the base is firm.

Serve with a salad.

Beef Burger Meatloaf

xxxxxxxxxxxxxxxxxxxxxxxxxxxxxxxxxxxxxxxxxxxxxxxxxxxxxxxxxxxxxxxxxxxxxxxxxxxxxxxxxxxx

SERVES 10

1 quantity Beef Burger *mixture (see p. 274)*

Place the Beef Burger mixture into a large loaf tin and firm down. Microwave for 14–15 minutes on HIGH.

Serve hot with the gravy of your choice or cold in sandwiches or with salads. (See colour plate opposite page 273.)

Cabbage Rolls

xxxxxxxxxxxxxxxxxxxxxxxxxxxxxxxxxxxxxxxxxxxxxxxxxxxxxxxxxxxxxxxxxxxxxxxxxxxxxxxxxxxx

MAKES 12

12 large green cabbage leaves

Filling

1 onion, finely chopped
½ teaspoon finely chopped fresh ginger
2 tablespoons/2 tablespoons plus 2 teaspoons water
575 g/1¼ lb lean minced beef or veal
½ teaspoon ground cummin
¼ teaspoon ground coriander
200 g/7 oz/1¼ cups finely grated carrot
100 g/3½ oz/¾ cup finely grated zucchini, juice squeezed out
280 g/10 oz/2 cups cooked brown rice

Tomato Sauce

425 g/15 oz canned whole tomatoes in natural juice, salt-free
75 g/2½ oz/¼ cup salt-free tomato paste
125 ml/4 fl oz/½ cup Vegetable Stock or Chicken Stock (see p. 14)
1 clove garlic, crushed
½ teaspoon ground cummin
2 teaspoons cornflour
finely chopped fresh parsley for garnishing

Place 6 cabbage leaves on a large glass platter. Cover, and microwave for 6 minutes on HIGH or until the cabbage leaves are tender and can be folded over. Repeat with the remaining 6 cabbage leaves.

To make the Filling, place the onion, ginger and water in a small casserole dish. Cover, and microwave for 3 minutes on HIGH. Stir. Add the meat and break up. Microwave for 5 minutes more on HIGH. Break up the meat again. Microwave for 5 minutes more on HIGH. Break up the meat again. Add all the other ingredients, and mix well. Divide the mixture evenly among the 12 cabbage leaves. Carefully roll up and secure each end. Place 6 cabbage rolls in a 20-cm × 30-cm/ 8″ × 12″ baking dish. Repeat with the remaining 6 cabbage rolls.

To make the Tomato Sauce, purée all the ingredients in a food processor or blender. Pour over the top of the cabbage rolls. Cover the baking dish with plastic wrap. Microwave for 10–12 minutes on HIGH or until the cabbage rolls are heated through. Serve hot with steamed baby carrots and new potatoes. (See colour plate opposite page 281.)

RICE, PASTA & GRAINS

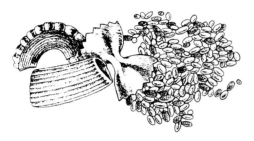

*T*he microwave oven cooks rice and pasta to perfection. (There is really not a time-saving factor in cooking rice and pasta in the microwave oven, but you use much less power, which is a saving in electricity expenses.)

You need to use dishes that hold large volumes, as rice and pasta expand in the cooking process. Your cooking water should be hot – boiling, to save cooking time – and you should always cover the rice and pasta when cooking so that they stay moist.

Gluggy rice will become a thing of the past if you use the microwave method. In fact, unless I wanted to cook rice for 20 people or more, I would not cook it any other way now. Brown rice retains its colour and its wonderfully nutty texture when cooked in the microwave.

The microwave oven is excellent for reheating pasta and rice because the food stays moist and loses none of its colour and nutritive value.

Rice and Corn Combination Salad

SERVES 8 – 10

350 g/¾ lb/2 cups brown rice
875 ml/1½ pints/3½ cups boiling water
225 g/½ lb/1 cup sultanas
½ teaspoon ground cummin
250 ml/8 fl oz/1 cup unsweetened
   orange juice
225 g/½ lb/¾ cup corn kernels
100 g/3½ oz/¾ cup chopped celery
100 g/3½ oz/¾ cup chopped green
   capsicum
100 g/3½ oz carrots, cut into julienne
   strips
225 g/½ lb/¾ cup canned baby corn,
   drained
large handful of finely chopped fresh
   parsley
90 g/3 oz/½ cup raw almonds
   (optional)

Place the rice and water in a 4-litre/7-pint/16-cup casserole dish. Cover, and microwave for 26–30 minutes on HIGH. Leave to stand for 10 minutes. Rinse under cold water until cold. Drain well.

Combine the sultanas, cummin and orange juice in a small glass jug. Cover, and microwave for 4–5 minutes on HIGH. Set aside to cool and stir occasionally as the ingredients turn to pulp. Leave to stand until completely cold. Drain, and reserve the juice. Combine all the remaining ingredients, and mix through thoroughly. Add some of the reserved liquid if the salad is too dry. (See colour plate opposite page 280.)

Brown Rice

MAKES 310 G/10½ OZ/2 CUPS

185 g/6 oz/1 cup brown rice
450 ml/15 fl oz/1¾ cups hot water

Place the rice and water in a 1-litre/1¾-pint/4-cup glass jug. Cover with plastic wrap. Insert some air holes in the plastic. Microwave for 15–20 minutes on HIGH. Leave to stand, covered, for 10 minutes to complete the cooking and absorb all the moisture.

To store the rice in the refrigerator, it should be very dry. Store in an airtight container for no more than 7 days.

Variations
- Add 1 teaspoon Vecon to the cooking water.
- Add 3 bay leaves before cooking.
- Add dried or fresh herbs before cooking.

Saffron Rice

SERVES 4

185 g/6 oz/1 cup brown rice
500 ml/16 fl oz/2 cups Chicken Stock
(see p. 14)
pinch of saffron powder
1 teaspoon grated lemon rind

Combine the rice, stock and saffron in a 1-litre/1¾-pint/4-cup jug. Cover with plastic wrap. Microwave for 20 minutes on HIGH. Add the lemon rind. Cover, and stand for 10 minutes or until the stock is absorbed.

Variation
- Add ¼ teaspoon ground cinnamon with the rind for extra flavour.

Spaghetti with Vegetable Sauce

SERVES 6

1 large onion, finely diced
2 tablespoons/2 tablespoons plus
2 teaspoons water
1 large green capsicum, finely diced
1 red capsicum, finely diced
2 sticks celery, finely diced
125 g/¼ lb/1 cup finely diced
mushrooms
150 g/5 oz/1 cup finely grated carrot
10 green beans, diagonally sliced
425 g/15 oz canned salt-free tomatoes
and juice, puréed
60 g/2 oz/¼ cup salt-free tomato paste
65 ml/2 fl oz/¼ cup water
½ teaspoon dried basil
½ teaspoon dried oregano
2 bay leaves
1 litre/1¾ pints/4 cups hot water
1 packet wholemeal spaghetti
freshly ground black pepper
finely chopped fresh parsley

Put the onion in a large casserole dish with the water. Microwave on HIGH for 2–3 minutes. Add all other ingredients, except the hot water, spaghetti, pepper and parsley, and microwave on HIGH for 10 minutes. Stir well. Microwave on HIGH for a further 10 minutes. Stir well. Microwave on HIGH for a further 5 minutes or until the vegetables are tender. Remove the bay leaves.

Put the hot water in a 4-litre/7-pint/16-cup casserole dish. Break the spaghetti in half and add to the water. Cover and microwave on HIGH for 20 minutes. Drain the spaghetti and wash under hot water to remove the starch.

Reheat the sauce and pour over the spaghetti. Season with pepper and garnish with parsley.

Spaghetti Pies

SERVES 12

1 quantity Spaghetti with Vegetable Sauce *(see p. 277)*
125 g/¼ lb/1¼ cups grated low-fat grating cheese
handful of finely chopped fresh parsley

Divide the cooked spaghetti evenly between two 20-cm/8″ pie dishes. Push the spaghetti up around the edges and over the base to create a spaghetti pie shell. Divide the spaghetti sauce evenly between the two pies, spooning it into the centre of each pie shell. Cover with the cheese and sprinkle half the parsley on top of each pie. Cover with plastic wrap and leave to cool. Store in the refrigerator until firm.

Place a serve on a serving platter and microwave for 1½ minutes on HIGH. Serve with a salad, and wholemeal bread with low-fat cottage cheese and herbs. (See right colour plate between pages 280 and 281.)

Porridge

SERVES 1

60 g/2 oz/½ cup rolled oats
250 ml/8 fl oz/1 cup water
fruit of your choice
unsweetened fruit juice or *skim milk*

Combine the rolled oats and water in a glass jug or pudding bowl. Cover with plastic wrap and insert several holes. Microwave for 2 minutes on HIGH. Stir. Microwave for 1–2 minutes more on HIGH. Spoon into a serving bowl. Top with the raw or lightly cooked fruit of your choice. Add some unsweetened fruit juice and serve immediately.

Apple Porridge

SERVES 1

60 g/2 oz/½ cup rolled oats
250 ml/8 fl oz/1 cup water
1 Granny Smith apple, grated
½ teaspoon ground cinnamon
skim milk

Combine all the ingredients, except the skim milk, in a glass jug or pudding bowl. Cover with plastic wrap and insert several holes. Microwave for 2 minutes on HIGH. Stir. Microwave for 2–3 minutes more on HIGH. Spoon into a serving bowl. Add some skim milk and serve immediately.

Fruit Porridge

SERVES 1

1 tablespoon/1 tablespoon plus 1 teaspoon unsweetened orange juice
1 small banana, peeled and chopped
2 tablespoons/2 tablespoons plus 2 teaspoons finely chopped dates
60 g/2 oz/½ cup rolled oats
250 ml/8 fl oz/1 cup water
a little ground cinnamon
a little non-fat or *low-fat yoghurt*

Place the orange juice, banana and dates in a glass jug or pudding bowl. Cover, and microwave for 1 minute on HIGH. Add the oats and water, and stir. Cover with plastic wrap and insert several holes. Microwave for 2 minutes on HIGH. Stir. Microwave for 1½–2½ minutes more on HIGH. Spoon into a serving bowl. Sprinkle the cinnamon on top and add the yoghurt.

SALADS

alads are an important part of every meal because of their high nutrient value, their moisture content and their natural fibre. By preparing vegetables for salads in the microwave you save not only time but also their goodness and colour.

Cauliflower and Broccoli Salad

SERVES 4

225 g/½ lb broccoli florets
225 g/½ lb cauliflower florets
½–1 teaspoon finely grated fresh ginger
2 tablespoons/2 tablespoons plus 2
    teaspoons Chicken Stock (see p. 14)
1–2 tablespoons low-salt soy sauce

Combine the broccoli and cauliflower in a casserole dish with the ginger and stock. Cover, and microwave for 8–12 minutes on HIGH. Stir once during cooking. Drain. Add the soy sauce, and toss the vegetables. Cool and refrigerate.

Cherry Tomato and Bean Salad

SERVES 4–6

450 g/1 lb green beans
2 tablespoons/2 tablespoons plus
    2 teaspoons water
225 g/½ lb cherry tomatoes
1 black olive
2 tablespoons/2 tablespoons plus
    2 teaspoons finely chopped fresh basil
2 tablespoons/2 tablespoons plus
    2 teaspoons finely chopped fresh
    parsley
65 ml/2 fl oz/¼ cup tarragon vinegar
black pepper to taste

Top and tail the beans and cut in half. Place in a casserole dish with the water. Cover, and microwave for 8–12 minutes on HIGH. Move the halved beans twice during cooking. Drain the beans, and plunge them into cold water until cold. Drain.

Place the tomatoes in a casserole dish. Cover, and microwave for 40 seconds–1 minute on HIGH. Chop up the olive as finely as possible. Combine all the ingredients and mix well without breaking the tomatoes. Cover, and stand until the tomatoes are cold. Season with black pepper.

Potato Salad with Mint Yoghurt

SERVES 4

450 g/1 lb new potatoes
2 tablespoons/2 tablespoons plus
    2 teaspoons water
250 ml/8 fl oz/1 cup low-fat yoghurt
2 tablespoons/2 tablespoons plus
    2 teaspoons finely chopped fresh mint
black pepper to taste

Wash the potatoes thoroughly, and cut into chunks. Place in a large casserole dish with the water. Cover, and microwave for 10–12 minutes on HIGH. Move the potato around once or twice during cooking. Drain, and leave covered until cool. Combine the yoghurt, mint and pepper, and pour over the potato. Chill well prior to serving.

Carrot, Zucchini and Mushroom Salad

SERVES 4

225 g/½ lb carrots, cut into julienne
    strips
2 tablespoons water
225 g/½ lb zucchini, cut into julienne
    strips
100 g/3½ oz mushrooms, finely sliced
handful of finely chopped fresh parsley
2 tablespoons/2 tablespoons plus
    2 teaspoons finely chopped fresh basil
2 tablespoons/2 tablespoons plus 2 teaspoons
    Tarragon Vinegar (see p. 144)
1 lettuce

Place the carrot in a shallow dish with the water. Cover, and microwave for 2½ minutes on HIGH. Add the zucchini. Microwave for 1–2½ minutes more on HIGH. Drain off the liquid. Add the mushroom, parsley, basil and Tarragon Vinegar. Cover, and leave to stand until cool. Refrigerate. (See colour plate opposite.)

Pasta Salad

SERVES 4 – 6

225 g/½ lb soyaroni noodles
750 ml/1⅓ pints/3 cups boiling water
75 g/2½ oz/½ cup chopped carrot
75 g/2½ oz/½ cup chopped celery
75 g/2½ oz/½ cup chopped red
    capsicum
75 g/2½ oz/½ cup chopped green
    capsicum
75 g/2½ oz/½ cup corn kernels
100 g/3½ oz/½ cup chopped red apple
2 tablespoons/2 tablespoons plus
    2 teaspoons finely chopped fresh
    parsley
2 tablespoons/2 tablespoons plus
    2 teaspoons finely chopped fresh chives
1 tablespoon/1 tablespoon plus 1 teaspoon
    Tarragon Vinegar (see p. 144)
1 tablespoon/1 tablespoon plus
    1 teaspoon unsweetened orange juice
1 tablespoon/1 tablespoon plus
    1 teaspoon low-salt soy sauce
    (optional)

Place the noodles in a large casserole dish and pour the boiling water over the top. Cover, and microwave for 14–16 minutes on HIGH. Drain and rinse the noodles in cold water until they are cold. Drain well. Mix all the remaining ingredients together. Chill well before serving. (See colour plate opposite.)

Rice and Corn Combination Salad (page 276); Pasta Salad and Carrot, Zucchini and Mushroom Salad (opposite page).

*Prawns in Chilli Sauce (page 267); Whole Stuffed Baby Trout and
Fish with Celery (page 269).*

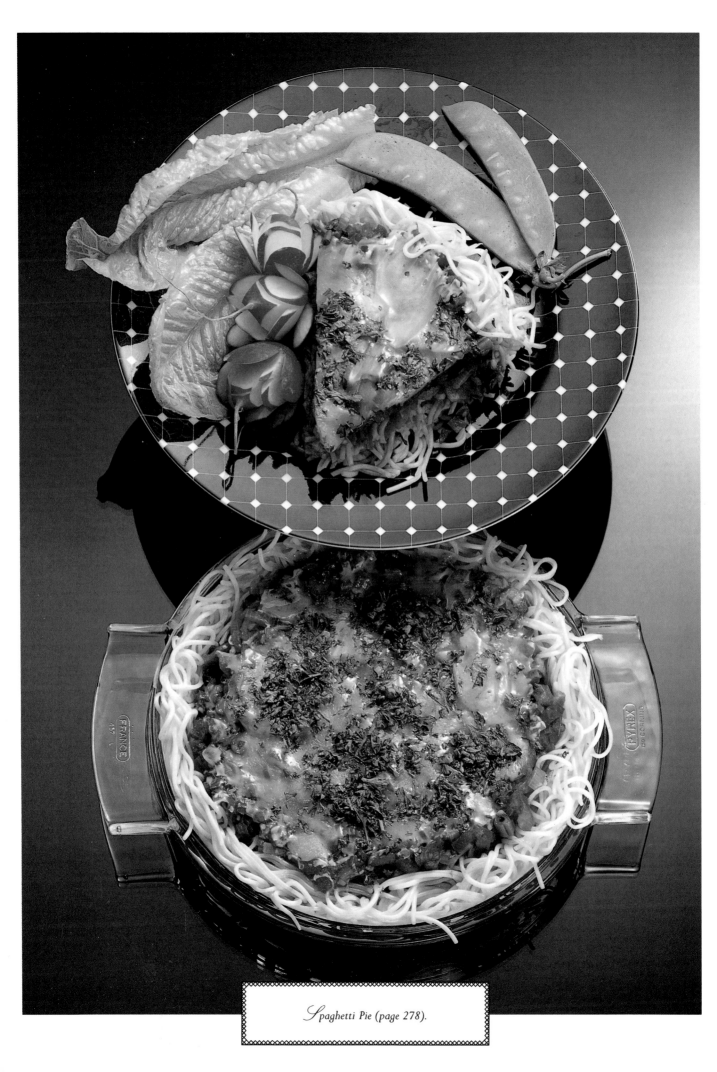

Spaghetti Pie (page 278).

Cabbage Rolls (page 275).

VEGETABLES

The most pleasure I receive from cooking in my microwave oven is undoubtedly when I cook vegetables. Because vegetables contain moisture, they create their own steam in the cooking process. If any liquid is added, it should be kept to an absolute minimum so that vegetables retain their natural colour and flavour.

Only minimal cooking time is required for crisp, crunchy vegetables that are power-packed with nutrition.

Pay particular attention to instructions regarding covering vegetables or leaving them uncovered. If you cut your vegetables into large chunky pieces they will take longer to cook and will need a short standing time before serving, so that they are cooked through. Always use your microwave oven manual for the special features offered by your model.

Asparagus

SERVES 1–2

225 g / ½ lb asparagus
2 tablespoons / 2 tablespoons plus
    2 teaspoons water or Chicken Stock
    (see p. 14)

The best results are achieved when using very fresh asparagus. The heads will snap away easily from the stems when fresh. Cooked asparagus should be tender but still slightly crisp. Cooking time will depend on the size of the asparagus spears. When serving asparagus cold, microwave until tender, drain and quickly plunge into cold water. Drain and towel dry.

Break off the woody stems of the asparagus. Combine the asparagus and water in a casserole dish. Cover, and microwave for 6–8 minutes on HIGH (thin spears) or 8–10 minutes on HIGH (thick spears). Stir once during cooking.

Variations
- Squeeze a little lemon or lime juice over the top after cooking.
- Add a little crushed garlic prior to cooking.
- Add freshly chopped herbs of your choice.
- Serve hot with White Sauce (see page 293).

Corn on the Cob

SERVES 2

2 large cobs of corn

Wrap the corn in plastic wrap. Place on the turntable of the microwave oven. Microwave for 4 minutes on HIGH. Turn over and microwave for 4 minutes more on HIGH.

French Beans

SERVES 4–6

450 g/1 lb green beans
2 tablespoons/2 tablespoons plus
   2 teaspoons water or Chicken Stock
   (see p. 14)

The best results are achieved when using very fresh beans. Fresh beans break cleanly with a crisp snap. They have a high moisture content, so they are excellent for microwave cooking. When cooking beans to add to a salad, microwave them, then plunge into cold water, drain and towel dry.

Top and tail the beans and cut into even-sized pieces. Add the water. Cover, and microwave for 8–10 minutes on HIGH. Stir once during cooking.

Variations
- Add finely grated fresh ginger prior to cooking.
- Crush 1 clove of garlic and add prior to cooking.
- Add 1 teaspoon sesame seeds after cooking.
- Add chopped fresh herbs of your choice, especially dill or coriander, after cooking.
- Serve with cherry tomatoes (see colour plate opposite page 273).

Beetroot

SERVES 4–6

450 g/1 lb beetroot
2 tablespoons/2 tablespoons plus
   2 teaspoons water or Chicken Stock
   (see p. 14) or unsweetened orange
   juice

The smaller the beetroot, the sweeter the flavour. The skins should be washed thoroughly before cooking.

Cut the beetroot into even round slices. Add the water. Cover, and microwave for 7–9 minutes on HIGH. Stir once during cooking.

Variations
- Add a little white wine vinegar combined with unsweetened orange juice while the beetroot is still hot. Cover, and let stand for the flavours to penetrate the beetroot slices.
- Add some finely chopped mild onion prior to serving.
- Add a dash of ground cinnamon.

Broccoli or Cauliflower Florets

SERVES 4–6

450 g/1 lb broccoli or cauliflower
2 tablespoons/2 tablespoons plus
   2 teaspoons water or Chicken Stock
   (see p. 14)

Cut the broccoli into even-sized florets with stems. Remove the woody ends of the stems. Add the water. Place the broccoli heads towards the centre of the dish. Cover, and microwave for 8–12 minutes on HIGH.

Variations
- Add finely grated fresh ginger prior to cooking.
- Add a little crushed garlic prior to cooking.
- Add ground nutmeg or coriander, or cayenne pepper, prior to cooking.
- Add 1 teaspoon sesame seeds after cooking.
- Combine broccoli florets with cauliflower florets.

Brussels Sprouts

SERVES 4 – 6

450 g / 1 lb Brussels sprouts
2 tablespoons / 2 tablespoons plus
  2 teaspoons water

Brussels sprouts are best eaten when young. They can develop a strong flavour and lose their nutrients if over-cooked. Buy only small to medium-sized Brussels sprouts and avoid any that are tinged with yellow.

Trim the base and outer leaves of the Brussels sprouts. Add the water. Cover, and microwave for 8–10 minutes on HIGH. Stir once during cooking.

Variations
- Add sliced water chestnuts and reheat 1–1½ minutes on HIGH to just heat through the chestnuts.
- Squeeze a little lemon or orange juice over the top after cooking.
- Add a dash of curry powder prior to cooking.

Red and Green Cabbage

SERVES 4 – 6

225 g / ½ lb shredded green cabbage
225 g / ½ lb shredded red cabbage
2 tablespoons / 2 tablespoons plus
  2 teaspoons water

Combine the cabbage and water in a casserole dish. Cover, and microwave for 8–10 minutes on HIGH. Stir once during cooking.

Variations
- Add 1–2 tablespoons of Tarragon Vinegar (see page 144) and finely chopped fresh tarragon after cooking.
- Add 1 teaspoon of caraway seeds after cooking.
- Add 100 g / 3½ oz / ½ cup of plumped raisins after cooking.
- Add a little chopped onion prior to reheating.
- Add sliced water chestnuts and reheat 1–1½ minutes on HIGH to just heat through the chestnuts.
- Finely sliced fresh fennel combines well with cabbage. Reheat to just heat through the fennel.

Cabbage and Apple

SERVES 4 – 6

450 g / 1 lb red cabbage, finely shredded
1 onion, finely chopped
1 large red apple, cored and sliced into
  thin wedges
2 tablespoons / 2 tablespoons plus
  2 teaspoons white wine vinegar
1 teaspoon apple juice concentrate
125 ml / 4 fl oz / ½ cup dry red wine
black pepper to taste

Combine all the ingredients, except the pepper, in a large casserole dish. Cover, and microwave for 8–12 minutes on HIGH. Stir twice during cooking. Add the pepper.

Spicy Baked Capsicum and Tomatoes

SERVES 4 – 6

1 large red capsicum, chopped
1 large green capsicum, chopped
1 onion, finely sliced into rings
1 clove garlic, crushed
¼ teaspoon chilli powder
¼ teaspoon ground coriander
¼ teaspoon ground cummin
425 g/15 oz canned tomatoes in natural
   juice, salt-free
2 tablespoons/2 tablespoons plus
   2 teaspoons salt-free tomato paste

Combine the capsicum, onion, garlic, spices and 3 tablespoons/3 tablespoons plus 3 teaspoons of the juice from the canned tomatoes in a casserole dish. Microwave for 3 minutes on HIGH. Chop the tomatoes and add with the tomato paste. Microwave for 5 minutes on HIGH. Stir. Microwave for 3–5 minutes more on HIGH.

This is a delicious vegetable accompaniment to chicken, fish, brown rice or wholemeal noodles.

Carrots or Parsnips

SERVES 2

225 g/½ lb carrots
2 tablespoons/2 tablespoons plus
   2 teaspoons water or Chicken Stock
   (see p. 14) or unsweetened orange
   juice

Wash the carrots thoroughly and cut into julienne strips or diagonal rounds. Add the water. Cover, and microwave for 6½–9 minutes on HIGH. Stir once or twice during cooking.

Variations
- Squeeze lemon juice on the top and add finely chopped fresh mint after cooking.
- Add 1 teaspoon of apple juice concentrate and a little finely grated orange rind after cooking.
- Add a pinch of ground nutmeg or cummin after cooking.
- Add finely chopped fresh parsley and chives after cooking.
- Add 1 teaspoon of apple juice concentrate and 1 teaspoon of sesame seeds after cooking.
- Add 1 teaspoon of poppyseeds after cooking.

Leeks

SERVES 4 – 6

450 g/1 lb leeks
65 ml/2 fl oz/¼ cup water or Chicken
   Stock (see p. 14)

Cut off the coarse green foliage and root ends of the leeks. Cut into 10-cm/4″ lengths and then cut in half lengthwise. Place the pieces, cut side down, in a casserole dish. Add the water. Cover, and microwave for 8–12 minutes on HIGH.

Variations
- Serve cold. Divide the leek equally between serving plates. Slice an avocado and place a quarter on each plate. Make up a vinaigrette dressing using tarragon vinegar and finely chopped fresh basil and tarragon. Spoon this over the leek and avocado.
- Add pine nuts and currants to the hot leeks.
- Serve with a meat dish with freshly grated horseradish or wholegrain mustard.
- Add pink peppercorns to taste.

Peas

SERVES 6–8

450 g/1 lb peas
2 tablespoons/2 tablespoons plus
  2 teaspoons water or Chicken Stock
  (see p. 14)

Combine the peas and water in a casserole dish. Cover, and microwave for 8–10 minutes on HIGH. Stir once during cooking.

Variations
- Crush 1 clove of garlic and add prior to cooking.
- Add finely chopped fresh mint after cooking.
- Add 40 g/1½ oz/¼ cup of finely chopped red and green capsicum after cooking.

Jacket Potatoes

SERVES 2

2 large potatoes
a little non-fat or low-fat yoghurt
finely chopped fresh chives or parsley

Celery and Cheese Filling
40 g/1½ oz/¼ cup finely chopped celery
2 tablespoons/2 tablespoons plus
  2 teaspoons grated low-fat grating
  cheese
½ teaspoon geska herb cheese

Celery and Tuna Filling
2 tablespoons/2 tablespoons plus 2
  teaspoons finely chopped celery
40 g/1½ oz/¼ cup flaked salt-free tuna
¼ teaspoon dried dill
1 heaped tablespoon grated geska herb
  cheese

Celery and Sunflower Seeds Filling
40 g/1½ oz/¼ cup finely chopped celery
1 heaped tablespoon sunflower seeds
¼ teaspoon dried coriander
2 tablespoons/2 tablespoons plus
  2 teaspoons low-fat cottage cheese

Apple and Capers Filling
60 g/2 oz/¼ cup finely chopped apple
2 teaspoons capers
½ teaspoon wholegrain mustard
2 tablespoons/2 tablespoons plus
  2 teaspoons grated low-fat grating
  cheese

When baking potatoes, prick them with a skewer so that the steam can escape and the potatoes will not burst. Place the potatoes evenly around the microwave glass turntable. Turn the potatoes over half-way through cooking. The potatoes need to stand for about 5 minutes after cooking to allow them to cook through to the centre.

Place the 2 potatoes on a small piece of paper towel. Microwave for 10–12 minutes on HIGH. Stand the potatoes for 5 minutes. Make a cross-shaped cut in the top of the potatoes. Squeeze open. Top with the yoghurt and chives.

To make stuffed jacket potatoes, remove the tops from the potatoes, scoop out some of the potato and mash together with the desired filling. Spoon back into the potato and reheat, uncovered, for 2–3 minutes on HIGH. Serve with a tossed salad.

Left-over casseroles or savoury sauces make excellent fillings. Top with just a little grated low-fat grating cheese or low-fat cottage cheese.

Mashed Potatoes

SERVES 4

800 g/1¾ lb potatoes
65 ml/2 fl oz/¼ cup water
2 tablespoons/2 tablespoons plus
    2 teaspoons skim milk
2 tablespoons/2 tablespoons plus
    2 teaspoons finely chopped fresh chives
black pepper to taste

Peel the potatoes and cut into chunks. Place in a large jug. Add the water. Cover, and microwave for 9 minutes on HIGH. Stir. Cover, and microwave for 3 minutes more on HIGH. Drain the potatoes. Add the remaining ingredients and mash or purée in a food processor or blender until smooth.

Creamed Spinach

SERVES 6

1 large bunch spinach
1 onion, chopped
60 g/2 oz/¼ cup pine nuts
1 tablespoon/1 tablespoon plus
    1 teaspoon sesame seeds
a little nutmeg

Wash the spinach thoroughly and remove the stalks. Chop up roughly. Combine the onion and spinach in a 4-litre/ 7-pint/16-cup casserole dish. Cover, and microwave for 7–8 minutes on HIGH. Toss the spinach half-way through the cooking time. Drain the spinach well, and purée in a food processor.

Place the pine nuts and sesame seeds on a piece of greaseproof or non-stick baking paper on the microwave glass plate. Microwave for 2–3 minutes on HIGH or until lightly browned. Add these to the spinach and add the nutmeg.

Baked Herbed Tomatoes

SERVES 2

4 tomatoes, cut in half
a little fresh or dried oregano or basil or
    parsley or thyme
black pepper to taste

Place the tomatoes in a round casserole dish. Space evenly around the dish. Sprinkle the herbs and pepper over the top before or after cooking. Microwave for 5–9 minutes on HIGH. Leave the tomato halves to stand for 2–3 minutes.

Note
Four whole tomatoes take 8–13 minutes on HIGH.

Tomatoes with Pine Nuts and Basil

SERVES 4

2 tablespoons/2 tablespoons plus
    2 teaspoons pine nuts
225 g/½ lb cherry tomatoes, cut in half
1 tablespoon/1 tablespoon plus
    1 teaspoon white wine vinegar
1 tablespoon/1 tablespoon plus
    1 teaspoon finely chopped fresh basil
1 tablespoon/1 tablespoon plus
    1 teaspoon finely chopped fresh chives

Place the pine nuts on a sheet of non-stick baking paper and microwave for 2 minutes on HIGH. Stir once during cooking. Place the tomatoes and vinegar in a shallow dish. Cover, and microwave for 40 seconds to a minute on HIGH. Add the pine nuts and herbs, and serve.

Pumpkin

SERVES 4

400 g/14 oz pumpkin
2 tablespoons/2 tablespoons plus
  2 teaspoons water or unsweetened
  orange juice or Chicken Stock (see
  p. 14)

Cut the pumpkin into four serving pieces. Add the water. Cover, and microwave for 8–10 minutes on HIGH. Turn over during cooking.

Variations
- Add 1 teaspoon of poppyseeds.
- Add 1 teaspoon of sunflower seeds.
- Add 1 teaspoon of sesame seeds.
- Add a little cayenne pepper, nutmeg or allspice.

Sherried Turnips with Dill

SERVES 4 – 6

450 g/1 lb turnips
2 tablespoons/2 tablespoons plus
  2 teaspoons dry sherry
250 ml/8 fl oz/1 cup non-fat or low-fat
  yoghurt, at room temperature
1 tablespoon/1 tablespoon plus
  1 teaspoon finely chopped fresh dill

Slice the turnips finely. Add the sherry. Cover, and microwave for 8–10 minutes on HIGH. Stir twice during cooking. Pour the yoghurt over the top and sprinkle with the dill. Reheat for 1 minute on HIGH, and serve.

Turnips with Mustard Lemon Sauce

SERVES 4 – 6

450 g/1 lb turnips
65 ml/2 fl oz/¼ cup unsweetened
  orange juice
2 teaspoons wholegrain mustard
1 tablespoon/1 tablespoon plus
  1 teaspoon lemon juice
1 tablespoon/1 tablespoon plus
  1 teaspoon dry sherry

Slice the turnips finely. Combine with half the orange juice in a casserole dish. Cover, and microwave for 8–10 minutes on HIGH. Stir twice during cooking. Combine the mustard, lemon juice, sherry and the remaining orange juice. Mix well. Spoon over the turnip. Reheat for 1 minute on HIGH, and serve.

Zucchini

SERVES 4 – 6

450 g/1 lb zucchini
1 tablespoon/1 tablespoon plus
  1 teaspoon water or Chicken Stock
  (see p. 14)

Combine the zucchini and water in a casserole dish. Cover, and microwave for 6–8 minutes on HIGH.

Variations
- Crush 1 clove of garlic and add prior to cooking.
- Add ½ teaspoon of dried basil after cooking.
- Add 1 teaspoon of capers after cooking.
- Add 1–2 teaspoons of finely chopped fresh dill after cooking.
- Add ½ teaspoon of dried marjoram after cooking.

DESSERTS & CAKES

*D*esserts and cakes can be produced very speedily when using a microwave oven – a great help when visitors pop in unexpectedly or the children arrive home from school hungry! While I think I will always prefer cakes cooked in a conventional oven, a micro-waved cake can be made so quickly that the ease of preparation often outweighs any disadvantages.

Fruit desserts, on the other hand, are even better when made in a microwave oven. Fruit cooks quickly without the need for a lot of added liquid. Cooking the fruit lightly and leaving it to stand in its own juice will produce delicious results every time.

Date and Carob Custard Strawberry Flan

SERVES 8–10

450 g/1 lb/3 cups strawberries

Base
225 g/½ lb/1 cup dates, stoned
225 g/½ lb/1 cup raisins or sultanas
150 g/5 oz/1 cup raw almonds
60 g/2 oz/1 cup shredded coconut
225 g/½ lb/2 cups rolled oats
100 g/3½ oz/½ cup carob buds
2 teaspoons vanilla essence
*2 tablespoons/2 tablespoons plus
   2 teaspoons apple juice concentrate*

Custard Filling
1 litre/1¾ pints/4 cups skim milk
125 g/¼ lb/1 cup cornflour
1–2 tablespoons carob powder
2 teaspoons vanilla essence
2 teaspoons orange zest
*125 ml/4 fl oz/½ cup apple juice
   concentrate*
250 ml/8 fl oz/1 cup low-fat yoghurt

Glaze
*250 ml/8 fl oz/1 cup unsweetened apple
   juice*
*1 tablespoon/1 tablespoon plus
   1 teaspoon apple juice concentrate*
¾ teaspoon agar powder

To make the Base, blend the dates and raisins in a food processor or blender until the mixture resembles breadcrumbs. Add the almonds, coconut, rolled oats and carob buds. Blend until the mixture again resembles breadcrumbs. Add the vanilla essence and enough apple juice concentrate to just bind the ingredients while the machine is still operating. Press the mixture into a 30-cm/12″ flan dish with deep sides. Firm down with your fingers and the palm of your hand. Refrigerate.

To make the Custard Filling, combine some of the milk with the cornflour and carob powder to make a paste. Add the remaining milk, vanilla essence and orange zest. Mix well. Place in a 2-litre/3½-pint/8-cup glass jug. Microwave for 9 minutes on HIGH. Stop every 2–3 minutes to stir thoroughly to avoid lumps. Let the mixture cool slightly before adding the apple juice concentrate and yoghurt, and stir until smooth. Pour into the Base and leave to cool. Top with the strawberries (leave them whole or slice finely).

To make the Glaze, combine the apple juice and apple juice concentrate in a glass jug and microwave for 3–4 minutes on HIGH. Add the agar powder and mix well. Microwave for 1–2 minutes more on HIGH. Cool slightly and then brush the glaze over the top of the flan. Refrigerate the flan. (See colour plate opposite.)

Variation
- Add 2 teaspoons of brandy with the vanilla essence when making the Custard Filling.

*D*ate and Carob Custard Strawberry Flan
(opposite page); Pear with Figs (page 290).

Quick Strawberry Jam Spread and Blueberry Sauce (page 292);
Lemon Topping (page 293).

Apple and Carob Cake

SERVES 10

250 ml/8 fl oz/1 cup boiling water
8 dried apple rings
a little ground cinnamon
125 g/¼ lb/1 cup unbleached white
    plain flour
100 g/3½ oz/¾ cup wholemeal plain
    flour
3 teaspoons baking powder
3 tablespoons/3 tablespoons plus
    3 teaspoons carob powder
1 teaspoon ground cinnamon
1 teaspoon mixed spice
1 large Granny Smith apple, coarsely
    grated
125 ml/4 fl oz/½ cup apple juice
    concentrate
75 ml/3 fl oz/⅓ cup cold-pressed oil
2 teaspoons vanilla essence
2 egg whites

Pour the boiling water over the dried apple and let stand for 5 minutes. Drain the apple and pat dry. Sprinkle the cinnamon over the base of a 20-cm/8″ cake ring. Place the apple rings evenly on the base. Sift the flours, baking powder, carob powder, ground cinnamon and mixed spice twice and return the husks to the mixture. Combine the apple, apple juice concentrate, oil and vanilla essence. Add to the flour and mix well. Beat the egg whites until stiff. Gently fold through mixture. Spoon the mixture into the cake ring, but do not smooth down. Microwave, covered with plastic wrap, for 7½ minutes on HIGH. Remove from the oven. Remove the plastic wrap, turn it over, replace on the cake and leave an air vent. Cool in the cake ring.

The cake is best eaten on the day it is made. Serve with Whipped Ricotta Cream (see Pancake Toppings, page 190).

Jamaican Bananas

SERVES 4

4 firm but ripe bananas, peeled
2 tablespoons/2 tablespoons plus
    2 teaspoons apple juice concentrate
65 ml/2 fl oz/¼ cup unsweetened
    orange juice
juice from ½ lemon
grated rind of 1 lemon
pinch of ground cinnamon

Place the bananas in a casserole dish. Combine the apple juice concentrate, orange juice, lemon juice and rind, and pour over the bananas. Sprinkle the cinnamon on top. Microwave, uncovered, for 2 minutes on HIGH. Move the bananas in the centre to the outside and the outside bananas to the centre. Microwave, uncovered, for 2 minutes more on HIGH.

Serve hot or cold with low-fat ice cream, non-fat or low-fat yoghurt, non-fat frozen yoghurt or low-fat whipped cream.

Blueberry Cake

SERVES 10

280 g / 10 oz / 2 cups wholemeal plain
  flour
3 teaspoons baking powder
1 teaspoon ground cinnamon
225 g / ½ lb blueberries (fresh or frozen,
  not canned)
65 ml / 2 fl oz / ¼ cup cold-pressed oil
125 ml / 4 fl oz / ½ cup apple juice
  concentrate
65 ml / 2 fl oz / ¼ cup non-fat buttermilk
2 teaspoons vanilla essence
2 egg whites
200 g / 7 oz / 1½ cups fresh blueberries

Sift the flour, baking powder and cinnamon twice. Add the blueberries and toss in flour to coat well. Combine the oil, apple juice concentrate, buttermilk and vanilla essence. Add to the flour mixture, and mix well. Beat the egg whites until stiff peaks form. Fold through. Pour the mixture into a lined and floured 20-cm/8″ cake ring. Microwave for 4–5 minutes on HIGH. Cool in the ring. Turn out.

Serve with Whipped Ricotta Cream (see Pancake Toppings, page 190) and fresh blueberries.

Winter Pears

SERVES 4 – 8

4 firm ripe pears, peeled
60 g / 2 oz / ¼ cup chopped dates
60 g / 2 oz / ¼ cup sultanas
rind of 1 lemon
½ teaspoon ground cinnamon
200 ml / 7 fl oz / ¾ cup unsweetened dark
  grape juice
10 raw almonds, chopped (optional)

Core the pears and cut in half. Arrange, with the top of the pears pointing to the centre, in a deep glass casserole dish. Add the remaining ingredients. Microwave for 5–7 minutes on HIGH. Turn the pears over. Microwave for 5–7 minutes more on HIGH. Spoon the sauce into the cored cavity and over the top.

Serve hot or cold with low-fat whipped cream, non-fat or low-fat yoghurt, or low-fat ice cream.

Pear with Figs

SERVES 1

1 ripe but firm pear
2 dried figs, finely chopped
1 teaspoon lemon juice
1 teaspoon apple juice concentrate
pinch of ground cinnamon

Core the pear, and fill with the fig. Spoon the lemon juice over the top. Drizzle the apple juice concentrate over the top and sprinkle with the cinnamon. Place on a small plate. Cover with plastic wrap. Microwave for 4–6 minutes on MEDIUM, depending on the size of the pear. Serve hot or cold with non-fat or low-fat yoghurt or fresh seasonal fruit. (See colour plate opposite page 288.)

JAM SPREADS, CHUTNEY & SAUCES

Sauces, gravies, custards and your favourite spreads can be made in no time in the microwave oven. Use a large glass jug or bowl for these recipes (it should be big enough to hold twice the capacity of the recipe). Most sauces and gravies are thickened with cornflour, which means that ingredients need to be mixed thoroughly, and checked and stirred frequently during cooking, to avoid lumps.

Apple Spread

MAKES 3 × 250-ML/8-FL-OZ JARS

225 g/½ lb dried apples, finely chopped
750 ml/1⅓ pints/3 cups unsweetened
*   pineapple juice*
½ lemon, finely sliced

Combine all the ingredients in a 2-litre/3½-pint/8-cup casserole dish. Cover, and microwave for 10 minutes on HIGH. Stir well. Microwave for 10 minutes more on HIGH. Remove lemon. Purée in a food processor or blender. Pour into sterilised jars, cover when cool and store in the refrigerator. The spread is excellent as a toast spread or a spread on day-old cakes, a porridge topping, in sandwiches, on pancakes, or in muffins.

Tropical Fruit Spread

MAKES 1½ × 250-ML/8-FL-OZ JARS

2 Granny Smith apples, peeled, cored
*   and finely chopped*
125 g/¼ lb/½ cup canned unsweetened
*   crushed pineapple, drained*
75 g/2½ oz/¼ cup dried bananas, finely
*   chopped*
¼–½ teaspoon ground cinnamon
¼–½ teaspoon mixed spice
1 teaspoon finely grated lemon rind
1 teaspoon finely grated orange rind
125 ml/4 fl oz/½ cup unsweetened
*   pineapple or pear juice*

Combine all the ingredients in a glass jug or bowl. Cover with plastic wrap. Insert some holes. Microwave on HIGH for 8–10 minutes or until the apple is quite soft. Purée in a food processor or blender. Spoon into sterilised jars, cover when cool, and store in the refrigerator.

Quick Strawberry Jam Spread

MAKES 125-ML/4-FL-OZ JAR

225 g/½ lb strawberries
1 tablespoon/1 tablespoon plus
   1 teaspoon lemon juice
1 tablespoon/1 tablespoon plus
   1 teaspoon apple juice concentrate

Place all the ingredients in a large jug (the larger the better, so the mixture does not boil over). Microwave for 5 minutes on HIGH. Stir. Microwave for 5 minutes more on HIGH. Stir. Microwave for 5 minutes further on HIGH. Stir. Pour into a sterilised jar, seal when cool, and refrigerate. (See colour plate opposite page 289.)

Variation
- Grate 1 Granny Smith apple, add to the strawberries, and cook the jam spread as above.

Mango Chutney

MAKES 2 × 250-ML/8-FL-OZ JARS

1 onion, finely chopped
1 teaspoon finely chopped fresh ginger
rind of 1 orange, finely grated
¼–½ teaspoon chilli powder
½ teaspoon ground cummin
65 ml/2 fl oz/¼ cup Chicken Stock
   (see p. 14) or unsweetened orange
   juice
flesh of 2–3 mangoes, chopped
2 Granny Smith apples, grated
75 ml/3 fl oz/⅓ cup brown rice vinegar
125 ml/4 fl oz/½ cup apple juice
   concentrate

Place the onion, ginger, orange rind, spices and Chicken Stock in a large casserole dish. Microwave for 3 minutes on HIGH. Add the remaining ingredients. Cover, and microwave for 10 minutes on HIGH. Uncover. Microwave for 10 minutes more on HIGH. Stir. Microwave a further 10 minutes on HIGH or until thickened. Pour into sterilised jars, seal when cool, and refrigerate.

The chutney is excellent as a sandwich spread, a dip for vegetable crudités or served with chicken or fish. (See colour plate opposite page 272.)

Blueberry Sauce

MAKES 2½ × 250-ML/8-FL-OZ JARS

500 ml/16 fl oz/2 cups unsweetened
   apple juice or pear juice
2 tablespoons/2 tablespoons plus
   2 teaspoons arrowroot
500 g/1 lb 2 oz blueberries (fresh or
   frozen, not canned)
2 teaspoons lemon juice
1 tablespoon/1 tablespoon plus
   1 teaspoon apple juice concentrate
   (optional)

Mix a little apple juice with the arrowroot to make a paste. Combine the remaining apple juice and the paste in a 2-litre/3½-pint/8-cup glass jug. Microwave for 3–4 minutes on HIGH. Stir thoroughly. Microwave for 2–3 minutes more on HIGH. Add the blueberries, lemon juice and apple juice concentrate. Microwave for 1 minute further on HIGH. Pour over cakes, pancakes and desserts. (See colour plate opposite page 289.)

Lemon Topping

MAKES 600 ML/1 PINT/2½ CUPS

30 g/1 oz/¼ cup cornflour
300 ml/10 fl oz/1¼ cups water
200 ml/7 fl oz/¾ cup lemon juice
125 ml/4 fl oz/½ cup apple juice
concentrate
½ teaspoon orange essence
grated rind of 1 orange (optional)

Combine the cornflour with 65 ml/2 fl oz/¼ cup of the water, and mix to a paste. Place the remaining ingredients and the cornflour paste in a 1-litre/1¾-pint/4-cup glass jug, and mix well. Microwave for 2 minutes on HIGH. Stir. Microwave for 2 minutes more on HIGH. Stir. Microwave for 1½–2 minutes further on HIGH.

Use the topping over wholemeal pancakes or fill your favourite wholemeal flan base to make a lemon-flavoured pie. (See colour plate opposite page 289.)

Pizza Tomato Sauce

MAKES 1.25 LITRES/2¼ PINTS/5 CUPS

3 onions, finely chopped
2 cloves garlic, crushed
65 ml/2 fl oz/¼ cup water
425 g/15 oz canned tomatoes in natural
juice, salt-free
225 g/½ lb/1 cup salt-free tomato paste
½ teaspoon dried basil
1 teaspoon dried oregano

Place the onion and garlic in a large casserole dish. Add the water. Cover, and microwave for 4–5 minutes on HIGH. Purée the remaining ingredients in a food processor or blender. Add to the onion mixture. Cover, and microwave for 5 minutes on HIGH. Cool and use as required. (See colour plate opposite page 273.)

White Sauce

MAKES 500 ML/16 FL OZ/2 CUPS

30 g/1 oz/¼ cup cornflour
500 ml/16 fl oz/2 cups skim milk or
reduced-fat soymilk
2 bay leaves
black pepper to taste

Mix the cornflour with a little milk in a 1-litre/1¾-pint/4-cup glass jug to make a paste. Add the remaining milk and ingredients and stir well. Microwave for 2 minutes on HIGH. Stir well. Microwave for 1½ minutes on HIGH. Stir well. Microwave for 1½ minutes further on HIGH or until the sauce reaches the desired consistency. Remove the bay leaves prior to serving.

Variations
- Fresh or dried herbs of your choice – for example, parsley – to make a white herbed sauce to serve over vegetables, fish or chicken.
- Grated low-fat grating cheese or geska herb cheese to make a cheese sauce.
- Salt-free tomato paste.
- Low-salt soy sauce.
- Paprika or cayenne pepper.
- Curry powder.
- Capers.

Chicken Gravy

MAKES 250 ML/8 FL OZ/1 CUP

2 tablespoon/2 tablespoons plus
2 teaspoons cornflour
1 tablespoon/1 tablespoon plus
1 teaspoon water
250 ml/8 fl oz/1 cup hot Chicken
Stock (see p. 14)

Mix the cornflour with the water in a 1-litre/1¾-pint/4-cup glass jug. Add the Chicken Stock and stir. Microwave for 2½–3 minutes on HIGH. Stir twice during cooking for a smooth gravy.

Beef Gravy

MAKES 250 ML/8 FL OZ/1 CUP

2 tablespoons/2 tablespoons plus
2 teaspoons cornflour
1 tablespoon/1 tablespoon plus
1 teaspoon water
250 ml/8 fl oz/1 cup hot Beef Stock
(see p. 15)

Mix the cornflour with the water in a 1-litre/1¾-pint/4-cup glass jug. Add the Beef Stock and stir. Microwave for 2½–3 minutes on HIGH. Stir twice during cooking for a smooth gravy.

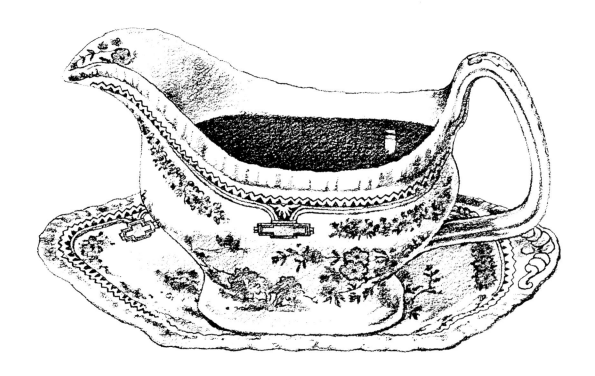

DRINKS

*W*hile the microwave oven is great for making a quick cup of tea, don't limit yourself! Try the following delicious drink recipes and then experiment. Many healthy combinations can be made in seconds; remember, though, to use caffeine-free substitutes for coffee and tea, and low-fat milk.

Caro Cappuccino

SERVES 4

500 ml/16 fl oz/2 cups cold water
500 ml/16 fl oz/2 cups cold skim milk
4 teaspoons Caro powder or other
    suitable caffeine-free beverage
250 ml/8 fl oz/1 cup boiling water
1 teaspoon extra Caro powder or other
    suitable caffeine-free beverage
1 teaspoon ground cinnamon
½ teaspoon nutmeg

Place the water in a glass jug. Microwave for 3–5 minutes on HIGH and bring to the boil. Place the milk in another glass jug. Microwave for 4–6 minutes on MEDIUM-HIGH. Place 1 teaspoon of Caro in the base of each mug. Add 65 ml/ 2 fl oz/¼ cup of the boiling water to each cup and stir well. Use a beater, food processor or blender to make the milk frothy and thick. Add 65 ml/2 fl oz/¼ cup of milk to each cup. Combine the extra Caro powder with the cinnamon and nutmeg, and sprinkle over the top of each drink. (See colour plate opposite page 225.)

Nutmeg Quench

SERVES 1

250 ml/8 fl oz/1 cup skim milk
½–1 teaspoon vanilla essence
1 tablespoon/1 tablespoon plus
    1 teaspoon Whipped Ricotta Cream
    (see Pancake Toppings, p. 190)
pinch of nutmeg

Place milk and vanilla essence in a cup and microwave for 2–3 minutes on MEDIUM. Top with Whipped Ricotta Cream and add a pinch of nutmeg to taste.

Vegetable Broth Pick-me-up

SERVES 1

1–2 teaspoons Vecon
1 tablespoon/1 tablespoon plus
    1 teaspoon boiling water
250 ml/8 fl oz/1 cup cold water
1 teaspoon finely chopped fresh parsley
½ teaspoon finely grated lemon rind
freshly ground black pepper

Dissolve the Vecon in the boiling water in a cup. Add the cold water and microwave for 2–4 minutes on HIGH. Stir through the parsley and lemon rind and season with pepper (cayenne pepper can also be used).

GENERAL INDEX

MICROWAVE INDEX